# THE BEST
# PLAYS
# FROM
# AMERICAN
# THEATRE
# FESTIVALS
# 2015

# THE BEST PLAYS FROM AMERICAN THEATRE FESTIVALS 2015

Edited by **John Patrick Bray**

APPLAUSE THEATRE & CINEMA BOOKS
An Imprint of Hal Leonard LLC

Published in 2016 by Applause Theatre & Cinema Books
An Imprint of Hal Leonard LLC
7777 West Bluemound Road
Milwaukee, WI 53213

Trade Book Division Editorial Offices
33 Plymouth St., Montclair, NJ 07042

Printed in the United States of America

Book design by Lynn Bergesen, UB Communications

Library of Congress Cataloging-in-Publication Data

Names: Bray, John Patrick, editor.
Title: The best plays from American theatre festivals, 2015 / edited by John
    Patrick Bray.
Description: Milwaukee, WI : Applause Theatre & Cinema Books, [2016]
Identifiers: LCCN 2016023286 | ISBN 9781495057748 (pbk.)
Subjects: LCSH: American drama—21st century.
Classification: LCC PS634.2 B475 2016 | DDC 812/.608—dc23
LC record available at https://lccn.loc.gov/2016023286

www.applausebooks.com

# Contents

# Introduction

## Who Tells Your Story?

### John Patrick Bray

Welcome to *The Best Plays from American Theatre Festivals 2015*. The plays collected in this anthology represent some of the most exciting and dynamic plays being presented in the US independent theatre scene. Before diving in, I just wanted to clarify some terminology for you:

**Theatre:** The theatre is an abstract place, where philosophies are debated, ideas and identities are deconstructed; where we can go to be entertained, or to learn from each other. In other words, theatre is a place in which meaning is simultaneously made and evaluated. A live performance is a conversation between spectator and actor. To paraphrase Pulitzer-winning playwright Paula Vogel, the theatre is a space in which we learn to become comfortable with being uncomfortable with each other.

**Festival Plays:** Theatre festivals have been popping up all around the United States. In fact, most budding playwrights will have at least one if not two productions in a festival prior to landing a slot with a company's mainstage season. Many Off-Off Broadway theatre troupes produce *exclusively* in festivals due to the low financial risk and ability (or at the very least, the hope) to reach a wider audience. Some festivals represented in this volume may not have received much national attention; others certainly have. It is my hope to show the variety of festivals in the United States to demonstrate different ways of staging humanity.

Many festivals operate as "bring your own production!" venues. Festival administrators select plays based on certain criteria (for each festival, the criteria differ). Some festivals invite pieces. Some festivals have long track records. Some are new! Some festivals are tied to a national movement (such as the Women's Voices project, which promotes exclusively work written by women). Other festivals are tied to universities, which have teamed up with equity theatres in order to showcase full productions of graduate student work (e.g., the Hollins-Mill Mountain Winter Festival of New Work in Roanoke, VA).

One of the many challenges in creating this anthology has been the sheer number of festival productions in the United States. Last year, the New York International Fringe Festival alone hosted more than two hundred productions of new work. I wanted to create some clear criteria in order to, quite frankly, narrow down my options. First, I decided to select works that had full productions rather than staged readings. In a festival, a full production is a play in which actors are off-book and an admission (or donation) is paid. Second, I decided the plays in this anthology needed to run between one and two hours. This eliminated a number of shorter plays, true; however, the Applause *The Best Short American Plays* series already offers a home to shorter works.

**The Best:** This is probably the toughest phrase to qualify. By using the term "the best," I am situating this volume within Applause's long-running *The Best American Short Plays* series. "Best" can mean many things. For my purposes, I hunted out plays that received critical attention (Lisa Lewis's *SCHOOLED* at the New York International Fringe Festival, Lauren Ludwig's *Hamlet-Mobile* at the Hollywood Fringe Festival), strong pieces that may have been overlooked in a flurry of production activity (Miranda Jonte's *St. Francis* was also produced in the New York International Fringe Festival, where it won the Excellence Award for Best Direction (Stephen Brotebeck); writing for *Theater Is Easy*, critic Sarah Moore laments, "The worst part about the NYC Fringe Festival is finding a gem of a show like *St. Francis*, only to discover it is closing the next day."), and other pieces that I've either read or seen over the past year that somehow begged to be published. In other words, some of the "bests" in here are subjective; however, following in the footsteps of William Demastes, who has edited the past four *The Best Short American Plays* anthologies, the plays all speak to a common theme. I hope the approach works as well here as it has for him.

## The Emerging Themes of the Included Works

In Lin-Manuel Miranda's Broadway hit *Hamilton*, the cast of characters (consisting of our Founding Fathers and some of their loved ones) asks the audience, "Who tells your story?" Miranda's piece is deeply entrenched in questions of history, memory, and legacy. The characters are asking us (and in a sense, the entire play is asking us, if that's not too metaphysical): What will we be remembered for? And more importantly, who will remember us? How will they remember us?

Miranda's *Hamilton* deals with themes of story, narrative, and who gets to tell the tale; however, it is not the only play that dives into these questions. In fact, it can be argued that *Hamilton* is part of a much larger theatre consciousness, as the plays presented here (many at the same time as the initial run of Miranda's runaway hit) also question issues of legacy and what we leave behind. As I curated this special collection, the themes of telling and listening, and living and dying, presented themselves in ways that were beautiful and exciting, horrifying and comforting—and at times, in a way that asks the audience to listen carefully, even when what we hear is too much to bear. In William Coleman's *Helvetica*, a stuffed bear guides the audience, in nonlinear order, through the life of a children's book author to demonstrate that our belief in fantasy helps us create the story of our lives. In E. M. Lewis's *Now Comes the Night*, a reclusive vet is haunted by a dead comrade-in-arms and a living journalist who wants the world to know his story. Bekah Brunstetter's *The Oregon Trail* gives us a look into the successes and defeats of a young woman, and what we put ourselves through in order to find our life's ideal place, via the popular 1990s computer game. *What Happened When* by Daniel Talbott is perhaps the most uncomfortable play in this anthology, bringing to mind the raw qualities of the in-yer-face playwrights of Britain from the late 1990s. Two siblings tell stories of their pasts, which include a number of acts of sexual abuse. It is the sort of play one may wish to put down but cannot help but finish. Can these characters find peace?

*Spit Like a Big Girl* by actress/playwright Clarinda Ross is a one-woman, autobiographical show (though it may be performed by two women) that focuses on Ross's father, a larger-than-life figure from the Appalachia region, and Ross's own struggles with raising a special-needs daughter in a complicated and fast-paced world. For residents of Appalachia and throughout the American South, storytelling is an important part of keeping the family history alive. *girls. in boys pants* is Kato McNickle's romantic (but rocky!) marriage of the world of words and the world of art; sometimes, a work of art just is, and that is its message. Lisa Lewis's *SCHOOLED* demonstrates the power dynamics in teacher/student relationships, particularly when the teacher is a well-regarded screenwriter, and the student is eager to learn by (almost) any means necessary ( . . . almost). One of the central debates in this piece involves whose stories get told, and which are important? How can the human act of storytelling be incorporated into making a Hollywood fortune? Is it even possible? And to what lengths are we willing to go in order to ensure our story is heard?

Miranda Jonte's *St. Francis* also deals with humanity versus commerce: Tessa, a veterinarian, creates a no-kill animal shelter but is being forced out by a Starbucks that seeks to lease the space. Tessa is forced to ask her estranged father for assistance. Lauren Ludwig's *Hamlet-Mobile* is a gorgeous hybrid of Shakespeare's masterpiece and a eulogy for Stephen Pine, the late artistic director for the experimental theatre company The Moving Shadow. The text of *Hamlet* operates as a "found piece" for this site-specific work, through which a company is able to mourn the passing of a beloved theatre colleague.

The last piece in this anthology is T. Anthony Marotta's puppet-play *(becoming) Hue-Man*. This piece is performed without dialogue and demonstrates the ways in which performances of masculinities are shaped, interrogated, made taboo, and (even in the best circumstances) read as "violent." In other words, we leave the anthology with the question, "What does it mean to be a man?"

Those of us who practice and study theatre are guided by the question, "What does it mean to be human?" These ten plays demonstrate different ways of asking the question, with an understanding that there is no one single answer. Welcome to the cutting edge of American theatre!

# Helvetica

## A play about stories

Will Coleman

# Will Coleman

Will Coleman is the artistic director of the Wheelhouse Theatre in Chicago. His play *Helvetica* won the 2015 Getchell New Play Award from SETC. Other plays include *Krugozori!*, *The Brooklyn Bridge (and other marvels)*, *A Crack in the Wall*, and the musicals *Zombie Boyfriend!* and *Squid Hunt!* He is currently an MFA candidate at the Playwright's Lab at Hollins University.

# Production History

*Helvetica* was produced as part of the Hollins-Mill Mountain Theatre Winter Festival of New Works. It ran January 16–25, 2015. The production was directed by Katie Mack and featured the following cast and creative team:

## Cast

**Myron**   Kevin McAlexander
**Past Helvetica**   Emma Sala
**Present Helvetica**   Bonny Branch
**Future Helvetica**   Kathy Clay
**Mother/Patient/Illustrator/Animal Shelter Employee**   Amanda Mansfield
**Father/Doctor/Agent**   Michael Mansfield
**Husband**   Jared M. Anderson

## Crew

**Scenic & Costume Designer**   Amanda Quivey
**Lighting Designer**   Ann Courtney
**Stage Manager**   Meredith Dayna Levy
**Hollins Technical Director**   John Forsman
**Mill Mountain Technical Director**   Karen Gierchak
**Producers**   Todd Ristau, Ernie Zulia
**Assistant Stage Manager**   Caroline Cromwell
**Production Assistants**   Maddie Buttitta, Katie Ward
**Light Board Operator**   Aileen Buckland
**Scenic Carpenters**   John Correll, Cole Tankersley, Katie Ward
**Box Office/House Manager**   Anna Goodwin

## Characters

**Past Helvetica**   Child. A young adult actress playing a precocious child. Very bright and energetic.
**Present Helvetica**   Adult. Anywhere from twenty-five to forty-five. Agitated, full of ennui.
**Future Helvetica**   Senior—Sixties to seventies, but fit, still a spark of youth.
**Myron**   A stuffed bear. He's played by an adult. No bear costumes, please.
**Mother**   Twenties to forties. She's tired. Troubled.
**Father**   Twenties to forties. Masculine. Works with his hands.
**Husband**   Twenties to forties. He's successful, and looks it.
**Patient**   Twenties to fifties. Female. Optimist.
**Doctor**   Any age. Any gender. Professional, with kind eyes.
**Illustrator**   Female, around the same age as Present Helvetica. She's fun. Enjoys life.
**Animal Shelter Employee**   Twenties to thirties. Either sex. Still enjoys their job.
**Agent**   Any age. Any gender. Helvetica's biggest fan.

## Notes

I think it is important to have a screen door as part of the set, possibly visible throughout the entire play.

Many parts should be played by the same actors—ideally, a cast of six to eight actors. One such combination could be the following:

Past Helvetica Mother/Illustrator/Patient/ Animal Shelter Employee
Present Helvetica Father/Doctor
Future Helvetica Husband/Agent
Myron

Or really any combination, as long as the actor playing Myron does not double as anyone else.

# SCENE ONE

[*Lights up on* MYRON, *a stuffed bear. He's played by a middle-aged man, somebody's beloved uncle. He's alone on an empty stage. He smiles and waves at the audience.*]

**MYRON** This is a story about my best friend.

[*PAST HELVETICA enters. She's a young adult actress playing a precocious eight-year-old. She stands, frozen in time.*]

This is Helvetica Burke. She is eight years old. This is the day her mother died.

[*SOUND EFFECT: Sharp, short.*]

[*PRESENT HELVETICA enters. She's somewhere between thirty and forty. She freezes.*]

Here she is today. The day her husband leaves her for a religious cult.

[*SOUND EFFECT: Longer, pained. Not a punchline.*]

[*FUTURE HELVETICA enters. Sixties to seventies, but fit, still a spark of youth. She freezes.*]

And this is the day she will die.

[*SOUND EFFECT: An unknown sound.*]

These are not the biggest events in her life. They are resonant, they are important, but they aren't everything. The biggest event in her life was on a quiet Sunday at home, when, after fixing that creaking sound that the screen door kept making, she decided she wasn't going to feel sorry for herself anymore, and she didn't. Like all people, Helvetica had her crises. When her husband left her, in the middle of her life, she thought it was his absence that sent her into a spiral of doubt, but it had really started long before then. But these moments, and all the ones in between, the 25,000 some-odd days that humans are blessed with, are what make up Helvetica, and she is our story.

[*All three HELVETICAs exit. Lights shift and we're in the past,* HELVETICA's *childhood home. The set is dressed in full view of the audience, or maybe by Kuroko.*]

[*SOUND EFFECT: The Sound of the Past.*]

[HELVETICA's MOTHER *is alone onstage.*]

Helvetica was born on the edge of a Large Midwestern City filled with space and time. Her parents were the ordinary sort of parents, as seen from the eyes of a child, with a masculine, outdoor-type father and the retiring wife. When she was born, they weren't quite sure what to do.

[MYRON *exits as* FATHER *joins* MOTHER *and they address* HELVETICA *in her crib.*]

**MOTHER**   Child, is it strange to still call her "child"?

**FATHER**   We'll think of a name eventually.

**MOTHER**   Darling.

**FATHER**   Sweetie.

**BOTH**   Child.

**FATHER**   I know that the world seems hard out there from the padded bottom of your crib . . .

**MOTHER**   Surrounded by bars . . .

**FATHER**   . . . But we want you to know that your mother and I are here for you . . .

**MOTHER**   Will always be here for you.

**FATHER**   Well, not always.

**MOTHER**   Almost always.

**FATHER**   For the foreseeable future, at least, we will be here for you, and help you, and guide you through the many strange turns a life may take.

**MOTHER**   You will have your first step soon, your first word, your first sentence.

**FATHER**   Your first doubt, your first tantrum, your first apology.

**MOTHER**   It's a strange and terrible place out there. There are countries that want to kill us.

**FATHER**   Other religions that would burn us to the ground.

**MOTHER**   I had a nightmare when I was pregnant that a man cut you out of my belly with an electric knife.

**FATHER**   Honey.

**MOTHER**   You know, like the ones you use at Thanksgiving? And he pulled you out of me, but it was too soon for you to be born yet, so you were just lying there on the floor while the man, not really more than a child, really, he just held on to his Thanksgiving knife and cried, and I stared at your cold little body on the carpet and then I woke up.

**FATHER**   Dreams are meaningless.

**MOTHER**   I was so relieved when you were born, because when I saw you, you looked nothing like the dead child from my dream. That was a relief.

**FATHER**   You had hair.

**MOTHER**    Such a lovely head of black hair.

**FATHER**    I wanted to pace in the waiting room like Ricky Ricardo and hand out cigars. But apparently they don't do that anymore.

**MOTHER**    Your father was right there by my side, feeding me ice chips and holding my hand.

**FATHER**    I was happy to do it.

**MOTHER**    When you were in my belly we called you Little Sprout, 'cause that's what you looked like on the sonogram.

**FATHER**    A little bean that had just sprouted.

**MOTHER**    She's four days old, honey, surely we'll think of a name soon.

**FATHER**    Until then, good night, little sprout.

**MOTHER**    Little bean.

**FATHER**    Little girl.

[*The lights go out on them. Lights shift to find* MYRON *and* MOTHER. *There could be a projection or some illustration of the story.*]

**MYRON**    Helvetica's mother grew up on a farm, so she loved animals. She could relate to them in a way that she never quite could with humans. She liked people well enough, she wasn't a shut-in, she had plenty of friends, but the pressure to talk, to keep up a conversation, was something that she always felt anxious about, in the presence of other humans. When she was alone with animals, her dog Bastion, for example, she loved the simple act of being silent with him. She also enjoyed brushing her family's dairy cows, playing with cats, geese, goats, and all of the other critters and crawlies that reside in the farmland of the Middle West. When she met Helvetica's father, they were both volunteering at the local animal shelter. [FATHER *enters.*] She was a junior—Art History—he was a year out of college—Literature— living with his parents, and trying to get a job. Times were tough all over. She graduated, and while her grades weren't quite admirable enough for Veterinary School, she did know one thing.

**MOTHER**    I want to do something with animals.

**MYRON**    And while Zoology and Marine Biology were outside her grasp, there was the job at the animal shelter.

**FATHER**    I've found a job.

**MOTHER**    No more substitute teaching?

**FATHER**    It's the Parks Service.

**MOTHER**    A Government job?

**FATHER**    Federal Benefits, good wages...

**MOTHER**   A Park Ranger? You love the outdoors.

**FATHER**   Sort of.

**MOTHER**   Well?

**FATHER**   I watch for forest fires.

**MOTHER**   Someone does that?

**FATHER**   It's me.

**MOTHER**   You're that someone.

**FATHER**   Now I am.

**MOTHER**   So, what, you sit and look through binoculars?

**FATHER**   Sometimes. I sit in a ranger station, high above the trees, and watch the horizon for impending forest fires.

**MOTHER**   Only you can prevent them.

**FATHER**   Exactly.

**MOTHER**   Well, sounds like you'll have plenty of time.

**FATHER**   I can work on my book!

**MYRON**   But as time wore on, as time must, Helvetica's parents found their vocations . . . less than they had hoped. He found he had plenty of time to write, but nothing to write about. He sat staring at the horizon, a beautiful one to be sure, and the thoughts in his head, always bursting to get out when he was younger, seemed to drift away over the tops of the trees.

**MOTHER**   You know I saw something the other day.

**FATHER**   Something great?

**MOTHER**   Yes.

**FATHER**   I saw a fox taking a bath.

**MOTHER**   It was a word. In the font selector.

**FATHER**   The what?

**MOTHER**   The fonts. It was a name.

**FATHER**   For our little sprout?

**MOTHER**   Helvetica.

**FATHER**   What does it mean?

**MOTHER**   I have no idea.

**FATHER**   I love it. Helvetica.

**MOTHER**   Helvetica.

**MYRON**   Helvetica's mother was good at her job. She enjoyed it immensely, and it showed, so she was promoted. Around the time Helvetica was beginning to gestate inside her, she accepted a promotion. It was now her job to personally euthanize the animals to whom she had grown so attached. She always knew it was happening. Too many animals, not enough people. And although she herself thought it might/should be the other way around, there was no changing the fact that the animals had to be killed, and someone had to do it. Older ones, mostly. The cute puppies and kittens would usually get snatched up, sometimes by the workers themselves. Helvetica's mother had a small menagerie herself at one time. It happened on Friday mornings. So while most people looked forward to the weekend, Helvetica's mother knew that Friday only brought death in the form of a small room and a crank of a dial. Gas was more efficient than needles. As the months . . . and years went on, she found that she had trouble looking her own animals in the eye. The silent comfort she once felt with Meg or with Pip, Hermione and Edmund, Huck and Scout eroded over time. She slowly gave the animals away, to good homes, of course. And she cried when each one was driven away, but they were tears of relief, for deep in her heart, she knew they knew. They could smell the death on her like they could smell fear. And although she still loved animals, she couldn't keep them at home any longer. Her grief had drowned the joy she had once found in the company of living things. So, as a compromise to herself, when Helvetica was one year old, she gave her a stuffed bear, a beautiful, handmade piece, with onyx eyes and soft, downy fur. Because his singular expression didn't remind her of any of her favorite protagonists, she decided on Myron. We were friends at first sight.

## SCENE TWO

[PAST HELVETICA *is alone onstage. Dancing, or playing on pieces of furniture.* MYRON *enters, and watches her for a time before speaking.*]

**MYRON**   Like all children with no siblings, Helvetica relied on her imagination more than most. She fought dragons and rescued handsome princes from evil wizards, she crash landed her spaceship on a hostile, alien planet, she even solved the mystery of Who Killed Barbie? Hint: It was Skipper. But her favorite game of all was Travel. More than anything, Helvetica loved to construct a sailboat out of household furniture, and sail around the living room, her trusty First Mate, yours truly, at her side.

[HELVETICA *begins building the sailboat out of furniture.*]

**PAST HELVETICA**   Put your back into it, Myron!

**MYRON**   Aye, Captain!

**PAST HELVETICA**   We have to get this cargo loaded before Cap'n Kloves figures out it's missing!

**MYRON**   Ah, the Dread Pirate Cap'n Kloves! Scourge of the Seven Seas, hated from Tripoli to Singapore!

**PAST HELVETICA**   He hasn't seen the last of Captain Helvetica! We may have to sneak away this time, but one day—

**MYRON**   We shall return to Black Island and have our revenge!

**PAST HELVETICA**   For now we will be satisfied by the liberation of these treasures.

**MYRON**   And you're sure none of these could go . . . missing?

**PAST HELVETICA**   Myron, I've told you! These treasures belong to the people of Hong City.

**MYRON**   But there's so much here. Surely they won't miss a little gold. Don't we deserve to be rewarded?

**PAST HELVETICA**   All the reward I need is seeing the delight in the people's eyes when I return what's been stolen.

**MYRON**   Sigh. And the look on Cap'n Kloves face when he realizes we stole it out from under him.

**PAST HELVETICA**   That too.

**MYRON**   Still we could use a new coat of paint, maybe a cannon or something.

**PAST HELVETICA**   Posh. The Condor is a fine ship. Fastest clipper in the Philippines.

[MYRON *looks through a spyglass.*]

**MYRON**   Avast! The pirate's gang approaches!

**PAST HELVETICA**   Retreat!

**MYRON**   If only we had a cannon!

**PAST HELVETICA**   Speed is as fine a weapon as any!

**MYRON**   They draw closer!

**PAST HELVETICA**   Then shove off, ya dog! Let the winds guide us home!

**MYRON**   Aye, Captain!

[*They sail away.*]

## SCENE THREE

[*SOUND EFFECT: The Sound of the Present.*]

[PRESENT HELVETICA *is sitting at a table at a restaurant, perusing a menu.* MYRON *enters.*]

**MYRON**   By the time she was in her late twenties, Helvetica had accumulated a variety of ex-boyfriends, and one, she was somewhat proud to note, on again, off again female lover. She didn't like to affix labels to herself or be "part of a cause," but looking back on it years later, she thought of the relationship fondly. But on this night, four years after graduating college—that relationship was over, and she found herself on a blind date. A setup courtesy of friends from work.

[HUSBAND *enters, looking around, and spots* HELVETICA. *He's masculine, successful, and looks it. A touch insecure, though. Probably some bullshit with his parents.*]

He didn't look like she expected. He was handsome, but in a unique way. He was also a little scattered. He looked like he wasn't in control of the situation. Helvetica found this appealing.

**HUSBAND**   Helvetica?

**PRESENT HELVETICA**   That's me! So you're him.

**HUSBAND**   I am indeed him.

**PRESENT HELVETICA**   Hi.

[*He sits down.*]

**HUSBAND**   It's nice to meet you.

**PRESENT HELVETICA**   Nice to meet you. The boys have told me a lot about you.

**HUSBAND**   Really? They seemed awfully tight-lipped about you.

**PRESENT HELVETICA**   I cultivate an air of mystery.

**HUSBAND**   That can be very appealing.

**PRESENT HELVETICA**   I've found that to be true.

**HUSBAND**   Does that make me a detective?

**PRESENT HELVETICA**   It makes me Agatha Christie and you some guy on a train with a book.

**MYRON**   The easy, flirtatious banter was second nature to Helvetica. While she found His Girl Friday charmingly outdated from a feminist perspective, there was no denying the dialogue. Her sparring partner, having not had the pleasure of experiencing Ms. Russel's superb delivery, felt like he was missing something.

**HUSBAND**   So did you uh—find the place okay, I mean, with the weather and all it's—

**PRESENT HELVETICA**   Oh, no I live close to here, I come here all the time.

**HUSBAND**   Oh yeah? My office is just down the street.

**PRESENT HELVETICA**   We could have passed each other a thousand times.

**HUSBAND**   Never even noticed.

**PRESENT HELVETICA**   So they said you're in finance.

**HUSBAND**   Yep.

**PRESENT HELVETICA**   What does that mean?

**HUSBAND**   You don't really wanna know, do you?

**PRESENT HELVETICA**   Oh god, I really don't.

**HUSBAND**   What do you do?

**PRESENT HELVETICA**   I come up with stories.

**HUSBAND**   Stories?

**PRESENT HELVETICA**   Short answer. I'm a writer.

**HUSBAND**   Long answer?

**PRESENT HELVETICA**   You don't want to hear about it.

**HUSBAND**   I really do.

**MYRON**   What Helvetica thought was:

**PRESENT HELVETICA**   Well . . . I think it would probably have been better to never be born at all. The world is nothing but suffering followed by death, and the only alleviation humanity has come up with is stories. Fantasies to make us believe that there's something worthwhile to this bankrupt existence.

**MYRON**   What she actually said was:

**PRESENT HELVETICA**   I try to make the world a little happier.

**HUSBAND**   You want a drink?

**PRESENT HELVETICA**   Yes.

[*Lights shift.*]

**MYRON**   It was a below average date, in her estimation. Her usual, cynical honesty had put him off, as it did many others. They ate, they drank, but conversation seemed forced, she was asking him questions, searching for mutual interests. They both liked "comedies" and "music" and "spending time with friends." Generic, non-threatening answers to engender the least possible amount of disagreement or controversy. But then something happened.

**HUSBAND**   This isn't working, is it?

**PRESENT HELVETICA**   I don't think so, no.

**HUSBAND**   Okay, then how about this? The chances of us seeing each other again right now are pretty low, right?

**PRESENT HELVETICA**   Low.

**HUSBAND**   Like single digits.

**PRESENT HELVETICA**   Agreed.

**HUSBAND**   So why don't we ditch the bullshit for a minute, huh? You have opinions?

**PRESENT HELVETICA**   Doesn't everyone?

**HUSBAND**   Unpopular ones?

**PRESENT HELVETICA**   Almost exclusively.

**HUSBAND**   All right, then. We trade unpopular opinions. Cut straight through the fat and really get into what we're like. What makes us individuals.

**PRESENT HELVETICA**   Sounds fun.

**MYRON**   It sounded like a lot more than just fun. It was straight out of a movie screen. Woody Allen asking Diane Keaton to start their first date with a kiss. Sentiment and Cynicism fought it out for a quick three rounds inside Helvetica's brain. Sentiment won on points.

**HUSBAND**   Okay. I'll go first. I love the Microsoft Office paper clip guy.

[HELVETICA *laughs. A real, honest laugh that melts the tension from her shoulders, and when she looks up at her future* HUSBAND, *she sees him in a new light.*]

Your turn.

**PRESENT HELVETICA**   I really like airports.

**HUSBAND**   Really.

**PRESENT HELVETICA**   I've always found them relaxing. They're so clean and organized. Plus I love the schedule. I've got two hours to kill, all alone, I can totally read a good chunk of my book before I board.

**HUSBAND**   What kind of books do you like?

**PRESENT HELVETICA**   No, no, we can talk about that later! Be more offensive!

**HUSBAND**   Um . . . I don't like Bob Dylan!

**PRESENT HELVETICA**   What?

**HUSBAND**   He can't sing!

**PRESENT HELVETICA**   He doesn't have to sing!

**HUSBAND**   Then he shouldn't!

[*This is extremely good natured, they're both laughing.*]

**PRESENT HELVETICA**   I don't believe in God.

**HUSBAND**   I'm Jewish, but I'm anti-Zionist.

**PRESENT HELVETICA**   I'm not really interested in the news. I just don't care.

**HUSBAND**   It's hard to care sometimes. I like Ben Affleck.

**PRESENT HELVETICA**   I like country music.

**HUSBAND**   I like Death Metal.

**PRESENT HELVETICA**   I didn't vote last time.

**HUSBAND**   I haven't voted in years.

**PRESENT HELVETICA**   What's the point?

**HUSBAND**   I can't fucking stand to look at myself in the mirror.

[*The laughter stops.*]

**PRESENT HELVETICA**   Who can?

**HUSBAND**   I think I used to be able to, but something . . .

**PRESENT HELVETICA**   I think everyone feels that way sometimes.

**HUSBAND**   No, really. Sometimes, I just think that there's . . . there's no point to anything, you know? I mean, what am I doing this for? Why am I making this money? To pay for nicer things, and then even nicer things, and what? So I can have a child, and hope that one day that child will have even nicer things? Is that we're doing? Progressively sliding up the economic scale? For what? To raise privileged monsters who hate us and then die of a drug overdose at twenty-four?

**PRESENT HELVETICA**   I don't know.

[*He reaches out his hand.*]

**MYRON**   And Helvetica made a decision.

## SCENE FOUR

[*SOUND EFFECT: The Sound of the Future.*]

[FUTURE HELVETICA *and another* PATIENT, *much younger, are waiting in a doctor's waiting room. An oncologist's office.* FUTURE HELVETICA *is holding a book in her hands, but she's not reading. Her eyes wander. The* PATIENT *is staring at her.*]

**PATIENT**   Hi.

**FUTURE HELVETICA**   Hello.

**PATIENT**   I'm sorry.

**FUTURE HELVETICA**   What's wrong?

**PATIENT**   It's nothing, I just—

**FUTURE HELVETICA**   Yes?

**PATIENT**   I don't mean to bother you.

**FUTURE HELVETICA**   Oh?

**PATIENT**   You're Helvetica Burke, aren't you?

**FUTURE HELVETICA**   Um, yes, yes I am.

**PATIENT** I'm such a big fan of your books.

**FUTURE HELVETICA** Thank you. That's ah—nice to hear.

**PATIENT** My mother read *Darkly Drear* to me when I was a kid, and I—

**FUTURE HELVETICA** How nice.

**PATIENT** I'm sorry, this isn't the right . . .

**FUTURE HELVETICA** Oh no, I . . . It's always nice to talk with fans.

**PATIENT** I'm sorry, I just—Are you here?

**FUTURE HELVETICA** I'm not sure yet.

**PATIENT** Oh. I uh, I have breast cancer.

**FUTURE HELVETICA** Oh. I'm sorry.

**PATIENT** They cut my tits off.

**FUTURE HELVETICA** Shit.

**PATIENT** Yeah. And then I think I'm fine for a year and . . .

**FUTURE HELVETICA** Oh.

**PATIENT** My scan comes back and they want to do another biopsy. Just To Be Sure, they said. To Be Safe.

**FUTURE HELVETICA** I'm . . .

**PATIENT** And today I—I find out if it's in my liver.

**FUTURE HELVETICA** Is there someone—

**PATIENT** My mom's across the country. She wants me to move home.

**FUTURE HELVETICA** I—I started getting these headaches so. They cut open my head and cut it out, they just want to make sure it's uh . . .

**PATIENT** Little things are persistent, aren't they?

**FUTURE HELVETICA** Tenacious.

**PATIENT** Good one.

**FUTURE HELVETICA** Shaved my head. For the surgery, you know? So I feel like a fraud, people think I've had chemo, but . . . I got off easy on the cancer lottery. So far.

**PATIENT** I'm sure it's fine. They catch it early?

**FUTURE HELVETICA** Yeah.

**PATIENT** They do that shit all the time.

**FUTURE HELVETICA** You too. C'mon, lots of people come back from what you—

[*Silence for a moment.*]

**PATIENT**   Anyway, I didn't want to unload on you, I'm sure you've got your own stuff going on and—

**FUTURE HELVETICA**   No, it's okay. It's good to talk.

**PATIENT**   Yeah. I just. I really liked your books. Even the Ballerina one.

[HELVETICA *laughs*.]

**FUTURE HELVETICA**   Yeah, I took a lot of flak for that one.

**PATIENT**   There's nothing wrong with telling kids the truth.

**FUTURE HELVETICA**   Thanks.

**PATIENT**   You scared?

**FUTURE HELVETICA**   Sure.

**PATIENT**   I'm scared.

**FUTURE HELVETICA**   That's okay.

**PATIENT**   Can you uh—you think you could a—

[FUTURE HELVETICA *moves to sit closer to the* PATIENT. *After a moment, she reaches out slowly, and takes the* PATIENT'*s hand*.]

**FUTURE HELVETICA**   When I was a little girl my mother told me something. She said that the hands were the window to the soul. Everyone says it's the eyes, I know, but . . . someone's hands really tell you what they're like. Our hands are how we interact with the world, and with others. Rough or smooth, hard or gentle, our hands, and the way we touch are the closest we can be to someone, and are our most valuable possession. So when we hold hands, it's a cooperation. Each hand must carry some of the weight of the other. We're carrying each other.

[*Before anything else can be said, the* DOCTOR *enters*.]

**DOCTOR**   Good afternoon, Ms. Burke.

**FUTURE HELVETICA**   Doctor.

**DOCTOR**   If you'll follow me, please.

[*The* PATIENT *lets go of* HELVETICA'*s hand and smiles*. HELVETICA *follows the* DOCTOR *to another part of the stage. The* DOCTOR'*s desk is a piece of the sailboat from earlier*.]

**DOCTOR**   Thanks for coming in.

**FUTURE HELVETICA**   Is it like last time?

**DOCTOR**   The MRI showed a small mass in your cerebellum.

**FUTURE HELVETICA**   Oh.

**DOCTOR**   We've been able to grade the tumor, Ms. Burke, and as far as these things go, you understand, things are looking good—

**FUTURE HELVETICA**   Good.

**DOCTOR**   It's really very minor. What we call a grade I astrocytoma.

**FUTURE HELVETICA**   Another one.

**DOCTOR**   Right.

**FUTURE HELVETICA**   But it's not cancer.

**DOCTOR**   It's not cancer, no.

[HELVETICA *sighs in relief.*]

**FUTURE HELVETICA**   So what do we do?

**DOCTOR**   Well, as I said, it's not cancer, but the fact that it's there at all can present some difficulties. I would schedule a surgery immediately.

**FUTURE HELVETICA**   Again.

**DOCTOR**   It's actually a fairly simple procedure. Easier than last time. Much smaller incision. They do it every day.

**FUTURE HELVETICA**   Okay.

**DOCTOR**   Let's take a look at the schedule, shall we? How about the nineteenth?

**FUTURE HELVETICA**   So soon.

**DOCTOR**   We need to get to it as quickly as possible. Is there someone who can pick you up?

**FUTURE HELVETICA**   I'll figure something out.

**DOCTOR**   Okay, we'll see you then.

**FUTURE HELVETICA**   Sounds good.

**DOCTOR**   You're gonna be fine.

[*They exit.* MYRON *enters.*]

**MYRON**   At Helvetica's funeral, there was a reading from her book *Petunia's Brain*.

Petunia's Brain was like any other brain, in terms of neurons and vessels and cells.

But the thoughts that it thought were unlike the thoughts thought by Sleeping Beauties and Snow Whites and Belles.

For Petunia, though named for a flower, was unlike any plant you may find in the ground.

She was smart, she was rough, and just full of the stuff that made her different from those all around.

But the teachers in school and the kids on the block didn't like someone special like that,

So they hit her with sticks and they played their mean tricks, and the teachers sat her down for a chat.

You need to try harder, the teachers explained, to be just like the others in school.

And though Petunia tried hard, [well maybe not all that hard], she ended up breaking their rule.

'Cause what could she do? You can't be someone else when your brain thinks things different than they.

So she danced her own dance and she wore funny pants and didn't care what those fuckers would say.

I may have changed it a bit.

# SCENE FIVE

[*SOUND EFFECT: The Sound of the Past.*]

[PAST HELVETICA *and her* FATHER *are fishing off of a dock.* MYRON *is with them.*]

**MYRON**   Vacation.

**PAST HELVETICA**   This is boring.

**FATHER**   It's not boring, it's peaceful.

**PAST HELVETICA**   That's just a word adults use to mean boring.

**FATHER**   Sometimes. But look at that view.

**MYRON**   Reminds me of my natural habitat. Sometimes I long to return there, and survive on nuts and berries and the slower woodland creatures.

**PAST HELVETICA**   It's pretty.

**FATHER**   Just pretty?

**PAST HELVETICA**   I like the way you can see the trees reflected in the water.

**FATHER**   There you go. What else?

**PAST HELVETICA**   We could be missing something on TV.

**FATHER**   I sure hope so.

**MYRON**   *Night Murder* is on!

**PAST HELVETICA**   You think Mom's back yet?

**FATHER**   It's at least an hour into town.

**PAST HELVETICA**   So we're just gonna sit here.

**FATHER**   We're gonna catch a fish.

**PAST HELVETICA**   Ugh.

**FATHER**   And then we're gonna eat it.

**PAST HELVETICA**    Can't you do it?

**FATHER**    I'm building our relationship, Helvetica. One day, you'll look back on this day and smile. We're making lasting memories.

**PAST HELVETICA**    You think I'll forget how bored I was?

**FATHER**    I hope I'll forget how rude you were.

**PAST HELVETICA**    Can I at least get a book?

**FATHER**    Nope.

[*She sighs dramatically.*]

**PAST HELVETICA**    Can you tell me a story, then?

**FATHER**    Now that might be something I can do.

**PAST HELVETICA**    Cool.

**FATHER**    You have to keep an eye on your line, though.

**PAST HELVETICA**    Deal, deal. Story.

**MYRON**    Tell a story about a courageous bear, long domesticated, suddenly on his own in the wild.

**FATHER**    Here's a story about a fish.

**MYRON**    It's like he's not listening to me.

**FATHER**    Once upon a time there was a little girl who didn't appreciate the nice things her father did for her.

**PAST HELVETICA**    Daaad!

**FATHER**    All right, all right. Once upon a time there was a fisherman.

**PAST HELVETICA**    Fisherwoman.

**FATHER**    Excuse me, a fisherwoman. And the fisherwoman had to provide for her family, but it was a very poor season, and they were very hungry. So one morning she was out at the stream, and she cast her line, and after a great long time—

**PAST HELVETICA**    As long as this?

**FATHER**    The fisherwoman was very patient, and she knew how to enjoy nature, and she thought deep thoughts and figured out many things while she was waiting for that line to move. But eventually it moved, and she hauled up into the air . . . a very small fish. A disappointing haul to be sure. And the fish said, "Please, noble fisherwoman, please! I am such a small fish, I can't provide for your family! But if you wait for a season, I will eat and grow larger, and then catch me again, sell me for a large profit!" And the fisherwoman narrowed her eyes. "I would be very simple indeed if I were to give up certain gain for uncertain profit."

**PAST HELVETICA** . . . Is that it?

**FATHER** That's it.

**PAST HELVETICA** That's stupid.

**MYRON** I bet I could catch a fish.

**FATHER** How is it stupid?

**PAST HELVETICA** It just is.

**FATHER** It's about how what you have is better than some uncertain thing you may have in the future.

**PAST HELVETICA** I get it, Dad, I'm just saying. Okay, okay. My turn.

**FATHER** Go ahead.

**PAST HELVETICA** The fisherwoman narrowed her eyes. "A talking fish," she shouted, and struck a deal with the little fish on the spot. "I will never let harm come to you, little fish," she said. "If you will agree to jump into this bowl here, and tour the country, and go on television, and make us both rich." "Hmm," said the fish. "The stream is pretty boring." "We'll see the world together," said the wonderfully bright and beautiful fisherwoman. "50/50." The little fish narrowed his eyes. "60/40." They agreed, and her family had plenty to eat, and the little fish was very happy, and in my story no one had to die or anything. The End.

[FATHER *laughs.*]

**FATHER** All right, your story is better.

**PAST HELVETICA** I know.

[HELVETICA *has discovered something.*]

## SCENE SIX

[*SOUND EFFECT: The Sound of the Present.*]

[PRESENT HELVETICA *is at a book store, with her* HUSBAND. MYRON *appears.*]

**MYRON** She published her first children's book at thirty-one, shortly after getting married. It's called *Sailing Around the Living Room*, and it was very well received. I'll bet you can guess what it's about. A courageous bear, long since—

**HUSBAND** That was fun!

**PRESENT HELVETICA** You think so? You think they liked it?

**HUSBAND** Yeah, it's a funny story, right?

**PRESENT HELVETICA** Something like that.

**HUSBAND** I've got to run.

**PRESENT HELVETICA** I thought we were getting dinner?

**HUSBAND**   Client meeting, got pushed back from yesterday.

**PRESENT HELVETICA**   Oh, uh. Okay.

**HUSBAND**   Sorry, babe. Gotta make money.

**PRESENT HELVETICA**   This is making money.

**HUSBAND**   It sure is.

[*He kisses her goodbye, and leaves.*]

**MYRON**   We can go to dinner.

**PRESENT HELVETICA**   I guess we'll have to.

**MYRON**   I'll stay in your purse.

**PRESENT HELVETICA**   Italian?

**MYRON**   I don't eat.

**PRESENT HELVETICA**   I know.

**MYRON**   I'll keep you company, though.

[*A female* BOOK STORE EMPLOYEE, HELVETICA's *future* ILLUSTRATOR, *walks by.*]

**ILLUSTRATOR**   Ms. Burke?

**PRESENT HELVETICA**   Helvetica.

**ILLUSTRATOR**   Great reading.

**PRESENT HELVETICA**   Oh, thanks.

**ILLUSTRATOR**   It's so . . . wistful. In a good way, though, right?

**PRESENT HELVETICA**   It is?

**ILLUSTRATOR**   I thought so. You know, the girl having these imaginary adventures, but there's that sense that one day it'll be over. 'Cause she starts school the next day, right? And that's such a symbol of change, about crushing the imagination and the creative impulse out of us?

**PRESENT HELVETICA**   Haha. Yeah, that's sort of what I was going for.

**ILLUSTRATOR**   But the kids don't get it.

**PRESENT HELVETICA**   Not right now, at least.

**ILLUSTRATOR**   I know! Like, these kids are gonna grow up loving this story, and then come back to it when they have kids of their own, and get this totally different level to the story later, you know?

**PRESENT HELVETICA**   You really think so?

**ILLUSTRATOR**   Oh, definitely.

**PRESENT HELVETICA**   Hey, are you off work?

**ILLUSTRATOR**   Oh yeah, I just stuck around for the reading.

**PRESENT HELVETICA**   My husband just had to run off to— You wanna grab something to eat?

**ILLUSTRATOR**   Uh, sure! Yeah, that'd be fun.

**PRESENT HELVETICA**   You can stop telling me how great I am, I promise.

**ILLUSTRATOR**   Deal.

**MYRON**   Helvetica and the Book Store Employee became great friends, eventually she became her second-best friend, and the illustrator of all the rest of her books. They were close, and discussed much in their lives, but the secret that she never revealed was that Helvetica didn't really think her story was all that wistful at all. Because she never had that spark snuffed out of her at school, or by her parents, or anyone else. She and her faithful, courageous, handsome stuffed bear were constant companions, well into adulthood. Until one day, after everything fell apart, he was placed in the attic. I was placed in the attic. Helvetica's work suffered after that. Her public appearances became less frequent, her output stopped altogether.

## SCENE SEVEN

[*SOUND EFFECT: The Sound of the Future.*]

[*Animal Shelter.* FUTURE HELVETICA *is looking at dogs, which can be portrayed in a number of ways, probably just mimed. Real dogs wouldn't really be worth it.*]

**FUTURE HELVETICA**   Well, hello there! Hey fuzzyface. Are you ready to get out of here? I'll bet you are. I can't imagine having to stay cooped up in here.

[*An* ANIMAL SHELTER WORKER *joins her.*]

**ANIMAL SHELTER WORKER**   Neither can I.

**FUTURE HELVETICA**   It must be so hard to work here.

**ANIMAL SHELTER WORKER**   Sometimes. Sometimes it's worth it, though.

**FUTURE HELVETICA**   This one's a sweetheart.

**ANIMAL SHELTER WORKER**   Oh, absolutely. Found him living in a dumpster behind a restaurant.

**FUTURE HELVETICA**   Probably eating well, at least.

**ANIMAL SHELTER WORKER**   Poisoned, actually.

**FUTURE HELVETICA**   . . . Oh.

**ANIMAL SHELTER WORKER**   Happens a lot. Dogs aren't really made to eat people food.

**FUTURE HELVETICA**   Well, neither are humans.

**ANIMAL SHELTER WORKER**   Haha. Yeah, I guess not.

**FUTURE HELVETICA**   Seems okay now, though.

**ANIMAL SHELTER WORKER**   Do you have kids?

**FUTURE HELVETICA**   Nope. Just me.

**ANIMAL SHELTER WORKER**   I think he'd be a great choice. Huskies aren't great with kids, but are usually very loyal. They just have to know you're the boss.

**FUTURE HELVETICA**   Shouldn't be too hard.

**ANIMAL SHELTER WORKER**   What kind of dogs have you had in the past?

**FUTURE HELVETICA**   None, actually. Not that I remember anyway. But my mother had dogs and . . . I've been thinking about her lately.

**ANIMAL SHELTER WORKER**   Oh, really? Well, there might be some other ones that might be a little easier for beginners . . .

**FUTURE HELVETICA**   I think I like him. He looks, well, not like a Myron . . . like a Joharis.

**ANIMAL SHELTER WORKER**   You a *Darkly Drear* fan?

**FUTURE HELVETICA**   You could say that.

**ANIMAL SHELTER WORKER**   Oh my god. You're . . .

[*She smiles.*]

**FUTURE HELVETICA**   I'm surprised you recognized me.

**ANIMAL SHELTER WORKER**   I'm reading it to my son. He loves you.

**FUTURE HELVETICA**   Oh, children don't know books by their authors, just the stories. He loves *Darkly*. He's probably not even aware I exist yet.

**ANIMAL SHELTER WORKER**   Maybe not.

**FUTURE HELVETICA**   Sometimes I wish it were still that simple.

**ANIMAL SHELTER WORKER**   Everybody has a job, right?

**FUTURE HELVETICA**   What?

**ANIMAL SHELTER WORKER**   Well, I mean, we all think that certain people, wow, those actors, they've got it made. They get paid for playing around in front of a camera. But if you know any of those people, it's a lot of work, right? And the press, and they have to be away from their families. And you think, wouldn't it be nice to be a famous author, and just make up stories all day?

**FUTURE HELVETICA**   And there ends up being so much more than that.

**ANIMAL SHELTER WORKER**   Yeah, you have to go on tour, and promotions and—

**FUTURE HELVETICA**   Always be thinking of something new.

**ANIMAL SHELTER WORKER**   And if it's not the same as *Darkly Drear*—

**FUTURE HELVETICA**   You get crucified.

**ANIMAL SHELTER WORKER**   Yeah.

**FUTURE HELVETICA**   Or isn't it wonderful to be able to work with animals all day, and take care of them and find them good homes?

**ANIMAL SHELTER WORKER**   Yeah.

**FUTURE HELVETICA**   But there's more to it than that, isn't there?

**ANIMAL SHELTER WORKER**   Yeah.

**FUTURE HELVETICA**   What do I need to sign?

**ANIMAL SHELTER WORKER**   Come with me.

## SCENE EIGHT

[*SOUND EFFECT: The Sound of the Present.*]

[PRESENT HELVETICA *and her* HUSBAND *are at home.* MYRON *enters.*]

**MYRON**   People always asked Helvetica why she never had kids.

**HUSBAND**   So he left. Not like I can blame him.

**PRESENT HELVETICA**   You don't think she had a right?

**HUSBAND**   A right to what? It was his kid too.

**PRESENT HELVETICA**   No, I agree. But ultimately it was her decision.

**HUSBAND**   Yeah but without telling him?

**PRESENT HELVETICA**   It's complicated.

**HUSBAND**   I don't think it's all that complicated.

**PRESENT HELVETICA**   What if it wasn't his?

**HUSBAND**   Well then, all the more reason—

**PRESENT HELVETICA**   What would we do?

**HUSBAND**   Oh, I get a say?

**PRESENT HELVETICA**   Let's imagine, for a moment, that you do.

**HUSBAND**   I don't know.

**PRESENT HELVETICA**   We have money.

**HUSBAND**   But we have lives.

**PRESENT HELVETICA**   Some would say that a baby is the most important thing you can do with your life.

**HUSBAND**   What do you think?

**PRESENT HELVETICA**   Well, we always said we wanted kids someday.

**HUSBAND**   Someday is now?

**PRESENT HELVETICA**   I'm not saying that.

**HUSBAND**   You're very carefully not saying anything at all.

**PRESENT HELVETICA**   It would be hard for me to write if I had to take care of a baby.

**HUSBAND**   I don't imagine you'd get much done for a couple of years.

**PRESENT HELVETICA**   Unless you quit your job.
[*He laughs.*]
Is that funny?

**HUSBAND**   Um, no . . .

**PRESENT HELVETICA**   It just didn't occur to you?

**HUSBAND**   No.

**PRESENT HELVETICA**   Why should I quit my job?

**HUSBAND**   Because.

**PRESENT HELVETICA**   Careful. 'Cause I'm the woman? 'Cause I work at home?

**HUSBAND**   'Cause you work at—

**PRESENT HELVETICA**   I get paid pretty well for what I do at home.

**HUSBAND**   I know that, just . . .

**PRESENT HELVETICA**   More than you.

**HUSBAND**   Oh Christ, Helvetica.

**PRESENT HELVETICA**   Oh, sorry. You like to forget that right?

**HUSBAND**   So you're deciding?

**PRESENT HELVETICA**   I haven't decided anything.

**HUSBAND**   I'm sorry I laughed.

**PRESENT HELVETICA**   No, it's fine. It's good to know how you really feel. It's not like you're feeding the hungry or anything.

**HUSBAND**   I like to think—

**PRESENT HELVETICA**   But you're wrong. You work for a bank. A collection of banks, actually. A conglomeration of banks, an abomination of banks, I don't know the collective noun for banks.

**HUSBAND**   Hel—

**PRESENT HELVETICA**   And we all know what banks do, don't we? Banks take. I'm working in my office, I'm giving. Every profession is either giving or taking. I'm making up stories, I'm putting something into people's minds, but you, you're taking. Banks take people's houses and their cars, and their family-owned restaurants and the libraries and the museums and the theaters and the schools. And one day there won't be anything left but the banks. And then what will they take? 'Cause there won't be anything left. And as much as I give, the banks can always take more.

**HUSBAND**   Very poetic. You should put that in a story. *Comrade Mouse and the Soul of the Proletariat.*

**PRESENT HELVETICA**   Fuck you.

**HUSBAND**   No, fuck you. You trade in fairy tales and tell yourself it's art. You're too selfish to have a kid and you want to blame it on me.

**PRESENT HELVETICA**   You're right.

**HUSBAND**   What?

# SCENE NINE

[*Lights shift.* MYRON *and* PRESENT HELVETICA *are telling a story.*]

**MYRON**   It was a day like any other. The day she put me into the attic. It wasn't so bad at first. There had been times, of course, when I was on display in the guest bedroom. Sometimes months would pass without her noticing me, but it was always . . . temporary. The attic felt permanent, it felt . . . personal. Sometime after the divorce. It was sudden, but somehow I saw it coming for a long time.

**PRESENT HELVETICA**   I'm sorry, Myron.

[*She puts him in the attic. This can be done in any number of ways.*]

**MYRON**   I don't wanna go away. Don't listen to him, you need something. You do. You're not who he thinks you are. No. Stop. Listen to me! Talk to me, Helvetica. Talk to me. Please. You do, you need me. Please. Please. Please. I know you can hear me.

[PRESENT HELVETICA *can hear him, but she ignores him. Maybe she even tells herself she can't hear him any longer.*]

Don't do this. I don't like it up here. Please let me out, I'm scared. I'm . . . I'm all alone.

[MYRON *exits.* PRESENT HELVETICA *sits down to write. As* PRESENT HELVETICA *narrates, two* DANCERS, *who may or may not be* PAST HELVETICA *and* HUSBAND, *act out the story through dance.*]

**PRESENT HELVETICA**   Once upon a time there was a Ballerina. And she was perfect. She was beautiful, and eternally young, and she danced all day and never got tired. Yes, she was perfect in all the ways you can be perfect. Except the most important way. She wasn't real. Instead of blood and bones and flesh and fingernails, she was made of wood and some clockwork parts, and when a small crank was turned, she danced to a number of different songs. She lived in a music box in the Toymaker's window, and little girls and boys loved to watch her dance, and their laughter made her happy. But one day she was sold to a rich man who worked in the heart of the Palace. An advisor to the Queen, they said. And when the advisor's wife opened the gift, she clapped her hands and laughed, and the Ballerina danced and danced. As the years passed, The advisor's wife would open her box every once in a while, and get a faraway look in her eye as the Ballerina danced, really giving it her all, her springs and gears straining for all they were worth, but then she would close the box again, sometimes for months at a time. When you're built to do one thing, any time not spent doing it is torture. And one day the advisor's wife died. There was a great funeral, and the day after the service, the advisor spent hours watching the Ballerina dance, over and over, watching her wear down, then turning the crank with tears in his eyes. It confused the Ballerina. Her dance was supposed to make people happy, not sad. So she changed. She didn't think she could do it, go against her own clockwork like that, but she pulled and she strained, and she managed a grand jeté in a totally new place. The advisor almost dropped the box in surprise. Could this little dancer really have changed her dance? Or was grief driving him mad? Late that night he dreamed a familiar dream. He was dancing in a great ballroom, but for the first time, instead of dancing with his wife, it was the Ballerina. They danced through the old clockwork steps, and then the new grand jeté, and then they were on their own, making it up as they went, and the Ballerina laughed. She had never danced with a partner before. So it went for some time. The advisor resigned his position, staying in his chambers most days, to watch the ballerina dance, and then meet her in a dream, where they would dance through the night. It was a year before he could admit to himself that he had fallen in love with her. He never said anything, not even in the dream dance. They let the dance talk for them; to ruin it with words would be something close to sacrilege. So he just watched her dance more and more. Hundreds of times a day, and all through the night. The Ballerina was in heaven. And then, the advisor realized that people would pay money to watch her dance. A music box ballerina should not be able to do a changement, but somehow, she could. The peasants would clap their hands and gasp and lay down their coins for the advisor, who began to demand more and more from the little ballerina. She didn't mind. All she ever wanted to do was dance, but strangely, after a number of years, just as the first strands of grey began to appear in the advisor's beard, she began to grow tired. The advisor had become very rich, but her schedule never wavered. She'd dance and dance, until her movements slowed, and the advisor would call an end to the day's entertainment, taking her home to rest. And while he begged her and pleaded to keep working, keep dancing, for just a few more days, a few more hours, a few more minutes, I need this, please, I need you to dance for me! Dance! Just a bit longer, and then we'll rest, I promise, then you'll only dance for me. And like a fool, like a little wooden-headed girl, she believed him. And she danced. And she stopped seeing him in her dreams, for now he only dreamed of himself. And then one day came, as these days always will. She missed a step once, jerking forward in her track like skipping forward in time, and the advisor gave a shout, and snapped the music box closed. He rushed into town, trying to find the old Toymaker's shop, finding it empty and dark, with a sign in the window that said "foreclosed." He was afraid of opening the music box himself, terrified of doing something irreparable. The Queen's great machinist took a look at the gears and the sprockets, and apologized. "It looks like she was loved," said the machinist, and the advisor just nodded. He took the Ballerina back to his room and watched her dance again and again, her steps faltering more and more, until the music and her body stopped short, stuck in place forever. The little Ballerina couldn't move, as much as she tried. The advisor put her back on the dresser, where she had spent so many years, locked away inside her box, but this time he didn't close the lid. She could still see him, every day, going about his business, waking and sleeping, but all the joy was gone. Without the dance, she became another piece of furniture, and sometimes he didn't even remember that they had shared anything at all. But the Ballerina did. And when she dreamed, she was still dancing.

## SCENE TEN

[*SOUND EFFECT: The Sound of the Future.*]

[FUTURE HELVETICA *is at lunch with her* AGENT.]

**AGENT**  I know it's a been a tough couple of years.

**FUTURE HELVETICA**  Decades?

**AGENT**  Okay.

**FUTURE HELVETICA**  You're gonna ask me to write another *Darkly Drear*.

**AGENT**  Not necessarily.

**FUTURE HELVETICA**  The story's over. He's grown up, what, you want me to write about his old age? *Darkly Depressed*?

**AGENT**  Please, no.

**FUTURE HELVETICA**  I was joking. No one wants another Ballerina.

**AGENT**  Actually it did well overseas.

**FUTURE HELVETICA**  I heard.

**AGENT**  People are more pessimistic there.

**FUTURE HELVETICA**  What, are you hurting for commissions or something?

**AGENT**  Why's it gotta be about that?

**FUTURE HELVETICA**  It's been ten years.

**AGENT**  And that's too long without a book. You haven't worked on anything?

**FUTURE HELVETICA**  I had something, but . . . too close.

**AGENT**  Too close?

**FUTURE HELVETICA**  Too close to home. I don't think I want it published.

**AGENT**  What's it about?

**FUTURE HELVETICA**  A girl and her father.

**AGENT**  Oh.

**FUTURE HELVETICA**  Right.

**AGENT**  Well, you be the judge of that. What about something new?

**FUTURE HELVETICA**  You don't have any authors?

**AGENT**  Not like you.

**FUTURE HELVETICA**  Oh, are you my biggest fan?

**AGENT**  If I wasn't your biggest fan you'd be in trouble.

**FUTURE HELVETICA**  Okay.

**AGENT**  Kids forget, Helvetica. The Darkly kids are all grown up, just like him. I'm not saying that's it, I'm not saying they're not classics. Kids will read them for the next century, but . . .

**FUTURE HELVETICA**  What?

**AGENT**  I think we deserve more.

**FUTURE HELVETICA**  Awfully demanding today, aren't you?

**AGENT**  I'm just saying . . .

**FUTURE HELVETICA**  I'm old.

**AGENT**  I want to read another Helvetica Burke book.

**FUTURE HELVETICA**  Before I die.

**AGENT**  It's always about death with you.

**FUTURE HELVETICA**  I'll think it over.

**AGENT**  It's not as bad as you think.

**FUTURE HELVETICA**  What's not?

**AGENT**  Everything.

**FUTURE HELVETICA**  Sometimes I just think I'm out of reasons.

**AGENT**   Reasons to write.

**FUTURE HELVETICA**   Excuses. Stories about better places, magic and romance?

**AGENT**   Have you thought about writing for adults ?

**FUTURE HELVETICA**   Ha. I have no interest in that.

**AGENT**   I think the cynicism would kill me.

**FUTURE HELVETICA**   Probably.

**AGENT**   Just think it over.

**FUTURE HELVETICA**   Maybe something will come to me.

**AGENT**   Call me. And get a dog or something. You'd be surprised.

**FUTURE HELVETICA**   I've always been afraid of dogs.

**AGENT**   A little too old to still be afraid of things, aren't you?

## SCENE ELEVEN

[*SOUND EFFECT: The Sound of the Past.*]

[PAST HELVETICA *is being tucked in by her* MOTHER. MYRON *is there, of course.*]

**MOTHER**   Did you have a good day today?

**PAST HELVETICA**   I love the zoo. Myron too.

**MOTHER**   Oh? Myron didn't scare anyone off, did he?

**MYRON**   I solve my problems with words.

**PAST HELVETICA**   No, he was nice.

**MOTHER**   He's a very good bear. You brush your teeth?

**PAST HELVETICA**   Yes.

**MOTHER**   Do I need to check it?

**PAST HELVETICA**   Sure.

**MYRON**   The trick is just to wet the brush.

[*They bump fists.*]

**MOTHER**   I need to tell you some things.

**PAST HELVETICA**   Dad already told me a story.

**MOTHER**   Oh. No. Not a story.

**MYRON**   No reason we can't have two stories.

**PAST HELVETICA**   Mom?

**MOTHER**   . . .

**PAST HELVETICA**   Mom?

**MOTHER**   What, baby?

**PAST HELVETICA**   Can I have another story?

**MOTHER**   Sure.

**PAST HELVETICA**   Thanks, Mom.

**MOTHER**   Okay. Um, let's see. Once upon a time, there was a woman who didn't know what she wanted. She wasn't a princess or anything, just a regular girl. But for some reason she grew up expecting to find all of those things from the stories, and the funny thing is she did. She found the handsome prince. Okay, he wasn't a prince, but he did all right, and he sure was handsome. And the beautiful castle was a split level in the suburbs, and it all seemed so great when she was twenty-three. And at thirty she realized that maybe she didn't want any of that, that maybe she didn't want anything at all, and that maybe . . . maybe she wanted everyone to just shut up, to just stop talking so goddam much. 'Cause there's the storm coming, and it's so dark, and it's so there, just hanging on the horizon, and no one seems to notice it but her, and maybe if everyone shut up she could finally get some rest then, and maybe she'd just go to sleep for a long, long time, maybe she'd just prick her finger on a spindle wheel or something and sleep for a long time, and when she woke up everyone would be gone. But then the sun comes out and the birds sing, and everything seems fine again, you know? For a while. For just a little while, everything seems fine and there's you, my love. You absolutely light up my sky. But the storm is so very dark, sometimes.

[*She takes* PAST HELVETICA's *hands in hers. Carrying her hands.*]

**PAST HELVETICA**   Mom?

**MOTHER**   Yes, baby?

**PAST HELVETICA**   What are you talking about?

**MOTHER**   Nothing.

**PAST HELVETICA**   I'm sleepy.

**MOTHER**   Honey?

**PAST HELVETICA**   Yeah?

**MOTHER**   Don't be afraid to be alone. Sometimes there's nothing better than being alone. Loneliness is underrated.

**PAST HELVETICA**   Um.

**MOTHER**   And don't trust perfect people, okay? Perfect people are liars. If you meet a man who claims he's got it all figured out, you run as far as you can, okay?

**PAST HELVETICA**   Okay.

**MOTHER**   And be sure he needs you as much as you need him. It's terrible to owe anybody anything. And do something you love, okay? Even if it's just for fun? Even if no one will pay you a cent for it?

**PAST HELVETICA**   Okay.

**MOTHER**   And you know about your period?

**PAST HELVETICA**   Mom!

**MOTHER**   Okay, okay. It's nothing to be ashamed of. Neither is sex. Sex is just like any other sport. Protect yourself and you won't get hurt.

**PAST HELVETICA**   What?

**MOTHER**   Nothing, I—I . . . I'll see you in the morning, love.

**PAST HELVETICA**   Okay, Mom.

**MOTHER**   I love you so much.

**PAST HELVETICA**   I love you, too.

[MOTHER *stands up. She sees something out the window. For the first time in a long time.*]

**MOTHER**   On a good day you can see the lake from here.

**PAST HELVETICA**   Yeah?

**MOTHER**   Not today, though.

**PAST HELVETICA**   Oh.

**MOTHER**   Goodnight, Little Sprout.

**PAST HELVETICA**   Goodnight, Mom.

[*She leaves.*]

## SCENE TWELVE

[*SOUND EFFECT: The Sound of the Present.*]

[*Sounds indicate a large, loud party. People talking, loud music, traffic.* PRESENT HELVETICA *is on stage with* ILLUSTRATOR. MYRON *is there, but not present in the scene.*]

**MYRON**   Helvetica hated parties.

**PRESENT HELVETICA**   [*Shouting over the noise*] I can never hear anything! I can barely hear myself think, excuse me, excuse me—I—Shit!
[HUSBAND *enters with two glasses of champagne.*]
Thank god.

**HUSBAND**   Do you know any of these people?

**PRESENT HELVETICA**   They're from the publisher.

**HUSBAND**   Ugh. Well, good turnout, I guess. All of these strangers seem to like you.

**PRESENT HELVETICA**   They have been fed a steady dose of lies and slanders.

**HUSBAND**   And money.

**PRESENT HELVETICA**   Can't forget that.

**HUSBAND**   Or maybe they just really like your work.

**PRESENT HELVETICA**   Maybe a mix of both.

**HUSBAND**   Well, It's a business, just like—

**ILLUSTRATOR**   Helvetica?

**PRESENT HELVETICA**   Hey!

[ILLUSTRATOR *hugs both* HELVETICA *and* HUSBAND.]

**HUSBAND**   Finally, someone we recognize.

**ILLUSTRATOR**   Oh, yes, these are very important people.

**PRESENT HELVETICA**   Did you shake some hands?

**ILLUSTRATOR**   A few. I met Hunter Graves.

**PRESENT HELVETICA**   Oooohh. You gonna try to hit that?

**ILLUSTRATOR**   By hit that, do you mean illustrate for him or . . . hit that?

**HUSBAND**   Whichever.

**ILLUSTRATOR**   I wouldn't turn down either.

**PRESENT HELVETICA**   We have the same editor, I'll put in a good word.

**ILLUSTRATOR**   Have you been schmoozing?

**HUSBAND**   She's been hiding by the shrimp.

**PRESENT HELVETICA**   The shrimp is more interesting.

**ILLUSTRATOR**   You have to try.

**PRESENT HELVETICA**   I'm not really a schmoozer. I think most of the people here think I'm somebody's assistant.

**ILLUSTRATOR**   It's 'cause you don't put your picture on the jacket.

**PRESENT HELVETICA**   No! Have you not seen the galleys for *Darkly the Great*? Big, ugly picture of me on the flap!

**ILLUSTRATOR**   Ha! Who talked you into that one?

**PRESENT HELVETICA**   Who do you think?

**HUSBAND**   It's a great picture. Took it myself.

**ILLUSTRATOR**   Are you standing on a cliff, holding a torch?

**HUSBAND**   That would've been good.

**ILLUSTRATOR**   Oh, what is that one?

**PRESENT HELVETICA**   Oh, yeah, Jessica Davis. She's got a necklace in her mouth!

**HUSBAND**   What?

**PRESENT HELVETICA**   I don't know who told her that was a good idea.

**ILLUSTRATOR**   Yeah, she's a great writer, I just don't think she cares about the business side of it. She just lets other people make decisions for her, and now she gets ridiculed at parties by her peers.

**PRESENT HELVETICA**   Okay.

**HUSBAND**   You see what she did there?

**PRESENT HELVETICA**   It was subtle.

**ILLUSTRATOR**   Thank you.

**PRESENT HELVETICA**   It's a nice picture, really. Just me in the house. Where I'd rather be right now.

**HUSBAND**   You wanna go home? We can go home. Fuck these people.

**ILLUSTRATOR**   Yeah, what is this anyway?

**PRESENT HELVETICA**   The American Library Association.

**HUSBAND**   Ugh, libraries.

**ILLUSTRATOR**   They're the worst.

**PRESENT HELVETICA**   Point taken.

**HUSBAND**   Seriously, though, we can duck out early if you need to.

**PRESENT HELVETICA**   I'm supposed to read, or . . . give a speech or something.

**ILLUSTRATOR**   You know what you're gonna say?

**PRESENT HELVETICA**   I don't know. Something about creativity?

**HUSBAND**   She's been not working on it for weeks, now.

**PRESENT HELVETICA**   Something will come to me.

**ILLUSTRATOR**   That's it?

**PRESENT HELVETICA**   I'll make it up when I get up there. Maybe I'll just read from the book.

**HUSBAND**   Now you're making me nervous.

**PRESENT HELVETICA**   It's not a big deal, I'll just tell people what they want to hear. I should have been a pair of ragged claws, scuttling across a silent sea.

**ILLUSTRATOR**   Oh yeah, that's popular. Peppy.

**HUSBAND**   That's my cue to get more drinks.

[*He exits.*]

**PRESENT HELVETICA**  People don't like to be reminded of the creeping inevitability of death? Is that not a thing?

**ILLUSTRATOR**  Not at a children's book launch.

**PRESENT HELVETICA**  I can never read these situations.

**ILLUSTRATOR**  Just give your speech.

**PRESENT HELVETICA**  You ever think you'd be happier as an animal?

**ILLUSTRATOR**  Like a puppy?

**PRESENT HELVETICA**  I've never liked dogs. Something mindless or something. A clam or a mussel or a—something with no responsibilities or actions, just—

**ILLUSTRATOR**  Scuttling across silent seas?

**PRESENT HELVETICA**  Alone.

**ILLUSTRATOR**  This is super depressing.

**PRESENT HELVETICA**  I don't think so. At least you don't have to worry about what you're supposed to do. Evolution has left us with too much free time, you know? Maybe it would be better. Can you see me as a clam?

**ILLUSTRATOR**  Maybe you should talk to your husband about this.

**PRESENT HELVETICA**  Ugh. Please.

**ILLUSTRATOR**  All right, do your reading and I'll draw you a picture. A mollusk or a crab or whatever you want.

[*The lights shift.*]

**PRESENT HELVETICA**  Hi, everyone. Thanks for coming. This is called *Warrior Girl*. The town of Errata was a terrible mess. People left their socks right on the floor. And soup in the bowl, and paste on the brush, and everything, right where it fell, stayed where it lay, forever. And no one was messier that Kenzie McFibb. Kenzie never combed her hair or washed her shirts or changed her underwear. And that suited Kenzie just fine, thank you very much, because there was no one there to tell her any different. Oh, did I forget to mention? No one in Errata had any parents.

## SCENE THIRTEEN

[*SOUND EFFECT: The Sound of the Past.*]

[PAST HELVETICA, MYRON, *and her* FATHER *are sitting on a bench outside a funeral home. They've just buried her* MOTHER. HELVETICA *hugs* MYRON *throughout.*]

**FATHER**  That was nice. She would have liked . . .

**PAST HELVETICA**  Everyone was crying.

**FATHER**  Yeah.

**PAST HELVETICA**  I didn't know Mom liked animals.

**FATHER**  She used to.

**PAST HELVETICA**  I mean, I know she works at the . . .

**FATHER**  We used to have so many animals. Pigs and chickens, an iguana—

**PAST HELVETICA**  An iguana?

**FATHER**  Sure did.

**PAST HELVETICA**  What was his name?

**FATHER**  Umm . . . Oh, uh Cloves? Oh, no that was the dog. He liked to eat them.

**PAST HELVETICA**  Iguanas?

**FATHER**  No, cloves. Yeah, he was an old retriever. We named him Captain Cloves.

**PAST HELVETICA**  I'm scared of dogs.

**FATHER**  Oh, that's silly. They won't hurt you.

**PAST HELVETICA**  Hey, Dad?

**FATHER**  Yeah, honey?

**PAST HELVETICA**  What happens when we die?

**FATHER**  . . . Fuck.

**MYRON**  The question Helvetica's father had been dreading for days now. All parents, really, they know there will one day be a question asked of them that they are profoundly unable to answer.

**FATHER**  I, uh . . . I don't know.

**PAST HELVETICA**  Well, what do you think happens?

**FATHER**  I guess I—I guess I hope something . . . something nice?

**PAST HELVETICA**  Heaven?

**FATHER**  Yeah.

**PAST HELVETICA**  That would be nice.

**FATHER**  Yeah. Heaven's nice.

**PAST HELVETICA**  Kinda stupid, though, isn't it?

[*Long Pause.*]

**FATHER**  Yeah.

**PAST HELVETICA**  I mean, not that nothing happens when you die, but it's stupid to think it's all clouds and harps and stuff, right?

**FATHER**  You're right. If something happens, if there's another place, it's not perfect.

**PAST HELVETICA**   Huh?

**FATHER**   Well, like here. Some days are good, and some are bad, right?

**PAST HELVETICA**   Yeah.

**FATHER**   Today was a bad day. The last few days.

**PAST HELVETICA**   Yeah.

**FATHER**   But one day, there'll be good days again, right?
[HELVETICA *nods.*]
So that's probably what it's like out there. Sometimes there's good days, sometimes there's bad, but it's . . . different.

**PAST HELVETICA**   Like a planet with cat-people?

**FATHER**   Or dinosaurs.

**PAST HELVETICA**   A black and white world.

**FATHER**   Right. Something different. That's what she wanted, just something different.

**PAST HELVETICA**   Are you gonna die now?

**FATHER**   Oh, honey.
[*He hugs her tight, pulling her from* MYRON.]
Baby, I'm going to be here a long, long, time. As long as I possibly can, okay?

**PAST HELVETICA**   But you're gonna die someday.

**FATHER**   Do we need to talk about this right now?
[*A look at her face tells him the answer.*]
Yes. Yes, everyone dies, Helvetica. Your mom, your grandparents, me, even you. But not for a long, long time. So long from now . . .

**PAST HELVETICA**   Even Myron?

**FATHER**   No. No, I think Myron gets to live forever, doesn't he? That's kind of the magic of him, isn't it?

**MYRON**   Damn straight.

**PAST HELVETICA**   So you'll never leave me?

**MYRON**   Promise. I'm here for good. Like the wooden ballerina, doing what I was built for, for all eternity.

**PAST HELVETICA**   What?

**MYRON**   Nothing. Tell you later.

**PAST HELVETICA**   If everyone's gotta die, I just wish I could die first. Then I won't have to see them die.

**FATHER**   Don't you say that.

**PAST HELVETICA**   What?

**FATHER**   Don't say that, that's what . . . that's what some people think, and that's . . . that's just wrong, okay? You're supposed to outlive some people, okay? You only get so long here, so don't start wasting it already . . . Some people think the world is full of ugliness and just can't get over all the terrible things that happen, but you know? That's just stupid, all right? There's a lot of great things that happen too, all right? Like the Beatles and fishing trips and Vladimir Nabokov and Hamlet and falling in love, and silk stockings and coffee and cigarettes and dogs and cats and birds and iguanas, and just . . . the capacity to love an animal is miraculous, isn't it? And they're . . . they're more than worth sticking around for. Okay?

**PAST HELVETICA**   Okay.

**FATHER**   I love you.

**PAST HELVETICA**   I love you.

**FATHER**   Always.

**PAST HELVETICA**   You really think there might be a cat-people world?

**FATHER**   . . . yeah.

**PAST HELVETICA**   That would be nice.

**FATHER**   Tell me about it.

**PAST HELVETICA**   What?

**FATHER**   Tell me about the cat-people world.

**PAST HELVETICA**   Oh. Okay. So the world is like a big ball of yarn, and when you step on it it's kind of bouncy, like a trampoline.

**FATHER**   I'll bet the cat-people love that.

**PAST HELVETICA**   Yeah.

## SCENE FOURTEEN

[*SOUND EFFECT: The Sound of the Present.*]

[PRESENT HELVETICA *and her* HUSBAND *are looking through some papers.*]

**PRESENT HELVETICA**   The Church of the Errant Light?

**HUSBAND**   Right.

**PRESENT HELVETICA**   What is that supposed to mean?

**HUSBAND**   It's not important.

**PRESENT HELVETICA**   No, tell me.

HUSBAND   Well, it's like, sometimes the light doesn't end up where it's supposed to, right? And that's what causes depression, and mental illness, and—and all the things that make you feel bad, really.

PRESENT HELVETICA   Are you serious?

HUSBAND   I knew! I knew you wouldn't take it seriously.

PRESENT HELVETICA   So what, by giving them a lot of money they redirect the "light," and then you're happy?

HUSBAND   It's more complicated than that.

PRESENT HELVETICA   Well I should certainly hope so.

HUSBAND   I don't expect you to understand.

PRESENT HELVETICA   What is that supposed to mean?

HUSBAND   It means . . . nothing.

PRESENT HELVETICA   No, really, I need to know.

HUSBAND   What do you think happens when we die?

PRESENT HELVETICA   Nothing. Probably.

HUSBAND   And that doesn't scare the shit out of you?

PRESENT HELVETICA   Sometimes. But there's nothing you can do about it.

HUSBAND   So what does it matter if I believe in this?

PRESENT HELVETICA   I—

HUSBAND   You think nothing happens after death, so all that matters is what we do now.

PRESENT HELVETICA   I don't—

HUSBAND   That's what you say, at least.

PRESENT HELVETICA   Yes.

HUSBAND   So, if this makes me happy, you can't be happy for me?

PRESENT HELVETICA   No, I just . . .

HUSBAND   What?

PRESENT HELVETICA   I want you to be better!

HUSBAND   Oh. Thanks.

PRESENT HELVETICA   You're not happy! This won't make you happy. You've collected faiths and new age bullshit and you wear them around your neck, and you're still unhappy.

HUSBAND   I just want to believe in something.

**PRESENT HELVETICA**   And you'll believe anything anyone tells you. You gave these people, what? A hundred thousand dollars? Are you insane?

**HUSBAND**   It's a donation! They're building a new center!

**PRESENT HELVETICA**   You are such an asshole.

**HUSBAND**   I'm the asshole? 'Cause I don't shit on other people's ideas? 'Cause I don't think what they tell you to think? You don't know the secrets of the universe, Helvetica. No one does. So, yeah, maybe it's ridiculous. Maybe there's no such thing as the Errant Light. But is it any more ridiculous than any other theory you might have? You think the universe just came about randomly, and we're all just here for no reason.

**PRESENT HELVETICA**   Not for no reason.

**HUSBAND**   Well I want to be part of something.

**PRESENT HELVETICA**   I thought we were.

**HUSBAND**   You know what I meant.

**PRESENT HELVETICA**   There's beauty in the facts.

**HUSBAND**   You have such an imagination in your stories. Why can't you have any when it comes to this?

**PRESENT HELVETICA**   Because it's a lie.

**HUSBAND**   So are stories.

**PRESENT HELVETICA**   Stories aren't lies. All the best stories are true. They're metaphors and fables, but they're about real life.

**HUSBAND**   Can't you just support me?

**PRESENT HELVETICA**   I'm not gonna let you give my money to crazy people.

**HUSBAND**   You don't believe in anything. Not me, not yourself, not us. You write these stories because you hate yourself so much, you're trying to come up with something better.

**PRESENT HELVETICA**   Don't be ridiculous.

**HUSBAND**   You think I don't know? I know you better than anyone. And you don't believe in anything.

**PRESENT HELVETICA**   I believe in me. I believe in stories! I believe in my father! I believe in—

**HUSBAND**   Me?

**PRESENT HELVETICA**   I thought I did.

**HUSBAND**   I think I'm gonna stay with some friends.
[HELVETICA *doesn't speak.*]
Did you hear me?

**PRESENT HELVETICA**   Yeah, fine, go stay with your friends. All your laughing, suited banker friends that—

**HUSBAND**   Where are your friends?

**PRESENT HELVETICA**   What?

**HUSBAND**   You have co-workers. You have publishers and agents and illustrators, but do you even talk to them when you're not working? So where are your friends?

**PRESENT HELVETICA**   Sometimes. I talk to—

**HUSBAND**   I'm your friend, Helvetica.

**PRESENT HELVETICA**   Don't do it.

**HUSBAND**   Don't what?

**PRESENT HELVETICA**   Don't feel sorry for me. I don't need friends, and I don't need a fucking cult to tell me I'm a complete person.

**HUSBAND**   You don't need anything, do you? You don't need me.

**PRESENT HELVETICA**   And you need everything so desperately.

**HUSBAND**   What's wrong with that?

**PRESENT HELVETICA**   It's pathetic.

**HUSBAND**   Nice.

**PRESENT HELVETICA**   That's what attracted me to you in the first place, you know. You needed me so badly.

**HUSBAND**   Oh, fuck this.

**PRESENT HELVETICA**   You are so phenomenally broken, you know that? And you need anything, doesn't matter what, that can hold you together. And I guess it wasn't me. I'm glad it's not me. I can't be your anesthetic anymore, I don't have the energy.

**HUSBAND**   I'm leaving.

**PRESENT HELVETICA**   Yeah.

**HUSBAND**   Stop me.

[*He waits for her to say something. She doesn't.* HUSBAND *exits.*]

## SCENE FIFTEEN

[*SOUND EFFECT: The Sound of the Future.*]

[FUTURE HELVETICA *is alone on stage. Silence. She's looking off into the distance. She thinks of something. She walks offstage. A moment passes. She returns, bringing* MYRON *with her. She hugs him tightly, and moves off to the screen door.*

*While* MYRON *begins speaking,* FUTURE HELVETICA *begins fixing the screen door, tightening a screw. It's an easy fix. Something she could have done years ago, but just let it pass, walking through it, hearing the squeak, hating the squeak, but not doing anything about it. Today she has done something about it.*]

**MYRON**   So what happened while I was in the attic? What did she do without me for all those years? The short answer is: I'm not sure. Such a large section of her life passed by when I was gone, but that's what happens to the past isn't it? Ten years can go by sometimes, without once thinking of your fourth grade teacher, Mrs. Strickland, and how you broke that potted plant painted by a former student, and how she cried. So Helvetica lived her life. She wrote a little, she took up and abandoned some hobbies. Her dad died. I was sorry I missed that. She got old. Maybe the two are related. Other things happened as well, big and small. She slept. She read some great books. She watched some dumb movies. She watched TV, which was somewhere in between. She ate. She made love with people she didn't care about. She fixed the screen door.

[*After a moment, she crosses to her desk, which is still a piece of the sailboat. She picks up a phone and calls her agent.*]

**FUTURE HELVETICA**   Hey. It's me. No, it's all clean. Just got home from the doctor's office. You were the first one. Who else am I gonna call? Yeah, hair's growing back and everything. I know. Well I think I'm gonna have something for you. It's been awhile, yeah. Fifteen years? Twenty? Oh. I spent some time in the attic. Found some old comforting things.

[MYRON *touches her hand.*]

I don't know, I just thought it would be nice. Yeah, my paralyzing fear of death. Hey, Madeline L'Engle wrote into her seventies and eighties. This may be the start of a whole new renaissance. Yes, I guess you could say I'm happier now. I'll call you when I have something.

**MYRON**   She would be dead in ten months.

**FUTURE HELVETICA**   Are you gonna help me with this?

**MYRON**   Sorry.

[*The two of them begin to move the furniture around. It's ritualized now, almost a dance. This is* HELVETICA *looking for ideas. This is how she writes.*]

Thanks for finally springing me, by the way.

**FUTURE HELVETICA**   You'd been in there too long.

**MYRON**   Why the change of heart?

**FUTURE HELVETICA**   Is "I missed you" too easy an answer?

**MYRON**   You're not growing soft, are you?

**FUTURE HELVETICA**   I'm sorry.

**MYRON**   Glad to be back.

**FUTURE HELVETICA**   Hoist the sail, stupid bear.

**MYRON**   Aye.

[*After a time,* PAST HELVETICA *joins them.*]

**FUTURE HELVETICA**   Thanks.

**PAST HELVETICA**   Where are we going?

**FUTURE HELVETICA**   I'm not sure yet. Where do you want to go?

**PAST HELVETICA**   A city in the clouds?

**FUTURE HELVETICA**   We've been there.

**PAST HELVETICA**   We can't go back?

**FUTURE HELVETICA**   Not today.

**PAST HELVETICA**   So treasure and pirates are out too, huh?

**FUTURE HELVETICA**   I'm afraid so.

**MYRON**   We're international thieves, betrayed by our accomplices, with no way to smuggle the jewels out of Monaco . . .

**BOTH HELVETICAS**   No.

**MYRON**   You guys never want to have fun.

**PAST HELVETICA**   What about the desert?

**MYRON**   A dashing prince.

[*The furniture now becomes a desert palace. Maybe some crenellations or a minaret.*]

**FUTURE HELVETICA**   A brilliant but flawed prince, at war with his evil brother.

**MYRON**   And a princess.

**FUTURE HELVETICA**   But not a love story.

**PAST HELVETICA**   A ghost story?

**MYRON**   What's the difference?

**PAST HELVETICA**   The soul of the dead king can't cross into paradise until the kingdom is at peace.

**FUTURE HELVETICA**   Magic, Good vs Evil.

**MYRON**   A talking tiger!

**FUTURE HELVETICA**   The soul of the dead king is the tiger.

[MYRON *roars sheepishly.*]

**PAST HELVETICA**   Then what happens?

[*The palace is complete.* FUTURE HELVETICA *starts to think.*]

# SCENE SIXTEEN

[*SOUND EFFECT: The Sound of the Present.*]

[PRESENT HELVETICA *sits at a table with her* FATHER.]

**MYRON**   Helvetica's father has long since retired from the forestry service. He's an old man now, sleeping in the old shaggy recliner that no one can seem to make him remove. He doesn't eat right, and although Helvetica worries he'll develop heart disease or diabetes, it's the cancer that'll kill him. Prostate, then liver and bone. But for now, he's still here, for another ten years or so, to listen to Helvetica's problems and offer the support he can.

**FATHER**   Happy Birthday.

**PRESENT HELVETICA**   Another one.

**FATHER**   They just keep coming, don't they?

**PRESENT HELVETICA**   Forty-five. And alone.

**FATHER**   You know I was only thirty-four when your mother died.

**PRESENT HELVETICA**   . . . Yeah. I uh, I didn't think about that.

**FATHER**   That means she was—

**PRESENT HELVETICA**   Thirty-two. Jesus.

**FATHER**   There's a lot worse things that can happen to you than a divorce at forty.

**PRESENT HELVETICA**   How come you never . . .

**FATHER**   Eh. It's not so big a deal. After a while, you just get used to being on your own, I think. I mean, I saw some women. When you were still around I tried to keep it a secret, but . . .

**PRESENT HELVETICA**   You never met anyone special?

**FATHER**   They're all special. Everyone's special, Helvetica. That's the problem. It wasn't that I couldn't find anyone that lived up to your mother. It was . . . I could see myself marrying any number of these women, and then I thought . . . well, I guess that makes the problem with me, doesn't it? I think I just wanted to be married. Anyone would do. You needed a mother, and I was trying to find you one.

**PRESENT HELVETICA**   I get it.

**FATHER**   I decided that I would make a better mother than some stranger.

**PRESENT HELVETICA**   You did.

**FATHER**   I . . . thank you.

**PRESENT HELVETICA**   I think I'll start an online profile.

**FATHER**   Take some time though.

**PRESENT HELVETICA**   Oh, I have no interest in jumping into another relationship.

**FATHER**   No, I mean, some time for you. When's the last time you finished a book?

**PRESENT HELVETICA**   Three years?

**FATHER**   Isn't it time?

**PRESENT HELVETICA**   What am I going to write about?

**FATHER**   I don't know.

**PRESENT HELVETICA**   What do you think?

**FATHER**   I can't tell you what to write.

**PRESENT HELVETICA**   Just a little?

**FATHER**   Some things you have to do for yourself.

**PRESENT HELVETICA**   Sometimes I feel like I can't do anything. The screen door's been broken ever since we moved in, and every time I pass it I think, I've gotta fix that thing. But I don't.

**FATHER**   So fix it.

**PRESENT HELVETICA**   Yeah. I will. Someday.

**FATHER**   And write.

**PRESENT HELVETICA**   It seems like I can't get there anymore.

**FATHER**   Where, to that little girl who didn't want the fish to die?

**PRESENT HELVETICA**   Something like that.

**FATHER**   Just be you, Helvetica. You'll find it again.

**PRESENT HELVETICA**   I've got a story. About a ballerina. It's different though. Dark.

**FATHER**   You have to write who you are. And you change. People will understand that or they won't.

**PRESENT HELVETICA**   And if I lose my adoring public?

**FATHER**   You'll still have me.

**PRESENT HELVETICA**   Thanks.

**FATHER**   And Myron.

**PRESENT HELVETICA**   Myron's in the attic.

**FATHER**   Oh, that's a mistake.

**PRESENT HELVETICA**   Time to put away childish things?

**FATHER**   Eh. Sometimes I think childish things are underrated. Why the attic?

**PRESENT HELVETICA**   You'll laugh.

**FATHER**   So?

**PRESENT HELVETICA**   Accusing me, looking at me with those eyes . . . I just . . . I couldn't look at him anymore.

**FATHER**   It's hard to look at sometimes. I had the picture of your mother on my nightstand turned down for years. It gets better after a while.

**PRESENT HELVETICA**   Maybe I'll fish him out one of these days.

**FATHER**   Well you've got us, in the attic, in the old folks' home, wherever.

**PRESENT HELVETICA**   Always.

## SCENE SEVENTEEN

[*SOUND EFFECT: The Sound of the Present.*]

[FUTURE HELVETICA *is in the sailboat.*]

**MYRON**   Helvetica died on a warm autumn Tuesday, of an aortic aneurysm in her sleep. She was seventy-three years old. Survived by an ex-husband on the West Coast, a husky mix named Joharis, an old stuffed bear, and millions of children, who grew up reading her stories. They might not have known her name, but they knew her stories, and named their pets Darkly and Cap'n Kloves and Veronica and Drake and they acted out her stories in their living rooms. Her last book, the labor of the last few months of her life, was finished a few weeks before her death. She didn't know it, but she had started it years before. Before the book about the desert, which was already at the printer's. This was something else, something different. It was on her agent's desk when s/he heard about the news. S/He opened it immediately, and noticed the weight. It was long. Very long for a children's book, indeed. If she hadn't died, it would be tough to sell, but for now she was on the covers of magazines, and the publisher would buy whatever s/he brought them. S/He turned to the first page, and with a sigh, knowing it would be the last book s/he would read by his/her favorite author, s/he started to read. The first image was of a little girl and a small, worn, stuffed bear.
[PAST HELVETICA *enters.*]
The girl said:

**PAST HELVETICA**   This is a story about my best friend.

[MYRON *joins* FUTURE HELVETICA *in the sailboat. Sounds of crashing waves.*]

**MYRON**   Where are we headed?

**FUTURE HELVETICA**   Not sure. Do we really have to go?

**MYRON**   We do.

**FUTURE HELVETICA**   You think there's something out there?

**MYRON**  There's always something more.

**FUTURE HELVETICA**  How do you know?

**MYRON**  I'm just a stuffed bear, Helvetica. I don't know the mysteries of the universe.

[*She reaches out, and takes his hand.*]

**FUTURE HELVETICA**  There's nothing left here anymore. Time to see what else there is to see.

**MYRON**  Across the ocean, new wonders await.

**FUTURE HELVETICA**  Endless forms most beautiful.

**MYRON**  I'll consult the astrolabe.

**FUTURE HELVETICA**  I don't think there are charts for this neck of the ocean.

**MYRON**  Uncharted waters.

**FUTURE HELVETICA**  My favorite kind.

[PAST HELVETICA *climbs aboard the sailboat.*]

**PAST HELVETICA**  How can I help?

**FUTURE HELVETICA**  Tighten the mizzen and hold fast, girl, there's rough seas ahead.

**PAST HELVETICA**  Aye.

**MYRON**  Are you scared?

[PRESENT HELVETICA *enters, and climbs aboard.*]

**PRESENT HELVETICA**  What's there to be scared of, bear?

**MYRON**  The Undiscovered Country?

**PRESENT HELVETICA**  We're explorers, Myron.

**FUTURE HELVETICA**  Discovery is in our blood!

**PAST HELVETICA**  All hands on deck!

**PRESENT HELVETICA**  Set course, dead ahead! Are we prepared for what comes?

**PAST HELVETICA**  Always—

**FUTURE HELVETICA**  —Always.

**PRESENT HELVETICA**  —Always!

**MYRON**  . . . Always.

[*Hands joined, they sail away.*]

END OF PLAY

• • •

# Books by Helvetica Burke

*Sailing Around the Living Room*
*Hester Sings Tonight!*
*Once Upon a Pirate*
*The Hamelin Town Musicians*
*Twice Upon a Pirate*
*Darkly Drear*
*The Monster Dance*
*Darkly Under Fire*
*The Moon Loved Me*
*The Most Miraculous Fish*
*Thrice Upon a Pirate*
*Two Treehouses*
*Darkly in the Deep*
*The Planet with No Children*
*A Bookful of Fables*
*Petunia's Brain*
*Darkly Disappears*
*Too Many Mice*
*Trouble with Dragons*

*A Houseful of Stories*
*Darkly Takes a Chance*
*A Cityful of Tales*
*Once More upon a Pirate*
*The Princess War*
*Warrior Girl*
*Darkly the Great*
*A Countryful of Lies*
*Snowman Parade*
*A Forest, Deep and Dark*
*Fairy Tale*
*Darkly Forever*
*The World Stopped Turning*
*The Ballerina*
*A Planetful of Legends*
*A Galaxy, Full of Myths*
*The Tiger's Tail*
*Always*

*The Witch, the Mouse, and the Boy Who Believed in Fairies*

# Now Comes the Night

E. M. Lewis

# E. M. Lewis

E. M. Lewis is an award-winning playwright and librettist. Her work has been produced around the world and is published by Samuel French. She is the recipient of a Hodder Fellowship from Princeton University, the Steinberg Award and the Primus Prize from the American Theater Critics Association, the Ted Schmitt Award from the Los Angeles Drama Critics Circle, and the 2016 Oregon Literary Fellowship in Drama. Plays include *Song of Extinction, Infinite Black Suitcase, Heads, True Story, The Study, Now Comes the Night, The Gun Show, Magellanica,* and *Apple Season.* Lewis is currently working on a new opera with composer Evan Meier, commissioned by American Lyric Theater. Lewis was born and raised in Oregon, where she now resides. She is a member of the Dramatists' Guild of America, Inc.

*www.emlewisplaywright.com*

# Production History

*Now Comes the Night* received its world premiere at 1st Stage in Tysons, VA, as part of the Women's Voices Theater Festival. The production was directed by Alex Levy and featured Dylan Morrison Myers, Jaysen Wright, and Sun King Davis. It ran from September 17to October 18, 2015.

• • •

"...and I only am escaped alone to tell thee."

—Herman Melville (*Moby Dick*)

"Television is not the truth. Television is a goddamned amusement park."

—Paddy Chayevsky (*Network*)

"If you can't find your courage in a war, you have to keep looking for it anyway . . ."

—Michael Herr (*Dispatches*)

"And what'll you do now, my blue-eyed son? What'll you do now, my darling young one?"

—Bob Dylan (*A Hard Rain's A-Gonna Fall*)

## CHARACTERS

**Michael Aprés** (36) A broadcast journalist. Formerly co-anchor of the *Hartford Evening News* with Brad Flanigan. While working in Iraq, he was taken hostage and held for eighteen months. He has been back in Hartford for twelve days. He is unshaven and pale and thin. His leg was badly injured when he was in Iraq, and he uses forearm crutches to get around.

**Jack Velazquez** (29) A photojournalist. Has a dark, three-day shadow and longish hair. Impatient and capable. His clothes are dirty and sweat-stained and torn, and there's a little blood on his shirt. He has no shoes or socks or belt.

**Brad Flanigan** (34) A broadcast journalist based in Hartford, Connecticut—anchorman on the local evening news. Well-dressed and handsome, in that clean-cut anchorman way.

## TIME

2006. Three o'clock in the morning. Memorial Day.

## SETTING

Michael Aprés's loft apartment in Hartford, Connecticut.

The split-level apartment is high-ceilinged and spartanly furnished. The furniture is of good quality, simple and masculine in style. There are no pictures or tablecloths or knickknacks. There is a kitchenette in one corner, and a sleeping alcove out of sight through a doorway. A cedar chest is being used as a coffee table in front of the couch. The door to the outside has three locks—two dead bolts and a chain.

Something about the quality of light suggests a cell.

At the top of the play, an imposing array of lights surround the couch and chair, along with a television camera. A very Barbara Walters setup. In Act II, when the lights and camera are in use, they will become invisible—or the couch and chair and coffee table will just be closer to us, somehow.

## NOTES

Michael and Jack can both see Brad, but Brad can't see Jack. When Michael and Jack talk with each other, it is like they are speaking on a different channel—Brad can't hear them, and time doesn't pass for him. Things get messier for Michael as the play goes on. He is having two conversations at once, both of which become increasingly heated. The channels will begin to bleed into each other.

The playwright encourages diverse casting.

# ACT I

[MICHAEL APRÉS's *loft apartment slowly becomes visible. The lights are dim. It's late. Very late. In the corner, there is a pile of television equipment, which has been hastily and incompletely packed up, but not yet removed. MICHAEL sits on the floor with his back against the wall. He is dressed in a very nice suit that doesn't fit him like it used to. He is thinner, now. His suit jacket lays crumpled on the floor. The top buttons of his slightly rumpled shirt are unbuttoned. MICHAEL's forearm crutches are lying beside him, too, but not obtrusively. We might not see them yet. What we do see is mail. A giant pile of bills and advertisements and magazines and professional correspondence and personal notes from well-wishers. A box of checks, a few books ordered from Amazon. Eighteen months' worth of mail. MICHAEL has been going through his mail, opening things and discarding them in such a way that it's difficult to tell the read pile from the unread pile. MICHAEL turns a package over in his hands that is different from the others. It is battered, covered in tape and foreign stamps, and ineptly wrapped. It is addressed to MICHAEL; there is no return address. JACK VELAZQUEZ stands in the shadows, leaning against the wall, watching MICHAEL.*]

**MICHAEL**   What is this?

**JACK**   What do you think?

**MICHAEL**   I don't know. [*Pause*] I don't like surprises anymore.

[*But he doesn't set the package down.*]

**MICHAEL**   Should I open it?

[JACK *doesn't answer. A moment.*]

**MICHAEL**   Yes? No?

**JACK**   [*Pause*] I don't know.

**MICHAEL**   Lots of stamps. [*Pause*] Two hundred and fifty dinars. Times . . . a lot. They still use dinars?

**JACK**   They prefer dollars.

[*A moment.*]

**MICHAEL**   The simplest things are so . . . [*Pause*] It's been the most screwed up day.

**JACK**   I know. [*Pause*] Don't think about it.

[MICHAEL *turns the package around, looking at it.*]

**MICHAEL**   Caroline is doing her push-ups now. [*Pause*] She does the most ridiculous version of a push-up you've ever seen.

**JACK**   Stop thinking about her.

**MICHAEL**   Does that ever work? "Stop thinking about . . ." Stop thinking about . . . Stop thinking about . . .

[*A moment.*]

**MICHAEL**   I had a dream last night.

**JACK**   You're telling me your dreams now?

**MICHAEL**   I'm floating on my back, on the ocean, staring up at the sky. [*Pause*] I know it's the ocean, because there isn't anything in any direction. Just blue and . . . blue. [*Beat*] I've been floating there for a long time. My eyes keep wanting to close, but I can't close them, because if I close them I'll sink. But I'm really tired. I'm really, really tired. And I have this feeling that . . . [*Beat*] . . . something is coming up behind me.

**JACK**   Don't think about it.

[MICHAEL *laughs.*]

**MICHAEL**   Yeah.

[MICHAEL *winces, and rubs his leg.*]

**JACK**   How's the leg?

[MICHAEL *doesn't answer.*]

**JACK**   Why are you sitting on the floor?

**MICHAEL**   I don't know. It feels . . .

**JACK**   What?

**MICHAEL**   It's just . . . strange. Being back. You know?

[JACK *doesn't answer.*]

**MICHAEL**   It feels like someone else's house.

**JACK**   It's your house.

**MICHAEL**   I know.

[*A moment.*]

**MICHAEL**   I want to . . .

JACK   Go swimming?

MICHAEL   [*laughs a little, but then . . .*] Ask you something.

[JACK *listens.*]

MICHAEL   How did you feel?

JACK   When?

MICHAEL   After you . . . after you told them you . . . [*Beat*] After you saved me?

[JACK *shakes his head.*]

MICHAEL   Tell me.

JACK   I'm a picture guy, not a word guy.

[MICHAEL *nods.*]

JACK   You thought it would feel different than this?

[MICHAEL *nods.*]

JACK   Told you not to do it.

MICHAEL   I didn't listen to you.

JACK   You never listen to me.

MICHAEL   Are you angry at me?

[JACK *doesn't answer.*]

MICHAEL   Jack?

JACK   I didn't save you just to let you destroy yourself.

[MICHAEL *looks away from* JACK.]

MICHAEL   Don't leave.

JACK   I can't leave.

MICHAEL   Don't be angry.

[JACK *doesn't answer.*]

MICHAEL   Talk to me.

[*A moment.*]

JACK   We should have gone left, at the top of the stairs.

MICHAEL   Oh, God.

JACK   No—I've been thinking about this.

MICHAEL   We're not talking about that again.

JACK   If I'd just—

MICHAEL   Stop! Will you stop? [*Beat*] You're never going to figure out what you should have done.

**JACK**   [*Beat*] Yeah.

**MICHAEL**   You did what you had to do.

**JACK**   Yeah.

**MICHAEL**   Stop thinking about it.

[JACK *laughs. A moment.*]

**JACK**   You want me to tell you my favorite movie?

**MICHAEL**   Yeah. Tell me your favorite movie.

**JACK**   Okay . . . It starts with a map of Africa and Arabia, and this music that's kind of fierce and ominous and sexy. And then a man's voice. [*Doing the voice.*] "With the coming of the second world war, many eyes in imprisoned Europe turned hopefully, or desperately, toward the freedom of—"

**MICHAEL**   Is this another war movie?

**JACK**   No. Yes. Kind of. Don't interrupt me. " . . . toward the freedom of the—"

**MICHAEL**   It sounds familiar.

**JACK**   You want me to tell you this, or—

[*There is a sudden knock at the door.* MICHAEL *and* JACK *both cringe at the sound.* MICHAEL *fumbles with the box, but keeps hold of it.*]

**MICHAEL**   Shit.

[MICHAEL *turns and looks at the door.*]

**MICHAEL**   [*Hushed, scared.*] Someone's here.

[*Another knock. Insistent.*]

**JACK**   It's okay.

[MICHAEL *turns and looks at* JACK.]

**JACK**   It's okay. You're okay.

[*Another knock. And from behind the door, a voice.*]

**BRAD**   [*Offstage*] Michael?

[*A moment. Another knock.*]

**BRAD**   [*Offstage*] Michael? [*Pause*] I know you're there.

[*A moment. Knocking.*]

**BRAD**   [*Offstage*] Michael!

[*A moment.*]

**BRAD**   [*Offstage*] I'm going to use my key, okay?

[*Keys, fumbling.* MICHAEL *sets the box aside. He looks down at the floor, then grabs his forearm crutches, fixes them to his arms, and gets up. It's an awkward maneuver for him; he's not used to them. The crutches both support and impede his movements.*]

*He stands there in the dark, breathing fast. Then the sound of a dead bolt turning. And another. The door opens a few inches, but stops against the chain. MICHAEL moves to the door. He stands there beside it, leaning against the wall on the hinge side, not the open side, out of BRAD's line of sight.*]

**BRAD**   Michael?

[BRAD *presses his face against the opening between the door and the lintel, trying to see in.*]

**BRAD**   If the chain is on, I know you're here.

**MICHAEL**   I'm here.

**BRAD**   [*startled by the closeness of MICHAEL's voice*] Shit!

[BRAD *pulls away. Then looks through the opening again. He still can't see MICHAEL. A beat.*]

**BRAD**   Are you going to let me in?

[MICHAEL *doesn't answer. A moment. MICHAEL doesn't move.*]

**BRAD**   I could get hypothermia out here.

**MICHAEL**   It's May.

**BRAD**   [*Offstage*] It's chilly.

**MICHAEL**   You're in the hallway.

[BRAD *sticks his hand through the door, and fiddles with the chain, but can't unhook it. He pulls his hand back. A moment.*]

**BRAD**   [*Offstage*] You're freaking me out a little.

**MICHAEL**   I'm sorry.

**BRAD**   [*Offstage*] Open the door.

[MICHAEL *reaches toward the chain, but then pulls his hand back.*]

**BRAD**   [*Offstage*] I want to talk about the interview. [*Pause*] Let me in.

[BRAD *pushes against the door, but the chain holds.*]

**BRAD**   [*Offstage*] I've never busted a door down before.

[MICHAEL *moves to push the door shut, but BRAD slides his arm through, blocking him.*]

**BRAD**   [*Offstage*] I am going to call the fucking police in thirty seconds on my cell phone for a "wellness check" if you don't let me through this fucking door.

[*A moment. Then MICHAEL moves where BRAD can see him.*]

**MICHAEL**   I'm fine. I'm . . . fine.

**BRAD**   Let me in.

[*A moment.*]

**MICHAEL**   I have to close the door to unhook the chain.

[*A moment. Then* BRAD *slides his arm out of the door.* MICHAEL *closes the door. A long moment.*]

**BRAD**  [*Offstage*] [*Loudly, audible through the closed door*] . . . eighteen, nineteen, twenty, twenty-one . . .

[MICHAEL *reaches over and unhooks the chain. A moment.* BRAD *pushes the door open, but* MICHAEL *doesn't move out of the way to let him enter.* BRAD *stands there for a moment, looking at* MICHAEL. BRAD *is wearing a winter coat and scarf over a finely tailored suit.*]

**BRAD**  Hello.

[MICHAEL *just looks at him.* BRAD *reaches out a hand toward* MICHAEL, *to touch his shoulder or hug him in greeting, but* MICHAEL *turns away and moves across the room to the kitchen.* BRAD *watches* MICHAEL *go.* MICHAEL *takes down a bottle of whiskey and one glass. He pours himself a drink. His hand shakes a little, and the bottle taps against the glass. He sets the bottle down and takes a drink.*]

**BRAD**  Yes.

[MICHAEL *looks up at him.*]

**BRAD**  Yes, I would like a drink.

[MICHAEL *doesn't get down another glass.* BRAD *comes into the apartment, leaving the door open behind him.*]

**BRAD**  Can I turn on some lights?

[*Without waiting for a reply,* BRAD *turns the overhead lights on.* MICHAEL *blinks against the sudden brightness of the room.* BRAD *notices the mail scattered around by the wall, but he doesn't see* JACK. *He doesn't ever see* JACK. MICHAEL *takes a large gulp of his drink.*]

**BRAD**  Should you be drinking, with your—

**MICHAEL**  Yes.

[MICHAEL *takes another drink.*]

**MICHAEL**  Did you forget something?

**BRAD**  No.

**MICHAEL**  Then what do you want?

**BRAD**  Ten years we work together, and that's what I get? "What do you want?"

**MICHAEL**  The interview's over.

**BRAD**  You made that clear when you kicked us out. [*Beat*] We're going to want the gear back.

**MICHAEL**  The guys can come and get it tomorrow. [*Beat*] I'm done talking. I can't talk anymore.

[MICHAEL *drinks.*]

**JACK**   Why is he leaving the door open like that?

**MICHAEL**   Close the door.

[BRAD *closes the door.*]

**MICHAEL**   What are you doing here?

**BRAD**   Are you okay?

[MICHAEL *laughs. Then he takes another drink.*]

**JACK**   What do you think, dumbshit?

**MICHAEL**   I'm fine. I'm fine. I'm . . . tired. We're done, right? We're done? You got your interview. It's in the can.

**BRAD**   You didn't say what I thought you were going to say.

**MICHAEL**   What did you think I was going to say?

[BRAD *doesn't answer.*]

**MICHAEL**   You get to choose who you interview. Not what they say. This isn't advertising.

**BRAD**   It kind of sounded like it.

**MICHAEL**   You didn't believe me?

[*A moment.* MICHAEL *takes a drink.*]

**MICHAEL**   It's not my fault you don't like my story.

**BRAD**   That's what I think it was. [*Pause*] That's what I think it was. A story. [*Pause*] You don't believe that shit.

**MICHAEL**   Get out. Okay? Get out. You have what you need.

**BRAD**   I'm worried about you. [*Pause*] You look like shit.

[MICHAEL *pulls at the collar of his shirt.*]

**MICHAEL**   [*Tensely*] I'm fine. You don't need to stay. You checked on me. I'm good.

**JACK**   Shh. Easy.

**BRAD**   I haven't had my drink yet.

**MICHAEL**   Have a drink at Palacki's.

**BRAD**   Palacki's closed six months ago.

**MICHAEL**   Somewhere else. Arch Street.

**BRAD**   It's late. [*Pause*] You're not going to give me a drink?

[*A moment. Then* MICHAEL *moves away from the kitchen, leaving his own empty glass behind.*]

**MICHAEL**   You know where the glasses are.

[BRAD *gets a glass and pours himself a drink.*]

**MICHAEL** Lock the door. If you're staying.

[MICHAEL *goes over to where he was sitting before. He leans against the wall, then slides down it, until he's sitting on the floor. He stretches his leg out carefully. Takes off his crutches and sets them beside him.* BRAD *locks the door.*]

**MICHAEL** All of them.

[BRAD *locks the dead bolt and puts the chain on the door. Then he looks at* MICHAEL *oddly.*]

**BRAD** You're safe now. [*Beat*] You know that, right? You're safe.

[*A moment.*]

**BRAD** This isn't how I thought it was going to be.

**MICHAEL** If I got back?

**BRAD** When you got back. [*Beat*] *When.*

**MICHAEL** You thought I was dead.

**BRAD** No.

**MICHAEL** Everybody thought I was dead after . . .

[MICHAEL *rubs his hand over his face.*]

**MICHAEL** Bring me my drink, will you?

[BRAD *refills* MICHAEL's *empty glass, and brings it over to him. He looks at the mail, scattered near the wall.*]

**BRAD** You've been opening your mail.

**MICHAEL** Someone saved it for me. [*Beat*] Thirty-seven first graders from Batchelder Elementary made me cards.

**BRAD** I know.

**MICHAEL** How?

**BRAD** I started opening some of your mail after a while. We got it forwarded to the station after your dad . . .

[*A moment.*]

**MICHAEL** It's illegal to open someone's mail unless you're like . . . his wife.

**BRAD** Yeah, well.

[*A moment.*]

**BRAD** I stopped opening the personal ones.

**MICHAEL** Why?

**BRAD** It's unseemly to cry in the office.

[MICHAEL *laughs.*]

**MICHAEL**   Don't laugh at me. You try opening thirty-seven cards handmade by first graders from Batchelder Elementary with glue and glitter that say "we hope you come home" and "we hope you're not dead" and see what happens to you.

[*A moment.*]

**BRAD**   What are you doing down on the floor?

**MICHAEL**   When I was sitting on my couch, you kept pelting me with questions.

[MICHAEL *looks over at the cameras and lights set up in his living room.*]

**MICHAEL**   [*Oddly, remembering how they used to begin their show before—back in the old days, before Iraq, before he was taken*] This is Michael Aprés and Brad Flanigan . . .

**BRAD**   Brad Flanigan and Michael Aprés . . .

**MICHAEL**   . . . here in Hartford, Channel Eight at Eleven. [*Pause*] You and me and the *Hartford Evening News.*

**BRAD**   [*referring to the interview they did earlier in the evening*] You just shit all over that.

[MICHAEL *winces.*]

**MICHAEL**   You're still pelting me with questions.

**BRAD**   That wasn't a question, it was a statement. "You just shit all over that."

**MICHAEL**   I don't like the news anymore. [*Beat*] It's not as fun when the stories are about you instead of by you.

**BRAD**   Gerry's never . . . after what you said, Gerry's never going to take you back.

**MICHAEL**   Maybe I don't want to go back.

**BRAD**   So you're burning all your bridges by making up a bunch of inflammatory shit on camera during my interview?

**MICHAEL**   [*Quickly, firmly*] That was all true.

**BRAD**   Bullshit.

**MICHAEL**   Nothing but the truth, so help me—

**BRAD**   Bullshit. That wasn't you.

**MICHAEL**   Who was it?

**BRAD**   Someone else. Them? Your . . . the people who were holding you must have—

**MICHAEL**   No.

**BRAD**   —brainwashed you or—

**MICHAEL**   No! It's me. It was me. That's what I think.

**BRAD** "Every single American soldier and journalist and engineer who is killed in Iraq deserves to die, because he shouldn't ever have gone there." You said. [*Beat*] That isn't you saying that.

**MICHAEL** Who else would it be?

**BRAD** I don't know.

**MICHAEL** You said it yourself. I'm safe now. [*Beat*] Will you leave me alone? Please? Will you please leave me alone?

**BRAD** No.

**MICHAEL** You're looming over me.

**BRAD** "America lost this war before it began." That's what you think?

**MICHAEL** That's what everybody thinks.

**BRAD** No.

**MICHAEL** Then they're idiots.

**JACK** Never get involved in a land war in Asia.

**MICHAEL** Never get involved in a land war in Asia. Or the Middle East. God help you if you try both at the same time. I don't know what President Bush thinks he's doing. I said that in the interview, didn't I?

**BRAD** I don't know if you had time. Things escalated pretty fast.

**MICHAEL** [*To* JACK] I don't want to talk to him anymore.

**JACK** Then kick him out.

**BRAD** What you said in the interview . . .

**MICHAEL** Yes?

**BRAD** That's not what I thought you were going to say.

[*A moment.*]

**MICHAEL** Yeah.

**BRAD** It wasn't even an interview. It was a carnival side show.

**MICHAEL** Gerry seemed happy.

**BRAD** Gerry is a television producer. As long as he gets it on tape, he doesn't give a shit what you say. He doesn't give a shit about you.

**MICHAEL** But you do?

**BRAD** How the hell can you ask me that?! We worked together for ten years. [*Pause*] Yes. Yes, Michael, I'm your fucking friend, even if you do abandon me at the first opportunity.

**MICHAEL** I didn't abandon you.

**BRAD** You were gone for eighteen months.

**MICHAEL**   Things went a little different than I planned.

**BRAD**   Why did you go?

[*No answer.*]

**BRAD**   I never asked you. Before you left. It seemed . . .

**MICHAEL**   Stupid?

**BRAD**   I didn't think that.

**MICHAEL**   Didn't you?

**BRAD**   It all happened . . . really fast. You said you were going. And then you were gone. [*Beat*] I think I was the last to know.

**MICHAEL**   No.

**BRAD**   No?

**MICHAEL**   It was just really fast.

**BRAD**   I wanted to ask you that in our interview.

**MICHAEL**   Why I went to Iraq?

**BRAD**   Yes.

**MICHAEL**   To prove my manhood. [*laughs, but not because it isn't true*] You should go. This is devolving into an—

**BRAD**   Actual conversation? You wouldn't want that.

**MICHAEL**   You're fine. You have Bobbi Ann.

**BRAD**   Bobbi Ann is not—[*Beat*] Jesus, I am so . . . [*Beat*] For ten years, it's me and you. It's the me and you show, not the random chick with . . . low-cut blouses, with her—

**MICHAEL**   You never mind low-cut blouses.

**BRAD**   —College Station, Texas, voice. She talks too slow, Michael. The rhythm is off. She's driving me crazy. And you just . . . I finally get you back, and everything is going to be like it was before, and then you go and . . . What the fuck was with that interview?

**MICHAEL**   It's not my fault you don't like Bobbi Ann.

**BRAD**   I'm done talking about Bobbi Ann. I want to know about the interview. What was coming out of your mouth?

[MICHAEL *smashes the end of his crutch against the floor three times.*]

**MICHAEL**   Nothing is ever going to be like it was before, Brad.

**BRAD**   And you thought, "Well, my leg's a little screwed up, so I'm just going to blow up myself and Brad and every single thing we've built together"—

**MICHAEL**   My leg is more than just a little—

**BRAD**  It doesn't fucking matter! You're a fucking anchor on the fucking *Hartford Evening News*. Your job is sitting down!

**MICHAEL**  I didn't blow you up. You're fine.

**BRAD**  I'm nothing without . . . Jesus, I'm not saying that. Yes, I am. It's our show. What we built together . . . and it was an accident, them putting us together, but it clicked, and it was fun, and people liked it. They liked us. It was fun to do and it was fun to be liked, but now it's just the same as everybody else's eleven o'clock news.

**MICHAEL**  And so are the ratings?

**BRAD**  Everybody is waiting to see this interview. They watched you for the last ten years on the evening news, sitting in their living rooms while you told them what the world is. They lit candles over at St. Joe's and St. John's after you were taken. They prayed for you every week at Union Baptist and Metropolitan A.M.E. and Windsor Avenue Congregational. They wrote letters to their congressmen. The whole fucking city has been waiting for you to be released, waiting for you to come back. You and me, we're not . . . We're not Walter Cronkite or Barbara Walters or Edward R. Murrow or Howard Cosell. But we "tell it like it is" here in Hartford. [*Beat*] They deserve to hear the truth.

[*A moment.*]

**BRAD**  If we air that interview tomorrow night—

**MICHAEL**  Tonight.

**BRAD**  [*looks at watch*] *Tonight*, there's no going back. You're done. Just as sure as if you had died there in Iraq, you're done. And we're done. There can't be any more Brad and Michael show.

**MICHAEL**  What do you mean, "if?"

[BRAD *doesn't answer.*]

**MICHAEL**  What do you mean, "if" we air that interview?

**BRAD**  We have a choice. Run it or don't run it.

**MICHAEL**  We don't have a choice. Gerry has it. It's in the can. The Memorial Day feature, immediately following and slightly more complicated than the Marine Corps Band, playing the national anthem. There is nothing that would stop him from running it.

**BRAD**  Except not having it.

**MICHAEL**  [*Beat*] Why would he not have it?

[*A moment.*]

**MICHAEL**  Gerry has the tape, Brad. It's in the can. It's a done deal. I did it. I did the interview. It's done. They're airing it at eight o'clock, preempting every fucking thing.

**BRAD**   Gerry doesn't have the tape.

**MICHAEL**   [*Beat*] What do you mean, Gerry doesn't have the tape?

[BRAD *goes over the kitchen and refills his whiskey glass. Takes a sip.*]

**BRAD**   Shawn and I finished editing it three hours ago. Then he went home. Everybody went home. And I was sitting there in the editing bay, staring at your face up on the big screen, and I thought . . . this is wrong. This isn't right. I don't know what you were doing in that interview, but it wasn't . . . [*Beat*] So I took it out.

**MICHAEL**   You took out the tape.

**BRAD**   Yes.

**MICHAEL**   Why did you take it out?

**BRAD**   Just in case.

**MICHAEL**   Just in case what?

**BRAD**   We change our minds about airing it.

[MICHAEL *gets to his feet, awkwardly.*]

**MICHAEL**   We're not going to change our minds, Brad.

[*A moment.*]

**MICHAEL**   You hear me?

**BRAD**   I hear you.

**MICHAEL**   The editing equipment backs everything up to three different places.

**BRAD**   I took care of that.

**MICHAEL**   What do you mean, you took care of that?

[*A moment. And then* BRAD *pulls a tape out of his coat pocket.*]

**MICHAEL**   What's that?

**BRAD**   The interview. Your interview with me, from . . . [*Looks at watch*] . . . ten hours ago. The only copy of your interview.

[*A long moment.*]

**BRAD**   I don't like it. I think we can do better.

**MICHAEL**   I'm not doing another interview.

**BRAD**   No?

**MICHAEL**   No! What the hell are you doing?

**BRAD**   Nothing smart. Gerry's going to kill me when he gets to the station in the morning and sees what I've done.

**MICHAEL**   You destroyed all the backups of the interview.

**BRAD**  Except this one. [*Pause*] Why did you lie?

**MICHAEL**  I didn't lie.

**BRAD**  Bull shit. You don't believe any of that crap you were spouting.

**MICHAEL**  How do you know?

**BRAD**  "9/11 was nothing compared to what's going to happen to America if we don't leave Iraq." You said. [*Pause*] I don't think this is what you want to say on your first feature on national television.

**MICHAEL**  It's not my first feature on national television. My first feature on national television was eighteen months ago when I had a fucking gun pointed at my head.

**BRAD**  The gun isn't there anymore!

**MICHAEL**  Yes, it is!

BRAD [*Beat*]  What?

[MICHAEL *covers his mouth with his hand to keep himself from saying anything else.*]

**MICHAEL**  I've had a lot to drink today. I don't know what I'm saying.

[MICHAEL *struggles to his feet, shoving the crutches onto his arms. He moves over to the kitchen and opens the whiskey bottle again.* JACK *follows* MICHAEL *to the kitchen. Bottle and glass make a tick, tick, ticking sound as* MICHAEL'S *hand trembles, pouring.* JACK *puts his hand on* MICHAEL'S *hand to stop the shaking.*]

**JACK**  What are you going to do, Michael?

**MICHAEL**  I don't know.

[*He raises his glass to his lips and drinks. He picks up a bottle of pills that are sitting on the counter and opens them, and swallows one down. Then another from another bottle.*]

**JACK**  He wants the truth.

**MICHAEL**  I can't talk to him. You know I can't.

**JACK**  Then you shouldn't have let him in.

**MICHAEL**  I shouldn't have let him in. [*Pause*] I didn't have any choice.

[BRAD *moves over to the kitchen, near* MICHAEL. JACK *veers away, but keeps an eye on what's happening.*]

**BRAD**  Talk to me. [*Pause*] Why won't you talk to me? [*Pause*] I waited so long to talk to you. [*Pause*] You can trust me.

[MICHAEL *shakes his head.*]

**BRAD**  Yes. You can trust me. You know that. [*Pause*] Don't you remember that?

**MICHAEL**  Everything can be taken away.

**BRAD**  What?

**MICHAEL**  What do you want from me?

**BRAD**  The simple truth about what happened over there.

**MICHAEL**  The truth isn't simple.

**JACK**  Maybe you should. Tell him.

**MICHAEL**  I can't.

**BRAD**  What did you say?

[MICHAEL *takes a drink.*]

**JACK**  Maybe if you tell him, he'll leave us alone.

**BRAD**  Michael.

[MICHAEL *turns to* BRAD.]

**MICHAEL**  Take the tape back to the station. Gerry doesn't have to know you ever took it.

**BRAD**  No.

**MICHAEL**  What's going to happen to you if he comes back and finds the biggest story he's ever had dropped into his lap has been stolen by his star anchorman?

**BRAD**  Nothing good.

**MICHAEL**  Take it back.

**BRAD**  No. [*Pause*] I'm trying to help you.

**MICHAEL**  Then take back the tape.

**BRAD**  No.

**MICHAEL**  I need a friend, here. Not a reporter. I wish you would . . . used to be friends.

**BRAD**  We *are* friends.

[*A moment.*]

**BRAD**  When we were working together, we were good. We did good. There's a reason they kept us together.

[*A moment.*]

**BRAD**  Do the interview again. With me. We'll do it right this time. We'll take our time. All the equipment is right here.

**MICHAEL**  I don't—

**BRAD**  Just us. Talking. You and me, without so many distractions, or . . . [*Beat*] I hadn't thought about what it must be like for you to have twenty people in your space after being alone for so long.

**MICHAEL**  I'm not alone. I have Jack.

[BRAD *Pauses a moment and looks at* MICHAEL, *trying to figure out what the present tense means here, trying to figure out . . .* ]

**BRAD**   Had.

[*A moment.*]

**BRAD**   I hadn't thought about how overwhelming all this would be to you. You've only been home . . .

**MICHAEL**   Twelve days. [*Beat*] I count things. Now. [*Beat*] I'm not crazy.

**BRAD**   I don't think you're crazy. [*Pause; carefully*] But I don't think you were acting like yourself on that interview. Which is why I want to give you another chance.

**MICHAEL**   You're a great friend, Bradley.

**BRAD**   I am. Actually.

[JACK *leans in and speaks to* MICHAEL.]

**JACK**   He sounds sincere.

**MICHAEL**   [*To* JACK] Shut up. [*Beat*] He makes his living in front of the television camera. He always sounds sincere.

[JACK *laughs.* BRAD *leans back in his chair. Remembering how it all began, his friendship with* MICHAEL.]

**BRAD**   How long have I known you? [*Pause*] We were just out of college. Gerry put us together when—

**MICHAEL**   [*To* BRAD] Yeah.

**BRAD**   —when Solly and Jill both came down with malaria.

**MICHAEL**   It wasn't malaria.

**BRAD**   It was something like malaria.

**MICHAEL**   Mononucleosis. No . . .

**BRAD**   Someone had to loan me a shirt. Because I didn't have a—

**MICHAEL**   Because you spilled something on your—

**BRAD**   I was nervous. They told us fifteen minutes before we went on, that we were going on, probably because they'd tried getting everybody—

**MICHAEL**   Anybody.

**BRAD**   —anybody else first. We were the only ones left who . . . [*Beat*] We were just out of college.

**MICHAEL**   [*Beat*] Yeah.

**BRAD**   I had no idea who you were. But . . .

**MICHAEL**   It worked.

**BRAD**  It worked. [*Pause*] Why don't you want to talk to me?

**MICHAEL**  I don't want to talk to anybody.

[MICHAEL *turns away from* BRAD. JACK *steps forward.*]

**JACK**  Except me.

**MICHAEL**  [*To* JACK] Except you. [*Pause*] What happened to you telling me about your favorite movie?

**JACK**  You got distracted. [*Pause*] It's called *Casablanca*. Humphrey Bogart is in it, and that beautiful chick—what was her name? Not Lauren Bacall, the other one.

**MICHAEL**  Ingrid Bergman.

**JACK**  You saw it?

**MICHAEL**  Everybody's seen *Casablanca*.

**JACK**  I thought everybody had seen *Butch Cassidy and the Sundance Kid*.

**MICHAEL**  Somebody's always leaving in all the movies you like.

**JACK**  One of the most important things you gotta learn in this life is how to say goodbye.

**MICHAEL**  I don't want to talk to you anymore, either.

[MICHAEL *takes a drink and turns back to* BRAD.]

**MICHAEL**  Don't pretend your motives are altruistic. You're here for the job.

**BRAD**  I'm here because I want to know what happened to you over there. I thought they . . . When they found Wolfe and Velazqu—

**MICHAEL**  Shut up!!

**BRAD**  You don't know what it was like to not know what was happening.

**MICHAEL**  You don't want to know what happened.

**BRAD**  Yes, I do.

**MICHAEL**  You just want a story.

**BRAD**  If that was true, I'd be using the one I've got.

**MICHAEL**  You want me laid out and weeping for your camera.

**BRAD**  I am your friend.

**MICHAEL**  Then take the tape back to the station.

[BRAD *doesn't move. So* MICHAEL *tries to take the tape away from* BRAD. BRAD *tries to get away from* MICHAEL *without hurting him, but is determined to hold onto the tape.* JACK *steps toward them, frustrated at his inability to do anything.* MICHAEL *falls, and lets out a terrible sound, gripping his leg.* JACK *goes to the wall and hits it with his fist.* BRAD *sets the tape on the counter and goes to try to help* MICHAEL *up.*]

**MICHAEL**  Don't touch me.

[*A moment.*]

**BRAD**  We used to be friends.

**MICHAEL**  That was before I was news. I don't trust you.

**BRAD**  You don't trust anyone.

**MICHAEL**  No. I don't trust anyone. I trust Jack. Have I told you about Jack yet? He sent me this package.

[JACK *turns and looks at* MICHAEL. MICHAEL *reaches over and pulls the package to him.*]

**BRAD**  [*long Pause, then says carefully*] Jack is dead.

**MICHAEL**  I know that. But still . . .

[MICHAEL *holds up the package for* BRAD *to see.*]

**BRAD**  Michael . . .

**MICHAEL**  He's a real journalist.

**JACK**  More or less.

**MICHAEL**  Our plan for getting out didn't, didn't go so well. You ever see *The Great Escape*?

**JACK**  What are you doing?

**MICHAEL**  They used to look in at us. Jack and I. When we shared our . . . Our cell had a little window in the door that they could look at us through, and I remember waking up, cold, I was cold, and then I . . . [*Beat; wards something away with his hand*] . . . because there was an eye pressed against the window in the door. When I looked over at the door. And I didn't know how long it had been . . .

**JACK**  Why do you keep telling him about us?

**MICHAEL**  I don't know. [*Beat*] I think we need another drink.

**BRAD**  Why do you think the package is from Jack?

**MICHAEL**  I shouldn't have let you in. But I was afraid things would escalate if I didn't.

**BRAD**  I wanted to make sure you were all right.

**MICHAEL**  You and your tape. Are you sure now?

**BRAD**  No.

[*A moment. Then* BRAD *gets the bottle, and pours more whiskey into both their glasses. The last of the bottle.*]

**JACK**  [*about the bottle*] Dead soldier.

[MICHAEL *laughs a little.*]

**BRAD**  I'm throwing myself on a grenade for you. [*Beat*] No . . . sorry. I
shouldn't . . .

[JACK *goes over to* BRAD *and looks him in the eye.* BRAD *still does not see* JACK.]

**MICHAEL**  Shouldn't what?

**BRAD**  Appropriate wartime metaphors when we're still in the middle of a
war. [*Pause*] I am throwing my career—

**MICHAEL**  Such as it is.

**BRAD**  —in the toilet for you, to give you another chance at this interview, to
give both of us another chance, you ungrateful shit.

[MICHAEL *takes a drink.*]

**BRAD**  People seem to be . . . [*Beat*] For months, everybody had yellow
ribbons tied around their key card lanyards, and we did daily updates on
military casualties. I kept your desk just like it . . . [*Beat*] But the war just
keeps . . . It's 2006. And it's still going, but people seem to be forgetting. We
got a new runner last month, in the office, and he didn't know who you are.
[*Pause*] He's nineteen. [*Pause*] The president sold his order to hide the
arrival of the coffins of dead soldiers from the press as a respect thing. But I
think it was the most disrespectful thing he could have done to them. And
to us. Because we're not paying attention to how much this war is costing.
On every front.

**MICHAEL**  I don't want you to throw yourself on a grenade for me.

**BRAD**  This interview was supposed to be a chance for the whole world to see
what this war is costing. In the person of someone who they know. And
instead, you made it another propaganda fest. [*Pause*] What would you do
with yourself if you weren't doing the news?

**MICHAEL**  I don't know.

**BRAD**  We don't know how to do anything else. [*Pause*] I'm trying to save you.

**MICHAEL**  Us.

**BRAD**  Same thing. [*Beat*] And I only have until dawn to do it.

**MICHAEL**  Then you turn into a pumpkin.

**BRAD**  [*Beat*] Something like that.

**MICHAEL**  That's *Cinderella*.

**BRAD**  I know it's *Cinderella*.

[JACK *looks over at* MICHAEL.]

**JACK**  How many of those pills did you take?

**MICHAEL**  One of each.

JACK   With how much booze?

[MICHAEL *looks at* JACK.]

MICHAEL   [*To* BRAD] Jack likes movies. We spend a lot of time talking about
movies.

[BRAD *takes a drink. Noticing that* MICHAEL *is putting* JACK *in the present tense
again, and not sure what to do about that. He goes and sits down cross-legged near*
MICHAEL.]

BRAD   Tell me what he was like.

MICHAEL   Jack?

BRAD   You keep coming back to him.

[MICHAEL *rubs his leg.*]

MICHAEL   He's crazy. I don't like him at all.

JACK   Liar.

BRAD   The fact that you keep referring to him in the present tense makes me
wonder about your—

MICHAEL   It's not my fault he keeps sending me presents.

[*A moment.* MICHAEL *pulls the package close.*]

BRAD   I remember when I saw the first pictures of the two of you on Al
Jazeera. It had only been a month. Not even a month, since you left. But I
didn't think it was you, until . . . until I heard your voice. [*Beat*] You looked
so . . . different.

MICHAEL   I am. [*Beat*] A little different.

[*A moment.*]

BRAD   Right around the time when you were taken—there was a lot of
activity. An air strike killed a high level terrorist insurgent named Zaid Al
Sadr and his whole family. And they couldn't figure out if your abduction
was retaliation, or some entirely separate action. Then Fallujah happened,
and the Abu Ghraib story broke, and it was impossible to find out anything
about what was happening to you.

MICHAEL   They moved us a few times.

BRAD   After the tape of Wolfe and Velazquez, and their . . . it was five months
before we knew anything about what happened to you and Conway.

MICHAEL   Presumed dead.

BRAD   I didn't presume anything. I presumed . . . I *thought* you were alive. I
imagined you alive.

MICHAEL   You imagined me?

**BRAD**   I imagined you back here with me. I imagined us at our desk like always, under the lights. Working. Talking to eight million people over the camera like they were in our living room.

**MICHAEL**   Our market share has never been eight million.

**BRAD**   It will be for this interview.

[MICHAEL *doesn't reply.*]

**BRAD**   It was months before we heard anything about you and Conway. [*Beat*] The next . . . video . . . after—

**MICHAEL**   After.

**BRAD**   —was just her. But she talked about you.

**MICHAEL**   I was . . .

[MICHAEL *grips his injured leg.*]

**MICHAEL**   . . . not available for interviews that day. [*Beat*] I'm really trying to cut down on the interviews.

[MICHAEL *drinks.*]

**MICHAEL**   What time is it?

**BRAD**   [*looking at watch*] Almost four.

**MICHAEL**   She's doing her exercises now. Caroline. [*Beat*] I keep track. I figured out the time difference. Which is seven hours. Iraq is seven hours ahead of us. Every morning—which we couldn't always figure out when it was—but after they brought food—which they didn't always—she would do sit-ups and push-ups. And then she would . . . [*Beat*] I have two clocks running in my head all the time, my clock and her clock.

[*A moment.*]

**MICHAEL**   She's still there.

**BRAD**   I know.

**MICHAEL**   They still have her.

**BRAD**   I know.

[*A moment.*]

**BRAD**   You could talk about her. In the new interview. [*Pause*] If we do it right, this interview can be . . . good for us. It could start a whole new—

**MICHAEL**   A whole new what? Nobody cares about this war. It's been going on for years. It's been going on forever. And five years after it's over, if it ever does get over, no one will remember there was a war.

**BRAD**   No one's forgotten Vietnam.

**MICHAEL**   Everyone's forgotten Vietnam. Or we wouldn't be in Iraq.

[MICHAEL *takes a drink.*]

**BRAD**   Tell me more about Jack.

**MICHAEL**   He's rude and annoying and opinionated and pushy. Which all sounds very fam—

**BRAD**   How long were you held with him?

**MICHAEL**   Eleven days.

**BRAD**   That doesn't seem like very long.

[MICHAEL *laughs, oddly.*]

**MICHAEL**   I know him better than I know anyone.

**BRAD**   We worked together for ten years.

**MICHAEL**   Yeah.

**BRAD**   What makes him so special?

**MICHAEL**   He died for me. [*Pause*] They thought I was working for the CIA.

**BRAD**   Why?

**JACK**   Don't tell him about the CIA!

**MICHAEL**   I don't know. There's a lot I don't know.

**BRAD**   They thought you worked for the CIA doing what?

**JACK**   Every true thing is a bullet, Michael.

**MICHAEL**   I don't know. I don't know.

**BRAD**   But they were going to kill you for it.

**MICHAEL**   Yeah.

**BRAD**   But then they killed Jack instead.

**MICHAEL**   I don't want to talk about that.

[MICHAEL *reaches over and runs his fingers over the stamps on the package.*]

**BRAD**   What is that?

**MICHAEL**   I don't know. I haven't opened it yet. [*Pause*] Jack sent it to me.

**BRAD**   Jack is dead.

**MICHAEL**   The United States Post Office is a miraculous organization. They have powers beyond—

**BRAD**   Did his family send it?

**MICHAEL**   Jack sent it. He thought I'd need it.

**BRAD**   [*Pause*] Do you want to get up off the floor now?

**MICHAEL**   No.

**BRAD**   I'm getting up.

**MICHAEL**   I don't care.

[BRAD *gets to his feet.*]

**BRAD**   This is the third time I've seen you since you've been back. And the first time, you were . . . [*Beat*] I talk my way into that hospital, using every bit of skill, leverage, manipulation and threatening that I can muster, and you were . . . [*Beat*] And then Thursday. When I think the deepest we got in our conversation was whether it was going to rain. Both of us sitting here like idiots. Okay, I was sitting here like an idiot. Because I didn't know how to say, "How are you, buddy?"

**MICHAEL**   I want to sleep. That's how I am.

**BRAD**   If you want to sleep, sleep. We can redo the interview when you wake up. I'm not leaving.

**MICHAEL**   I want you to leave me alone.

**BRAD**   I can't do that.

**MICHAEL**   I don't know what you want from me!

**BRAD**   I want to do the interview again.

**MICHAEL**   I can't.

**BRAD**   I want to know that you're okay.

**MICHAEL**   I'm not okay.

[*A moment.*]

**MICHAEL**   I didn't mean that.

**BRAD**   You did mean that. [*Beat*] I don't know what the fuck to do about it. But I know you meant it. [*Beat*] It's like somebody must feel . . .

**MICHAEL**   [*Pause*] Must feel . . . ?

[BRAD *shakes his head.*]

**MICHAEL**   Like what!?

**BRAD**   I don't understand why I can't just do this with you. Okay? Just let me sit here and drink your cheap whiskey, and—

**MICHAEL**   Tape me for the evening news? "It's like somebody must feel" who . . . ?

**BRAD**   Whose girlfriend was raped. And he can't be there and he can't not be there, and everything is fucked forever, but he can't leave, because then he'd be the biggest dick ever, and he doesn't want to leave, but sometimes he does, and mostly he just wants to kill somebody, because all he can see behind his eyes is red. [*Beat*] And I know you're not my girlfriend.

**MICHAEL**  And I wasn't raped.

**BRAD**  I think the comparison is apt. [*Pause*] Which I never thought about before this.

**MICHAEL**  I wasn't raped.

**BRAD**  You were tied up and thrown in the back of a car and blindfolded and starved and hurt and held hostage for eighteen months in a foreign country, and you thought they were going to kill you, and they killed the guy beside you instead.

**MICHAEL**  None of that is rape.

**BRAD**  Show me your leg.

**MICHAEL**  No.

**BRAD**  I want to see it.

**MICHAEL**  You want to film it? A little blood and skin for the camera?

**BRAD**  That's not what I—

**JACK**  If it bleeds, it leads.

**BRAD**  I don't want to film it, I just want to see it.

**MICHAEL**  You want me to take off my pants?

**BRAD**  I want to understand what they did to you.

**MICHAEL**  And you think me taking off my pants is going to clear it all up?

**BRAD**  It's not about your pants.

**MICHAEL**  Then what is it about?

**BRAD**  I want to know who hurt you, and how they hurt you. I want to know who Jack was, because you've been acting like he's your dead fucking lover. I want to know if you're permanently fucked in the head, or just temporarily. I want to know when you're coming back to the show. And most of all, even if it's totally irrelevant and stupid, I want to know why you abandoned me.

**MICHAEL**  I didn't abandon you. I just . . . took a little trip.

**BRAD**  Is that what we're calling it now? Michael's little—

**MICHAEL**  "That is the stupidest idea you ever had."

[BRAD *turns away. But then back again.*]

**BRAD**  If I said that—

**MICHAEL**  You did say that. Those were your exact—

**BRAD**  If I said that, it was . . . That's how we *start* a conversation about something.

**MICHAEL**  You didn't want to go. You didn't want me to go.

**BRAD**  Why the fuck didn't you let me talk you out of it?

**MICHAEL**  Because I knew you could.

**JACK**  Tell him.

**MICHAEL**  [*Overlapping*] I can't tell him. You have to tell him.

**JACK**  [*Overlapping*] He's trying to help you. He's trying to save you.

**MICHAEL**  [*To* JACK] It's not me who needs saving. [*Beat; to both*] Fuck. [*Pause; to himself*] Four here is eleven there.

**BRAD**  What?

[MICHAEL *mutters something under his breath, fiercely, strangely, low and unintelligible.*]

**MICHAEL**  [*Under his breath*] Tell him, don't tell him, fuck, I don't know, Jesus, Caroline, I don't know what to do, I don't know what the fuck to do, and you won't stop pushing, he doesn't understand, you have to make him understand.

**BRAD**  What did you say?

[BRAD *moves over to where* MICHAEL *is sitting, and crouches down near him.*]

**MICHAEL**  [*To* BRAD, *intensely*] We have to use that interview. The one I did.

**BRAD**  Why?

[MICHAEL *grabs* BRAD *by the collar and hauls him close, speaks right to him in a whisper that we can hear.*]

**MICHAEL**  If I say something, if I say anything, about, about, about what happened, what happened to me there, in Iraq, when I was a prisoner in Iraq, they're going to kill Caroline. If I say anything other than what they told me to say, they're going to . . .

**BRAD**  [*Beat*] What?

**MICHAEL**  They still have Caroline! They are still holding Caroline! Don't you understand?

**BRAD**  No.

**MICHAEL**  Told me . . . He . . . [*Begins to hyperventilate*] He . . . uh . . . he . . .

**BRAD**  Easy. Here. Put your head down. Breathe.

[BRAD *puts a hand on* MICHAEL's *shoulder, but* MICHAEL *pulls away.*]

**MICHAEL**  Don't touch me!

**BRAD**  It's okay. It's okay. Easy.

**MICHAEL**  That's why. I can't talk to you. [*Pause*] They pulled down my blindfold and put a gun to her head and said . . . [*Pause*] I'm . . . I'm . . . I'm not going to say anything more. I did what I was supposed to do. I'm just going to . . .

**BRAD**  Let them get away with it?

[MICHAEL *pulls away from* BRAD.]

**MICHAEL**  The only reason Caroline is alive is because they're waiting to see if I do what I'm supposed to do. They only let me go because I swore I would only say what they told me to say.

**BRAD**  They only let you go because the American military was closing in on your position, and your leg was so fucked up you were slowing them down. You had a one-hundred-and-five-degree fever. They probably thought you were going to die before anybody found you. You almost did.

**MICHAEL**  They put a gun to Caroline's head.

**BRAD**  And may they burn in hell for that little maneuver. But that doesn't mean you should . . . Jesus. It means . . . it means you have to talk. You have to tell people the truth about what they tried to make you do. About what's happening over there.

**MICHAEL**  How do I know what's happening over there?! I spent the whole time in a five–foot-by-five-foot cell I couldn't stand up in. I couldn't lie down except corner to corner. What the fuck do I know about this war? It's fucked. Everything over there is fucked.

**BRAD**  Michael, you have no control over whether or not they kill Caroline. Zero control.

**MICHAEL**  Yes, I do. They said they'd—

**BRAD**  And they always do everything they say?

[MICHAEL *doesn't answer.*]

**BRAD**  They've found a way to let you go and keep you locked up at the same time.

**MICHAEL**  They'll kill her. Just like they . . . they killed Jack. And Harold. [*Pause*] Her life is in my hands.

**BRAD**  You really believe that?

**JACK**  Michael.

**MICHAEL**  [*to* JACK] Shut up. You did what you had to do. Now I'm doing what I have to do. All right?

[MICHAEL *lurches to his feet, balancing on his crutches. He can see the tape on the counter, but* BRAD *is standing between him and it.*]

**MICHAEL**  Do you know what it's like not to be in control of anything? Of when you eat and when you shit and whether the light is on or off for eleven days in a row, because the bulb burns out, or the generator runs out of gas, and when the light finally comes back on, that single bulb blinds you,

and you don't sleep for three days because you don't want to close your eyes
and have it be dark again?

**BRAD** No. I don't know about any of that. But I know that you don't have
control over this.

**MICHAEL** Am I just supposed to let him die?

**BRAD** Him?

**MICHAEL** Her. Caroline. Caroline.

[*But he's looking at* JACK.]

**BRAD** You can't save Caroline.

**MICHAEL** If we just let the interview we did earlier air tomorrow—

**BRAD** Michael, she's probably dead already.

[MICHAEL *turns to* BRAD.]

**MICHAEL** Is that what you said about me?

[*A moment.*]

**MICHAEL** She took care of me after . . . after Jack. They put me in with her.
[*Beat*] She's not very maternal, really, but I . . . [*Beat*] A little kindness is a
long way. [*Beat*] I'll do anything to save her.

**BRAD** The best thing you can do for her . . . I believe this. Do you hear me? I
want you to tell me your story. Your real story. We can do the interview
again. Okay? Right now. Right fucking now. Tell me—tell the world—what
happened to you. What they did to you. What they threatened to do to
Caroline.

**MICHAEL** On your show.

**BRAD** On OUR show.

**MICHAEL** *No.*

**BRAD** If they keep her alive, it will be because they need her for something. If
they kill her, it will be because they decided that's how she'll be of the most
use to them, not because of anything you do or don't do.

**MICHAEL** How can I know that? They watch. They're watching us.

**BRAD** If you lie for them, if you say these terrible things for them, are they
going to let her go free?

**MICHAEL** I don't know.

**BRAD** What do you think?

**MICHAEL** Maybe!

**BRAD** *No!* They can kill her any time they want, for any reason they want,
and say it's your fault!

**MICHAEL**   I can't keep not having control over anything. I can't.

**BRAD**   You have control over yourself.

[MICHAEL *laughs helplessly.*]

**BRAD**   Do you think she wants you to help them?

**MICHAEL**   Do you think she wants to die? [*Beat*] I don't have anything more to say.

**BRAD**   Because of Caroline or because you're a coward?

**MICHAEL**   Fuck you. You have your interview. I'll take it back to Gerry myself.

[MICHAEL *takes a step toward* BRAD, *reaching for the tape.* BRAD *throws the tape to the floor, shattering it into pieces.* JACK *recoils at the explosive sound.* MICHAEL *looks down at the broken tape, his face a tangle of fear and horror. The lights go out.*]

END OF ACT I

# ACT II

[*Although there isn't a clock visible in* MICHAEL's *apartment, there is the sound of a clock ticking. We hear it, and* MICHAEL *and* JACK *hear it. Perhaps it was ticking, subtly, all through intermission, without us quite realizing it. The lights and camera are there, but no longer visible to us. We are further inside the room, or the couch and chair and coffee table are closer to us, somehow. There is nothing between us and them.* BRAD *sits in one of the Barbara Walters chairs. But our attention is with* MICHAEL *and* JACK, *who are sitting with their backs to the wall again, back by the messy pile of mail.*]

**JACK**   I like the scene where everybody stands up and sings.

**MICHAEL**   Everybody likes the scene where everybody stands up and sings. Just like everybody likes the scene about the whistling.

**JACK**   That's the wrong movie.

**MICHAEL**   It is?

**JACK**   Yes! You don't watch enough movies.

**MICHAEL**   It's not Humphrey Bogart?

**JACK**   It is Humphrey Bogart, but it's not that movie. He was in a lot of movies. [*Pause*] My mom always liked the boat one.

[MICHAEL *smiles. Remembering the boat one.*]

**MICHAEL**   You two went to the movies a lot, didn't you?

**JACK**   Every Sunday. It was her day off. We'd put on our good clothes, and go to Mass, and then eat our sandwiches in the park, then go to the movies. The Palace—it was called the Palace, the movie theater over on Montgomery—this is when I was like, eight to ten, when we were there—

they showed old movies cheap. Three dollars, and you could stay all day if you wanted. [*Pause*] You can learn a lot about how life works from the movies. [*Pause*] You go to the movies with your folks?

**MICHAEL**  No.

**JACK**  Your dad never took you to the movies?

**MICHAEL**  My dad was always . . . far away.

**JACK**  He traveled? For work?

**MICHAEL**  No. No. He was there. He was just . . . [*Beat*] In family pictures, like for Christmas, or somebody's wedding, you can see him standing in the back, which is right, because he's . . . he was tall. But he was also . . . like . . . one step back. And away.

[*A moment. MICHAEL looks over at BRAD, who is sitting in the big chair in front of the camera. JACK follows MICHAEL's gaze; he looks at BRAD, too, for a moment.*]

**JACK**  You told me about him.

**MICHAEL**  Brad?

[*JACK nods.*]

**MICHAEL**  He's screwing everything up.

[*A moment.*]

**MICHAEL**  What did I tell you?

**JACK**  The night he found out about his sister . . .

**MICHAEL**  Emily.

**JACK**  And the two of you walked all night. How he stopped on the bridge—

**MICHAEL**  The Bulkeley Bridge.

**JACK**  The Bulkeley Bridge. And looked over the side.

[*A moment.*]

**MICHAEL**  Things shift. With people. When you . . . stand on bridges with them in the middle of the night, looking over the side.

[*MICHAEL reaches out and traces the stamps on the package.*]

**JACK**  What are you going to do?

**MICHAEL**  [*with sudden strength and emphasis*] I'm going to say what I have to say. I'm going to say the same thing I said before. Right?

[*JACK looks away.*]

**MICHAEL**  She's reciting dirty limericks now. Caroline. [*Pause*] She didn't know any proper poetry by heart, but she could recite dirty limericks until the cows come home. I don't think her family has cows, but she says that.

[*Pause*] There once was a fellow McSweeney. Who spilled some gin on his weenie. Just to be couth, he added verm—

JACK    [*Cutting MICHAEL off*] Yeah.

MICHAEL    You already heard that one?

[*A moment.*]

JACK    If I'd made us wait another day, before we tried to escape, we would have made it out.

MICHAEL    Shut up.

JACK    We could have made it out. There wouldn't have been so many—

MICHAEL    Stop.

JACK    I'm trying to figure this out.

MICHAEL    I know.

[BRAD *gets up, goes to the camera, and puts in a new tape.*]

JACK    It's time.

MICHAEL    No.

JACK    He's ready to get started.

[MICHAEL *sits there for a moment. But then he gets up. He looks at* BRAD.]

MICHAEL    I'm going to say what I have to say. [*Pause*] I could use another drink.

JACK    Better not.

MICHAEL    Better not. Okay. Okay.

[MICHAEL *checks the locks on the door.* JACK *hands* MICHAEL *his suit jacket.* MICHAEL *puts the* JACK*et on—maybe needing* JACK*'s support as he takes off each crutch, slips his arm through the sleeve, and presses it back onto his forearm again.* JACK *runs his fingers through* MICHAEL*'s hair to straighten it, like you would your kid.*]

MICHAEL    [*Warily*] What are you doing?

JACK    Hair and makeup.

[JACK *steps away from* MICHAEL.]

MICHAEL    What about you?

JACK    I'm behind the camera. You're in front of the camera.

[*And suddenly, they are.* JACK *has stepped back, out of view of the television camera, watching.* MICHAEL *is in front of the camera, in front of his chair, across from* BRAD. *He stares out at the camera. It is the new eye, watching him.*]

JACK    Are you ready?

[MICHAEL *looks at* JACK *a moment, then sinks down into his chair, and takes off his crutches, setting them carefully beside him, out of sight, but close at hand.* BRAD *uses a remote control to turn on the lights and camera. They all come on at once, with a single click, blindingly bright and humming. And they're rolling.* BRAD *smiles encouragingly at* MICHAEL. *But he doesn't say anything. And he doesn't say anything. And he doesn't . . . So finally* MICHAEL *opens his mouth to say something, anything, and—*]

**BRAD**   Why is hazelnut and salted caramel ice cream the only food in your kitchen?

**MICHAEL**   [*To* JACK] Why did he ask me that?

**JACK**   Ask him.

**MICHAEL**   [*To* BRAD] Why did you ask me that?

**BRAD**   The first time we did this, I asked the wrong questions.

**MICHAEL**   "What's in my refrigerator?" That's the right question?

**BRAD**   I know what. I want to know why.

[*A moment.*]

**MICHAEL**   It tastes good. [*Pause*] I missed it. [*Pause; ramping up*] America is doing things in Iraq—

**BRAD**   I don't want to hear about America.

**MICHAEL**   I have things to—

**BRAD**   I want to hear about you.

**MICHAEL**   I don't want to talk about me.

**BRAD**   Don't you want people to know what happened to you over there?

**MICHAEL**   People?

**BRAD**   People. People.

**MICHAEL**   No. No, I really don't.

**BRAD**   Everyone wants to hear your story. You're a hero.

**MICHAEL**   *No.*

**BRAD**   You survived a terrible—

**MICHAEL**   That doesn't mean I'm some kind of—

**BRAD**   What *does* it mean?

**MICHAEL**   Having something bad happen to you doesn't make you a hero.

[*A moment.*]

**MICHAEL**   Jack is a . . .

**BRAD**   Hero?

**MICHAEL**   He did all the right things for all the right reasons. He saved me. And then he kept saving me. He's a hero.

**BRAD**   You lived.

**MICHAEL**   That doesn't matter.

**JACK**   [*Overlapping*] It matters to me.

**BRAD**   [*Overlapping*] It matters to me.

**MICHAEL**   Surviving isn't heroic. Trying to escape isn't heroic if you don't give a damn if you die trying, you just can't bear to keep—

**JACK**   You have a lot of rules in your head about what a hero is.

**BRAD**   Maybe the best we can hope for in any war is . . . complicated. Complicated motives. Complicated actions. [*Pause*] When did you try to escape?

**MICHAEL**   I don't want to talk about that. [*Pause*] I want to talk about the actions the US has taken in the Middle East, that have led to—

**BRAD**   I'm not going to let you.

**MICHAEL**   What?

**BRAD**   I didn't realize, the first time we did this, that you were a hostile witness.

**MICHAEL**   I'm not a hostile witness. I'm a—

**BRAD**   I'm not going to have you saying things to undermine the confidence of our American soldiers in Iraq, like some . . . Hartford Rose.

**MICHAEL**   Don't you think our confidence should be undermined? Not our soldiers' confidence. It's not their fault they're there. Our—our—confidence. America's confidence. Confidence gets us into trouble.

**BRAD**   Are you talking about the country right now, or yourself?

**MICHAEL**   I'm talking about this country's attitude about itself, that makes us feel like every other country in the world is our business, in a continuing game of Empire that's straight out of the—

**BRAD**   That may be true—

**MICHAEL**   That is true.

**BRAD**   —but I'm less interested in a bunch of anti-American propaganda that a bunch of terrorists coerced you into—

**MICHAEL**   Shut up!

**BRAD**   —saying than I am about what happened to you, personally, when you were in Iraq.

**MICHAEL**   You can't say that on the tape.

**BRAD**   I'll edit it.

**MICHAEL**   You'll edit it?

**BRAD**   Yes.

[*A moment.*]

**BRAD**   Why are you working so hard to avoid the question?

**MICHAEL**   I'm not. [*Beat*] I don't remember what the question was.

**BRAD**   You were telling me about Jack.

**MICHAEL**   Jack.

**BRAD**   You said he was a hero. What makes him a hero?

**MICHAEL**   He's not like us. [*Beat*] He's a real reporter.

**BRAD**   What do you mean by "real"?

**MICHAEL**   He's a photojournalist. Boots on the ground. Going where the news is. [*Beat*] Seeing for himself, not just parroting what someone else put together. Taking pictures of what's happening over there, what we're doing over there.

**BRAD**   Until he died.

**MICHAEL**   [*Beat*] Yes. [*Beat*] Pictures don't lie.

**JACK**   Is that what you think?

[MICHAEL *looks over at* JACK.]

**BRAD**   They scooped the two of you up at the same time. November 14th, 2004.

**MICHAEL**   Yes.

**BRAD**   From a caravan of cars.

**MICHAEL**   [*Beat*] Safety in numbers, for journalists. They said.

**BRAD**   Not so much.

**MICHAEL**   Not so much.

**BRAD**   What happened?

[*A moment.*]

**BRAD**   Tell me what happened.

**MICHAEL**   [*Pause*] We were at the tail end. Of the caravan. And . . . somehow our cars got separated from the rest of the cars. His car and my car.

**BRAD**   They took you and Jack.

**MICHAEL**   Drug me out of the car. They were wearing . . . [*gestures at face*] . . . over their faces. Guns—

**JACK**   Rifles.

**MICHAEL**  Rifles, they had . . . One of them shot my fixer, right in . . . he . . . I had blood, there was blood on my . . . And then someone hit me with the butt of his rifle, and . . . [*Beat*] That was . . . [*Beat*] That was how I was taken hostage.

**BRAD**  If they . . . did that to you, why do you want to help them?

**MICHAEL**  I don't want to help them.

**BRAD**  Yourself?

**MICHAEL**  No. [*Beat*] Caroline. [*Beat*] I'm not going to talk about that.

**BRAD**  Caroline Conway, who worked at the British Embassy as a secretary—

**MICHAEL**  Personal assistant. She doesn't like being called a secretary.

**BRAD**  She was held with you for the last eighteen months that you were a hostage.

**MICHAEL**  Yes. Most of the last eighteen months.

**BRAD**  Then why is Jack Velazquez the one you want to talk about?

[MICHAEL *doesn't answer.*]

**BRAD**  You told me he sent you something.

**MICHAEL**  [*Beat*] Yes.

**BRAD**  A box.

**MICHAEL**  Yes.

**BRAD**  I think we should open it.

**MICHAEL**  Now?

**BRAD**  Don't you want to know what he sent you?

[MICHAEL *looks over at* JACK.]

**JACK**  No.

**BRAD**  I want to know.

[*A moment.*]

**BRAD**  Tell me about Caroline Conway.

[*A moment.*]

**BRAD**  She worked at the British Embassy in Iraq before she was taken hostage.

**MICHAEL**  Yes.

**BRAD**  And she's still being held in Iraq, by the same people who—

**MICHAEL**  I don't want to—

**BRAD**  She's still being held there.

**MICHAEL**  Yes. [*Pause*] America is—

**BRAD**  Tell me about her.

**MICHAEL**  You're not letting me—

**BRAD**  Forty-one years old. Married.

**MICHAEL**  Separated.

**BRAD**  Born in Manchester. They interviewed her father last year, who is not your typical buttoned-up Englishman, and he said she's probably giving them hell. Is she?

**MICHAEL**  [*Beat*] She gives everyone hell.

**BRAD**  Including you?

**MICHAEL**  When I needed it. [*Pause*] This is a terrible strategy.

**BRAD**  Why do you think so?

**MICHAEL**  Because you're making me miss her.

**BRAD**  [*Beat*] You miss Jack Velazquez.

[MICHAEL *just looks at* BRAD.]

**BRAD**  Tell me what he was like.

**MICHAEL**  You're going out of order.

**BRAD**  We'll fix it in editing.

**MICHAEL**  Why didn't you fix the first one in editing?

**BRAD**  The first one was five minutes of phony, followed by twelve minutes of crap. There was no fixing that.

**MICHAEL**  [*With stronger voice.*] I would like to make a statement about America's involvement in the Middle East, by which I mean the war the United States started in Iraq in the wake of the destruction of the World Trade Center in New York City on September 11, 2001.

**BRAD**  This sounds memorized. Did someone write it out for you?

**MICHAEL**  No! I—

**BRAD**  You were in Iraq for eighteen months.

**MICHAEL**  Yes, I—

**BRAD**  Held by Shi'ite insurgents in Iraq for eighteen months.

**MICHAEL**  I wasn't—

**BRAD**  Held for eighteen months?

**MICHAEL**  Yes, I was held for eighteen months.

**BRAD**  By terrorists.

**MICHAEL**  America is responsible for terrible atrocities in Iraq, perpetrated against—

**BRAD**  How do you know?

**MICHAEL**  [*Beat*] What?

**BRAD**  You spent eighteen months in a five-foot-by-five-foot cell. You were taken hostage about five minutes after you arrived in Iraq.

**MICHAEL**  [*Beat*] Two weeks.

**BRAD**  I don't care what America did.

**MICHAEL**  What kind of reporter are you?

**BRAD**  I'm an anchorman for a third-tier urban market located in Hartford, Connecticut. This isn't *Frontline*.

**MICHAEL**  As journalists, we have a responsibility to—

**BRAD**  I'm not MacNeil. You're not Lehrer. And this interview is not with the people who started this war, or the people who are fighting this war, on this side or on that side, it's about one man from Hartford, Connecticut, who went to Iraq to see what this war was all about and got in over his head.

**MICHAEL**  We shouldn't be in Iraq.

**BRAD**  You shouldn't have been.

**MICHAEL**  Because I got myself captured five minutes after I got there?

**BRAD**  Because they hurt you there. And you are my friend.

**MICHAEL**  [*Beat*] A lot of people are getting hurt over there. Military and civilians. American and Iraqi.

**BRAD**  Jack Velazquez got hurt over there.

[MICHAEL *doesn't reply.*]

**BRAD**  He was a freelance photojournalist. Right? Selling pictures to anyone who would buy them. He was from New York?

**JACK**  No.

**MICHAEL**  No. He just landed there sometimes.

**BRAD**  Why don't you want to talk about him?

[MICHAEL *doesn't reply.*]

**BRAD**  Your captors murdered him and American engineer Harold Wolfe.

**MICHAEL**  [*Long pause*] Yes.

**BRAD**  [*Beat*] Do you feel a responsibility to speak for the dead?

**MICHAEL**  I feel a responsibility to speak for the living!

**BRAD**  What do you mean by that?

[MICHAEL *doesn't reply.*]

**BRAD**   Are you talking about Caroline Conway?

[MICHAEL *grabs his crutches and puts them on. He gets to his feet.*]

**BRAD**   Where are you going?

**MICHAEL**   I can walk into any newsroom, anywhere in America right now, and someone will let me say what I need to say.

**BRAD**   Not without me shouting to the rooftops what you told me. [*Beat*] Sit down.

[*A moment. But then* MICHAEL *sits down. He grabs his injured leg as a wave of pain runs through it.*]

**BRAD**   Are you okay?

[MICHAEL *laughs.*]

**MICHAEL**   I'd like a drink.

**JACK**   Not a good idea.

**MICHAEL**   [*To* JACK] I don't give a shit.

[BRAD *hesitates, but then goes over to the kitchen to find another bottle of liquor and pour them each a glass. He brings* MICHAEL's *glass over and holds it out to him, but pulls it away when* MICHAEL *reaches for it.*]

**BRAD**   Tell me what made you decide to go to Iraq.

**MICHAEL**   I read the news off the teleprompter. That was my job, and I did it. That's what they paid us to do. Keep our hair cut short, our nails neatly manicured, our suits well cut, and read the news off the teleprompter. [*Beat*] And then there was 9/11. Right over there. Close enough that we could smell the smoke. [*Pause*] And maybe I didn't know what it meant to read the news off the teleprompter anymore. [*Pause*] And then there was a war.

[*A moment.*]

**MICHAEL**   And I had this brilliant idea to go over there. Brad said, "Don't be an idiot, Michael." Tell them how you said it.

**BRAD**   [*Gently*] Don't be an idiot, Michael.

**MICHAEL**   No, you said it much louder than that.

**BRAD**   Not loud enough.

**MICHAEL**   I remember packing up my suitcase with what ended up being all the wrong clothes for the Middle East. Because I had no idea what I was getting into. [*Beat*] Lots of people were going over there to see what was happening, and I wanted to see what was happening. Because in some fundamental ways, I had suddenly realized I didn't understand what was happening. What we were doing over there, and why we were doing it. [*Beat*] What we were doing over there, and why we were doing it.

[BRAD *hands* MICHAEL *his drink.* MICHAEL *drinks deeply.* BRAD *sits down.* JACK *leans toward* MICHAEL.]

**JACK**  [*Softly, coaching, helping.*] Before I could figure anything out . . .

**MICHAEL**  Before I could figure anything out . . .

**JACK**  I was taken . . .

**MICHAEL**  I was taken . . .

**JACK**  Hostage.

**MICHAEL**  Hostage.

**JACK**  By . . .

**MICHAEL**  By . . .

**JACK**  Say the fucking words, Michael.

**MICHAEL**  Before I could figure anything out, I was taken hostage by a small band of Iraqi insurgents. [*Beat*] It was my own fault.

**JACK**  No, it wasn't.

**BRAD**  Why do you say that?

[MICHAEL *looks down. Sets down his drink. Veers in another direction.*]

**MICHAEL**  They wanted me to change my name to Michael Apple.

**BRAD**  What? [*Beat*] The network?

**MICHAEL**  Yeah. Back when you and I first—

**JACK**  That's just stupid.

**BRAD**  Michael *Apple*?

**MICHAEL**  I fought them on it.

**BRAD**  And won.

**MICHAEL**  Gerry said—

**JACK**  Your producer?

**MICHAEL**  Gerry said, "Nobody in America likes foreign people. Just foreign places. And they hate French people."

**JACK**  Only because French people are assholes.

[MICHAEL *laughs.*]

**BRAD**  You're not French. You're like . . . a quarter French.

**MICHAEL**  Yeah.

**JACK**  Why didn't you want to change your name?

**MICHAEL**  [*To* JACK] It's my name.

**JACK**  It's your father's name. *Après.*

**MICHAEL**  It's who I am.

**JACK**  You hate your father.

**MICHAEL**  No, I don't.

**JACK**  He got you into this. The whole Vietnam macho father thing.

**MICHAEL**  Stop it!

**JACK**  It's his fault you're here.

**MICHAEL**  It's your fault I'm here. [*Pause*] I didn't mean that.

**JACK**  I think you did. [*Pause*] I did what I had to do. You know that, right?

[MICHAEL *doesn't answer.*]

**JACK**  Michael.

**MICHAEL**  [*Bursting out to both* JACK *and* BRAD] Quit badgering me.

[BRAD *looks at him, bewildered.*]

**BRAD**  I'm not. I just want to . . . I'm just trying to . . .

[*A moment.*]

**BRAD**  I started reading everything I could get my hands on about the war after . . . after they took you. It had gotten so . . . theoretical. [*Beat; strongly*] I want to know what happened to you.

**MICHAEL**  There are things I don't remember.

**BRAD**  Things you don't remember, or things you don't want to remember?

**MICHAEL**  I can't talk to you.

**BRAD**  Why not?

**MICHAEL**  You . . . you know why not. There's more at stake than—

**BRAD**  Why don't you tell our viewers what's at stake?

[MICHAEL *turns away from the camera.*]

**BRAD**  When I got here tonight, you were opening your mail. But there was one package you didn't open.

**MICHAEL**  [*Beat*] I'm afraid to open it.

**JACK**  You think I'd send you something bad?

**MICHAEL**  [*To* JACK] No, but . . . [*Beat*] Pieces of you . . . [*Beat*] I can't . . . I couldn't . . .

[BRAD *looks over at the package from Iraq. He takes a sip of his whiskey.*]

**MICHAEL**  Why are you fighting me?

**BRAD**   I'm not fighting you. I'm trying to . . . I'm trying to help you acknowledge that this is a war you can't win. [*Pause*] I'm trying to get you to stop fighting and come home.

[MICHAEL *looks around the room.*]

**MICHAEL**   This doesn't feel like home anymore.

[BRAD *takes another drink, then sets down his glass. Then he goes over to the pile of mail by the wall. He picks up the package from Iraq, brings it over, and sets it on the coffee table between him and* MICHAEL. *Then he sits down.*]

**BRAD**   What is this?

**MICHAEL**   [*Beat*] A package.

**BRAD**   It has Iraqi stamps on it. And it's addressed to you. [*Beat*] Where did it come from?

**MICHAEL**   Iraq.

**BRAD**   Who sent it?

**MICHAEL**   Why are you doing this?

**BRAD**   You know why.

**MICHAEL**   Jack. Jack sent it. Jack Velazquez . . . sent it to me.

[*A moment.*]

**MICHAEL**   Are you trying to make me look like I'm crazy? So you can . . . so you can discredit me? Anything I say?

**BRAD**   No. [*Beat*] That's just the back-up plan.

**MICHAEL**   What's the plan?

[BRAD *doesn't answer.* MICHAEL *takes another drink.*]

**MICHAEL**   Make me look like I'm a drunk?

**BRAD**   No.

**MICHAEL**   I missed drinking. [*Looking straight into the camera.*] Whiskey and hazelnut caramel ice cream are two things that you should never take for granted, America. Remember that.

[BRAD *takes a small Swiss Army knife out of his pocket, opens it, and lays it on top of the package.* MICHAEL *picks up the knife.*]

**JACK**   Don't open it.

**MICHAEL**   [*To* JACK] Why not?

**JACK**   Pandora.

[MICHAEL *laughs.*]

**JACK**   We could run away some place.

**MICHAEL**  Casablanca?

**JACK**  Casablanca isn't real.

**MICHAEL**  Yes, it is. It's in Morocco.

**JACK**  The Casablanca you're thinking about isn't real.

**MICHAEL**  Imaginary places with imaginary friends.

**JACK**  Is that what you think I am?

**MICHAEL**  I don't know. [*Pause*] But I don't want you to go anywhere.

**JACK**  You shouldn't open the package.

**MICHAEL**  Does it have bad things in it?

[MICHAEL *looks at the knife in his hand.*]

**MICHAEL**  I could . . .

**JACK**  No.

[JACK *goes over to* MICHAEL, *takes the knife out of his hand, and lays it back on the table.*]

**JACK**  No.

[MICHAEL *picks up the package and shakes it gently beside his ear.*]

**MICHAEL**  It would be nice to have something . . . tangible. I don't have anything of Jack's. You know? Nothing that I can . . . All I have is this . . .

**JACK**  Complicated.

**MICHAEL**  [*To* BRAD] . . . complicated tangle in my head, of memories and voices and pictures. I see him . . . [*Smiles*] . . . and then I see him . . . [*Puts hand out as if to touch.*] . . . bloody and . . .

**JACK**  Don't remember me that way.

**MICHAEL**  [*To* JACK] I can't help it.

[MICHAEL *looks down at the box for a moment. Then he tears the brown paper off carefully, and opens it.* BRAD *watches, waiting to see what's inside.* MICHAEL *takes a camera out of the box, from its protective nest of bunched up glossy Spanish magazine pages and sheets of newspaper in Arabic. It's a good camera—a professional Nikon or Canon, with a zoom and satellite hookups and a battered case.* BRAD *looks oddly at the camera.*]

**BRAD**  Whose camera is that?

[MICHAEL *smiles as he turns it over in his hands, looking at it.*]

**MICHAEL**  It's Jack's.

[*He turns to* JACK.]

**MICHAEL**  Why didn't you want me to open it?

[JACK *moves away from* MICHAEL. MICHAEL *turns the camera on. He flips a switch.*]

**MICHAEL**   It has pictures on it. Jack's pictures.

**BRAD**   Can I see it?

[MICHAEL *hands the camera to* BRAD. BRAD *turns the camera over in his hands. It doesn't have a name tag on it. But it does have pictures;* MICHAEL *was right about that.* MICHAEL *is still looking at* JACK.]

**MICHAEL**   [*To* JACK] What are they?

**JACK**   What do you mean?

**MICHAEL**   The pictures. What are the pictures? [*Pause*] Jack?

**JACK**   Complicated.

[BRAD *looks through the viewer.*]

**BRAD**   I know this picture.

**MICHAEL**   [*To* BRAD] What do you mean, you know it?

**BRAD**   I know it.

**MICHAEL**   Give it to me.

[BRAD *hands* MICHAEL *the camera.* MICHAEL *looks through the viewer.*]

**BRAD**   It was on the cover of *Newsweek* after . . .

**MICHAEL**   [*Beat*] After we were taken?

**BRAD**   [*Beat*] After he was killed.

**MICHAEL**   It's . . .

**JACK**   Good.

**BRAD**   It's Jack Velazquez's picture.

**MICHAEL**   [*To* BRAD] I told you. It's his camera. [*Beat*] The boy's eyes are . . .

[JACK *looks out into the distance, remembering taking the picture.*]

**JACK**   This tiny little boy ran out the door. Maybe—

**MICHAEL**   [*To* JACK] Two years old?

**JACK**   Two years old. And his father grabbed him up, like . . . instinct. Instinct to do . . . And as he turned to go back into the house, the boy looked straight at me over his father's shoulder and reached out his hand like . . .

[JACK *reaches out his hand.* MICHAEL *looks at* JACK.]

**JACK**   I gave the camera to Marty for safekeeping after I sold the pictures on it. Then I visited him in a dream, and told him to send the camera to you.

**MICHAEL**   You wanted me to see your pictures?

**JACK**   Yes. No. I can't decide.

**MICHAEL**   You always know what to do.

**JACK**   No. No, I really don't.

[BRAD *looks over at* MICHAEL.]

**BRAD**   Are there more on there?

**MICHAEL**   [*To* BRAD] More pictures?

[BRAD *nods.* MICHAEL *looks at the camera, then up at* JACK.]

**MICHAEL**   [*To* JACK] Are there more pictures, Jack?

[*A moment. Then* JACK *nods.* MICHAEL *clicks the "back" button on the camera, and looks at the viewer. He scans through the pictures.*]

**MICHAEL**   [*To both* BRAD *and* JACK.] A boy and his father. Standing in the doorway of a house, somewhere in Iraq. [*Beat; scanning through the pictures.*] Then just the father.

[MICHAEL *makes the picture larger, so he can see the face of the man more clearly.*]

**MICHAEL**   I know him.

**BRAD**   Who?

**MICHAEL**   [*To* BRAD] The father. The . . . Al Sadr. [*Beat*] It's Zaid Al Sadr.

[MICHAEL *thrusts the camera into* BRAD's *hands and lurches to his feet. He moves away from* JACK. BRAD *takes the camera from* MICHAEL *and looks at the pictures, clicking through them.* MICHAEL *turns to* JACK.]

**MICHAEL**   What did you do?

**JACK**   Nobody saw me.

**MICHAEL**   Saw you—

**JACK**   Nobody saw me take those.

**MICHAEL**   No?

**JACK**   I didn't think anybody saw me.

**MICHAEL**   You told yourself nobody saw you, so you wouldn't have to . . . [*Pause*] Somebody saw you. And then they . . .

[MICHAEL *turns to* BRAD.]

**MICHAEL**   Sometimes he sells pictures to the CIA. Did I mention that?

**BRAD**   What? [*Beat*] Jack? Jack Velazquez sells . . . sold . . .

**MICHAEL**   Pictures. To the CIA.

**BRAD**   I don't understand.

**JACK**   I take pictures and I sell pictures.

**MICHAEL**  You're a *journalist*.

**BRAD**  Sometimes he sold pictures to the CIA?

**JACK**  The AP buys pictures. Sometimes I sell one to *Newsweek* or Gannett. And sometimes I have something the CIA might be interested in.

[*A moment.*]

**MICHAEL**  [*To* BRAD] This is how it goes. [*To* JACK] Right? [*To* BRAD] This is how it goes. Jack takes a picture of a boy and his father in a doorway and sells it to *Newsweek*. But the father isn't just a father. He's Zaid Al Sadr, second in command in the insurgency. [*To* JACK] Did you know it was him you were shooting?

**JACK**  I had a tip.

**MICHAEL**  You had a tip.

**JACK**  I followed a guy.

**MICHAEL**  [*To* BRAD] He followed a guy. And took his picture.

**JACK**  That's my job.

**MICHAEL**  And sold the picture of the boy to *Newsweek*. And sold the rest of the pictures to the CIA. [*To* JACK] Is that your job, too? [*To both*] He sold the rest of the pictures to the CIA. Because the father wasn't just a father, he was—

**BRAD**  Zaid Al Sadr.

**MICHAEL**  And an air strike is called on the house in the picture.

**BRAD**  Seventeen confirmed dead. [*Pause*] Twelve of them were enemy combatants.

**MICHAEL**  Twelve?

**BRAD**  Five of them were noncombatants.

**MICHAEL**  How many of them were children?

[*Neither* BRAD *nor* JACK *answers.*]

**MICHAEL**  [*To* JACK] What kind of journalist are you?

**JACK**  A really fucking practical one. [*Pause*] Al Sadr wasn't a good guy. You know that, right?

**BRAD**  Oh, God. [*Pause*] Jack is the one who got you captured.

[MICHAEL *nods, folding in on himself.*]

**JACK**  I didn't ask you to make me into a hero.

**MICHAEL**  But I did.

[*A long moment.*]

**JACK**  Newsweek bought that one picture. The one with the boy. The rest I sold to the CIA for seven hundred.

**MICHAEL**  Seven hundred dollars?

**JACK**  Yeah. [*Beat*] Yeah. [*Pause*] Four. [*Pause*] Four of them were children. They showed me pictures of them when we were being held in the . . . [*Pause*] If I'd just—

**MICHAEL**  Just what? [*Pause*] You're always choosing. Aren't you? What people see and what they don't see. Every picture is a choice about what story to tell. And sometimes it's not the whole story, is it? [*Beat*] You left a few things out.

**JACK**  Nobody else was supposed to be involved! If your car hadn't followed our car . . . If. Fucking "if."

[*A moment.*]

**JACK**  Your car got behind our car, somehow, in the caravan.

**MICHAEL**  I was late.

**JACK**  When we turned off, you turned off, instead of following the caravan.

**MICHAEL**  I was talking to a man in the bar.

**BRAD**  The bar at the Palestine Hotel?

**MICHAEL**  There was an AP stringer who was sitting at the bar every time I went into the bar. At the Palestine. Four in the morning. Two in the afternoon. Eleven o'clock at night. He'd stopped going out. I think he'd stopped sleeping, too. That morning I bought him a glass of bourbon and he told me he'd started making it all up. His stories.

[*A moment.*]

**MICHAEL**  He only spoke French.

**BRAD**  [*Beat*] The man in the bar?

**MICHAEL**  [*"I started making it all up. My news stories. This is the story now. I shouldn't be telling you this. Go buy me another drink, boy. Don't trust anyone."*] Je me suis mis à tout inventer. Mes reportages. C'est ça l'histoire maintenant. Je ne devrais pas vous dire tout ça. Offrez-moi un autre verre, jeune homme. Ne faites confiance—

**BRAD**  Michael.

**MICHAEL**  —à personne. [*Beat*] His arms bled. He had these little scabs on his arms. He'd pick at them while he drank, then dab at them with the white linen napkins.

**JACK**  You weren't supposed to follow us. Nobody was supposed to follow us.

**MICHAEL**  [*To* JACK] It was an ambush.

**JACK**  [*Beat*] Yeah.

**MICHAEL**   They set a trap for you.

**JACK**   Yeah. [*Pause*] Eyes for eyes. Teeth for teeth.

**MICHAEL**   You told them . . . what you did. When they had us. When they were threatening to kill me because I was—

**JACK**   Network.

**MICHAEL**   No. Because I was with you. Because they thought I was with you. [*Beat*] You told them what you did. So they'd kill you, and not me.

**JACK**   Yeah.

**MICHAEL**   Did you do it because it was right, or did you do it to save me?

**JACK**   Does it matter? [*Pause*] Sometimes things . . . collide. [*Pause*] I don't know.

**MICHAEL**   I let them kill you. [*Beat*] Because I wanted to—

**JACK**   You didn't let them do anything. They had Kalashnikov rifles and we didn't even have socks. They did whatever the fuck they wanted.

[MICHAEL *shakes his head.*]

**JACK**   We're always making choices inside of no choices. We're always working against a ticking clock. In the newsroom, the digital clock up above the booth clicks off the tenths of seconds. The clock in your head that you've been carrying around for Caroline is so loud even I can hear it, tick, tick, tick. Every person on this planet is ticking, ticking, ticking, losing time. You put your ear to any chest and you can hear it.

[JACK *steps away from* MICHAEL.]

**JACK**   You let me own my shit. Is what you did. [*Pause*] They took us because I was selling pictures to the CIA. They beat the shit out of us because I led us on a crazy, stupid escape plan.

**MICHAEL**   I helped with the crazy, stupid escape plan.

**JACK**   They killed me, because when you're outmanned and outgunned, the only weapon you have is terror.

[BRAD *touches* MICHAEL's *arm. He jerks away, startled.*]

**JACK**   It's very effective.

**BRAD**   You okay?

**MICHAEL**   I don't know.

[MICHAEL *sits back down. Clutches his leg.*]

**MICHAEL**   Bring me my pills, will you?

[BRAD *goes to the counter. Gets* MICHAEL's *pills, and hands them over.* MICHAEL *takes one of each pill, washing them down with whiskey.* MICHAEL *nods.* BRAD *watches* MICHAEL *holding his leg, gritting his teeth until the pills take effect.*]

**BRAD**  You haven't told me what happened to your leg.

**MICHAEL**  You haven't asked.

**BRAD**  We're on the same side, Michael.

**MICHAEL**  The same side of what?

**BRAD**  What happened to your leg?

**MICHAEL**  After my third escape attempt, they nailed it to the floor with an iron spike.

[*A long moment.*]

**MICHAEL**  Don't ask if you don't want to know.

**BRAD**  I want to know. I just . . .

**MICHAEL**  For what? What good does this do, is this going to do, you, me, or anybody else?

**BRAD**  It's important.

**MICHAEL**  Why?

**BRAD**  Truth is important.

**MICHAEL**  I laid there for four days. I would have crapped myself if they'd given me any food, but you don't get food if you're bad. Sometimes you don't get food if you're good. [*Beat*] That's when Jack came back.

**BRAD**  [*Beat*] When you were . . .

**MICHAEL**  I woke up, and he was . . . [*Pause*] It was so nice to see him. [*Pause*] This isn't what I want to talk about.

**BRAD**  Yes, it is. [*Beat*] I think it is.

**MICHAEL**  He came back when I was lying there in my own . . . And he hasn't left. He followed me home. Or I dragged him back here with me. [*Beat*] He's right over there.

[MICHAEL *turns and points at* JACK. *Then he goes over to* JACK. *They look at each other, as* MICHAEL *continues to talk with* BRAD.]

**MICHAEL**  Everything is out of control. I shouldn't be drinking, because it's not helping me feel more in control, but it's something I can do. I don't know what to do.

[BRAD *steps toward* MICHAEL.]

**BRAD**  Michael . . .

[MICHAEL *turns to* BRAD.]

**BRAD**  He's not real.

[JACK *reaches out and runs the back of his hand down* MICHAEL's *arm.* MICHAEL *shudders.*]

**MICHAEL**   He seems pretty real.

[*A moment.*]

**JACK**   You're holding onto me like . . . Not like a boat, like one of those big—

**MICHAEL**   —bright hot air balloons.

**JACK**   You have hold of my string and you won't let go.

**MICHAEL**   I'm so angry. [*Beat*] I can't be angry at you.

**JACK**   Why not?

**MICHAEL**   You saved me. You're not allowed to be angry at someone who saves you.

**JACK**   You have so many rules.

**MICHAEL**   I grew up in suburban Connecticut. My whole life is rules.

**JACK**   We have absolutely nothing in common, you know that? [*Pause*] You gonna drag me around forever like this?

**MICHAEL**   I never wanted you to leave.

**JACK**   Tough shit, buddy. [*Pause; gestures at* BRAD] You get him.

**MICHAEL**   He's not you.

**JACK**   Let's face it . . . nobody is. I'm spectacular.

[MICHAEL *smiles.*]

**JACK**   The same string that's holding me here is holding you here. [*Pause*] I'm . . . sorry I wasn't the hero you needed me to be. [*Beat*] I would have been if I could have been. But it was kind of too late before we even started. I'd already made all the choices that ended you up there. [*Beat*] I keep going over it all in my head, over and over, and that's what I keep coming up with. [*Pause*] I really hate failing.

**MICHAEL**   You didn't. [*Beat*] You didn't. [*Beat*] I ended myself up there.

**JACK**   No. You didn't. You didn't end. You got a whole life here you can choose. Laid out in front of you like a feast, and all you gotta do is choose it.

**MICHAEL**   I don't know how.

[*A moment.*]

**MICHAEL**   I'm sorry I failed you. I'm sorry I didn't save you. I didn't know how. Maybe I . . . maybe I don't have control over that. Over whether you and Caroline get saved. [*Beat*] Do I? [*Beat*] Do I have control over that?

[JACK *doesn't answer.*]

**MICHAEL**   You're not going to answer me?

**JACK**   I don't know. [*Beat*] I don't know.

[MICHAEL *nods.*]

**JACK** Come here.

[MICHAEL *doesn't move.*]

**JACK** What? You don't trust me?

[MICHAEL *doesn't answer.*]

**JACK** Come here.

[MICHAEL *goes over to* JACK. *A moment. Then* JACK *pulls a picture out of the bottom of the box, and holds it out to* MICHAEL. *It's a photograph of himself.*]

**MICHAEL** The last thing in Pandora's box is a picture of you?

**JACK** Remember me by.

[MICHAEL *nods.*]

**JACK** You get to pick the picture you take with you. [*Pause*] Take this one. Okay?

[MICHAEL *takes the picture from* JACK.]

**MICHAEL** Why did you send me the box?

**JACK** I can't . . . change what happened. What I did. Everything I did. Anything I did. But maybe the one thing I can change is telling you the truth.

[JACK *reaches out and puts his hand on the back of* MICHAEL's *neck, and pulls him close. A moment.*]

**JACK** Be okay. Okay? [*Beat*] Go do something good.

[*And then* JACK *steps back. And back. And back. And then he's gone.* MICHAEL *makes a small sound. He keeps losing more than he can bear to lose.*]

**MICHAEL** I don't want to be the one who lives all by myself.

**BRAD** You're not all by yourself.

[MICHAEL *turns back to* BRAD. *A moment.*]

**MICHAEL** If you could go back in time and save your sister, would you?

**BRAD** [*Beat*] I can't believe you said that.

[MICHAEL *just looks at* BRAD.]

**BRAD** Yes. Yes.

**MICHAEL** Then—

**BRAD** But I can't. I can't go back in time and . . . save Emily. She's dead.

**MICHAEL** Caroline isn't.

**BRAD** You can't transport yourself back to Iraq and swoop in and save Caroline. You have no idea where they took her. You're not in the military. You're not Superman.

**MICHAEL**  Who am I if I can't save her?

**BRAD**  Human? [*Pause*] I tried to help Em.

**MICHAEL**  I know.

**BRAD**  I really did. She was—

**MICHAEL**  Really screwed up.

**BRAD**  She was my sister.

**MICHAEL**  I'm trying to help Caroline.

**BRAD**  You can't. [*Beat*] I really, truly believe you can't. You're fooling yourself if you believe you can.

[MICHAEL *sinks down into his chair. He has the picture of* JACK *in his hand.*]

**BRAD**  That picture . . .

[MICHAEL *hands it to* BRAD.]

**BRAD**  Where did you get this?

**MICHAEL**  Jack gave it to me. It was in the box. [*Pause*] I want to tell you about Jack. And . . . and Caroline.

[MICHAEL *looks at* BRAD *for a moment. Then he picks up the clicker and turns off the lights and camera. He sets the clicker down.* BRAD *gets up.*]

**BRAD**  What the hell are you doing?

**MICHAEL**  I'm not going back on the air, Brad. [*Pause*] I'm not that person anymore, who can do that. The *Hartford Evening News*. Read words off the teleprompter. Make jokes about breakfast cereal in between segments on the girls basketball coach who was molesting his players, and the latest suicide bombing in Afghanistan.

**BRAD**  [*Beat*] I don't know how to do anything except this.

**MICHAEL**  We're not stupid people.

**BRAD**  I don't know what anything else looks like. We've always done this. This is what we are.

**MICHAEL**  No. This is what we do. What we are . . . is a little bigger than that.

[*A moment. Through the following, a warm, natural, early morning light washes over the apartment through the windows as the sun rises outside.* MICHAEL *reaches out . . . and instead of picking up his drink, he picks up the clicker. He turns the lights and camera back on. Everything is light again. Everything hums.* BRAD *looks at* MICHAEL, *not sure what he's doing.*]

**MICHAEL**  Sit down.

[BRAD *sits.* MICHAEL *sets the clicker on the coffee table, and gathers himself up. He puts on his television self—back straight, eyes focused—and we can suddenly see what he was before.* BRAD *responds without thinking—turning toward* MICHAEL, *back straight, eyes focused. We can see a glimpse of what they were like before.*]

**MICHAEL**   Hello, Hartford. [*Pause*] I've missed you. [*Pause*] Did you ever think you'd hear me say that?

**BRAD**   [*Beat*] We missed you, too. Michael Aprés.

**MICHAEL**   This is my last broadcast with my friend and colleague Brad Flanigan. [*Pause*] So we're going to make it a good one. [*Pause*] Brad has a few questions about what happened to me when I . . . when I decided to go to Iraq and see what this war was all about. Right?

**BRAD**   [*Beat*] I have a few questions.

**MICHAEL**   Brad's going to ask every question he's got. About . . . about Jack. Velazquez. And about Caroline Conway. And about . . .

**BRAD**   Everything.

**MICHAEL**   Everything. [*Beat*] And then he's promised to take me over to Palacki's, and we're going to get blotto together.

**BRAD**   Nobody has used the word "blotto" since Frank Sinatra.

**MICHAEL**   I like Frank Sinatra.

**BRAD**   So does my grandmother. [*Beat*] Palacki's closed six months ago.

**MICHAEL**   Because of the roaches or the underage drinking?

[BRAD *smiles.*]

**BRAD**   We'll have to get drunk together some place else.

**MICHAEL**   I think we can figure it out. [*Beat*] We'll find a new place.

**BRAD**   Yeah. [*Beat*] Yeah. We'll figure it out.

[BRAD *squares his shoulders and lifts his chin—and looks, now, entirely like the professional he is.*]

**BRAD**   Michael Aprés. A year and a half ago, you went to Iraq to cover the war there.

[BRAD *hands* MICHAEL *the picture of* JACK. MICHAEL *looks at it.*]

**MICHAEL**   Yes. Yes, I did.

[MICHAEL *out at the camera. A moment.*]

**MICHAEL**   It seemed like a good idea at the time.

[MICHAEL *looks over at* BRAD. *And they begin.*]

END OF PLAY

# The Oregon Trail

Bekah Brunstetter

# Bekah Brunstetter

Bekah Brunstetter's plays include *Going to a Place Where You Already Are* (South Coast Rep Commission), *Cutie and Bear* (Upcoming, the Roundabout), *A Long and Happy Life* (Naked Angels Commission), *Be A Good Little Widow* (Ars Nova, Collaboraction, the Old Globe), *Oohrah!* (the Atlantic Theater, Steppenwolf Garage, the Finborough Theatre / London), *Nothing is the end of the World (except for the end of the world)* (Waterwell Productions), *House of Home* (Williamstown Theatre Festival), and *Miss Lilly Gets Boned* (Ice Factory Festival). She is an alumni of the CTG Writers Group, Primary Stages Writers Group, Ars Nova Play Group, the Playwright's Realm, and the Women's Project Lab. She has previously written for MTV (*Underemployed, I Just Want My Pants Back*) She wrote for ABC Family's *Switched at Birth*, and is now writing for Starz's upcoming *American Gods*. She received a BA from UNC-Chapel Hill and an MFA in Dramatic Writing from the New School for Drama.

# Production History

*The Oregon Trail* was developed during a residency at the Eugene O'Neill Theater Center's National Playwrights Conference in 2013.

Executive Director: Preston Whiteway
Artistic Director: Wendy C. Goldberg

Developed at the Lark Play Development Center, New York City.

*The Oregon Trail* received its world premiere in September 2015 at Flying V (Jason Schlafstein, Flying V Artistic Director; Jonathan Rubin, Flying V Managing Director) as part of the Women's Voices Theater Festival in DC, directed by Amber Jackson, with the following cast, crew, and creative team:

William Hayes   *Billy/Matt*
Ryan Tumulty   *Clancy*
Madeline Whiting   *Jane*

Julia Klavans   *Mary Anne*
Kelsey Meiklejohn   *Then Jane*
Zachary Fernebok   *Voice of the Game*

Derek David   Assistant Stage Manager
Tia Shearer Basset   Audience Designer
Kathryn Kawecki   Costume Designer
Devon Ross   FOH Manager
Phil da Costa   FV Company Manager/ Asst. Production Manager
Dan Mori   FV Education/Internship Manager
Kim Goldberg   FV Grant Manager
Susanna Pretzer   FV Literary Manager
Heather Whitpan   FV Media and Marketing Manager

Liz Tuxbury   FV Production Manager
Kristin A. Thompson   Lighting Designer
Ashley Wagoner   Master Electrician
Bekah Brunstetter   OT Playwright
Melody Taylor   Props
Britney Mongold   Scenic Charge
Kathryn Kawecki   Scenic Designer
Neil McFadden   Sound Designer
Corie Bruins   Stage Manager
Andrew Berry   TD/Master Carpenter
Julie Roedersheimer   TD/Master Carpenter

## CHARACTERS

### Present

Jane, an angsty, contemporary young lady, prone to sadness
Mary Anne, her slightly OCD sister, a violinist
Billy, the hottest pre-pubescent guy in school

### 1848

Then Jane, a young girl traversing the country with her family, via the Oregon Trail
Mary Anne, her seemingly perfect sister (played by contemporary Mary Anne)
Clancy, their father
The Omnipotent Voice of the Oregon Trail

# PART I

## GAME GOING BACK TO 1997

[*A computer lab at a nice private K-12, where privileged kids go. A wall clock's hands read 3:27 pm: that weird time after school where you're there for rehearsal, or practice, or you're just—weird.* JANE, *13, an angsty loner who is growing into her body in a bad way, sits at a desk, on her sweet-ass giant Nokia cell phone. She is calling someone for the tenth time who is just not picking up. She leaves a message.*]

**JANE**  Mom. MOM. MOMMMMM. Are you home? MOM PICK UP. You were supposed to be here an hour ago. Mary Anne's got violin and I'm still here and if you're not here in ten minutes I am going to *kill* myself. Or whatever, I can just walk home, and then I'll get hit by a car, and everyone will be really sad,  you'll be sad, whoever hit me will be sad, Mary Anne'll be sad and then you'll have to bury my body in the *ground.*

[*Beat.*]

I'm in the computer lab now if you even care. Bye.

[*She aggressively pushes the end button. Tosses the phone in her bag. She turns to look at the sleeping computers, her friends. She peers around to make sure no one is looking, then makes her way to her favorite computer by the window. She reaches for a disc in her bag, pops it in, and THE GAME BEGINS. A smile crosses her face. This game soothes her. It's one of the few things that makes her happy.*]

**GAME/JANE**  [*Booming*] THE OREGON TRAIL!

**GAME**  You may: 1. Travel the Trail. 2. Learn about the Trail. What is your choice?

**JANE**  [*Clicking*] Travel that shit.

**GAME**  Many kinds of people made the trip to Oregon.

**JANE**  No der.

**GAME**  You may: 1. Be a Banker from Boston. 2. Be a Carpenter from Ohio. 3. Be a Farmer from Illinois. 4. Be a completely ineffectual middle schooler who has yet to excel at anything and who also cannot manage her body odor.

**JANE**  That one's new. Carpenter because they can fix the wagon axle things. [*Punching a key.*] Carpenterrrrrrr.

**GAME**  What is the first name of the wagon leader?

**JANE**  [*Typing*] Me, duh. Jane.

**GAME**  What are the first names of the four other members in your party?

**JANE**  Jared. Blossom. Claire Danes. Andddddddd . . .

[*The cursor blinks.*]

Billy.

**GAME/JANE**  [*Booming*] GOING BACK TO 1848.

[JANE's *big sister,* MARY ANNE, *17, passes by. She's effortlessly pretty, seemingly per-fect, and carries a violin in a case. She's a bit manic, constantly covering something she's not old enough to yet name.*]

**MARY ANNE**  What're you doing?

**JANE**  Living my life.

**MARY ANNE**  You're supposed to be out front. Mom said to meet her out front/so you need to be out front.

**JANE**  She called the office. She's going to be like 100 years late which is so stupid because she doesn't even have a *job*.

**MARY ANNE**  Neither do you.

**JANE**  Neither do you.

**MARY ANNE**  *We're* her job.

**JANE**  I'm not a job! I'm self-sufficient, I trim my own bangs.

[JANE *angrily continues to play the game.* MARY ANNE *goes to* JANE, *watches the game. She twirls* JANE's *ponytail in her fingers.*]

**JANE**  Stop it.

**MARY ANNE**  [*Proudly*] We had ancestors on the Trail.

**JANE**  [*Who the fuck cares.*] I *know.*

**MARY ANNE**  I just think it's cool, it's a fun fact thing that I like to think about!

**JANE**  Can I have a dollar?

**MARY ANNE**  What for?

**JANE**  Vending machine.

**MARY ANNE**  Jane, soda is SO bad for you.

**JANE**  My body my choice and my choice is a Mountain Dew.

**MARY ANNE**  You have got to build good habits now. If you're not careful you'll get really fat in college.

**JANE**  That's like in 100 years.

**MARY ANNE**  It's sooner than you think.

[MARY ANNE *smells her. Makes a face.*]

**JANE**  . . . What?

**MARY ANNE**  Nothing.

**JANE**  Do I smell?

**MARY ANNE**  A little bit, yep.

**JANE**  [*Horrified*] What kind?

**MARY ANNE**   Like you've been running.

**JANE**   I haven't been running. It's just how I smell.

**MARY ANNE**   I got this, it's okay—

[MARY ANNE *starts to rummage through her bag.*]

You gotta start wearing deodorant. Mom got you some Teen Spirit, you gotta start using / it or people are gonna keep saying things—

**JANE**   I DO, I DO USE IT.

**MARY ANNE**   I'm not—I'm just trying to help.

**JANE**   Well you're not.

**MARY ANNE**   If you wanna make friends, you have to—

**JANE**   I have friends! They're back at Whitaker!

**MARY ANNE**   Well, you go *here* now.

[MARY ANNE *pulls out some terrible spray, sprays it all over her sister.*]

**JANE**   Ahhhh STOP it! Now I smell like Bath and Body Works freaking died in my hair!

**MARY ANNE**   You smell *better.* You smell like [*looking at bottle*] honeysuckles at sunset—melon.

**JANE**   I smell like a whore baby.

[MARY ANNE *sprays herself so she too smells like honeysuckle melons at sunset.*]

**MARY ANNE**   You gotta take care of yourself, you gotta pay attention to yourself. You should let Mom take you shopping for some new clothes!

**JANE**   If I ever had a scrunchie that matched my shirt I would kill myself.

**MARY ANNE**   But maybe if you felt *better* about your *appearance* then—

**JANE**   [*Quickly*] Guys don't like me.

**MARY ANNE**   Yeah they do.

**JANE**   Who?

[*Beat.*]

**MARY ANNE**   But also, who cares? It doesn't matter.

**JANE**   I wanna go home. Why can't you just drive me it'll take like two seconds!

**MARY ANNE**   I have lessons 'til 5.

**JANE**   [*Groaning*] Guhhhhhhhhhhhh I'm going to kill myself.

[*Beat.*]

**MARY ANNE**   You shouldn't say that. Didn't they show you the video in health class?

JANE   Yeah so I'm obviously not serious or I'd be giving away all my CDs.

MARY ANNE   Mom'll get here when she gets here.

JANE   Do you ever wish you were adopted from someplace like really far away like your real parents were Eskimos or royalty or wolves?

MARY ANNE   What's going on with you? Ever since you got your / period

JANE   Don't say p—

MARY ANNE   You've been all—

JANE   I *know* I don't know leave me alone.
[*Beat.*]
I think when you get your p—when you get it—it's like when your body starts to tell you the truth about your life.
[*Beat.*]
Sometimes something heavy comes out of nowhere and it just sits on me.
[*Beat.*]
You ever feel it? Even way deep down?

MARY ANNE   [*Uncomfortable*] I don't know. Maybe. I don't know.

JANE   What do you think it is?

MARY ANNE   I have to get to practice. If I'm late Mr. Parham makes me do scales.

[MARY ANNE *kisses* JANE *on the top of her head, and goes.*]

JANE   [*After her*] Don't get hit by a car. Because then I would be the girl whose sister died. And then people would feel sorry for me. And then I would have a name for whatever this is. "Loss."
[*She turns back to* GAME. *The cursor blinks.*]
Continue on the Trail.

[*The music RESUMES.*]

GAME   That was your SISTER? DAMNNNNN. She's hot.

JANE   Could you please not? Continue on the TRAIL.

GAME   1848. INDEPENDENCE, MISSOURI.

[*Lights warm to include* THEN JANE, *staring suspiciously at a wagon. She is a prairie girl with once tight braids that are falling out. The wagon is not a cartoon version of the trail blazer, but like the actual thing, a Conestoga built from light, sturdy wood to carry a medium to light load. This is not a game or cartoon, this is real. Her father,* CLANCY, *and her cheery as shit sister,* MARY ANNE, *stand next to the wagon.*]

THEN JANE   . . . You wanna do *what*?

CLANCY   We're gonna Head West, daughter!

**MARY ANNE**   [*So excited*] To West Linn, Ore-gone!

**THEN JANE**   Why'd you tell her and not me?

**MARY ANNE**   I'm the oldest, Jane, I get the first wave of information, it's logic, strict.

**CLANCY**   We're gonna join your Uncle Elijah. Got post from 'im, Says there's free land in Oregon. Six hundred acres a free land for every man.

**MARY ANNE**   My letter from cousin Joseph says RIVERS and FORESTS.

**THEN JANE**   What're we gonna do with 600 acres of land?!

**CLANCY**   Gonna farm it!

**MARY ANNE**   We're gonna grow COTTON or CORN! And we're gonna build a new HOUSE! With a sittin room—a wash room—a room just for books—a sittin room for guests—gentlemen guests—a whole cold room for just cheese—

**THEN JANE**   You're a *carpenter*, Pa. How're you gonna grow a thing?

**CLANCY**   I can learn! Your Uncle Elijah said he'd teach me. If they can teach the Injuns howta, I can learn it, too.

**MARY ANNE**   Jane, look at the positive.

**THEN JANE**   I'm tryin ta but I just don't see it.

**CLANCY**   [*Firm*] Find it, and look at it.

[*Beat.*]

**THEN JANE**   I guess I once dreamt I were the type that longed for adventure.

**CLANCY**   There ya go!

**THEN JANE**   But that wagon's kinda small.

**CLANCY**   Shore's smaller than others, but we only need two oxen ta pull this fella. I know she ain't the best but she was all I could get for Lucy.

**THEN JANE**   What happened to Lucy?!

**CLANCY**   She ain't dead, daughter, she just don't belong to us anymore. Simple as that. I traded her.

**THEN JANE**   What?! Why didn't you tell me so I could say goodbye?!

**CLANCY**   'Cause you're the sensitive type and I know you woulda drug out the farewell. Lucy was a cow, daughter, t'weren't a person.

[*Beat.*]

**THEN JANE**   Well how would we fit all our things insida there?

**MARY ANNE**   We'll havta sell some of it, Pa says. Only bring with us the precious and important items. Then when we get west, fresh start!

**THEN JANE**   I wanna die.

**CLANCY**   Careful what you wish for there, daughter. Don't tempt God, now.

**MARY ANNE**   Don't be glum, Jane, we're gonna see ALL the states! All of the fabrics and all the flowers and all the cultures and all the fields and all the little rabbits, I bet each new state is different, with a different type a land, a different type a tree—

**THEN JANE**   Or maybe it all looks like Missoura so why leave?

**CLANCY**   Listen ta me. Your Ma—she woulda wanted us to join her family, and Oregon's where they are. There's a whole new life for us out there. Nothin left for us in Independence.

**THEN JANE**   This is where I've grown up. This is where my roots are.

**CLANCY**   S'true. But I gotta—I need a change, daughters. Everywhere I look I still see your Ma.

[THEN JANE *and* MARY ANNE *are quiet at this rare and potent glimpse of* CLANCY's *emotion.*]

I walk past the post e'ry day I see the hill where she's buried, and my folks buried, my sister and my brother and my brother's wife. Each day I wanna stop and—I wanna rest there, for a moment.

**THEN JANE**   Well then you should.

**CLANCY**   Don't got time for that. Each day? For that sort of reflection? No, ma'am. Gotta move on. Please trust that I know what's best for ya. I'm tryin to change your life here, now. I gifted it to ya and now you gotta trust me with it. You'll thank me some day, daughter.

[*Beat.*]

**THEN JANE**   . . . How long will it take to get there?

**CLANCY**   Got about two thousand miles to go—Elijah says you can make 'bout 15 miles a day—

**MARY ANNE**   Ooh! Ooh! [*Quick math*] Carry the—four months! Four!

**CLANCY**   That's right.

**THEN JANE**   *Months?* I don't agree with this.

**CLANCY**   I'm not askin you your opinion, daughter, I'm tellin you my plans. It's decided. Now. We gotta get on. If we move through the night we can catch up with the group left a few days ago. Now go help your sister, start packin up.

**MARY ANNE**   OH PA, CAN I BRING MY FIDDLE? CAN I?

**CLANCY**   Course you can.

[CLANCY *goes.* MARY ANNE *inspects the sky.*]

**MARY ANNE**  Rain's comin in. Come on. Help me with the packin. I'm going to put everything in boxes and take my pencil and write on each box what's inside of each box. That way when we get to the promised land—

**THEN JANE**  Has it been promised?

**MARY ANNE**  . . . When we get there, we'll take all of the boxes out of the wagon and there will be a box for each room and the name will be on the box. And we'll take that box into that room and unpack it and it'll all make such pretty sense.

[*She takes a deep, soothing breath.*]

**THEN JANE**  I'm going to go behind you to all of the boxes and erase all the names.

**MARY ANNE**  Don't you dare.

[MARY ANNE *starts packing obsessively.*]

**JANE**  Can you imagine a world with no boxes? I want you to stand right there and imagine that world.

[MARY ANNE, *ignoring her, produces her FIDDLE. She starts to play, calming herself.*]

**MARY ANNE**  [*Singing*]
LOU LOU
SKIP TO MY LOU
LOU LOU
SKIP TO MY LOU
LOU LOU
SKIP TO MY LOU
SKIP TO MY LOU MY DARLING

**THEN JANE**  You done?

**MARY ANNE**  [*Singing*]
LOU LOU
SKIP TO MY LOU
LOU LOU
SKIP TO MY LOU
LOU LOU
SKIP TO MY LOU
SKIP TO MY LOU MY DARLING

[*Back to the computer lab.*]

**GAME**  It is 1848. Your jumping off place for Oregon is Independence, Missouri. You must decide which month to leave Independence. 1. March. 2. April, when the world is full of dresses and popsicles and possibility. 3. May, when the sun starts to smolder and your bangs stick to your face no matter what you do, and you are disgusting.

**NOW JANE**   I'm growing them OUT.

**GAME**   4. Ask for advice. What is your choice?

**NOW JANE**   March 'cause of less hot months and you skip storm season.

**GAME**   Before leaving Independence, you should have equipment and supplies.

**NOW JANE**   Really? 'Cause I was going to traverse the country with NOTHING!

**GAME**   Just as you are unequipped to traverse life.

**NOW JANE**   Touché, game.

**GAME**   You have $1600 in cash, but you don't have to spend it all now. You can buy whatever you need at Matt's General Store. Press Space Bar to continue.

**NOW JANE**   Hi Matt. Will you be my boyfriend, Matt?

**GAME**   That is not the answer!

**NOW JANE**   Is it part of the answer?

**GAME**   I cannot tell you!

**NOW JANE**   What. Is. It.

**GAME**   Cannot reveal! [*Resuming*] MATT'S GENERAL STORE. INDEPENDENCE, MISSOURI. March 1, 1848.

[MATT's *general store.* MARY ANNE *and* JANE *wait as* CLANCY *orders supplies.*]

**MATT**   What can I get for ya?

**NOW JANE/CLANCY**   Eight hundred pounds of food.

**NOW JANE**   [*Overlapping*] Blowpops. Cheezits. Guns.

**CLANCY**   [*Overlapping*] Flour, sugar, bacon, coffee.

**CLANCY/NOW JANE**   Two Yokes of Oxen.

**MATT**   Good choice. They spook less easy than horses, tire less too. I got some right strong ones for ya. Don't need oats, just grass.

**MARY ANNE**   I'm gonna give each oxen a name suited to their personality. Each day I'm gonna note characteristics of each oxen, and select a name from the universe that corresponds with their nature!

**MATT**   Shore, they'll like that. Just make sure they get their water or they might go crazy 'n run you off a ravine! Straight to your death!
[*Hearty laughter.*]
What else can I get for ya?

**NOW JANE**   Ten boxes of bullets for those pesky Injuns and wolves.

**NOW JANE/CLANCY**   Wagon Wheel, Wagon Axel, Wagon Tongue, 2 of each.

[MATT *hefts and lifts and presents them with each part.*]

MATT   Here ya are. These parts'll start ya. Once you get to Ft. Kearny you can trade for more. And if ya come across a wagon that's been abandoned, it's trail rules you can pillage it for parts, if ya need be. And make sure ya boil your drinking water or you might catch the Cholera!

[*Again, they all laugh, but less. More so just—politely avoiding the reality of their potentially impending doom.*]

CLANCY   This'll do us, Matt. We thank you kindly.

MATT   Good luck, Clancy. I wish luck to you all.

MARY ANNE   And we wish luck to *you*!

CLANCY   We'll send letters.

THEN JANE   No we won't.

MATT   Oh yeah, why not?

THEN JANE/NOW JANE   Because we'll/you'll never make it.

THEN JANE   Because America ends after Missoura. It drops off like the lip of a table into a fiery sea. Because there is no place in the world but Missoura, where what's left a my Ma's body lay in the ground.

[*Beat.*]

MATT   Well, watch out for bears!

   [*They all laugh, heartily, except for* THEN JANE.]

   You're ready to start. Good luck! You have a long and difficult journey ahead of you!

NOW JANE   Thanks Matt! Clearly you have feelings for me.

GAME   Now loading the wagon . . .

[MARY ANNE *and* CLANCY *load the wagon.* THEN JANE *drags on a LARGE AND BEAUTIFUL ROCKING CHAIR.* CLANCY *spots it—the sight of it saddens him.*]

THEN JANE   We almost forgot Ma's chair.

CLANCY   We're all full up, daughter.

THEN JANE   But shouldn't we keep some part a her?

[MARY ANNE *runs her hands over the wood, remembering.*]

MARY ANNE   Oh Pa—Is it true that when you made this very nursin' chair for Ma when she was full a me was when you *knew* you wanted to be a carpenter?

THEN JANE   Thank for you for the exposition.

MARY ANNE   I just like remembering that. It's a good memory that I'm fond of.

CLANCY   'Strue. But we don't got room. Get west I'll make you a hundred rockin chairs.

**THEN JANE**  So we're just gonna leave it back here like she never was?!

[*This lands on* MARY ANNE, *makes her sad, but she shakes it off.*]

**MARY ANNE**  [*Diverting*] She's watchin us from heaven and she's in our hearts. And the framed likeness a her will go on the mantle, first thing.

**THEN JANE**  [*Desperate*] Pa. *Please.*

**CLANCY**  Time to get going.

[MARY ANNE *happily gets into the wagon.*]

**MARY ANNE**  Jane, c'mon. It's actually kinda nice in here! It's kinda cozy! It's like a little house inside, it's like a little story!

**THEN JANE**  STOP. TALKIN'.

**CLANCY**  'Bout to be a real crimpy night, we gotta get goin. Get in.

**THEN JANE**  Nope. Not gone do it, Pa.

[CLANCY *stares at his daughter, who won't budge, who clings to her mother's chair.*]

**CLANCY**  GET IN THE WAGON, JANE.

**THEN JANE**  I'm staying here, independent.

**CLANCY**  You are getting in this wagon if I have to throw you in it and tie you to it.

**THEN JANE**  That's abuse.

**CLANCY**  Not abuse if I fathered you.

**THEN JANE**  I hate you.

**CLANCY**  [*Hard*] Hate me from inside this wagon! Go on!

[*Pissed,* THEN JANE *crawls into the wagon. From inside:*]

**MARY ANNE**  So that part's my room, and that part's *your* room, and there's the parlor—

**THEN JANE**  Smells like old potatoes in here.

**CLANCY**  Good. That's the old potatoes.

**THEN JANE**  Smells like tears.

**CLANCY**  Good, that's the—I don't know what that is.

[CLANCY *starts to mount the front of the wagon—but spots the rocking chair, resting there in the dirt. He exhales. A part of him doesn't want to leave it, either, this thing he made that once held his daughter and wife. He picks up the chair, TIES it to the top of the wagon. It's sloppy, but it'll do.* THEN JANE *sees this.*]

**THEN JANE**  [*Breathless*] Thank you—thank you, Pa—

**GAME**  Here you are, you're ready to go! Care to say farewell?

**NOW JANE**  Hey, sure, why not. Later, assholes!

[CLANCY *gets on the front of the wagon. Readies his oxen. Before he proceeds, he stops to pray.*]

**CLANCY**   Dear Lord I have often doubted but I know is there:

[*Beat. He looks up the trail that awaits them.*]

I know there have been—dark hours. Hours when I din't know how to carry on. When Abigail up and head for the River. No explanation, no— When all I see is loss and most everyone I loved choking out their last bits of life. Drownin. Fevers. Carryin on. But I got these daughters, here. You give me these daughters, here. Gotta go on for them.

[*A HAWK flies by, crying, like an omen.*]

And so I ask you to put in all of us the will to go on, no matter how rough. That is our *nature*, that you have given us. To keep goin. And we thank you for that blessing. Amen.

**MARY ANNE**   [*Suddenly, from inside wagon.*] AMEN.

[CLANCY *faces the town one last time.*]

**CLANCY**   Farewell, Missoura!

**MARY ANNE**   Farethee well!

**THEN JANE/NOW JANE**   Goodbye, forever.

[*He goes to his oxen, driving them.*]

**CLANCY**   HAW! HAW!

[*They begin their mile, the first of thousands, as night falls.*]

**GAME**   Independence, Missouri. March 1, 1848. You may: 1. Continue on the Trail. 2. Check supplies. 3. Hitchhike home with an immigrant, which will make a great story to tell in adulthood, over and over and over, after 6 of your drinks of choice. 4. Walk to the gas station, and steal and eat your weight in Charleston Chews. What is your choice?

**JANE**   The gas station is really far. Continue on the Trail.

**GAME**   Continuing on the Trail.

[*The travelers move through the dust, persevere, push forward. BILLY has a snakebite.*]

**JANE**   Aww man—

**GAME**   Continuing on the trail. You have lost Billy. Here lies Billy.

**JANE**   So sad. Now we'll never marry.

[*Suddenly, BILLY passes by. He is the hottest pre-pubescent dude this school has to offer, the kind of hot that in retrospect was really not that hot at all. It was just that perfect flip of hair, the perfect sag of the soccer shorts. He comes up behind her. His mid-practice sweat drips onto the keyboard.*]

**BILLY**   [*Looking at screen.*] No way, I died?!

[*Clearly this is the first time* BILLY *has addressed her in a year, though she's dreamt of its happening multiple times and it's usually happening inside of an Abercrombie and Fitch against a rack of jean jackets that smell of woods.* JANE PAUSES *the game.*]

**JANE**  No, um—it wasn't you. I didn't name it after you.

**BILLY**  Yeahhhh, there's lots of Billys.

**JANE**  No they're not, you're the only one!

[*Beat.*]

**BILLY**  So what's up, bus buddy?

**JANE**  [*Flattered*] I'm your bus buddy?

**BILLY**  Well you were before I got my license. Boom.
[*He whips his license out of his pocket, so proud, and shows it to her.*]
Official member of the great state of Oregon. Nailed it on the first try.

**JANE**  Cool. I saw your car, the wheels're really big.

**BILLY**  Yeah, I lifted that shit. Yeah, it's a great car, yeah. I did the down payment myself with my job money. I got a job. My Dad was gonna get me one, but then I was like, hell nah, I can get it for myself, I don't want your money.
[BILLY *stops, suddenly feeling he's revealed too many feelings.*]
So whatever.

**JANE**  I miss seeing you on the, I mean I miss talking to you on the, I mean I haven't talked to you in—

**BILLY**  Huh?

**JANE**  What?
[*Beat.*]
Nothing. So.

**BILLY**  So what's your deal?

**JANE**  What?

**BILLY**  When I see you you always look so sad.

**JANE**  This is just my face.

**BILLY**  Cool, so what're you still doing here?

**JANE**  My Mom's late picking me up.

**BILLY**  Sucks, yeah. I'd give you a ride home when I'm done but I gotta meet my buddy after practice.

**JANE**  You would?

**BILLY**  Sure! We're neighbors right?

**JANE**   Yeah. I just got a trampoline. That we could jump on sometime. Simultaneously. That means at the same time.

**BILLY**   Yeah, sounds good, your sister's Mary Anne Goodrich, yeah?

**JANE**   Yeah.

**BILLY**   Cool, cool. She seems / cool.

**JANE**   What're *you* still doing here?

**BILLY**   I got practice late. Coach has been killing us, man, we're running laps. We're on a ten. I think I pulled a hammie.

[*He stretches. Yay. He drinks his Gatorade, his Adam's apple bobbing.* JANE *takes in this glorious sight. He then takes a load off in the wheeley chair next to her, wheels in close to her.*]

How far're you?

**JANE**   What?

**BILLY**   In the game.

**JANE**   Oh, Pretty far, / I—

**BILLY**   Man. I always get dysentery.

**JANE**   [*Boldly*] I'm really good at it. [*Then*] The game. Not at getting dysentery. It's good to be a carpenter 'cause you start with more money and you have more skills. And don't pick farmer cause then you're really poor.

**BILLY**   Cool, so what happens at the end?

**JANE**   Oh um. I've never gotten to the end. Computer class always ends, but I bet you're just—there. And probably most of your family is dead. But like you have character.

**BILLY**   Cool, cool, so what's your sister's deal?

**JANE**   [*Not getting it.*] What's her deal how?

**BILLY**   [*Gee, I'd like her to take my virginity.*] Like what's her deal?

**JANE**   She sucks, she's okay.

**BILLY**   Cool, cool. Just wondering, whatever.

[*Beat.*]

What time is it, I gotta head out—

**JANE**   [*Suddenly bold*] Your Dad's an idiot.

[*Beat.*]

Sorry, um. My mom is friends with your mom. They do jazzercise together. So I heard, about.

[*Beat.*]

He's an idiot for leaving.

[*Beat.*]

And that's all I have to say about that.

**BILLY**  [*Weirdly touched*] Yeah.

[*Beat.*]

He showed up at one of my games and I was like. Whatever.

[*Beat.*]

I think I'm like, traumatized.

[JANE *hears this. This is the hottest thing she has ever heard.* BILLY *blossoms in front of her into Jordan Catalano, damaged, hair in his eyes.*]

**JANE**  Totally. [*Then*] Well look at the bright side.

**BILLY**  What's that?

**JANE**  Now you have something to overcome. Instead of just like, being fine. Which is the real tragedy.

*# same*
*at 13*

**BILLY**  Who says?

**JANE**  Me. Just now.

[BILLY *smiles, feeling strangely understood.* JANE *cannot believe this is happening, this conversation. She wants to make a home inside of it.*]

**BILLY**  What're you gonna put on my tombstone?

**JANE**  I—I don't know—

**BILLY**  Put something awesome on it. Here, I'll do it.

[*He leans over her to type and she dies the middle school death of longing and lust.*]

Pepperoni.

[*He laughs.*]

**JANE**  Ha ha—pizza joke!

[*They laugh together.*]

**BILLY**  Wait, hold on—

[*He leans over her further, typing.*]

And—sausage.

[*When he brings his hand back, he accidentally touches* JANE'*s boobs.*]

Whoa, sorry.

**JANE**  [*Bold*] I'm not.

[*Compelled by something,* JANE *leans in and kisses him, which she's never done, and has learned mostly from episodes of* My So Called Life. *He pushes her off, reels back, repelled, horrified, like his sister just kissed him.*]

**BILLY**  That was weird.

**JANE**  I—sorry—I thought—

**BILLY**  Uh, I gotta head out.

[*He heads for the door.*]

**JANE**  But if you ever wanna come over / and jump on the trampoline—

[*But she just sits there. BILLY goes. JANE turns back to her computer, his smell lingering on her, her heart racing. She is quietly horrified and devastated.*]

**GAME**  YOU HAVE REACHED THIS MOMENT. WOW, THAT JUST HAPPENED. THIS IS NOT A MEG RYAN MOVIE. PEOPLE DO NOT JUST KISS EACH OTHER. OH MAN. YOU REALLY PUT YOURSELF OUT THERE. WAY TO GO. BUT YOU SHOULD PROBABLY NEVER DO THAT AGAIN. You may: 1. Wallow in the moment. 2. Write a poem about this moment. 3. Move past this moment. What is your choice?

**JANE**  . . . Wallow.

**GAME**  You have chosen to wallow in this moment.

[*She reaches into her backpack, finds and puts on her Discman. Selects a track. Listens. Sings. It's like Bush's "Glycerine." She sings, badly, with full heart. THEN JANE, trailing behind the wagon, joins her, exhausted, singing to the same song to herself.*]

**MARY ANNE**  Jane? What is that nonsense you're singing?

**THEN JANE**  Dunno.

[*Outside, a car horn honks and honks. JANE ejects the disk, shoves it in her bag.*]

**JANE**  I'M COMING, GOD!

[*THEN JANE, MARY ANNE, and CLANCY are frozen. Gradually they turn to dust and blow away with the wind. JANE heads towards the door, but she is stopped. Trapped. Suddenly:*]

**GAME**  [*Booming*] GOING FORWARD IN TIME.

**JANE**  Wait—I'm not playing right now, I turned it off—

**GAME**  Many kinds of people live their lives. You may: 1. Continue to sit in the middle of your life and wallow in it. 2. Sit in the shadow of your sister's life. 3. Live your life.

**JANE**  Uh . . . live it?

**GAME**  GOING FORWARD IN TIME!

**GAME**  Most people graduate high school. Most privileged people with the opportunities that your sort of privilege afford. You may spend high school: 1. Being focused on your studies and excelling academically. 2. Being focused on attention from boys but never getting it. 3. Doing Drama Club and getting cast as boy parts because there are too many girls. 4. A combination of 2 of 3.

**JANE**  Definitely the focusing on my studies one?

**GAME**  Number 1 is not an option.

**JANE**  You just said it was an option.

**GAME**  Number 1 is not an option. Please select another option and press space bar to continue.

**JANE**  A combination of 2 and 3?

**GAME**  You have forged high school. You have lost your virginity.

**JANE**  How?

**GAME**  Dysentery.

**JANE**  Can I start / over?

**GAME**  [*Booming*] GOING FORWARD IN TIMEEEEEEEEE. You have reached College.

**JANE**  Wait—slow down—

**GAME**  Most people with the opportunities that your sort of privilege afford attend college. You may: 1. Attend a well-regarded liberal arts school tucked in the mountains far away where you'll truly find yourself and be the first person since the 19th century to make a living as a poet. Driven by the clean mountain air, you start training for marathons, invent pumpkin pie pops, and eventually meet and fall in love with a kind and bearded European whom, when you marry him, gifts you with dual citizenship and you live, happily ever after, at home and abroad. You live Everywhere. 2. Attend the mediocre state school where your sister went. What is your choice?

**JANE**  Definitely 1.

**GAME**  You do not get accepted.

**JANE**  But—

**GAME**  Please select an option and press space bar to continue.

**JANE**  ControlAltDelete. ControlAltDelete.

**GAME**  You have selected option 2.

**JANE**  WAIT—

**GAME**  GOING FORWARD IN TIMEEEEEEEEEE. You are now in college, would you like to look around?

**JANE**  . . . Fine.

[*We are transported to a college quad.* JANE *looks around.*]

**GAME**  What do you want to study? This could determine the rest of your life. Decide now. Deciderightnow.

**JANE**  I don't know / I

GAME   DECIDE RIGHT NOW.

JANE   I don't know, I guess I want to take some linguistics, maybe poetry, and French—

GAME   You study Media Studies, which means nothing. Also you gain fifteen pounds. That fucking food court.

[JANE *looks down at her body.*]

GOING FORWARD IN TIMEEEEE

JANE   Wait—stop—

GAME   You have reached the end of college. You may: 1. Get a job. 2. Don't get a job.

JANE   I definitely wanna get / a job—

GAME   CONGRATS YOU GET A JOB.

JANE   Sweet, what job do / I

GAME   . . . I'M SORRY. YOU HAVE BEEN FIRED FROM YOUR JOB.

JANE   . . . What?

GAME   You are a not a team player! You do not have a good attitude! And also, downsizing!

JANE   But I can do that, I can have a good attitude—

GAME   NO YOU CANNOT.

JANE   Why not?

GAME   IT IS NOT IN YOUR NATURE.

JANE   What does that even mean?

GAME   Go home and live with your parents while you "figure things out." Eat their free food and watch their free television.

JANE   I don't wanna play anymore—

GAME   THAT IS NOT AN OPTION. PLEASE SELECT A VALID OPTION.

JANE   Can I try and find another / job

GAME   USELESS Degree! You got a USELESS Degree! Useless Degrees are a PRIVILEGE of the PRIVILEGED! Please select Option 2.

JANE   I can't get *any* job?

GAME   You are too arrogant for both menial labor and also Starbucks! You sign with a temp agency, instead. You stuff envelopes which barely pays your rent.

So GO HOME AND LIVE WITH YOUR PARENTS.

JANE   Okay, *fine*!

[*Beat.*]

**GAME**   But your parents do not want you there.

**JANE**   They don't?

**GAME**   They do not want to appear to perpetuate your laziness which they otherwise definitely do. Also, they've just started having sex again! Move into your sister's office slash guest room instead! At the ripe age of 25, you have already made a mess of your life and wasted your privilege.

**JANE**   Can I go back and try again?

**GAME**   Never. *Never.*
[*Beat.*]
Instead, while still under your parents' health insurance, start therapy, medicate accordingly.

**JANE**   Wait why am I in therapy?

**GAME**   For your "sadness," in quotes.

[*Beat.*]

**JANE**   . . . I always thought that would go away when I grew up.

**GAME**   Nope.

**JANE**   But what if I tried really hard to be happy?

**GAME**   Your efforts are futile!

**JANE**   But *why*? Is there something wrong with me?

**GAME**   Cannot reveal. You have reached your sister's apartment.

**JANE**   CONTROL—ALT—DELETE.

**GAME**   Cannot recognize commands. Date: Now. Weather: Rain. *Cheers* reruns. Health: Meh. Food: An entire box of Easy Mac and one third bottle of lukewarm chardonnay. Next Landmark: 30. Miles traveled: None except for trips to the pharmacy, [*And he SINGS!*] where everybody knows your name! Press space bar to continue.
[*Beat.*]
Press space bar to continue.

**JANE**   [*Reluctantly*] . . . Space bar.

## PART II

[MARY ANNE's *apartment forms around* JANE. *It is well appointed and optimistic in its colors, but cluttered with boxes of* JANE's *unpacked stuff. The TV drones on the background, something like* America's Next Top Model. *On the coffee table in front of her, there are remnants of an Easy Mac feast, PBR, tissues.* MARY ANNE, *weary from a long day of working and doing, enters the apartment. She wears scrubs. She stops for a moment when she sees* JANE *on the couch.* JANE *sits up, almost eagerly.* MARY ANNE *sorts through the mail.*]

**JANE**  How's it going, sister?

**MARY ANNE**  Good, I'm good.

**JANE**  What're you up to tonight?

**MARY ANNE**  Nothing I'm just going to go to yoga run some errands do some laundry make some cookies for my co-workers clean the kitchen and start my taxes.

**JANE**  Cooookies!!!!!!

**MARY ANNE**  What're you doing home?

**JANE**  . . . Took a personal day.

**MARY ANNE**  [*At fridge*] Did you eat my Lean Cuisine?

**JANE**  No?

[*She shuts the freezer door. Her eyes land on the sink, suspended in space, littered with dishes. She's frustrated, but covers, smiles.*]

I'm gonna do those later.

[MARY ANNE *surveys her living room, all of the boxes.*]

**MARY ANNE**  Hey do you think maybe tonight you could unpack your stuff and move it into your room and stuff?

**JANE**  Yeah. Sorry. I will.

[MARY ANNE *starts to absentmindedly clean.*]

**JANE**  . . . Did you always know what you wanted to do with your life?

**MARY ANNE**  Not really, I just did something with it.

[*This stings* JANE.]

Sorry. I watched this old lady die today.

**JANE**  Damn.

**MARY ANNE**  They sure let you take a lot of personal days.

**JANE**  They're flexible.

**MARY ANNE**  How flexible?

**JANE**  I got let go.

**MARY ANNE**  You got fired?! You're a temp, you like barely even have to be a person!

**JANE**  They didn't need me anymore. And thanks for making me feel like shit on top of already feeling like shit about it. Speaking of, cat shit on the floor.

[MARY ANNE *regards the mess.*]

**MARY ANNE**  Um—When?

**JANE**  What time is it?

[*Silently,* MARY ANNE *cleans up the mess.*]

**JANE**  Sorry, I was gonna clean it up but I didn't know how.

**MARY ANNE**  "How?"

**JANE**  I didn't want to mess up your floor.

[MARY ANNE *cleans.*]

Since when do you have a cat, have you always had a cat?

**MARY ANNE**  It was Doug's.

[MARY ANNE *cleans.*]

**JANE**  They let a bunch of people go, it wasn't like some—

[*Beat.*]

I need to take some time to figure out what I really want to do and then like really actively pursue that.

**MARY ANNE**  Yeah! I don't know.

**JANE**  What?

**MARY ANNE**  Maybe you need to stop obsessing over whether or not it's the right job, and you just need to *work.*

**JANE**  I think my serotonin's low. Mom and Dad said they'd pay for me to start seeing my therapist lady again but she takes everything I say out of context.

**MARY ANNE**  But maybe you should stop expecting them to pay for things?

**JANE**  They owe me.

**MARY ANNE**  How?

**JANE**  Trauma.

**MARY ANNE**  Okay, that's—I'm not going to respond to that.

[MARY ANNE *starts to stack magazines aggressively.*]

Please could you just unpack like one box tonight?

**JANE**  . . . Yes.

**MARY ANNE**  Thank you.

[MARY ANNE *heads into her room.* JANE *doesn't move, eyes glued to her computer.*]

**JANE**  I'm doing it!

**MARY ANNE**  You're on Facebook.

**JANE**  I'm networking!

[MARY ANNE *gives her a look.*]

Fine.

[*JANE goes to a box. MARY ANNE closes her door. Sighs. Sinks to the ground. Opens it. Starts to dig through it. CDs, notes, scrapbooks, trophies. It's all too depressing. She opens ANOTHER. She finds her DISCMAN. SWEET. She keeps digging. It's all too depressing. She returns to the couch, to her computer. Lies on her back, scrolls and scrolls. Suddenly, her eyes light up.*]

**GAME**  You can now play the Oregon Trail online for free! Get yer wagon ready and let's hit the trail!

**JANE**  Oh, helllllllll yes . . .

[*Eagerly, she clicks. The GREEN from the game screen lights her face as it explodes into a nostalgic smile. Game music RESUMES.*]

**GAME**  HELLO AGAIN.

**JANE**  Hello to you too.

**GAME**  You look exactly the same but older.

**JANE**  You look weird now. I liked you better before.

**GAME**  I liked YOU better before. Oh look. Your boobs are the exact same size. Is that weird for you?

**JANE**  Could we just—

**GAME**  The Oregon Trailllllllll! You may: 1. Read the news. Become a more grounded and intelligent person. 2. Sign up to give a micro loan to struggling single mothers in developing nations, you great person you! 3. Like seven thousand pictures.

**JANE**  I wanna finish this game.

**GAME**  You are technically an adult technically! Do you really want to finish this game right now?

**JANE**  [*Determined, firm*] I am going to finish this game. I am good at this game and I am going to FINISH IT.

**GAME**  Fine. You have selected to stay inside and regress to your childhood and be one of those people who finds corn chips in their hair. Okay, great. You may: 1. Start a new game. 2. Resume your old game.

**JANE**  Do over.

**GAME**  That is not an option.

**JANE**  Fine, resume.

**GAME**  CONTINUING ON THE TRAILLLLLLLL

[*We find the FAMILY trudging up the trail, some weeks later. They are weary, worn down, exhausted. Dust whips into their eyes, the sun burns and blisters their lips. The wagon moves through shrubs and dust. Eventually* THEN JANE *and* MARY ANNE *get out and follow behind it. The wheels whine. They are going and going but it seems like they've gotten nowhere. Their feet and the wheels sink into dust.*]

**MARY ANNE**   [*Singing*]
FOUND A PEANUT
FOUND A PEANUT
FOUND A PEANUT, JUST NOW
JUST NOW I FOUND A PEANUT
FOUND A PEANUT JUST NOW
[*Beat.*]
FOUND A PEANUT
FOUND A PEANUT
FOUND A PEANUT, JUST NOW
JUST NOW I FOUND A PEANUT
FOUND A PEANUT JUST NOW

**THEN JANE**   I wish you really had found a peanut. I'm so sick a beans.

**MARY ANNE**   Did that sound good Pa? I'm getting better! Figure I'd keep my practicing up—

**CLANCY**   Sounded real nice. C'mon, let's get a move on, pick it up. Just 'til dusk then we'll make camp. Feelin wolfish.

**THEN JANE**   Where's the other party, Pa?

**CLANCY**   We'll find 'em.

**THEN JANE**   We lost track a their trail days ago.

**CLANCY**   . . . We'll find 'em, Jane.

**THEN JANE**   What if we don't?

**MARY ANNE**   You gotta keep your spirits up!

[*They walk.* CLANCY *directs the* OXEN *around a bend.*]

**CLANCY**   Gee! [*Right*] Haw! [*Left*] I said HAW! HAW!

[*They keep moving, dragging their feet through the dust.*]

**MARY ANNE**   I like to slice time into tiny moments, like little buttons or beads. And then I just take them one by one and I just—
[THEN JANE *is just staring at her.*]
So that's how I like to think about time.

**NOW JANE**   Guhhhhh this is so harddddddd

[*They carry on.*]

**GAME**   You have reached the Platte River. You must cross the river in order to continue. The river is currently 646 feet across and 2.3 feet deep in the middle. You may: 1. Attempt to ford the river. 2. Caulk wagon and float it across. 3. Get more information.

**JANE**    [*Distantly, from couch.*] Ford! Ford! Ford!

[CLANCY *inspects the RIVER.*]

**CLANCY**    We'll have ta ford it. No bridge in sight.

[*They attempt to ford. He sweats, pushing on his oxen.*]

GET ON NOW! GET ON, BOYS!

**MARY ANNE**    C'mon Landon! C'mon Bernard!

[*The* OXEN *pull and pull, but the wagon meets quicksand in the middle of the river. It starts to sink. It's frighteningly real.*]

**GAME**    River is too deep to ford. You lose: 9 sets of clothing, 890 bullets, 2 wagon wheels, 2 wagon axles, 1 wagon tongue.

**CLANCY**    No—please God no—

[*Bags of flour, bundles of clothes, boxes of bullets litter the river.* MARY ANNE *near drowns as* CLANCY *fights through the water, pulling her to safety.*]

**CLANCY**    JANE. GET THE WARES. HELP ME.

[THEN JANE *struggles through the water, retrieving wares. She drags a bag of flour to shore, collapses on it.* CLANCY *pulls* MARY ANNE *to shore, then goes back to the wagon. He unloads wares to lighten the load, then rescues the sinking rocking chair. Finally, the oxen pull the wagon out of the muck.*]

**CLANCY**    Lost a frightful. Help me pack it back up.

**THEN JANE**    Can't we rest here a moment? Mary Anne near drownded—

**MARY ANNE**    I'm okay, I'm dandy!

[MARY ANNE *coughs up water.* THEN JANE *helps her to her feet.*]

**GAME**    What would you like to do? You may: 1. Continue on the trail. 2. Stop and rest. 3. Watch *Extreme Makeover Home Edition*, the one where half the family's in wheelchairs so they build lots of ramps and you cry. What is your choice?

**NOW JANE**    [*From couch, motivated*] Continue on the trail.

[*She stands. She tries. She sits back down.*]

Actually, stop and rest. It's been a long day. You earned it.

[NOW JANE *lies on the couch, away from the computer. She curls into a ball. Night falls. Open air, stars.* THEN JANE *sits by a dying fire.* CLANCY *and* MARY ANNE *sleep nearby. Faraway wolves, storms.* MARY ANNE, *once asleep, wakes up. She looks radiant. Stretches, adorably.*]

**MARY ANNE**    What're you doin?

**THEN JANE**    Can't sleep. Thinkin all grandly. Too much space out here for thoughts.

**MARY ANNE**   Pa's gonna hear you and come out here and read you a page from the good book if you don't get to bed.

**THEN JANE**   'Mnot hurtin anybody.

[MARY ANNE *joins her.* JANE *bursts into tears.*]

**MARY ANNE**   Jane. Stop that!

**THEN JANE**   I can't.

[THEN JANE *tries to dry her eyes on her skirt.*]

I miss Ma. I miss the house. I miss Lucy.

**MARY ANNE**   You shouldn't waste time thinkin about those things.

**THEN JANE**   Don't you miss Ma?

[*Beat. This stings* MARY ANNE. *She covers.*]

**MARY ANNE**   Time has passed, and we gotta move on.

**THEN JANE**   It's just been a year. That is a mere one-thirteenth of my life.

**MARY ANNE**   Of course I miss her. I miss her every *second* if I let myself.

**THEN JANE**   Why don't you ever talk about it?

[*Beat.*]

**MARY ANNE**   Well how would that help, if I carried on about it? Waste a strength.

[*Beat.*]

I just think there are other things. To be done. With our time. On this earth. So. That's what I think about that. So. Hey. We should scrub up tomorrow, you stink.

**THEN JANE**   . . . Do you think it were intentional?

**MARY ANNE**   What?

**THEN JANE**   When Ma—

[*Beat.* MARY ANNE *gets what she means.*]

**MARY ANNE**   It was an accident.

**THEN JANE**   Yeah but she knew how to swim. And what was she *doin* out there? Don't you ever wonder that?

**MARY ANNE**   Why wonder about it?

[*Beat.*]

**JANE**   What if we have a sorrow in us—like her?

**MARY ANNE**   Why would you think that?

**THEN JANE**   'Cause sometimes I just—I just don't know how I'm going to keep going. I just don't see why.

**MARY ANNE**   What do you mean *why*? To move on. To keep goin.

**THEN JANE**   But why?

**MARY ANNE**   . . . Because.

**THEN JANE**   Yeah but why?

**MARY ANNE**   Because we're alive?

**THEN JANE**   But why?

[*Beat.*]

**THEN JANE/NOW JANE**   Why?

[*A rustling nearby.*]

**MARY ANNE**   Now you gone and woke Pa.

[CLANCY *sits up tired, pissed, disoriented.*]

**CLANCY**   Whatsa matter?

**MARY ANNE**   Jane says she's "got a sorrow."

**CLANCY**   Well, you don't. Time to sleep.

**THEN JANE**   But I'm feeling troubled, genuine.

**CLANCY**   [*Trying*] Want me to tell ya a story?

**THEN JANE**   No, Thank you.

**CLANCY**   Aren't you wore out from walkin all day?

**THEN JANE**   Sure I'm tired but my heart's not. I'm sad, Pa—

**CLANCY**   You can't use it as no excuse. You see to the grease 'n beans in the morning. You help your sister. We make Beaver early, 'fore sunset.

[*Obediently,* MARY ANNE *goes back to her bed.* THEN JANE's *tears don't stop.*]

**CLANCY**   I'm not gonna tell you again.
    [CLANCY *sees his daughter crying. For a moment, he can't help but melt a bit.*]
    I'm—fond of you, Jane.

**THEN JANE**   I'm fond of you too.

**CLANCY**   Yeah. Good.
    [*Beat.*]
    You are *strong*. It's in your nature.

**THEN JANE**   Was Ma strong?

**CLANCY**   [*Breaking slightly.*] You got every piece a her. You got her nose, you got the same face when you cry.

**THEN JANE**   I do?

**CLANCY**   Spittin image.

**THEN JANE**  Do you miss her? Do you think about her?

**CLANCY**  [*Firm*] Enough a this.

[*Beat.*]

I can't have all this carryin on.

**THEN JANE**  WHY NOT.

**CLANCY**  I CAN'T THINK ABOUT IT.

[*Beat.*]

We gotta focus on the task at hand, we gotta get ourselves onto Oregon.

Now you gotta buck up and pull your weight afore I leave you on back with the coyotes.

Because I will do that, daughter. Do not test me.

[THEN JANE *nods, trying.* CLANCY *goes back to sleep.* THEN JANE *sits alone, studying the stars, her* FATHER'S *words hanging on her. Lights shift back to* MARY ANNE'S *apartment. The Middle of another Night. Darker.* JANE *has changed positions. No work has been done or boxes unpacked. She watches* Family Matters. *On the coffee table in front of her, her laptop rests, Game PAUSED.*]

**JANE**  [*Singing*]

IT'S A RARE CONDITION

IN THIS DAY AND AGE

[*Beat.*]

Get up. Get up right now.

[*Beat.*]

Stop being sad.

[*Beat.*]

StopitstopitstopitstopitSTOPIT.

[*Beat.*]

[MARY ANNE *enters, half asleep, in sweet pajamas. She's got her glasses on, she's tired and pissed.*]

**MARY ANNE**  No progress on the boxes, I see.

**JANE**  I'm going to start tomorrow.

**MARY ANNE**  [*To herself*] Which you said last week.

**JANE**  Hey did I show you? I found this old / game I used to play online—

**MARY ANNE**  So awesome. Hey so, I'm sleeping and you've officially interrupted my REM sleep and I have a 24-hour shift in 3 hours.

**JANE**  Sorry. Hey remember *Family Matters*?

**MARY ANNE**  What time is it?

**JANE**  Almost four.

**MARY ANNE**   Can you turn it down?

[JANE *does so.* MARY ANNE *moves sleepily off to the bathroom. She Pauses when she sees the dishes, the pile of which has definitely grown.*]

**JANE**   I'm gonna do them before I go to bed.

**MARY ANNE**   Did you look online today?

**JANE**   For what?

**MARY ANNE**   Online. For jobs.

**JANE**   YES. I responded to like 900 posts. I'm trying. I don't even know if they're even getting opened though.

**MARY ANNE**   That's why you have to follow up.

**JANE**   But my resume sucks. It's like "Went to high school. Went to college. Made a few sandwiches. Cried a few times." I have no character, no specificity, I'm just this wash of a person.

**MARY ANNE**   Well then think about your strengths, and beef it up.

**JANE**   Yeah.
   [*Beat.* MARY ANNE *is glaring at her.*]
   You mean like right now?

**MARY ANNE**   Yeah.

**JANE**   Okay. Here I go.

**MARY ANNE**   Good night.
   [MARY ANNE *goes into her room. Shuts the door.* JANE *reaches for laptop. Pulls up her resume. She just—can't. Her defeat is palpable. Her eyes return to the TV.*]
   Urkel just walked into a door. Poor Urkel. Small, well-intentioned man. This show's DARK. You know? It's dark. Like when he turns into Stefan. Why should he have to change himself? Why, just because he's got his ears pierced and a deeper voice, how is he then more worthy of Laura's love?
   [*Beat.*]
   Why do I feel so—? That's the worst part. It has no name. What is it? It throbs. It hurts, right here. [*She places a hand on her gut.*] And here.
   [*She puts a hand on her heart.*]
   I was gonna do my laundry today but I looked outside and I saw a lion in the street.

[*She resumes the GAME, the only thing she feels like doing right now.*]

**GAME**   You have reached this moment. Another day and you didn't die. Hey: congrats. You coulda been hit by a car—oh wait. You did not leave the house today. Just kidding! Way to play it safe.

**JANE**   [*Weak*] A *lion.*

**GAME**   Sure! You can: 1. Fester here, in this moment. 2. Start a blog. 3. Please. Do not start a blog. 4. Say it with me.

**JANE/GAME**   Continue. On. The Trail.

[*We find the FAMILY trudging up the trail, some weeks later. They are weary, worn down, exhausted. Dust whips into their eyes, the sun burns and blisters their lips. Flush. MARY ANNE re-emerges from the bathroom and heads straight for her room. Door shuts, hard. JANE sinks further into the couch, as night turns to a beautiful, optimistic morning on the trail. Whimsical clouds. THEN JANE sits up, stretches. She observes the sky. A genuine and determined smile spreads across her face. She gets a fire going. She cuts wood. Lugs logs from a stack, focusing intently on her work. She sings a song she should not know, a song of optimism, of resolve—like Alanis's "One Hand in My Pocket." THEN JANE struggles lighting the fire. It just won't light. NOW JANE sings from the couch, remembering the song, singing listlessly. The song drifts off, as NOW JANE loses focus.*]

**GAME**   You have a broken spirit. Would you like to try and fix it?

**NOW JANE**   Yes.

**GAME**   How would you like to fix it? 1. An entire bottle of lukewarm chardonnay. 2. Unpack a few more boxes therefore earning your sister's love and respect. 3. Respond to this Facebook message from Billy Butler from middle school WHICH I STRONGLY DO NOT ADVISE UNLESS OF COURSE YOU LOVE PAIN.

**NOW JANE**   Wait, say WHAT?

[*And her phone DINGS. She looks. Her face morphs to joy.*]

**BILLY**   'Sup, weary traveler. How long's it been? You still in town? We should get a drink sometime. Here's my number, text it, call it, fax it.

[*Finally, THEN JANE gets her fire LIT. SUCCESS.*]

# PART III

[*Back on the trail. THEN JANE sets to work making breakfast. Quite the feast. Feast cakes, potatoes, venison. She takes a quenching sip of water from her oil sack. MARY ANNE wakes up.*]

**THEN JANE**   Hey sleepyhead! Beautiful morning!

**MARY ANNE**   . . . What're you doin?

**THEN JANE**   Makin breakfast!

**MARY ANNE**   But I always start breakfast. It's my function.

**THEN JANE**   I was up early, I thought I'd make it.

[*MARY ANNE goes to the fire, inspects.*]

**MARY ANNE**  We're 'sposed to be savin the rest a the venison for the winter!! It's my favorite thing in the winter! Warm venison! It makes me SO. HAPPY.

**THEN JANE**  We can trade for more, this is a special occasion!

**MARY ANNE**  Pa's gonna have a storm bout this. PA! PA! JANE'S COOKIN UP ALL THE MEAT!

[CLANCY *emerges from his bed.*]

**CLANCY**  What's all this?

**MARY ANNE**  JANE's cookin up all the MEAT!

**THEN JANE**  It's a special occasion, I told ya! I have an announcement! Sit, please. Make me an audience.

[CLANCY *and* MARY ANNE *reluctantly sit.* THEN JANE *serves them coffee.*]

**THEN JANE**  This morning I was woke up by the sun. A pure and innocent Sun. It woke me up like a friend come ask me to play. I heard what you said to me, Pa. You're right. We gotta keep going no matter what, because we got no choice but to do so.

[CLANCY *nods, agreeing, firm, proud.*]

And so I announce to you today a new leaf that has turned over. I—am—attempting happiness. Please hold your applausing.

[*She smiles.*]

**MARY ANNE**  That's nice but you're burning the last of our meat.

**THEN JANE**  Shoot.

[THEN JANE *attends to the venison.* CLANCY *kisses the top of her head.*]

**CLANCY**  That's my girl.

**MARY ANNE**  And me also!

**CLANCY**  And also you.

[CLANCY *and* MARY ANNE *settle in for a feast as* JANE *finishes up the cooking. They all eat together, happy, having found this moment of peace among hardship. Time moves as they eat. We find them full and happy.* MARY ANNE *grabs her fiddle. Fiddles with it.*]

**MARY ANNE**  [*Singing*] CAMPTOWN LADIES SING THIS SONG.

**CLANCY/THEN JANE**  [*Singing*] DOO DA! DOO DA!

**MARY ANNE**  [*Singing*] CAMPTOWN RACETRACK'S TWO MILES LONG.

**CLANCY/THEN JANE**  [*Singing*] ALL THE DOO DA DAY!

**ALL**  [*Singing*] GOIN TO RUN ALL NIGHT
GOIN TO RUN ALL DAY!
BET MY MONEY ON A BOB TAILED NAG
SOMEBODY BET ON THE GRAY!

[*They laugh, joyous.*]

**THEN JANE**     BERRIES! We need berries for an arbitrary breakfast dessert. I'll be swift.

[*She grabs a bucket, goes.* CLANCY *calls after her.*]

**CLANCY**     Not too far, now!

[THEN JANE *goes.* MARY ANNE *takes a sip of water from a JUG.*]

She's a strange girl.

**MARY ANNE**     I just don't know what's gotten into her. You want some water, Pa?

**CLANCY**     Please and thank you.

[MARY ANNE *hands him the JUG.*]

[*Then: The back bar of your local Applebee's where the margaritas are face-sized and the potato skins have only been frozen twice.* BILLY, *27, having grown a gut and a deep awareness of the reality of all things life, sits at the bar, nursing a beer and two whiskies. He stares off. He burps. He stares.* JANE *approaches. She's put on a dress and done up her hair. She spots him immediately. She can't help it. She smiles, huge. This is the moment. It's finally here.*]

**GAME**     You have reached this moment. You should have worn the better bra, but okay. Sure. You can: 1. TURN AND RUN AS FAST AS YOU HUMANLY CAN. 2. Take a step forward. Maybe he's the love of your life.

[BILLY *burps.*]

3. But also maybe not.

[*Determined, trying to quiet the* GAME, *she takes a step forward.* BILLY *senses her eyes and turns to her. She tries to play it cool.*]

**BILLY**     'Sup Jane Goodrich.

**JANE**     Not much, it's great / to

**BILLY**     It's two for one apps, we're gettin double nachos.

**JANE**     Okay, I'm in!

**BILLY**     You look great.

**JANE**     I do?

**BILLY**     Yeah!

**JANE**     Yes I do. I look great.

**BILLY**     Well c'mere! Hug it out, man—

**JANE**     Yeah, let's do that—

[*They hug it out,* JANE *sliding nicely into his nook as she's done so many times in her dreams.*]

**BILLY**     You wanna sit / down?

**JANE**   Yep! I love to sit. So much better than standing.

[*She joins him, scooting out a stool. He slides his whiskey to her.*]

**BILLY**   Got this for you.

**JANE**   Ahhhh thanks. I'm not a big whiskey drinker / but

**BILLY**   F that, bottoms up, it's good for your bones. This is some trail shit!

[*She takes a sip.*]

Hey you still play the violin?

**JANE**   Uh—nope! That was / my sister—

**BILLY**   I've been teaching myself the guitar again.

**JANE**   Nice—

**BILLY**   Played it a little bit in high school, me and Jimmy Linville, remember Linville?

**JANE**   Yeah, totally, with the—

**BILLY**   Yeah we're starting a band.

**JANE**   Cool.

[*She waits for him to ask her what she's been up to, but he does not. She sips her whiskey. She winces, unaccustomed to it.*]

Yeah so, I've just been uh—yeah, hanging out. Finished college, went / to—

**BILLY**   Yeah I did a year at State but messed up my knee, lost my scholarship, started doing some general stuff at Forsyth Tech, gotta get back up with that. Been working too much though.

**JANE**   Yeah, where do you work?

**BILLY**   Home Depot.

**GAME**   WOW. OKAY. You can: 1. AGAIN I SUGGEST THAT YOU TURN AND RUN. 2. Pretend like that's a totally great place to work. I mean it is a great store with great customer service and I mean you have to work somewhere. 3. No really, maybe you could work there too.

**JANE**   [*Trying*] Great store.

**BILLY**   Yeah I help people put their windows and lawnmowers in their cars. It never all fits and they act like it's my fault, but it's not. They always buy too much shit to fit in their cars. But my wife doesn't wanna work, so.

**JANE**   Oh—

**BILLY**   Remember Ashley, Ashley Shue?

**JANE**   Yeah, yeah, you two were—? Are? Married?

**BILLY**   Were.

[*He downs his whiskey, motions for another.*]
Separated right now.

**JANE**   I'm so sorry . . .

**BILLY**   Yeah it was going great for a while but now she's a cunt.

**GAME**   PLEASE LOCATE THE NEAREST EXIT. HAILSTORM AHEAD.

**JANE**   [*Leaning in, ignoring.*] Yikes.

**BILLY**   Yeah, I don't use that word lightly but it's like, I didn't marry this cunt. She changed. Happened all the sudden. There was some shit going on with her and some guy.

**JANE**   Oh man, I'm so sorry—

**BILLY**   It was good for a while, then, ah—She just uh, stopped seeing me. Like she used to.
[*Beat.*]
It hurts, you know?

[*He rings his head in his hands, pressing on his temples.*]

**JANE**   I know.

**BILLY**   I think I'm like. Traumatized.

[JANE *is drawn in.*]

**JANE**   Totally.

**BILLY**   I got a son.

**JANE**   Yeah? I saw some pictures, I wasn't looking or anything, but I saw—

**BILLY**   You wanna see?

[BILLY *gets out his phone, shows pictures.*]

**JANE**   Aw, He looks just like you—

**BILLY**   He's my life. Only reason I don't drive my car into oncoming traffic somedays, you know? Scary how easy that'd be.

**JANE**   Yeah, to just drive with your eyes closed.

**BILLY**   Yeah.

**JANE**   He's beautiful.

**BILLY**   Thanks. I want to do something awesome, so he can look at me and be like: I also want to do something awesome. I just wanna be awesome for him.

**JANE**   Yeah, like, pass something down.

**BILLY**   Exactly.

**JANE**   I feel like I'm wasting whatever life was given to me. So.

**BILLY**  Yeah, for sure, for sure.

[*Beat.*]

[*Taking her in.*] Jane.

**JANE**  That's me.

**BILLY**  It's good to see you.

**JANE**  To the bus!

**BILLY**  To the bus!

[*They cheers. Drink.* BILLY *smiles at* JANE, *which emboldens her.*]

**JANE**  Remember seventh grade?

**BILLY**  Ha, I try not to.

**JANE**  No, me, seventh grade, you, tenth grade? The computer lab.

**BILLY**  Yeah?

**JANE**  Remember?

**BILLY**  [*But not*] I uh—sure?

[*Beat.*]

**JANE**  I've been a little uhh, depressed actually. So! I wasn't going to tell you that, but now I'm telling you. So. That's what's been going on with me.

**BILLY**  Sucks, man, sorry to hear that.

**JANE**  Yeah.

[*They drink.*]

**BILLY**  Like actually depressed? Like clinically?

**JANE**  No, I mean, like.

**BILLY**  Or just like. Sad.

**JANE**  It's not "just" . . .

[*Beat.*]

It's just like—my whole life, I've felt this—

**BILLY**  Least you're not going through a divorce.

**JANE**  Yeah, but it's still . . .

[*She trails off. He puts his hand on her knee, sliding it presumptuously between her legs. She tries to close them.*]

**BILLY**  You wanna get outta here or what?

**JANE**  . . . What.

**BILLY**  Jane? You wanna get outta here?

**JANE**  . . . Are you serious?

**BILLY**  I'm really serious Goodrich, are you serious?

[*She downs her whiskey. She thinks.*]

**GAME**  THIS IS NOT THE ANSWER.

**JANE**  [*As if there's no choice; as if she's trapped*] Yeah. Let's go.

[*Back on the trail.*]

**CLANCY**  She should be back by now. Gettin dark.

**MARY ANNE**  [*Off into the distance.*] JANE!

[*Nothing. Faraway storms, wolves.*]

**CLANCY**  JANE!

[*SUDDENLY, a cloud comes over both of them.*]

**MARY ANNE**  I don't feel so good, Pa—

**CLANCY**  I just—need to sit—

[*He does. He turns and throws up violently. He stands, trying to regain his strength, but he falls over, back into a pool of his own vomit.*]

**MARY ANNE**  Pa—

[*She goes to him, trying to help him up, but collapses onto him. MARY ANNE doubles over in pain, turns and vomits. A hawk cries as it passes.*]

[*Then: NOW JANE and BILLY on the couch, back in the apartment. He's fucking her and it's not pretty. There's an open bottle of nice whiskey in front of them. She's trying to enjoy it or at least let it be what she wanted it to be, but it just isn't, because it never is. He's finishing.*]

**JANE**  Don't—in my—I'm not on the—

[*But he does. He lays there, laughing. JANE is stunned. Isn't quite sure what to do as she processes what just happened.*]

Did you—?

**BILLY**  Aw man, you're a dirty birdy.

[*He laughs and laughs.*]

**JANE**  Why're you—it's not funny—

**BILLY**  I'm sorry—

[*He laughs and laughs.*]

**JANE**  It's not *funny*.

**BILLY**  Girls're turned on by misery, why is that? "Just got separated from my wife," you think they'd head for the hills, man, but no, they're all, *cry on me, fuck me, cry on me*—

[*JANE reaches for her clothes. BILLY lays there, reflecting, catching his breath.*]

**JANE** [*Fighting tears.*] You need to go.

**BILLY** Yeppp.

[*Drunk, he reaches for his pants.*]

Full circle, Dirty Birdy. I was comin for ya.

[*He pulls on his pants, shoes, heads for the door. Stops there.*]

You can take the thing, right, the morning after thing?

[*Beat.* JANE *does not respond.*]

Do you want money for it?

[*She does not respond.*]

Hey don't think I'm like—I thought this was what we were doing.

**JANE** I didn't.

**BILLY** Just don't think bad a me, you know? I'm just going through a lot right now, I'm a mess, I've been really sad—

**JANE** That's no excuse. Please just go.

**BILLY** "Sgood to see you.

[BILLY *goes. She crumbles.*]

**GAME** THAT WAS NOT THE ANSWER.

**JANE** I KNOW. What is it. TELL ME WHAT IT IS.

**GAME** I CANNOT TELL YOU.

[JANE *goes to the computer.*]

**JANE** WHAT. IS. IT.

**GAME** CANNOT REVEAL.

[*She TOSSES the computer. She sinks to her knees, breathing, destroyed. The sun comes up.* JANE *is on the couch, in the same position, numb.* MARY ANNE *enters—seems surprised to see* JANE STILL *on the couch. She spots the dishes, even more dishes, still dirty in the sink.*]

**JANE** How was your shift?

**MARY ANNE** Fine.

[MARY ANNE *starts to clean up, picking up the bottle of whiskey. She clocks the two glasses.*]

**JANE** We uh. I drank some of your whiskey but I'll replace it hope that's cool.

[*Beat.*]

Why'd you have whiskey anyways, you hate whiskey.

[MARY ANNE *goes to the sink, sees the dishes, sighs. Tosses the glasses in the sink.*]

I'm gonna do them tonight.

[MARY ANNE *sighs aggressively.* MARY ANNE *takes the trash out of the trashcan by herself. Closes it. It's hard.* JANE *watches* MARY ANNE *wrestle with the bag.*]

**JANE**  [*Not moving.*] Let me help you.

**MARY ANNE**  I got it.

[MARY ANNE *tosses the bag against the sink and heads toward her room.*]

**JANE**  Hey—do you ever stop and / think—

**MARY ANNE**  No.

[MARY ANNE *goes into her room.*]

**JANE**  [*Broken*] I miss treat bags from birthday parties. Yo-yos and Reese's Cups and Airheads. Hit up a few parties in a weekend you got candy for a month.

[*Then, to no one:*]

What is wrong with me . . .

[MARY ANNE *emerges from her room, dressed for yoga.*]

**MARY ANNE**  It was Doug's whiskey.

**JANE**  . . . Doug.

**MARY ANNE**  Yeah. Doug. My boyfriend. Ex-boyfriend. Remember? Turns out he was sleeping with my friend? "Fun Stacey?" He moved out. And you moved in. Where have you been?

**JANE**  [*Guilty*] I—forgot—

**MARY ANNE**  Oh my god.

**JANE**  What is wrong with me?!

[MARY ANNE *moves to the dishes, starts to wash them violently.*]

I'm gonna do those for real—I wish you / wouldn't—

[*Violently,* MARY ANNE *throws a dish onto the floor. She stops. She breathes.*]

**MARY ANNE**  You wanna know what's wrong with you? You are selfish and you are lazy and you smell like PARMESAN CHEESE FOR NO REASON. I work hard all day, I come home, I want *home*, I want QUIET, and there you are, sitting there all day, doing nothing.

**NOW JANE**  [*Meek*] Sometimes I do things.

**MARY ANNE**  YOU ARE NOT CUTE. You suck. You make me sick. Mom and Dad let you get away with this shit, but not me, I RUN A NINE-MINUTE MILE. And you sit around with my futon up your ass, watching my TV, that I NEVER get to watch, I pay for it! I GET UP AT FIVE AM, and you are PATHETIC. I AM VERY TIRED.

[*She stops, breathes hard. Both are stunned. Quietly,* MARY ANNE *dries her hands. She exits quickly toward her room. A door shuts.* JANE *stands up. She moves toward the dishes. She stares at them, unable to make herself do them.*]

**GAME**  You have reached rock bottom. You may: 1. Continue on the Trail. 2. Continue on the Trail. 3. Continue on the Trail. 4. Continue on the Trail.

**JANE**  No. I'm done.

**GAME**  THAT IS NOT AN OPTION. PLEASE SELECT A VALID OPTION.

**JANE**  Stop—I don't wanna play anymore.

**GAME**  PLEASE SELECT AN OPTION AND PRESS SPACE BAR TO CONTINUE.

**JANE**  I don't wanna play anymore!!

**GAME**  CONTINUING ON THE TRAIL.

**JANE**  NO—

[NOW JANE *returns to the couch. She picks up the bottle of whiskey. She takes a DEEP SIP. She Pauses, winces. She takes ANOTHER. She then takes ANOTHER, pulling on it hard. She gags. Tears in her eyes. Back on the Trail,* THEN JANE *returns with an apron full of berries.*]

**JANE**  Sorry, sorry, I strayed off, got lost, I got some—
[*She spots* CLANCY *and* MARY ANNE, *lying next to each other by the dying fire in pools of their own puke and shit.*]
What—

**CLANCY**  Jane.

[MARY ANNE *chokes and pukes.*]

**THEN JANE**  I'll get some—

[*She grabs a jug of water, rushes over.*]

**CLANCY**  Bad water, daughter—

**THEN JANE**  I still got some—from the stream—

[*She pours water from her water skin into* CLANCY's *mouth, then* MARY ANNE's.]

**JANE**  [*Frantic*] What should I do, Pa?

**CLANCY**  You gotta keep goin'—

[*Frantically, she runs to the wagon, tearing around for medicine, grabbing blankets, anything. Helpless, alone.*]

**THEN JANE**  It's gonna be okay.

[*She fights back tears as she helplessly, worthlessly wraps them in blankets which they kick away, dying, writhing, expelling.*]

[MARY ANNE *enters from her room.*]

**MARY ANNE**  Jane, I—
[*She spots* JANE, *chugging the whiskey, gagging.*]
What're you doing?

[JANE *throws up, then goes for more whiskey.*]

STOP! Stop it—

[MARY ANNE *tries to take the whiskey from* JANE, *but* JANE *is fierce, fighting her off, trying to bring it again to her lips. Finally,* MARY ANNE *wrestles the bottle away from* JANE. JANE *HEAVES into a trashcan. She then lies there, writhing, expelling, as* MARY ANNE *processes what just happened.*]

**JANE**  [*Groggy*] Going forward in time—Forward—in—time—

[JANE *considers this. Softly, she starts to cry. Back on the trail, helpless and alone,* THEN JANE *erupts.*]

**MARY ANNE**  What was that?

**THEN JANE**  HELPP!!!! HELP ME PLEASE SOMEBODY HELP!!!!!!

**JANE**  [*Meek*] . . . Help.

[*She starts to cry.*]

*Help.*

**MARY ANNE**  [*Determined*] Okay.

[*Beat.*]

Okay.

[*She strokes her sister's hair, and thinks.*]

# PART IV

[*The Trail.* THEN JANE *has finished burying* MARY ANNE *and* CLANCY. *She hefts large* ROCKS *to mark each grave. She is exhausted from digging, from crying. She lies at their feet, and soundlessly weeps out all that's left inside of her.*]

[*Lights switch to include* NOW JANE *sitting on a stump in the same space. It's nighttime, on the top of a massive hill.* MARY ANNE *is arranging a sleeping bag.* JANE *watches her.*]

**GAME**  Mt. Pisgah, Oregon. Weather: Sure. Food: 2 Luna bars. Nearest Landmark: that Exxon before you head up the hill. Morale: . . . Nope. Press space bar to continue.

**JANE**  [*Weary, defeated.*] Space bar.

[MARY ANNE *looks at her watch. She pulls a piece of paper out of her pocket, looks at it, begins to collect rocks.*]

What is that, what're you doing?

**MARY ANNE**  I'm collecting rocks for the healing circle you're going to make.

**JANE**  Nope. Don't want that.

**MARY ANNE**  You asked for help. This is me helping you.

**JANE**  So what do I do, do I just light myself on fire, or—

**MARY ANNE**   I looked up lots of different—first you write down all the things that're troubling you. Then you burn the clothes you've been wearing and with them, you burn the spirits of negativity that have been—like— clogging your—Yeah. Then there's some stuff with sage. [*Handing to her.*] Here's a print-out of the directions. [*Handing again.*] And here's the sage. It's a cleanse thing.

**JANE**   This is stupid.

**MARY ANNE**   *You're* stupid.

**JANE**   Do I have backup clothes or do I sit here naked after?

[MARY ANNE *tosses her a backpack.*]

**MARY ANNE**   Backup.

[MARY ANNE *places the last rock, and stands, gathering her things.*]

**JANE**   You're leaving me here?

**MARY ANNE**   I have a night shift.

**JANE**   How'm I getting home?

**MARY ANNE**   This'll be good for you. Our great great great whatevers made it all the way across the country on a freaking wagon, I think you can handle it. Take a bus, figure it out.

**JANE**   What if I get murdered?

**MARY ANNE**   Well maybe then you'll snap out of your whatever it is.

**JANE**   If I was MURDERED?

**MARY ANNE**   No one is going to murder you. But here's some mace.

[*She hands it to her.*]

**JANE**   [*Weak*] Why're you being so mean to me?

**MARY ANNE**   Because somebody has to be. You have not experienced tragedy, okay? The woman who brought her dead two-year-old into the ER last night after she accidentally ran over him with her secondhand minivan right after her husband was killed overseas, SHE gets to not get out of bed. Not you.

[*Beat.* JANE *hears this.*]

Mom and Dad won't say this to you, but I will. I can't live with you anymore like this. And I know you don't have anywhere else to go. But I mean it, if you don't at least TRY to change your—perspective, your—whatever it is, then you are out, because I love you but you look stupid when you're sad and you have no good reason to be. So I need you to figure out what's wrong and I need you to fix it.

[*This silences* JANE.]

**THEN JANE**   But—

**MARY ANNE**  FIX IT.

[MARY ANNE *goes.*]

**NOW JANE**  [*After her*] This is NOT the answer!!!

[*Frustrated, she settles into the dirt. A HAWK cries. She jumps. She pulls the sleeping bag around her.*]

**GAME**  May 1. Mt. Pisgah—

**JANE**  I KNOW WHERE I AM.

**GAME**  You may: 1. Continue on the Trail. 2. Learn about the Trail. What is your choice?

**JANE**  I have nothing to learn.

**GAME**  3. Learn about the Trail. 4. Learn about the Trail. 5. Learn about the Trail.

**JANE**  OKAY. LEARN ABOUT THE TRAIL.

**GAME**  You will now learn about the Trail.

[JANE *waits. Nothing happens.*]

**JANE**  Great.

[*She reaches into her backpack, pulls out her DISCMAN. Selects an old track, tries to comfort herself with the nostalgia. She digs for her journal, starts to write.*]

I watch too much TV. I can't decide whether or not I believe in God, and how there's no way to decide that but just decide that. I have little to no self-respect. Microwavable breakfast burritos. I will never be like my sister.

[THEN JANE *returns with a fistful of wildflowers. She kneels by a makeshift grave, and gently lays the flowers by each headstone. She isn't quite sure what to do next. She then finds and digs through CLANCY's SATCHEL. Finds a knife. Considers it. The easy way out. A HAWK cries. THEN JANE is terrified. She sinks to the dust. Gives up. Gives in.*]

**NOW JANE**  Good jeans don't fit me. Nothing is fair.

**THEN JANE**  My family is dead—my whole family is dead—

[*She lies down by the fresh graves. She whispers to them.*]

I'm staying with you. Forever.

[*She restacks the headstones. Straightens them, tries to make them perfect. She starts to gather headstones for herself.*]

**NOW JANE**  This is stupid.

[*She drops the journal. It's not working. She returns to arranging the STONES for the circle. She reaches for another STONE, just as NOW JANE reaches for the same one. And suddenly—THEY SEE EACH OTHER. They both jump with fear. THEN JANE shrieks.*]

**NOW JANE**  What the—

**NOW JANE / THEN JANE**  Who're you?

[*Beat.*]

**THEN JANE / NOW JANE**  I'm Jane.

[*Beat.*]

**THEN JANE / NOW JANE**  Wow.

**THEN JANE**  Am I dead? Have I gone up to heaven?

**NOW JANE**  I don't think so, are you real?

**THEN JANE**  I think so, are you?

**NOW JANE**  Pretty sure.

    [*Beat.*]

    This is a dream. Okay, cool.

[*They stare at each other, taking each other in, not sure how to continue.*]

**THEN JANE**  [*Of rocks*] What're you doing with those?

**NOW JANE**  It's a "healing circle." It's a cleanse thing.

**THEN JANE**  A "cleanse"? You're gonna take a bath with no water?

**NOW JANE**  No for like sadness and just—yeah.

**THEN JANE**  You mean like melancholy?

**NOW JANE**  . . . Yeah.

    [NOW JANE *spots the knife in* THEN JANE's *hand.*]

    Cool knife.

**THEN JANE**  It's for protection.

    [*She knows this is a lie. She feels compelled to tell this girl the truth. Tears come to her eyes.*]

    And for maybe takin my own life which is a great sin, as it's a great gift, life is.

**NOW JANE**  . . . Yeah. Been there.

    [*Beat.*]

    Why were you gonna do it?

**THEN JANE**  Because my whole family is dead.

**NOW JANE**  . . . They are?

**THEN JANE**  [*Tears coming now.*] My ma first, some years ago. Then my sister and my Pa. Here they are, I buried 'em here.

    [*She shows* NOW JANE *their gravestones.*]

And now I'm all alone and it's the middle a nowhere and I don't know where to go or how to get there.

**NOW JANE**   . . . I'm sorry.

[*Beat.*]

What were you doing out here?

**THEN JANE**   We were trying to get to Oregon.

**NOW JANE**   . . . You're in Oregon.

**THEN JANE**   . . . What?

**NOW JANE**   You're here.

**THEN JANE**   WE'RE HERE?!

**NOW JANE**   Yep!

**THEN JANE**   West Linn?

**NOW JANE**   Yeah, like a hundred miles north.

**THEN JANE**   . . . That's really far.

**NOW JANE**   It's really not.

**THEN JANE**   But I'd have to go the rest of the way all by myself.

**NOW JANE**   [*Realizing*] My great-grandma did.

**GAME**   DING DING DING!

[NOW JANE *smiles. They stare at each other. It's too strange to say out loud but they just—know.* THEN JANE *spots* JANE'*s Discman.*]

**THEN JANE**   What's that?

**NOW JANE**   It's a Discman.

**THEN JANE**   That's a man?

**NOW JANE**   It's music.

**THEN JANE**   [*Intrigued, scared*] Oh—

**NOW JANE**   I'll show you.

[*She takes the headphones off, and gently places them around* THEN JANE'*s ears. Presses PLAY. Soft from the Discman, we can hear something like Aerosmith's "Amazing."* THEN JANE *listens, liking this. Softly, she starts to sing along. They sing together. The song ends. They stare at each other, linked.* THEN JANE *turns to dust and blows away in the wind.* NOW JANE *stands, renewed.*]

[*THEN:* MARY ANNE'*s apartment, the next morning.* MARY ANNE *sits on the couch, numb from crying. Her violin sits next to her like an old friend she barely knows anymore.*]

**MARY ANNE**   [*Covering*] Hey, how'd it go?

**JANE**   Good! Actually, really good, I—

[*She sees the look on* MARY ANNE'*s face. A hollowness, a defeat that looks familiar to her.*]

You okay?

[MARY ANNE *crumbles, but fights it.*]

**MARY ANNE**   . . . I got stuck on this elevator today. For like two hours. I didn't have my phone or anything. It was just me. And there was nothing else to do, except think and wait, and *think*. So much thinking. So slow. I thought about—what I said to you, and then I thought more, I thought about the knife block in the kitchen. And I thought about Doug and how he would always—his beard in the sink—

[*Beat.*]

But it's all so stupid because I have a good job, I have a good life, everything's fine in the grand scheme of things, so why am I *so*—why do I feel so—

**JANE**   It's okay to be sad.

**MARY ANNE**   It's *not*.

**JANE**   But maybe it is.

[*Beat.*]

It can't be fixed. And it doesn't need to be. It's supposed to be there. It's bigger than us.

[MARY ANNE *nods, dries her tears.*]

**MARY ANNE**   Yeah. Maybe.

[*Beat.*]

**JANE**   I see you found your violin.

**MARY ANNE**   I was reorganizing my closet / and it

**JANE**   Why were you reorganizing your closet?

**MARY ANNE**   Because I LIKE to, I LIKE to reorganize my closet, that is my idea of fun.

**JANE**   You're a crazy person.

**MARY ANNE**   I know.

[*Beat.*]

I took it out to play it but I can't even play it anymore. I barely remember how.

**JANE**   Let's hear it.

**MARY ANNE**   No.

**JANE**   C'monnnnnnnn.

[MARY ANNE *hesitates, but then sniffing, picks up the violin. She plays "Skip to My Lou." She's terrible. As she plays, we see* THEN JANE, *dragging her* MOTHER's *rocking chair through the dust, determined, pushing on towards Oregon.*]

**MARY ANNE**  [*Singing*]
LOU LOU
SKIP TO MY LOU
[JANE *laughs, delighted.*]
LOU LOU
SKIP TO MY LOU
LOU LOU
SKIP TO MY LOU
SKIP TO MY LOU MY DARLING.

**JANE**  Wow. You suck.

**MARY ANNE**  [*Laughing now, too.*] Yeah I do.

[*She keeps playing.*]

**GAME**  GOING FORWARD IN / TIMEEEEEE

**JANE**  NO.

**GAME**  GOING—

**JANE**  NO. Resting here in this moment.

[*Beat.*]

**GAME**  Congratulations. You have made it to Oregon.

[*Back on the trail,* THEN JANE *spots something in the distance. Something familiar, heaven-like, warm and welcoming. She picks up her pace, exhausted, overjoyed, and moves towards it. The* JANEs *smile. END OF PLAY.*]

# What Happened When

## [A Memory Play]

Daniel Talbott

# Daniel Talbott

Daniel Talbott is an actor, director, and writer, as well as an artistic associate of Rattlestick Playwrights Theater, the associate artistic director of {Your Name Here}, and the artistic director of the Lucille Lortel and NYIT Award-winning Rising Phoenix Rep. His plays include *Slipping* [Rattlestick, The Side Project], *Yosemite* (Rattlestick), *Afghanistan, Zimbabwe, America, Kuwait* (Rattlestick/piece by piece, Encore), *What Happened When* (Rattlestick, {Your Name Here}, Rising Phoenix Rep/HERE), *Someone Brought Me* (Quince Productions), *Mike and Seth* (Quince, Encore, The Side Project), *Extraordinary Things* (RPR), and *Gray* ({Your Name Here}). Recent directing work includes *Thieves* (Weathervane/RPR/Rattlestick), *F\*\*king Immaculate* (RPR), *A Fable* (piece by piece/ RPR/Rattlestick), *Gin Baby* (IRT), *Scarcity* (Rattlestick/Hill Town Plays), *Lake Water* (Neighborhood Productions), *Eightythree Down* (Hard Sparks), *Much Ado About Nothing* (Boomerang), *Squealer* (Lesser America), and *The Umbrella Plays* (the teacup company/ FringeNYC—Overall Excellence Award: Outstanding Play). Upcoming productions include directing the world premiere of *First Born* by Lyle Kessler at the Actors Studio, and a new play by Charlotte Miller for NYU/Strasberg. He received a 2011 Theater Hall of Fame Fellowship, a 2007 New York Innovative Theatre Award for directing, a Drama-Logue Award, two Dean Goodman Choice Awards and a Judy Award for acting, and was also named one of the 15 People of the Year by nytheatre.com. He is a graduate of Juilliard and teaches at NYU/Strasberg and Primary Stages/ESPA. He is a proud member of Lesser America and a member of the Actors Studio.

# Production History

*What Happened When* was produced as part of the 2015 F*cking Good Plays Festival at Rattlestick Playwrights Theater in New York, NY, with {Your Name Here} as associate producer. The production was directed by Daniel Talbott, and featured Will Pullen, Samantha Soule, and Jimi Stanton. Additional credits include scenic design by John McDermott, costume design by Tristan Raines, lighting design by Kia Rogers, sound design by John Zalewski, fight choreography by David Anzuelo, and stage management by Hannah Delmore and Danny Morales. An earlier version of *What Happened When* was also produced by Rattlestick West as part of the 2015 Fall Festival at the Sherry Theater in Los Angeles, CA. It was directed by Daniel Talbott and featured Will Pullen and Jimi Stanton.

## Notes

The use of "............": this constitutes a beat, a breath, a change in thought, a shift, maybe a thought within a thought.

The line-spacing change in Scene 6 is deliberate.

## SCENE 1

*[January 2009. 1:35 a.m. A farmhouse and wind chimes. Snow. JIMI's bedroom. A window, a twin bed, and a dresser with a lamp. A radio alarm clock. JIMI and WILL are on the bed, wrapped in blankets 'cause it's freezing out. WILL is sitting up with his back against the headboard. JIMI is lying with his knees up and his head facing the footboard. Their older sister SAM is lying next to them on her side, facing out. JIMI has a flashlight on that he moves across the ceiling as they talk.]*

**WILL**    Somewhere warm. On the beach. There's big sliding glass doors you can open and hear the ocean. Kids playing and dogs and families. We've got two cars. A Suburban and a Porsche. And a boy. He's two and she's pregnant again. You're in school somewhere nearby. A really good school. Like a UC. You live in the dorm and then stay with us on weekends. You're studying art or marine biology. You're always there though, like every day. Sam's traveling.

*[She smiles slightly, far away somewhere else. WILL talks to her.]*

You work in another country teaching. Helping kids. You have a room with all your stuff.

*[She smiles more, quietly.]*

Your books. Downstairs with a door and steps down to the beach. I've got a really good job. Like a construction company. We build houses. Like nice houses and do development. We're careful. We don't got to worry about money. And we've got season tickets to the local baseball team.

**JIMI**    And basketball.

**WILL**    Yeah. We go all the time.

**JIMI**    It's a big house.

**WILL**   Yeah. There's like five bedrooms. A huge living room. A couple decks. And at night we leave the doors open. Listen to the waves. Light some candles. Put a movie on. Something stupid like fucking *Ghostbusters* or something. We make popcorn and crack up. Say all our favorite lines. She falls asleep with her head on my lap. My wife. I kiss her and carry her to bed. Come back and we stay up. Put on something else and keep watching.

**JIMI**   What type of car do I have?

**WILL**   I don't know. But I'm getting you something really good when you graduate.

[WILL *hears something and stops.* JIMI *turns off the flashlight and sits up on the edge of the bed, listening to something downstairs.* SAM *stays lying on her side and turns her head to face the bedroom door.*]

**JIMI**   What is it?

**WILL**   Be quiet.

[WILL *gets up and walks around the side of the bed toward the bedroom door. He stops and listens.*]

**JIMI**   Is it Dad?

[WILL *doesn't answer.* SAM *sits up and sits on the edge of the bed with* JIMI.]

Is he up?

**WILL**   I don't know.

**JIMI**   Maybe it's Mom.

**WILL**   No. She's asleep. I checked on her when I took a piss.

[*They all stand and sit in silence, listening, waiting, just in case. Terrified. After a long time,* WILL *comes back to the bed and takes a pillow and hands it to* JIMI. SAM *takes another pillow, gets under the blankets, and lies back down where she was before.* WILL *sits back on the bed cross-legged, as* JIMI *continues sitting and staring at his bedroom door, holding the pillow. They sit and lie like that in silence. Snow and wind.*]

And it stays like that. You get older and meet someone. A really cool girl. Kind of quiet. She does art too. Or she's a teacher or a fucking scientist. You love her so much. She makes you so happy. You smile all the time. You're always holding her hand. Sam meets a guy. He's really tall and they move back. Get a small house in town with a garden and white Christmas lights on the porch. He's got big ears and curly hair. He's gentle and he always lets her talk first.

[*Tears begin falling down* SAM*'s face.*]

You guys live close by and our kids grow up together. All of them. We double date a lot. They go to the same school and we go to their dance shows and games. Do stupid shit. As a family. Go on vacations to Florida and Disneyland. Cruises together. None of us are exceptional in any way.

But we're good parents and good husbands. A good wife. We're best friends. And we've got each other's backs. Always. We live a long time. We get to see a lot of things. We go to Italy and Paris. Hawaii. We even try skydiving. We watch our kids grow up and go through shit. But they're healthy. We watch them get married and have grandkids. We spend every Christmas and Halloween together. It's a priority. We celebrate each other's birthdays and anniversaries. And in the end. It was worth it. Everything. Sometimes we think about the past. All the shit. The things that happened. And it doesn't matter anymore. Sometimes we can even laugh about it. It's gone. Like it was never there. Like it never happened.

[*They sit and lie in silence.* WILL *turns off the bedside lamp and* JIMI *turns off the flashlight.*]

Good night.

**JIMI**  Good night.

[*They lie together in the dark. Snow. Blackout.*]

# SCENE 2

[*Late May 2010. Early summer. A Sunday morning. The farmhouse. Wind chimes.* JIMI's *bedroom. A window, a twin bed, and a dresser with a lamp and an antique toy fire truck on it. A radio alarm clock.* JIMI *in bed with his back facing away from* SAM. SAM *sitting on the edge of the bed with her arm wrapped over the footboard and her feet on the floor.*]

**SAM**  You sure?

**JIMI**  Yeah.

**SAM**  They'll be home soon.

**JIMI**  I know.

**SAM**  You don't have a fever.

[JIMI *doesn't answer.*]

Are you going back to school tomorrow?

[JIMI *doesn't answer.*]

They said they need a doctor's note if you don't come back.

[JIMI *doesn't answer.*]

They'll know you're not sick.

[JIMI *doesn't answer.* SAM *pulls her feet up and sits on the bed.*]

Did you do your homework?

**JIMI**  Yeah.

**SAM**  If you don't go I can turn it in.

**JIMI**  Thanks.

[*Silence.*]

**SAM**  We could see some movies. Karen's working. She can get us in. Steve'll get us free popcorn.

**JIMI**  No.

**SAM**  If you don't come with me they're going to make you come down for dinner.

[JIMI *rolls onto his back and faces her.*]

**JIMI**  I thought you had work.

**SAM**  I lied.

**JIMI**  I thought you didn't lie to anybody.

**SAM**  I don't usually. I lie to them.

**JIMI**  Where's Will at?

**SAM**  Probably at Amber's. He said he'd be home tonight.

**JIMI**  What's playing?

**SAM**  *Shrek Forever* and *Robin Hood*.

**JIMI**  I thought you saw it already.

**SAM**  I have. I'd see it again.

**JIMI**  Did you like it?

**SAM**  I liked it more than here.

**JIMI**  Did Eric ask you out again?

**SAM**  No.

**JIMI**  Liar.

[SAM *smiles.*]

He's a good guy.

**SAM**  He's okay.

**JIMI**  You got to date somebody.

**SAM**  No I don't. But at least he gives us free popcorn.

**JIMI**  And Coke.

**SAM**  And Coke.

**JIMI**  We can steal some candy from the grocery store.

[SAM *smiles and looks at* JIMI.]

**SAM**  You got to go back to school tomorrow.

**JIMI**  I know.

**SAM**  I have work. Will's got practice. I don't want you here alone all day. Okay?

[*They look at each other. He knows what she's saying, or trying to say. Silence.*]
I want you to get up and get some clothes on and come with me.

**JIMI**  Nothing's clean.

**SAM**  I did your laundry last night. It's folded downstairs. I can get it for you.

**JIMI**  No. I'll do it.

**SAM**  You can't stay here by yourself right now. You know that. And I'm going to go fucking crazy if I sit here all day.

**JIMI**  I know.

[SAM *looks away from him, out the window.*]

**SAM**  I'm sorry.

**JIMI**  Don't be.

**SAM**  I don't know what else to do. I don't know what to say.

**JIMI**  You don't have to say anything.

**SAM**  Yeah I do.
[*Silence.*]
Are you okay?
[JIMI *doesn't answer.*]
Should you see somebody? Like a doctor.

**JIMI**  No.

**SAM**  You sure?
[*She looks at him, wanting to push. He can't meet her eyes and stares down at the bedding. She looks away, not knowing what to do. Silence.*]
I've been asking for more shifts. I've been trying. I applied at the movie theater and the drugstore. No one else is hiring.

**JIMI**  I know.

**SAM**  I want to get my own place. So we can live together. Will said he'd help when school's done. You could finish. You can start working in a year. We could fucking even move somewhere else.

**JIMI**  You did that already.

**SAM**  What?

**JIMI**  Moved.

**SAM**  I know.

**JIMI**  You were gone for almost the year.

**SAM**  Not really.

**JIMI**  You worked in a lighthouse.

SAM   I didn't work in a lighthouse. I worked at a hostel. At the check-in desk and the gift shop there.

JIMI   You said there were whales everywhere.

SAM   There were.

JIMI   You don't talk about it.

SAM   No.

JIMI   Why'd you come back?

SAM   'Cause being alone. Being without you guys was worse than being here.

JIMI   Yeah.

SAM   Yeah.

JIMI   You said you met people.

SAM   I did. Everyone was kind. From somewhere else. They were all going somewhere. They had something big to do or someone waiting for them when they left there. I didn't know how to start, you know? No one ever told me. I'd never . . . I didn't know how to begin anywhere. I didn't know who I was without here. Everyone had something remarkable to share. I just talked about my brothers. How much I missed them. Things that were important to me. How my brother could build a car. Or my other brother. My youngest brother would stop to help anyone. No matter what he was doing. How he had the biggest heart. And really beautiful brown eyes. And how he could imitate almost anyone and make you laugh. Do all your favorite lines from movies. Things I thought were cool. And they just weren't important in the real world. They'd say it was nice to meet you. The conversation usually ended there.
[SAM *looks at him, helpless. She starts laughing.*]
Maybe they'll die on the way home.

[JIMI *starts laughing with her.*]

JIMI   Yeah.

SAM   He'll fuck with the radio or try to find some cigarettes and hit a tree.

JIMI   Yeah.

SAM   Or they'll both realize we're better off without them. They'll blast some Christian music and hold hands. Drive into the fucking ravine. Sink to the bottom and become like a fucking Christmas tree for the fish and algae.
[*They finish laughing. Exhausted.*]
We'll never get that lucky.

JIMI   Nope.

SAM   We can hang out there. See when Will's coming home.

**JIMI**  Yeah.

[*Silence.*]

**SAM**  We could always tell somebody.

[SAM *looks at her little brother. They both know the answer. Silence. She gets off his bed. And hesitates.*]

I'll grab your clothes and bring 'em back up so you can get ready.

[SAM *leaves.* JIMI *sits alone. Blackout.*]

# SCENE 3

[*May 2012. The farmhouse. 1:30 a.m.* WILL, *fully clothed, asleep on his stomach in* JIMI's *bed.* SAM, *barefoot in sweats and a worn out oversized Patti Smith T-shirt, stands with a candle, watching him sleep. She stands completely still, almost without blinking, not sure whether to wake him or leave. She stands like that for a long time. There's an old cracked iPhone next to the bed. It's playing Lynyrd Skynyrd's "Simple Man." She listens to it. The sounds of the farm at night pouring through an open window.* WILL *wakes suddenly from a nightmare. He turns and sees her and freezes. They stare at each other, breathing. The music still playing.*]

**WILL**  I thought you were dead.

**SAM**  No.

[*The music still playing.*]

I love that song.

**WILL**  Me too.

[WILL *sits up and turns it off.*]

You scared the shit out of me. Fucking Jimi always talking about ghosts and how fucking haunted this place is. What are you doing up?

**SAM**  I couldn't sleep.

**WILL**  What time is it?

**SAM**  I don't know.

**WILL**  Are you going to stand there?

**SAM**  No.

**WILL**  You're being fucking creepy.

**SAM**  Stop being so mean.

[SAM *walks over to the bed stand and puts the candle down. Her brother scoots over for her and she gets on* JIMI's *bed.* ]

Why are you in here?

**WILL**  I don't know. I fell asleep I guess. I can't remember.

**SAM**  Did you go out?

**WILL**   Yeah earlier. I was fucking tired though. I fell asleep at like six.

**SAM**   Weren't you supposed to go out with Amber?

**WILL**   She was being a fucking bitch. I didn't want to go out with anybody.
[*Short silence.*]
Did you work tonight?

**SAM**   Yeah. I got home a few hours ago.

**WILL**   You still smell like popcorn.

**SAM**   I know. I hate it.

**WILL**   It smells good. I want to eat your fucking shirt.

**SAM**   It's Mom's. I stole it.
[*Short silence.*]
You talk to Jimi?

**WILL**   No.

**SAM**   We said we'd call him every day.

**WILL**   I know.

**SAM**   Why didn't you call him then?

**WILL**   I don't know. Get off my fucking ass.

**SAM**   I'm not on your ass. I want you to do what you say. He wants to talk to you.

**WILL**   I know.

**SAM**   Then fucking call him.

**WILL**   Okay.

[*Short silence.*]

**SAM**   Aunt Dee's going to take him to Disneyland.

**WILL**   Yeah?

**SAM**   Yeah. She promised. I sent her some money so he could get stuff. He's really excited. He wants to get a watch and a pin book or something.

**WILL**   How much is that?

**SAM**   I don't know. I took everything out of my account and closed it. And sent it to him.

**WILL**   Why'd you do that?

**SAM**   I think they're going to stay for like two days. I want him to be able to buy stuff.

**WILL**   We still have to pay the cable. It's past due. It's over three hundred bucks.

**SAM**   Let Mom do it.

**WILL** She won't.

**SAM** Then there won't be cable. Have her get a job and pay for it herself.

**WILL** Are you going to tell her?

**SAM** No. She'll figure it out in a few days.

[*Silence.*]

**WILL** Is he having a good time down there?

**SAM** Yeah. He misses us. They've been going to the water park a lot. They went to the fair. He's been riding the neighbors' horses.

**WILL** I'll call him tomorrow.

**SAM** Good.

**WILL** Did you talk to her about keeping him for the school year?

**SAM** No.

**WILL** Are you going to do it?

**SAM** No.

**WILL** Why?

**SAM** I need you to do it.

**WILL** Why?

[*She doesn't answer him.*]

Okay.

[*Short silence.*]

They're not going to be cool with it. They're already pissed off that we left him down there.

**SAM** So.

**WILL** So? What the fuck are you going to do when they're like go down there and get him? Or they fucking go down to Modesto themselves?

**SAM** I'm going to have you have a really honest conversation with them. And let them know you're going to have a really honest conversation with his principal. And the police if we have to.

[*The air falls out of the room.* WILL *looks down at his knees. They both sit in silence. Neither of them can speak.*]

I can write them a letter if you need me to.

**WILL** No.

**SAM** I kept some things. They're in my bed frame. A couple pairs of underwear. When I was doing the laundry. I think all we'd have to do is have the school send him to a doctor and do a physical.

[WILL *can't speak.*]

I know you know.

[*Silence.*]

I think it happened to you too.

**WILL**   It didn't.

[*Silence.*]

**SAM**   Say something.

[WILL *doesn't. They sit in the dark in silence. The sounds of the summer night fall into the room.*]

**WILL**   Did Eric ask you out again?

**SAM**   No. I don't think he likes me.

**WILL**   Yeah he does.

**SAM**   No he doesn't. No one likes me like that.

**WILL**   Did you watch a movie tonight?

**SAM**   Yeah. *Dark Shadows.*

**WILL**   Is it good?

**SAM**   Not really. You should see it though. Take Amber. Stop hanging out at Tommy's place.

[WILL *looks away from her.*]

You both look like shit. You look like you haven't slept in weeks.

[WILL *doesn't respond.*]

Don't ignore me.

**WILL**   What do you want me to say?

**SAM**   I want you to say I'm lying.

[WILL *can't.*]

**WILL**   What are you doing this weekend?

**SAM**   I'm going to the waterfall. With some friends. I'm supposed to work tomorrow night. I probably won't make it.

**WILL**   Karen'll cover for you?

**SAM**   Yeah.

**WILL**   You going with Janet?

**SAM**   Yeah.

**WILL**   She still pissed at me?

**SAM**   Yeah. She fucking hates you. You fucked her sister. And then you started fucking Amber. You lied to her. Some people don't get over that.

**WILL**   She was fucking other guys too.

**SAM**   Not while she was with you.

**WILL**   We weren't really together.

**SAM**   You guys got tattoos. You told her you wanted to have babies together. She said you begged to come in her.

**WILL**   Why the fuck is she telling you that?

**SAM**   She told everyone.

**WILL**   People say stupid shit.

**SAM**   She said you'd cry after.

**WILL**   I didn't fucking cry. What the fuck is that?

**SAM**   That's what she's telling everybody.
[WILL *looks like he could punch something.*]
She said you loved her. That you told her that.

**WILL**   I didn't fucking love her.

**SAM**   Do you love anybody?

**WILL**   I love you and Jimi.

**SAM**   That's not what I mean.

**WILL**   No.

**SAM**   Do you want to?

**WILL**   I don't know.
[*He can't look at* SAM.]
You're going to find somebody.

**SAM**   You say that to everybody.

**WILL**   It's true.

**SAM**   You want the world to fall in love. That's what I love about you. You come off like this . . . I don't know. But in the end you believe everything's possible.

**WILL**   It is.

**SAM**   Sometimes it's not. I keep thinking that's something they told us as kids. When they were going out. When they weren't going to be home for a week. In case they didn't make it back. That way we wouldn't feel it was our fault. If something bad happened. Or maybe they just wanted to make themselves not feel so bad.
[*They sit in silence.*]
I used to believe it. You know? You'd tell us these stories and I'd feel. They'd become true. You put something in my head that made it okay. I'd wake up thinking. We live on the beach. Or we're going to. We're going to live somewhere great. This little coastal town. Together. It'd get me through the

day. But then you get older and it's . . . How are you going to buy a house on the beach when you don't have a job? When you can't afford gas or fucking cigarettes at the store?

**WILL**  I'm trying.

**SAM**  No you're not.

[*He smiles at her, sadly. Silence.*]

**WILL**  Let's get out of here.

**SAM**  Where we going?

**WILL**  I don't know.

[*He looks at her, smiling.*]

To the ocean. To Big Sur. The redwoods. We can meet Jimi at Disneyland. Ride Space Mountain and the Matterhorn. Watch the fucking fireworks. Walk on the beach and get tacos. Swim. Go to Baja and Mexico.

[*He laughs. She doesn't.*]

It's never fucking happening.

**SAM**  No.

[*Silence. She takes his hand.*]

Look how big these hands are. You remember that?

**WILL**  No.

**SAM**  Grandpa used to say that. If you had big hands. You'd go far. I loved that your hand was the size of my head. It made me feel safe and proud that you're my brother.

[*She looks at him. He begins to cry.*]

When I look at you. I see that kid. So fucking cocky. You'd piss in public. You'd piss anywhere. All that hair. Blond. Your skin brown. I'd say "Where are we going to sleep if they don't come back?" And you'd be like, "Under the fucking stars. We'll steal some towels and listen to the seals." And you meant it. I'd be so scared and you'd make it fun.

**WILL**  I'm sorry.

**SAM**  For what?

**WILL**  That I'm not that. That I'm not that kid anymore.

[*They sit together. Blackout.*]

## SCENE 4

[*Late June 2012. Early summer. 3:20 a.m. The farmhouse and wind chimes. JIMI's bedroom. A window, a twin bed, and a dresser with a lamp and an antique toy fire truck on it. A radio alarm clock. JIMI sits on his bed, staring at the floor. WILL sits next to him.*]

**JIMI**  Is it yours?

**WILL**  Yeah it's fucking mine. It better be mine.

**JIMI**  How do you know?

**WILL**  Because.

**JIMI**  Because?

**WILL**  Because I just fucking know. 'Cause she's not like that.

**JIMI**  You're like that.

**WILL**  Not with her.

**JIMI**  Does she know?

**WILL**  What?

**JIMI**  About everyone else? All the other girls?

**WILL**  No.

**JIMI**  Are you going to tell her?

**WILL**  No I'm not going to tell her.

**JIMI**  You should.

**WILL**  What the fuck is wrong with you?!

**JIMI**  Nothing.

**WILL**  Why would I ever tell her about that?!

**JIMI**  Because you love her.

**WILL**  So.

**JIMI**  Because she should know.

**WILL**  No she fucking shouldn't! She should never fucking know! And if you ever fucking say anything! I swear to god!

**JIMI**  I won't.

**WILL**  You better not!

**JIMI**  I wouldn't.

**WILL**  What the fuck is wrong with you?!

**JIMI**  I don't know.

[*Short silence.*]

**WILL**  When do Mom and Dad get home?

**JIMI**  Tomorrow.

**WILL**  And what are you going to say?

**JIMI**  I don't know.

**WILL**   What did we talk about?

**JIMI**   That I woke up and . . . you just weren't here.

**WILL**   And . . .

**JIMI**   And everything seemed fine. Seemed normal.

**WILL**   Cool.

[*Short silence. Wind chimes.*]

**JIMI**   Where are you going?

**WILL**   I don't know I'll call you when we get there.

>  [JIMI *starts to cry.*]
>  Don't cry.
>  [JIMI *holds the back of his head with both of his hands and looks at the floor.*]
>  Oh, fuck.

[WILL *puts his hand on his little brother's back.*]

**JIMI**   I'm sorry.

**WILL**   Don't.

**JIMI**   I'm sorry.

>  [*Catching his breath.*]
>  I don't want you to go.

**WILL**   I know.

**JIMI**   I'm stupid.

**WILL**   You'll be fine.

>  [*Silence.* JIMI *continues staring at the floor.*]
>  Do you need any money?

**JIMI**   No.

**WILL**   You sure?

**JIMI**   Yeah.

[*Silence.*]

**WILL**   You going to play basketball next year?

**JIMI**   Probably not.

**WILL**   Why?

**JIMI**   'Cause I suck.

**WILL**   You're fast.

**JIMI**   Not fast enough.

**WILL**   You should try. You can't just fucking sit here.

[*Short silence.*]

**JIMI**  Why won't you let me come?

**WILL**  'Cause you're too young. I'd get in trouble.

**JIMI**  What if Mom would let me?

**WILL**  She wouldn't.

**JIMI**  You could ask her and see?

**WILL**  No.

**JIMI**  Why not?

**WILL**  'Cause I don't want you to.

[*Silence.*]

**JIMI**  What time are you getting Amber?

**WILL**  Now. I'm supposed to be there already.
[JIMI *looks back down at the floor.*]
Don't start again.

**JIMI**  I'm not.
[*Short silence.*]
Are you going to get married?

**WILL**  I don't know. I haven't thought about it.

**JIMI**  Can I come if you do?

**WILL**  Yeah. You'll be my best man.

[JIMI *smiles.*]

**JIMI**  What are you going to name it?

**WILL**  What?

**JIMI**  The baby.

**WILL**  I haven't thought about it.

**JIMI**  Will you name it Sam if it's a girl?

**WILL**  I don't know.

**JIMI**  Do you love her?

**WILL**  Who?

**JIMI**  Amber?

**WILL**  Yeah. I think so.

**JIMI**  I wish I had someone like that.

**WILL**  You will.

**JIMI**  No I won't.

**WILL**   Yeah you will. I promise. Some fucking weird, cute girl with all this hair and glasses. And really nice eyes. She's going to make you smile. She's going to get all this shit and let you know without having to say a word, that it's okay. You're going to hold her. In bed. And everything else. Is just going to fucking die away. I promise.

[*Silence.*]

**JIMI**   Do you see her?

**WILL**   Who?

**JIMI**   Sam?

**WILL**   No.

**JIMI**   Sometimes I think she's sitting on the couch. Or I'll look up and she's standing there. I want her to talk to me.

**WILL**   What does she look like?

**JIMI**   I don't know. Like she did I guess. She looks happy.

[JIMI *looks at* WILL, *wants to say something, but can't.* WILL *looks away from* JIMI, *out the window.*]

**WILL**   I got to go.

**JIMI**   I know.

**WILL**   It's late.

**JIMI**   Are you going to stay at Amber's tonight?

**WILL**   No. I'll drink some coffee. Get a Red Bull or something. Start driving.
   [*Beat.*]
   Amber believes in ghosts.

**JIMI**   I know. She told me.

**WILL**   She thinks when you love somebody so much. That you're . . . It's not possible for them to leave. They sit with you 'cause you need them. They sit with you 'til you're ready for them to leave. Or something like that. I don't know. Something stupid.

[*Short silence.*]

**JIMI**   I like Amber.

**WILL**   She likes you. She thinks you're sweet. She says you're going to be better looking than me.

**JIMI**   I am already.

[WILL's *cell phone begins to vibrate. He picks up.*]

**WILL**   Hey baby. Yeah—No I'm coming. I'm just talking to my little brother. Yeah. No. No I will. Okay.

[*He hangs up.*]
She says hi.

**JIMI**  Hey.

[*They sit.*]

**WILL**  Take my stuff.

**JIMI**  I will.

[WILL *wants to say something but can't.*]

**WILL**  You remember that house Mom dropped us off at when we were kids? When she was after Dad?

**JIMI**  Yeah.

**WILL**  She said we'd find a key under the mat in the front.

**JIMI**  Yeah.

**WILL**  Whose house was that?

**JIMI**  She never said.

**WILL**  It was so beautiful. Like no one had ever touched it. Fucking hot tub and apple orchards. I was so sad when they came back.

**JIMI**  Me too.

**WILL**  Sam couldn't stop crying. She didn't talk for a week.

**JIMI**  I wonder if Mom actually knew.

**WILL**  Who cares?

**JIMI**  I always thought maybe she just dropped us off at some random house and guessed.

**WILL**  It was the two best days of my life. I thought when I grow up I want that. A house like that. Some property and a couple dogs. And you guys just there. Sam with her own room. Somewhere quiet with lots of light. You'd have a fish tank.

**JIMI**  Salt water.

**WILL**  Yeah. With sea anemones.
[*Silence.*]
I want you to be all right.

**JIMI**  I will.

**WILL**  I don't believe you.
[*Short silence.*]
I need to do this.

**JIMI**  I know.

**WILL**   I want you to understand.

**JIMI**   I do.

**WILL**   No you don't.

**JIMI**   I'm trying to.

**WILL**   I feel like . . . like no matter what I'm fucked. It's like . . . I don't know. I can fucking stay with you. And what the fuck? What do I have here? Or try to start with her. Somewhere else. Fucking grow up. Leave you.

**JIMI**   I'll be okay.

**WILL**   No you won't.

**JIMI**   I don't know what to say.

[WILL *looks at his brother.*]

**WILL**   Don't say anything.

[*Silence.*]

**JIMI**   I'm glad she kept it. You're going to be a great dad.

**WILL**   You're going to be an uncle.

**JIMI**   That's crazy. Will you send me a picture?

**WILL**   Of course.

**JIMI**   How am I going to meet it?

**WILL**   I don't know.

**JIMI**   I hope it looks like Amber.

**WILL**   Me too.

**JIMI**   You got to go.

**WILL**   Yeah.

**JIMI**   What the fuck are you still doing here?

[WILL *looks at the floor and laughs. He can't get up.*]

**WILL**   I wish so fucking much. I wish . . . Fuck man . . . I'd give anything . . .

**JIMI**   I know.

**WILL**   For Sam to be here . . . to still be alive . . . For everything to just . . .

**JIMI**   Me too.

**WILL**   It just doesn't . . . I don't know . . . It doesn't seem real yet to me. That she's gone.

[WILL *can't finish.*]

I do see her. I talk to her. All the time. I mean she's not really there, but . . . I talk to her about everything. Like I used to. She was that for me, you know?

I didn't tell her. I didn't say anything, but she knew. She knew and she'd forgive me. She knew, you know? She knew . . . I don't know. I don't know what the fuck I'm saying.

[WILL *looks at the room.*]

I think years from now. We'll get a chance. To laugh about everything.

**JIMI**  Things can always get worse.

[WILL *begins to laugh.*]

**WILL**  Exactly.

[WILL *hugs his little brother to him.*]

If you need me call me.

**JIMI**  I will.

**WILL**  You're strong.

**JIMI**  No I'm not.

**WILL**  You're going to be the one that makes it. You'll see.

[*Blackout.*]

# SCENE 5

[*December 2013. The farmhouse. 12:20 a.m.* JIMI's *bedroom.* WILL *is lying on his side, naked except for wool socks, passed out.* SAM, *fully dressed, sits on the bed next to him with her legs stretched out or crossed, looking at* JIMI. JIMI *stands near the door of his room staring at* SAM. *He just got home from work. It's snowing out. After a while,* JIMI *slowly takes off his backpack and sets it on the floor. He quietly goes to the chair and sits. They continue to watch each other. He begins taking his socks off and laying them on the arm to dry out. He takes off his baseball cap and sets it on the floor by his backpack. He looks at* SAM. *They both look at* WILL *and then back to each other.*]

**JIMI**  Will.

[WILL *doesn't answer.* JIMI *tries again, a bit louder.*]

Will.

[WILL *continues to sleep.* SAM *stands up from the bed and walks out through the bedroom door into the hallway.* JIMI *watches her go. She's gone.* JIMI *sits, breathing hard. After a moment,* JIMI *gets up and walks to his brother. He touches his arm.*]

Will.

[WILL *still doesn't stir.* JIMI *follows* SAM *out of the bedroom door.* WILL *stays on his side. The snow continues to fall. After a moment,* JIMI *comes back in with a pair of boxers and some jeans and a T-shirt. He goes to the bed and lays them down, and then shakes* WILL's *arm.*]

Will. Will!

[JIMI *continues shaking him hard.* WILL *begins to move, barely. He's groggy and slow.* JIMI *turns on the side lamp by the bed.* WILL *shields his eyes.* JIMI *helps his brother sit up. He grabs the T-shirt and helps put it over his head. WILL is still drunk and high, and is having a hard time understanding where he is or fully waking up and coming to.*]

Will—

**WILL** Yeah.

**JIMI** You're in my bed.

[*WILL, confused, lies back down and curls up.*]

No. You've gotta sit back up.

[*JIMI tries to sit his brother back up. WILL can hardly keep his eyes open.*]

Do you want me to get you some water?

[*WILL doesn't answer. JIMI leaves the room again. WILL sits there awkwardly, starting to wake up a bit more. JIMI comes back in with a cup of water. He hands it to WILL and then grabs the boxers. He sits on the floor in front of his brother and puts in one foot and then the other. He then stands and helps WILL pull his boxers all the way up. WILL finishes the cup of water.*]

Want some more?

[*WILL shakes his head no.*]

It's really late. I got to get to bed. I'm working again tomorrow.

**WILL** Don't you got school?

**JIMI** It's Saturday.

**WILL** Where were you?

**JIMI** At work.

**WILL** That sucks.

**JIMI** It was fine. It was good.

**WILL** Why'd you wake me up?

**JIMI** 'Cause you're in my bed.

**WILL** Oh. Do you got school?

**JIMI** No. You asked me that already.

**WILL** I fucking hated school.

**JIMI** I know.

**WILL** I was terrible at it. I never felt dumb 'til I fucking started there. The teachers didn't get what I know. You know? Like I couldn't do all the math and stuff, or like name the presidents. But there's a lot of shit I can do. Like I can put together a car. I can fucking hunt and winter proof a house.

**JIMI** I know.

**WILL** I'm not fucking stupid.

**JIMI** I know.

**WILL**  They can't do that shit. They don't realize all the fucking shit they're teaching isn't going to pay your fucking light bill. Or get your kid to school.

**JIMI**  You want to sleep in here?

**WILL**  Yeah. I have to.

**JIMI**  Why?

**WILL**  To protect your fucking ass. Like I used to.

**JIMI**  Get your pants on.

**WILL**  I don't want my pants.

**JIMI**  Do you want your sweats?

**WILL**  No.

**JIMI**  It's cold in here.

**WILL**  My fucking balls need air.
[JIMI *stops. He doesn't know what to do.*]
Did Mom give you money for a tree?

**JIMI**  No.

**WILL**  She was supposed to give you money. She said you were going to bring one home. And some new lights.

**JIMI**  She didn't tell me.

**WILL**  We'll get one tomorrow. Sam said . . .

[WILL *stops himself.*]

**JIMI**  She's dead.

[*Silence.* WILL *looks out the window at the snow.*]

**WILL**  Is Amber still here?

**JIMI**  No. Was she here earlier?

[WILL *doesn't answer.*]

**WILL**  What time is it?

**JIMI**  After twelve.

**WILL**  Is it Friday?

**JIMI**  It was. Yeah.

**WILL**  Have I been sleeping here?

**JIMI**  Not for the last few nights. No.

**WILL**  Where was I?

**JIMI**  I don't know. You've been spending a lot of time down at Jake's place. You've been partying a lot down there.

**WILL**  I think he made me fuck his sister.

**JIMI**  Why?

**WILL**  I think she sucked my dick.

[JIMI *doesn't say anything.*]

I think we pissed on her.

[JIMI *doesn't know what to do.*]

I've been fucking Nick Sabi's mom. She fucking lets me sleep there. She lets me come in her. She used to buy us pizza after Little League. Sometimes she makes me dinner.

**JIMI**  Gino's.

**WILL**  Yeah. You remember her?

[JIMI *nods his head.*]

She used to be pretty.

[*They both sit in silence.*]

How'd I get here?

**JIMI**  I don't know.

**WILL**  Is my car outside?

**JIMI**  No.

**WILL**  You got my pants anywhere?

**JIMI**  Yeah. Right there.

[WILL *takes his pants and begins digging through his pockets. He finds something in his front right pocket and pulls out a dime bag. He digs his finger in it and gets what he can on the end and then snorts it, and gums his finger.* JIMI *watches him.*]

Do you want me to wash 'em.

**WILL**  No.

**JIMI**  I can get you clean ones.

[WILL *ignores* JIMI *and closes his eyes, holding onto his jeans like they're a blanket or teddy bear.*]

**WILL**  I think Amber's coming here. You should call her.

[*Short silence.*]

I think she changed her number.

**JIMI**  She did.

**WILL**  How the fuck do you know?

**JIMI**  You told me.

**WILL**  You fucking see her?

**JIMI**  No.

**WILL**  Behind my back?

[JIMI *doesn't answer.*]

Her fucking mom made her do it. She said I hit her.

**JIMI**  You did.

[WILL's *quiet.*]

**WILL**  I don't remember.

[*Short silence.*]

Was it bad?

**JIMI**  Yeah.

**WILL**  Did I hurt her?

**JIMI**  Yeah.

**WILL**  Were you there?

**JIMI**  No.

**WILL**  Good.

[WILL *looks down at his hands.*]

Our baby died.

**JIMI**  I know.

**WILL**  I was a terrible fucking dad.

**JIMI**  No you weren't.

**WILL**  Yeah I was.

[WILL's *quiet.*]

I got her a ring.

**JIMI**  Yeah.

**WILL**  I wanted to marry her. Now I'm never going to marry anyone.

**JIMI**  Yeah you will.

**WILL**  No I'm not. I'm going to be dead by the end of the year.

[JIMI *can't speak.*]

Do you know what it's like?

**JIMI**  What?

**WILL**  To look at someone's eyes when you're in them?

**JIMI**  No.

**WILL**  To know you have to go slow 'cause she's been hurt. So she can feel you?
You hold her ass with your hand and pull her up so you can go all the way
in. And not cause you're fucking, I don't know . . . but because you want her
to have everything you have to give. You push in as deep as you can and

hold yourself there. And you go . . . that's it. That's what it feels like to really trust someone. To be . . . I don't know. And you make a baby like that. It's like you've fallen through her it feels so good.

[WILL *can't speak. He looks at his hand. He stares at it.*]

I'm just like them. You know that?

**JIMI**   No you're not.

[*He shows* JIMI *his hand. There's an address and number written on his palm in black marker.*]

**WILL**   Yeah I am.

[*Blackout.*]

# SCENE 6

[*February 2015. Darkness. Moonlight. Snow and wind. The farmhouse and wind chimes. The same room—*JIMI's *bedroom. A window, a twin bed, and a dresser with a lamp, an antique toy fire truck on it, and a plastic funeral box or urn full of ashes. A radio alarm clock.* JIMI, *awake in bed in the dark.* WILL *sits in a chair in the corner of the room with a worn-out baseball cap and Converse. He's sitting permanently still, staring. A long silence. The sound of breathing.*]

**WILL**   What time is it?

[*Short silence.*]

You cut your hair off.

[*Silence.*]

Say something.

[JIMI *doesn't. Snow and wind. Silence.*]

You get your car fixed?

**JIMI**   No. Mom drives me.

**WILL**   There's Dad's pickup?

**JIMI**   No engine in it.

**WILL**   We used to sleep back there. When we were kids? Remember that?

**JIMI**   . . . . . . . . . .

**WILL**   Go fishing.
Have Grandpa drive us around.
You could fix it.
It's a good truck.
[*Silence.*]
The horses are gone.

**JIMI**   She sold them.

A few months ago.
Nice couple with a daughter lookin' to ride.
We had to.

**WILL**   Cute?

**JIMI**   Okay. Big tits, weird teeth. Kind of shy.

[*Short silence.*]

**WILL**   Still bowling?

**JIMI**   Sometimes. Sometimes with Robby.

**WILL**   You still hang out with that fuck?

**JIMI**   Yeah. We'll go down, throw a few games. Get some nachos and cheese
fries. Some Cokes.

**WILL**   He still with Linda?

**JIMI**   No. Not after he found out you fucked her.

**WILL**   She fucked everybody. She was a fucking hole.
She used to suck guys off at the truck stop for money.

[*Short silence.*]

**JIMI**   Her dad was a trucker.
Used to beat the shit out of her mom.
He used to arm wrestle for money.
    [*Beat.*]
She still comes into work sometimes, says hi.
I think she misses Robby.
I think she's lonely.

[*Silence.*]

**WILL**   It's cold.

**JIMI**   The heat's off.

**WILL**   Why?

**JIMI**   Couldn't afford to pay it.

**WILL**   I can hear the TV.

**JIMI**   She leaves it on. She likes the noise. Sounds like there's people.

[*Short silence.*]

**WILL**   Still a virgin?

**JIMI**   Still a faggot?

[WILL *laughs.*]

**WILL**   Still piss like a girl?

**JIMI** Sometimes. When I'm tired.

[*Silence.*]

**WILL** My bed's not made.

**JIMI** It's the same.
It hasn't been cleaned.
She left it.

**WILL** Why?

**JIMI** I don't know.

[*Short Pause.*]

**WILL** You take my money?

**JIMI** No.

**WILL** You should take it. See a movie.
[*Short Pause.*]
You should open the window. It fucking stinks in there.

**JIMI** I can't. Mom nailed it shut.

[*Silence.*]

**WILL** I used to jerk off in your shoes. When we were little.

**JIMI** Why?

**WILL** 'Cause.

**JIMI** 'Cause?

**WILL** Yeah 'cause.
[*Beat.*]
To fuck with you. Be a dick.
I used to rub it in so you couldn't tell.
[*Short silence.*]
I fucked your bear too.

**JIMI** I thought I lost it.

**WILL** I fucked it.

[*Silence.*]

**JIMI** Amber's pregnant.

[*Short silence.*]

**WILL** Yeah?

**JIMI** Yeah.

**WILL** Tommy's?

**JIMI**  Think so. She's moving back to Wyoming. She stopped by work to tell me. She misses you. She couldn't stop crying. She thinks, you know? Maybe. If you guys had worked. If the baby didn't die. You know? Things'd be different.

**WILL**  It wouldn't.

**JIMI**  I think she wants to be closer to her mom and her sister. They seem happy.

[*Beat.*]

**WILL**  It's snowing.

[*They watch the snow. Silence.*]

**JIMI**  It hasn't in days. It's been too cold.

**WILL**  Dad hated snow.
He used to say his cousin was Cuban.
Used to cut out all those travel magazines. Tape them to the bathroom mirror. Trees. Fish. Towels. Fucking nets.
Shells.
[*Beat.*]
He wanted to take us to Hawaii.
Buy stupid fucking shirts. Go whale watching. Scuba diving. Eat pig.
[*Silence.*]
Ever think this place is haunted?

**JIMI**  ...........

**WILL**  I used to hear shit when I was a kid. When I was little. When I was here by myself. Used to think I'd see shit too.
[*Short silence.*]
Why didn't you play basketball this year?

**JIMI**  Not tall enough.

**WILL**  But you're fast.

**JIMI**  Not fast enough.

**WILL**  You need to do something.

**JIMI**  I do.

**WILL**  What?

**JIMI**  Work.

**WILL**  You can't afford to pay the fucking heat bill.

**JIMI**  I'm saving.

**WILL**  For what?

[JIMI *doesn't answer. Short Pause.*]
I used to fuck Coach Lachey's daughter.

**JIMI**  Which one?

**WILL**  Brenda.

**JIMI**  She's cute.

**WILL**  Yeah?

**JIMI**  Yeah.

**WILL**  I wanted to fuck Stacey but she wouldn't let me.
[*Short silence.*]
Ever measure your dick?

**JIMI**  Yeah.

**WILL**  How big?

**JIMI**  I don't know. A little over six.

**WILL**  Seen others?

**JIMI**  Yeah. Yours.

**WILL**  You measure up?

**JIMI**  I don't know. About the same. Yours is bigger.

**WILL**  Ever been in love?

**JIMI**  I don't think so.

**WILL**  Ever want to?

**JIMI**  Haven't really thought about it.
Were you in love with Amber?

[WILL *doesn't answer. Short silence. Wind.*]

**WILL**  Old man Keith used to pay me.
He used to have me sit on his bed and jerk off while he watched.
Gave me fifty bucks every time I did it.
Told me he'd give me a hundred if I brought a friend.

**JIMI**  Did you?

**WILL**  He used to tape it.
He had them organized next to his bed.
[*Short silence. Snow and wind.*]
I miss pussy. I miss the smell.
Fucking getting down there.
Rubbing my face in it. Having a girl fucking sit on me. Giving it to her slow from behind.
Trying not to cum too fast.
[*Short Pause.*]
You ever go down on a girl?

**JIMI**   No.

**WILL**   You should find some really fat chick and muff dive her till she passes out.

[*Short Pause.*]

I can't feel my legs.

It's like there's nothing there.

I can feel my face and hands but I can't feel my feet.

[*He looks at his brother.* JIMI *looks away.*]

You remember hunting?

When we were kids? With Dad?

**JIMI**   ...........

**WILL**   That game we played?

**JIMI**   No.

**WILL**   Liar.

Counting?

In the woods?

Taking turns by ourselves?

With him.

**JIMI**   ...........

**WILL**   You remember.

[*Silence.* WILL *can't look at him.*]

Did Mom ever tell you how her and Dad met?

**JIMI**   No.

**WILL**   She found him in a parking lot with no pants on.

He couldn't remember how he got there.

Couldn't remember where he lived. She felt sorry for him.

He had his address written on his hand.

Like he knew he'd forget. Like he knew he'd be there.

**JIMI**   I thought he played football.

**WILL**   He did.

**JIMI**   I thought they listened to "Crimson and Clover."

**WILL**   They did.

It was her favorite song.

[*Short silence.*]

They were fucking drug addicts.

Then they found God.

**JIMI**   And each other.

**WILL**   And us.

> [*Beat.*]
>
> Why don't you have any friends?

**JIMI**   I have friends.

**WILL**   Not Robby.

> Like real friends. Friend friends.
>
> Like guys you hang out with and go camping and get stoned and shoot things and shit.

**JIMI**   I don't like hunting. I don't like killing things.

[*Beat.*]

**WILL**   I saw you. With Robby. When you were like ten.

> [*Beat.*]
>
> You like that?

**JIMI**   ..........

**WILL**   You like that stuff?

**JIMI**   What?

**WILL**   Don't fucking "what?"!

**JIMI**   No.

**WILL**   Did he make you?

**JIMI**   No.

**WILL**   You sure?

**JIMI**   Yeah.

**WILL**   On your knees.

> Like a little girl.
>
> [*Beat.*]
>
> You fucking swallowed.

**JIMI**   I did not.

**WILL**   I didn't see you spit it out.

> [*Short Pause.*]
>
> Is that why you don't like girls?

**JIMI**   I like girls.

**WILL**   You've never fucked one. I never see you with one.

> You never go the movies or take anybody out.

**JIMI**   I don't know what to say. I don't know anybody.

> [*Short Pause.*]

There's no one who likes me.
I don't know how you know.

**WILL**   You just know. They . . . they send it out. They give you signals and shit.

**JIMI**   Like what?

**WILL**   I don't know, you just know. They let you know.
[*Beat.*]
You ever let him fuck you?

**JIMI**   No.

**WILL**   You sure?

**JIMI**   Yeah.

**WILL**   You lying?

**JIMI**   No.

[*Short Pause.*]

**WILL**   Your hair tucked behind your ears. Fucking eyes open. Fucking makes me sick. Thought I was going to throw up.
[*Silence. Snow.*]
What you have for dinner?

**JIMI**   Pizza.

**WILL**   What kind?

**JIMI**   Pepperoni and sausage.

**WILL**   Gino's?

**JIMI**   Yeah.

**WILL**   They still have those balls?

**JIMI**   The dough balls?

**WILL**   Yeah.
With butter and garlic?

**JIMI**   Yeah.

**WILL**   I'd hang out there as a kid. Play Galaga. Fuck around.
They used give me free refills on Coke.
[*Beat.*]
I used to steal quarters out of Mom's underwear jar. Walk there.
[*Silence.*]
I don't have a lot of time.

**JIMI**   I know.

[*Snow and wind.*]

**WILL**   Remember Dad and those puppies?

**JIMI**   No.

**WILL**   Fucking bag and the shovel?
The snow?

**JIMI**   ...........

**WILL**   Carried them over his shoulder. His gloves. Cigarette in his mouth.
Behind the barn in the woodpile.
[*Short Pause.*]
Fucking made you watch. Made me hold your head. Made me hold you so
you wouldn't look away.

**JIMI**   ...........

**WILL**   Fucking took a piss.
Finished his cigarette. Kicked the snow off his boots and walked home.
Made us clean 'em up.
[*Short Pause.*]
I used to steal shit out of his truck. Bury it in the backyard. Tie notes on it.
Like, "If you find this you know what a piece of shit you are."
Piss on his toothbrush. Wipe my dick in his mug. Move his shit around.
Drive him crazy.

[*Silence.*]

**JIMI**   Do you see Sam?

**WILL**   ...........

**JIMI**   Mom says you see her now. That you're together.

**WILL**   ...........

[*Silence.*]

**JIMI**   They said they were playing the butt game. At the waterfall.
Sliding on their asses to the edge. Flipping back on the branch.
[*Short Pause.*]
They said she sat there. That she ...
She didn't even try to put her arms up.
[*Short silence.*]
We never talked about that.

**WILL**   We didn't talk about a lot of things.

**JIMI**   We should've.
[*Short silence.*]
Do you think it's true?

**WILL**   What?

**JIMI**  That she wanted to?
That she wanted to die?

**WILL**  I don't know.

**JIMI**  I wish I did.

**WILL**  What?

**JIMI**  Know.

[*Snow and wind.*]

**WILL**  Remember the pond? The rope swing when we were kids?
Barbecues? Bandanas? Roach clips with Indian feathers on 'em?

**JIMI**  Yeah.

**WILL**  Taking the raft around the island? Keeping watch while we kissed
girls?
[*Short Pause.*]
First time I saw pussy hair? I got so hard I jerked off in the bushes?

**JIMI**  Yeah.

**WILL**  Playing catch and frisbee. Pink Floyd. The Allman Brothers Band.

**JIMI**  I remember the rides home. The three of us asleep in the back of the car
in sleeping bags and jackets. The window down. The radio. Mom and Dad
holding hands and smoking cigarettes. Laughing.

[*Snow and wind.*]

**WILL**  I asked him to go the store with me that night. Dad.
I said I needed cigarettes and Coke. That I'd buy him another six-pack so I
didn't have to drive alone.
[*Short Pause.*]
He wanted to take the van. I lied. Told him the tires were bald. That there
was no gas in it. That I couldn't find the keys. That we had to take my car.
My seatbelt was broken. In the passenger seat.
I grabbed my hat. Kissed Mom's head. Turned down the TV.

**JIMI**  ..........

**WILL**  We listened to music. A mix tape. Guns N' Roses.
"Patience." "One in a Million." "Rocket Queen." Smoked cigarettes.
The front window kept fogging up so we had to keep the windows down.
You could see our breath. The moon was huge.

**JIMI**  I remember.

**WILL**  It was pouring snow. There was no one out. No one on the road. No
lights on. There was ice everywhere. On the trees. Everything was frozen.

[*Short Pause.*]
I need you to know what I'm saying.

**JIMI**  I do.

**WILL**  I kept hoping it would just happen, you know? That it would sneak up on us.
My hands were shaking. I thought I was going to pass out. My heart was punching my chest. I kept turning the music up 'cause I was afraid he could hear it.

**JIMI**  ...........

**WILL**  Fucking Mr. Brownstone, you know?
There's that turn? That turn onto Colombia? The fucking sign with the deer on it? Someone painted on a big cock and balls.

**JIMI**  Bambi?

**WILL**  Yeah, fucking Bambi.
I kept going. The fucking music. Just pushed down my foot. As hard as I could. Took my hands off the wheel.
[*Both brothers breathing hard. Silence. Wind and snow. Wind chimes.*]
I heard him with you.
Dad. The night before. In the bathroom. Like a fucking pig. The shower still on. His zipper. The sink. When he was finished.
Clearing his throat. Flushing the toilet.
Washing his hands.
[*Silence.*]
The showers as kids.
Soap. Tape measure. Shoestrings. Making us get hard for him.

**JIMI**  Haircuts.

**WILL**  In the summer.

**JIMI**  Three-quarter inch, close to the scalp. Trim.

**WILL**  Push-ups. Sit-ups.

**JIMI**  Yeah.
[*Silence.*]
Do you think he loved us?

**WILL**  Does it matter?

[*Short pause.*]

**JIMI**  He taught me how to throw a baseball.

**WILL**  Me too.
How to align my knuckles when you swing.

[*Silence.*]

They ever find those kids?

**JIMI** The Barretts?

**WILL** Yeah. Went fishing Old Stones Bridge. Disappeared.

**JIMI** No.

[*Short Pause.*]

**WILL** She should sell this place. Move back to Fresno. Pack up our things.

[*Short silence.*]

**JIMI** I applied to college.

**WILL** Yeah?

**JIMI** Yeah. Community college. Night classes in the spring.
Study English. Writing. I could go there a couple years and transfer. Save
some money.

[*Snow.*]

I hate you. You know that right?

[WILL *can't speak.*]

I hate you both for leaving me.

I have fucking nothing.

[WILL *looks at* JIMI *and then at a box full of ashes on the dresser.*]

**WILL** Is that me?

**JIMI** Yeah. When you died. Mom asked me if you wanted to be buried. I said
you always wanted to be cremated. Like a fucking Viking.

[*Silence.*]

**WILL** I sat there. Waiting. I could see everything. Like both sides . . . I kept
thinking I should move. Or call someone. I wanted a cigarette. I really
wanted a smoke. The music was still on. Fucking "Used to Love Her"
playing. The horn was stuck. The car was on its side against a tree. I think I
was still in it.

[*Short Pause.*]

I could see Dad on his back in the snow. His leg bent under him. He looked
like he was sleeping.

His mouth open. Eyes up. Forehead caved in.

[*Short Pause.*]

I felt. It's over. It's over now.

I felt happy.

I felt relieved.

[*Silence. Snow and wind.*]

**JIMI** Remember the field? In winter? Late at night when we were kids? All three of us? The fort?

Sam, you, and me?

**WILL** Yeah.

**JIMI** We'd work on it for days. Digging. Building.

[*Short Pause.*]

We'd always crawl backward. Erasing our tracks with our hands to the back. No words. Flashlights on.

[*Short Pause.*]

We'd spread blankets and pillows down. Lay out our sleeping bags. Sammy would bring books. You'd bring cards and a yo-yo. Do tricks for us.

We'd lay together and tell stories and jokes. Eat chips. Make animals on the wall. You'd always let us fall asleep first. And we'd lay there like that. Under the snow.

[*Short Pause.*]

I'd dream about. Long car rides in the summer. The Snake River. Trips to the boardwalk and the beach. Eating cotton candy and begging people to buy us tickets so we could ride the roller coaster and the log ride. We'd put out your hat and make up songs and dance. Ask people for money. And you'd buy us corn dogs with extra ketchup so we could eat. I never felt. I don't know . . . When you were both . . . When we were together . . . I always felt . . . No matter what. So able to . . . So happy.

**WILL** Yeah.

**JIMI** No one could touch that you know?

**WILL** Yeah.

**JIMI** It was always just us three.

[*Short silence.*]

And now . . .

**WILL** I know.

**JIMI** There's . . .

**WILL** I know.

[*Snow falls.*]

**JIMI** I wish. I wish so much . . .

**WILL** Me too.

**JIMI** I'd give anything.

[*There's nothing left to say. Silence. Blackout. END OF PLAY.*]

# Spit Like a Big Girl

### or

## Life is what happens on the way to where you're going

Clarinda Ross

# Clarinda Ross

Clarinda Ross is a veteran actress. She lives with her family in suburban Los Angeles. She has authored two full-length plays, *From My Grandmother's Grandmother Unto Me* and *Spit Like A Big Girl*, for which she was named the 2014 Tennessee Williams Scholar at the Sewanee Writers' Conference. She is the recipient of the Barbara Seranella Scholarship for excellence in creative writing at the University of California at Riverside's Palm Desert MFA Program. Ms. Ross is a member of Actors' Equity Association, SAG-AFTRA, and the Dramatists' Guild. For more information, please visit her website www.clarindaross.com.

*for Googy*

# Production History

*Spit Like A Big Girl* premiered at the Rubicon Theatre Company in Ventura, CA. Producing Artistic Director Karyl Lynn Burns, Director Jenny Sullivan, Production Stage Manager Christina Burck. The play was remounted by the Civic Light Opera of South Bay Cities, directed by Stephanie Coltrin. The touring production is produced by Googy Gress; the Production Stage Manager is Julie Richardson, with Sound Design by Kevin Goold. In 2015, the play was the featured act of the Appalachian Festival of Plays and Playwrights at the Barter Theatre with Ms. Ross in the lead.

## Production Note

The play can be performed solo or with two actresses. If there are two actresses, the Act One actress should be in her late 20s, and the Act Two actress should be late 40s.

## Setting

Two platforms. Stage Right platform with an acting cube represents "home." Stage Left platform with 2 cubes arranged like stairs represents all other locations: offices, hospitals, etc. Upstage Center there are 4 sturdy identical chairs which represent all the cars.

# ACT I

[*In darkness, a song such as Nanci Griffith's "Southbound Train" plays. We see slide projection images of father's handwriting.*
SOUND: *Pre-recorded VO of the dedication plays.*

*For my father,
who read me the great stories of history when I was too young to really understand them. He taught me life is hard but not impossible. I'm teaching my daughter simpler things, like how to eat with a spoon, brush her teeth, step up to the sink,
and
SPIT like a big girl.*]

**CLARINDA**   Have you ever heard that saying: *"Life is what happens on the way to where you're going"?* Well, I really believe it's true. Life is made up of those tiny moments in between the big plans and the dreams. Big things in life make us *stop* and notice the tiny moments. It takes a few births, deaths, car wrecks, or natural disasters, before we're even paying attention. Life will just sneak up behind you and sit down at your kitchen table while you're fixin' supper.

It's 1988. It's August. It's Atlanta. It's HOT and I'm pregnant. I'm really pregnant. I'd just closed the play *Steel Magnolias* and it had been a big hit. The women in our cast became very close and we used to go out together after shows. And, sometimes people would recognize us and send flowers or champagne to our table. I was talking on the phone to my daddy telling him all about it.

**YOUNG CLARINDA**   Daddy, I'm locally famous, but I'm not rich.   He said,

**DADDY** [*A deep, booming baritone.*] Me too, Deb. Me too!

**CLARINDA** The one thing I can tell you about my daddy: he's *just tickled* to be him. As we hung up the phone, he said,

**DADDY** I never worry about you, Deb. You're gonna be all right.

**CLARINDA** My husband, Patrick, and I went to our last birthing class. [*Lamaze breathing.*] HA-HA-HEE-HEE. HA-HA-HEE-HEE. I graduated with flying colors. My registered nurse-midwife, an aging flower child, said,

**FLOWER CHILD NURSE** You're certainly a great little breather.

**YOUNG CLARINDA** Thanks. I'm an actress.

**CLARINDA** We get home late. There is a message on the machine from Daddy.

[*SOUND: Answering machine.*]

**DADDY** Just calling to check in. Call when you can.

**CLARINDA** The next morning, I slept late . . .

[*SOUND: Phone ring.*]

. . . or tried to. The phone kept ringing. I was in that dreamy state, between sleep and wake. I thought that's my old daddy calling me . . . I'll call him back. Finally, I picked up.

[*SOUND out.*]

It's my friend, a director named David Thomas. He asked,

**DAVID** Hi—uh, how are you doing?

**CLARINDA** I launch into the perils of pregnancy.

**YOUNG CLARINDA** It's so hot, I'm so fat, my feet are swollen. David, why did I cut my hair?

**CLARINDA** I'm prattling; he's listening, but not really. Really, he is trying to keep me on the phone because he knew what I didn't. Oh! Call waiting.

**YOUNG CLARINDA** David, I gotta run.

**CLARINDA** It is my friend Bill, a playwright from Los Angeles, by way of Alabama. I had just done a reading of his new play. He's writing the true story of his sisters. And, in real life, his daddy died of cancer.

**BILL** Claire-In-duh I've got to find a way to end this here play.

**YOUNG CLARINDA** Well, Bill. It seems like, to me, you'll have to tell the truth in your play. You'll have to talk about your daddy dying.

**CLARINDA** Patrick pulled up in the driveway. What was he doing home in the middle of the day? Patrick walked into the house with his arms outstretched.

**PATRICK** Your mom found your dad . . . dead.

**CLARINDA**  And I remember thinking in that moment, what a *weird* way for him to word it, creepy, like Daddy had been murdered or something. I backed away from him. I wanted to put as much distance as possible between me and that news. I stood for a long time and looked out the window. I didn't cry for two hours. And, you know I loved my daddy. But there were people and things to take care of: call my mama—which was awful, call my mamaw, my daddy's mama—which was worse. The funeral. The memorial. Pick the casket. What should he wear? Where will he be buried? I was on the phone all day. Everybody was worried about me that I would miscarry, or go on a hunger strike. I ate a steak that night! But, Sherry never called me. Sherry is my very best friend in the whole wide world and I knew that she knew. Boone, North Carolina, is a small town, and . . . Daddy really was locally famous. At nine o'clock that night, I called Sherry.

[*Picks up the phone.*]

**SHERRY**  Clarinda, oh God, oh God, I was hoping you wouldn't call me.

**YOUNG CLARINDA**  Why? Why didn't you call me?

**SHERRY**  Because, I knew if you told me, it would be true.

[*Hangs up phone.*]

**CLARINDA**  Daddy used to comb his hair straight back when he got out of the shower. My mama didn't like it that way. She'd always run her fingers through it and mess it up, making it not so every-hair-in-place.

[*Approaches platform as if it is the casket.*]

The last thing Mama did, before they closed the casket, was reach in and mess up his hair.

[*Mimes that action.*]

Things were bad. They were really bad. But, to make matters worse, we couldn't find my father's will. I knew he had a will. He was a *historian*. He was detail-oriented. He was Department Chair at the University. He had a will. I just had to find it. Wasn't with his lawyer. Wasn't in the safety deposit box. I was turning the house upside down, running from room to room looking. And while I was doing this, this friend of mine, from high school, [*whispered*] who I never really liked anyway, came over to console me. *Kiki!* Ugh. Don't you just hate that name? Kiki talks in this . . .

**KIKI**  [*A screechy falsetto voice*] . . . real high squeaky voice.

**CLARINDA**  And, in some bizarre effort to console me—

**KIKI**  —she is telling me about this affair that she's having with a married man with two kids.

**CLARINDA**  Now, this is a crisis. My dad is *dead*. My mother is going on and on about how she's going to become this *homeless* person, and Kiki is talking to me—

**KIKI** —in her real high squeaky voice!

**CLARINDA** Something snapped. Kiki, Kiki! Kiki—HUSH! I'm sorry. I've got to go lay down!

I slam the door in her face and *hide* in my old room. And while I was in there *hiding* from Kiki—I found it! I *found* my father's will. There, in the bottom of a big dresser drawer, in my old room, inside my girlie 1970s Broyhill chest of drawers—there it was.

[*Kneels, picks a stack of notebooks.*]

Buried under forty or fifty *Fish and Game* magazines, shotgun shells, arrowheads, pocketknives, a pair of binoculars, and a camera that didn't work. There it was, tucked inside a college-ruled, spiral-bound notebook. I gave the will to Mother, which calmed her down considerably.

[*Opens a notebook and reads a bit, looks up with surprise.*]

My father kept journals. I waddled myself, heavy with child, down onto the blue shag carpet of my old room. And I read these notebooks cover to cover for three days—stopping only to pee.

[*IMAGE: College-ruled spiral-bound notebook circa 1968.*]

My father kept journals for over *twenty* years and none of us knew. They dated back to the late sixties when we were kids. Mostly he talked about his hunting trips. As a historian, he was very scientific. He'd note: the date, the time, the temperature, who went with him, what caliber of gun they toted, what they had for lunch, the names of the dogs, and how each performed.

Sometimes he'd *wander* . . . just kind of *wander* off the topic. He'd talk about places he'd pass through and *people* he met on the way. And, in the later notebooks, in the '80s, he talked more about traveling, and lecturing, and about us. Finding these notebooks was just like finding a part of him, a tangible piece that I could hold on to. I can look in here and see that on a windy Thursday, in 1967, he went hunting.

**DADDY** Didn't get anything, but he had a good time anyway.

**CLARINDA** He ate watermelon, and it was good. This is my favorite entry:

[*IMAGE: Daddy's handwritten entry.*]

November 5, 1986

**DADDY** Today, I am fifty-five years old. I had a wonderful time. Went to Valle Crucis to look at some property along the Watauga River with two friends and had a pleasant time. The staff and students had a birthday party for me at the Center for Appalachian Studies. Visited with a good friend. Talked with some people and came home.

**CLARINDA** I think that is the fear—when you lose someone you love—you think you're gonna *forget*. And, I didn't want to forget anything about my daddy. So, after my precious daddy died, I went out and I bought myself a college-ruled, spiral-bound notebook.

[*Holds up a newer notebook.*]

I started writing down everything I could remember about my childhood. Sometimes in the middle of the night I'd hop up and grab my notebook 'cause I'd remember tiny things about him like . . . his index finger was crooked right here, and when he laughed he didn't make noise—he just shook his shoulders. And, though I am named for his beloved grandmother, Deborah Clarinda, he always used to call me *Deb* or *Debber dear*. When he'd come home from a trip, he'd bring me a little something with the number *three* because my birthday is March third.

My writing isn't scientific or historically accurate and I am quite certain that I *wander*. Daddy's journals, which I found by *accident*, give me a lot of comfort, and teach me to slow up some, and notice people and things, on the road to where I'm *going*. I can tell you this—if my house is ever burning somebody will have to hold me down to keep me from going after these college-ruled, spiral-bound notebooks penned in my father's scrawling hand.

[*SOUND: Country song.*]

My very first memory is in a car with my daddy, I was two. My brother, Tyler, had just been born, and my father was driving me from Dubuque, Iowa—where he taught history at the university—back to the farm in Georgia to stay with my grandparents. I remember, it was this enormous white car with blue vinyl interior.

[CLARINDA *climbs into passenger seat.*]

It had a blue steering wheel, with a silver horn, and a *radio* in the dash. Daddy told me the radio was really a "*secret telephone*" and I could talk to anybody I wanted to just by pushing the buttons. And, there was this handle on the dashboard so you could *hang on!* This was back before they had seat belts, so, anytime we'd come to a stop sign, or a curve in the road, my father would fling out this enormous arm covered in strawberry blond hair and freckles. He'd brace me with his massive palm and say,

**DADDY** "Hang on, Debber, dear! Hang on!"

**CLARINDA** And, I'd say,

**TODDLER CLARINDA** I'm a hanging, Daddy. I hangin'.

[*Exits car.*]

**CLARINDA** My parents were very different, dangerous in a way. They were the first ones, in either of their families, to leave Murray County, Georgia, and get a college education. Let alone, a PhD.

**DADDY** Deb, there's alotta folks don't know what to make a me . . . [*Snicker*] I reckon it's 'cause I got book learning, and walking around sense. There's nothing more dangerous than an educated redneck.

**CLARINDA**  They threw lots of parties, and there were always interesting people hanging around our house. Writers, artists, scholars, and, really dramatic people— wearing long scarves, drinking wine. I loved it. My brother, Tyler, hated it. He hid out in the basement where he taught himself to play the guitar, the banjo, the dulcimer, the piano, the harmonica, and the trumpet. So, while Tyler was in the basement becoming this musical prodigy, I was upstairs at the feet of the grown-ups—*eavesdropping*.

No doubt, they were not the same as my friends' parents. They kind of treated my brother and me like short adults. For instance, the first movie they ever took us to see was not *Bambi*, not *Dumbo*, but *DOCTOR ZHIVAGO*!

[*SOUND: A song such as "Somewhere My Love" from* Doctor Zhivago]

I will never forget, as long as I live, Omar Sharif with those icicles in his beard, running through that house, busting out those windows so he can watch Julie Christie ride away . . . ooooh. It had a profound effect on me. And I'm convinced *Dr. Zhivago* is responsible for the phenomenon I call

[*SOUND: Movie Moment bell.*]

"Movie Moments." That's when a scene in your life reminds you exactly of a scene in a movie. Does that happen to y'all too?

My parents liked to go on long drives. Just get in the car and go, go, GO! I had seen every single *historical* marker in the southeastern United States by the—

**8-YEAR-OLD CLARINDA**  [*Doing a 3-finger Girl Scout pledge sign*]—age of eight!

**CLARINDA**  And, on these drives, they'd always have me

**8-YEAR-OLD CLARINDA**  Ask for directions, or pay the money at the coffee shop. It taught me to talk to anyone. And anyone will talk to me. I have one of those faces.

**CLARINDA**  In a crowded park, if a small child is lost, he finds me. Complete and total strangers will tell me their entire life stories. It's not my fault; it's the way I was brought up. My parents liked to have what they called:

**8-YEAR-OLD CLARINDA**  "Cultural experiences."

**CLARINDA**  Oh, that doesn't mean you have to go to the opera; you can have a cultural experience just driving across town to get a barbecue sandwich. You just have to be *awake, aware, engaged* in life. Most of my going, at an early age, was in the back seat of this . . .

[*Points to the "car."*]

. . . white, 1966 VW Beetle Bug. Whew, I remember this back seat.

[*SOUND: Car sounds.*]

**6-YEAR-OLD CLARINDA**  This is my daddy. He teaches history at the university. He is six foot three inches tall and has red hair and a red beard and he is soooooo BIG he can barely fit inside this car. This is my mama.

At 2:30, when all the mamas come to pick up, she's the prettiest one. She has big hair, and earrings. She wears pantsuits. This is my brother, Tyler. He's two years younger than me. [*To* TYLER.] AND I AM THE BOSS OF HIM! We drive all over having [*Stumbles*] "kultorul exsperiences." I don't mind it. Tyler, he don't like it; he gets bored. He always brings magnetic tic-tac-toe and Dr. Seuss books. And while we're driving along, Daddy pats Mama on the leg—like that—and rubs it and calls her, "Darlin'." We drive all over the place. But, I don't mind it. Sometimes, we take picnics and, I've been wading in every creek between North Carolina and Georgia. Sometimes, we drive so far that we stop and buy toothbrushes and spend the night at a motel! I don't mind it, except when Tyler gets car-sick. Him and Mama gets car-sick. Me and Daddy, we don't never get car-sick. We got cast-iron stomachs! And, all the time we're driving, they're always talking to us about who we're named for, and where we're from, and where wars were fought, and where Indians are buried!

[*Falls over in backseat like a dead Indian—then pops up.*]

**6-YEAR-OLD CLARINDA**   And, Mama's always saying:

**MAMA**   [*A mellifluous southern drawl*] Children, sit up straight, pay attention, look out the window. Look out at the world.

[*Exits the car.*]

**CLARINDA**   I always try to. I sure do love to go. I remember the only time my mother ever slapped me. We were on a drive, of course, and I was fighting with my brother Tyler in the back seat.

[*Enters the car, in the backseat. CLARINDA, as a child, kicking her brother.*]

**6-YEAR-OLD CLARINDA**   Get on your side of the line!

**CLARINDA**   And I said the word

**6-YEAR-OLD CLARINDA**   "n-i-g-g-e-r"

**CLARINDA**   And my MOTHER reached across the seat and . . . [*Gasps, reacts to a slap, holds cheek.*]

**DADDY**   Hold on there, Charlotte, she doesn't even know what that means.

**MAMA**   Well, Carl, she's about to find out!

[*Exits car.*]

**CLARINDA**   Then she told me the story of when she was pregnant with me. It was the year they integrated the University of Georgia. Daddy was working on his doctorate in history and Mama was a journalism major. And, her fellow journalism major, Charlayne Hunter, now Charlayne Hunter Gault, the first black lady to attend the University, was getting military escorts to class. I was born at the Catholic Hospital there in Athens. That was back before they let the fathers come into the room with the mothers. So,

Daddy's in the lobby—waiting. And Mama, who was just twenty, was back there screaming all by herself. And the only person from the journalism department to visit Mama and me in the hospital was Charlayne Hunter.

[*Returns to the backseat.*]

**CLARINDA**   So that's how come my mama reached across the seat and—

[CLARINDA, *six years old, feels the impact of the slap, gasps and holds her cheek. Exits car.*]

My parents, the college professors, living a life of the mind. They did not judge based on race, creed, religious affiliation, or sexual orientation. What mattered to them was if a person was good at their job, kind, and intellectually curious. They believed in everybody's right to privacy. My daddy was "Don't ask, don't tell" way before Bill Clinton. There are some things even "educated" rednecks are uncomfortable talking about. Mama is ten years younger than Daddy and was not afraid to hit the "touchy" subjects head-on. I'll never forget when she gave me the talk . . . you know, *the* talk. I was twelve years old . . .

[CLARINDA *becomes twelve, gangly, walks around the platform.*]

. . . and mortified as my mother knocked on my bedroom door.

[*She then adopts the very lady-like walk of* MAMA]

Now, Charlotte is an intellectual. So, Charlotte is prepared.

[*Picks up pink box.*]

She comes in carrying this PINK! cardboard box and she sits down beside me on the bed and we open up the lid of the PINK! cardboard box. Inside, there are sanitary items: Tampax, Kotex and one of those little belts. [*Speaking directly to a female audience member.*] Do *you* remember those? We go over the pamphlet with diagrams of the reproductive organs. We talk about the menstrual cycle, and how all of this will be starting soon, and finally she closes the lid on the PINK! cardboard box:

**MAMA**   Clarinda, sex is wonderful. It's just one of the best things in life. And because it is so wonderful, well you just don't want to go around having it with just anybody. Now, I'm not saying that you have to be married to him, but you should love him. He should *matter* to you. More importantly, YOU should *matter* to him. That's what makes it so wonderful. So, if you decide you are so crazy about some boy that you absolutely must have sex, you must promise to come to me first so we can get you the proper birth control. DO YOU UNDERSTAND ME?

**CLARINDA**   My best friend, Sherry, is the sister I never had. We have been best friends since the second grade when she brought a bunny rabbit to school for "Show and Tell." And it went to the bathroom . . . on my desk. All four years of high school, we were inseparable. I lived at her house or she lived at mine. Sherry inherited my *parents* who marched down to Watauga

County High School and changed her courses from Cosmetology to College Prep. They recognized genius when they saw it and they had that vested interest in educating rednecks. And I inherited Sherry's parents, Russell and Cosby Cornett. Sherry Lynn is a late-in-life baby. She snuck up on her mama, Cosby, well after forty. Cosby spoiled us rotten. She was a phenomenal cook, her kitchen never closed. And, her shoulder was always ready if you needed a good cry. But Cosby was my grandmother's age, so there was a definite generation gap going on.

[CLARINDA *becomes a teenager.*]

**TEENAGE CLARINDA**   Many a Friday night, you could find me in Sherry's den watching SHOCK! [*Scary laugh*] . . . *wah-hah-hah!* THEATRE—scary movies. I *hated* scary movies, but Sherry liked them and *she* was the boss of us. We'd sit up there in matching vinyl recliners watching SHOCK!—*wah-hah-hah!*—THEATRE, eating barbequed Fritos, chocolate icing from a can with two spoons, and drinking Diet Pepsi—

**CLARINDA**   —'cause that was back before they had invented Diet Coke and who can stand Tab?

**TEENAGE CLARINDA**   One night we were watching SHOCK—*wah-hah-hah!*—THEATRE and her mama, Cosby, came in . . .

**COSBY**   [*A soft sweet hillbilly voice*] Girls, I've got to talk to you, uh, I'm gonna run downstairs and get me a cup of uh coffee . . . I'll be right back.

**TEENAGE CLARINDA**   Sherry and I kinda looked at each other, 'cause she seemed so serious. Sherry said,

**SHERRY**   C'rinda, I bet she's gonna try and give us the talk. You know the sex talk!

**CLARINDA**   We started giggling because we were seniors in high school. By this time Sherry was already having sex and I was living vicariously through her.

[*Cosby returns.*]

**COSBY**   Girls, you know, I'm your Mama, and that I love you, and I wouldn't never tell you nothing that wont true. And you're fixing to leave me. You're fixing to go off into the big world, and go to the college. I need to warn you that they is thangs in this world that you have got to look out for . . . you've got to be very kerful and keep a close eye out . . . 'cause they look normal. But they're not. Girls, they is thangs in this world called, HOM-E-O-SEXUALS, and you've got to say that real fast or it will dirty up your mouth! You've got to be very kerful and not never let one get after ye, because if they do they will force ye to have . . . oral sex, and it will choke you. And you will die. It's God's way of punishing 'em.

**CLARINDA**  Now it's just all Sherry and I can do to hold it together. I mean we were expecting *where babies come from*. I elbowed Sherry under my breath and said, "If it's true about that oral sex part then you're a dead woman." But I am my parents' child, and I just had to ascertain *where* Cosby happened up on this information. "Cosby, who told you this?"

**COSBY**  I can see you don't believe me. You think you're so smart. Well! If you don't believe me, why don't you just go on down yonder and ask that man at the gas station?

**CLARINDA**  We're thinking: What man? *Which* gas station? What is she talking about? We never did get a *straight* answer from Cosby about the *mysterious* man at the gas station. Sherry and I did however become *fascinated* with this *idea* of this person, this man, "*out there*" with all the answers. Years from then, if we'd be lost or we just didn't know the answer to a question about the state of world affairs, Sherry'd say,

**SHERRY**  Well, C'rinda, I reckon we better stop and ask that man at the gas station.

**CLARINDA**  Back when I was growing up there actually was a MAN at the gas station.

[*IMAGE: Gas station attendant with bow-tie.*]

**CLARINDA**  *Full-service.* Remember that? He might be grungy and dirty, or he might be pristine in a little bow-tie. He'd change your oil, check your fluids, wash your windows, give you change for the Coca-Cola machine. He'd give you direction if you were lost. He was there for you. You could count on him. You could depend on the man at the gas station.

My daddy, my first dependable man, taught me to drive in the mountains of North Carolina, where I grew up. Daddy taught me how to drive in the *snow*.

**DADDY**  Deb should you ever find yourself in a fishtail spin NEVER slam on the brakes.

**CLARINDA**  He taught me how to bank just right in the curves. Winding mountain roads. Some weren't even paved—just rocks and dirt and ruts—bump-bump-bumping along. Those roads demanded respect. Those roads said, "Pay attention to me." My daddy taught me those roads.

After school, Sherry and I'd wheel into Shirley and Regan Exxon, that's back when it was still okay to go to Exxon before that whole Valdez mess, and . . . we didn't even have a BP station. An' . . . you didn't even have to *pay*. You'd just sign your daddy's name.

[*Rolls down car window, signs credit slip, and hands it back to the man.*]

Thank you! And *Daddy* would pay for it later! It was a *beautiful* system, and it is *gone*. It's gone forever. No man's coming to save the day. There is no one with all the answers. *Life* is *self-serve*.

[CLARINDA *exits the car.*]

Between my freshman and sophomore year of college, I had a great opportunity. I could go to Mexico with my daddy and a group from the university and get a semester's worth of college credits.

**CLARINDA**  We studied anthropologia, geografia, historia, y espanol! I wasn't remotely interested in any of these subjects and none of them applied to my major, but it gave me a chance to travel, and spend time with my daddy. The drawback was we had to *drive* down to Mexico in a university van. And, there were a lot of earthy anthropology majors on this trip.

[*SOUND: Waltz music.*]

Every pueblo we'd visit, my father would take me to the *plaza*—to the best restaurant. It was like a little date with my dad. In Oaxaca, we ate dinner overlooking the twinkling lights of the *zócalo*, the main square. Afterwards, we went down onto the plaza and *danced*.

[*Waltzing.*]

Daddy loved to dance. He wasn't the best dancer, but Mother used to say he had no fear of it, which made him fun.

[*SOUND out.*]

By the end of that summer, I'd had a really great time, spoke pretty passable Spanish, made new friends, Hane y Birhinia. That's Jane and Virginia for those of y'all who don't speak Spanish, and I have memories of my father that I will cherish always, especially the *dancing*.

When I got home from Mexico with Daddy, I was craving two things: a *cold* glass of milk and an American boy taller than me. There was one American boy over six feet tall I was especially interested in seeing. His name was Gary Culler, he had blond curly hair and I dated him at the end of my freshman year and I could not wait to get back to school and *date* him some more. But, before I started school, I had to go and visit my grandparents. I used to spend every summer with my grandparents on the farm. My grandparents came up through the Depression and it shaped their whole psyche. They had zero tolerance for laziness or waste. They didn't *believe* in credit. They thought the stock market was *evil*, and, *yeah*, see now . . . they mighta been right.

My grandmother, Willie Sue, a southern lady—who never appeared in public without lipstick and matching accessories—had me *convinced* there were "*rules of etiquette*" that a good little southern girl ought to follow. And, if I'd just adhere to the *rules*, I'd have a much easier time of it in life.

**CLARINDA**  [*Directly to the audience.*] We have done y'all a favor. We put my Grandmother's Rules right here in your program!

Hey, [*Insert name of stage manager here.*] _____?

**STAGE MANAGER**  [*The actual stage manager of the show, over the God Mic.*] Yes, Clarinda?

**CLARINDA**  [*To the audience.*] This is my stage manager _____. Y'all can say "hey."

[*Invariably the audience says, "Hey, _____."*]

[*Walks forward into the audience.*]

Honey, can I see your program for a minute?

[*Takes program from patron and flips through it. Then calls up to SM.*]

_____, What page are Grandmother's Rules on?

**STAGE MANAGER**  [*From the God Mic.*] Page_____.

**CLARINDA**  Thanks, honey.

[*She finds the page.*]

Oh, here they are. [*Reads a few rules from the following list.*]

Know how to set the table properly. which fork to use and when

Be nice to your help [they're doing your work]

Don't forget to tip [if you don't have the money to tip you don't have the money to go out]

Know basic sewing skills [how to thread a needle, use a thimble, pull a pull back through an open-weave sweater]

Clean as you go in the kitchen [makes life a whole lot simpler]

Separate your laundry for a really clean wash

Write thank you notes, birthday cards, and condolence cards promptly

Can't wear white before Memorial Day or after Labor Day

If you're going on a date after 6:00 pm you don't wear a watch. Because your gentleman is supposed to take care of you.

Your shoes, your belt, and your bag should always match

Buy one good dress instead of three trendy ones

Always wear clean underwear and panties and bra that match

Return phone calls promptly, and you must go out with the first boy who calls and invites you to the dance [I hated this rule basketball players never call first]

Don't be the first to arrive at a function or the last to leave

Fix your hair and your face when you go to town, you never know who you're gonna run into

Dress up when you travel, you never have a second opportunity to make a first impression

Hold your shoulders back and your tummy in

Remember you are as good as anybody, but better than none

Be nice to old people . . . you will be old one day

[*On the way back up to the stage,* CLARINDA *ad-libs with the audience: "My Grandmother Willie Sue lived until she was ninety-six! She knew a thing or two. So y'all ought to take these home. Get a magnet—put 'em up on your fridge. I hope they help you out."*]

[*She returns to the stage.*]

**CLARINDA**   While I was on my visit with my grandparents, Sherry called,

[*SOUND: Phone rings.*]

and she told me that this beautiful blond boy, Gary, that I had been dating . . . had . . . been in an . . . *accident*. His Jeep flipped over on the way home from a concert . . . He was dead. I was in shock. No, no, no! This is not right. I'm supposed to date him in three days. I grab the keys to my daddy's four-wheel-drive Ford Bronco, and decide to go for a drive. Big Mistake.

[*IMAGE: Creek.*]

[*SOUND: Small river.*]

[CLARINDA *gets into the car. It is a bumpy ride.*]

[*SOUND: Throughout following there are multiple layered sounds to create the thud of hitting a log and car being submerged in water.*]

Now, in the country we don't put a bridge over every little creek that runs through every little pasture. You just find a shallow place and drive on through. But remember I had been gone all summer and it had rained a lot. I found my usual little crossing place, drove in, *hit* a log and began to *sink*. Then, I did something that was not very bright, I *opened* the door. Water came rushing in. My granddaddy called a wrecker. We watched as they pulled my father's beloved Ford Bronco out of the water.

My daddy *loved* that car. When he died we seriously considered getting a backhoe, digging a big hole in the woods and *burying* him at the wheel of that Bronco. For weeks after my *accident* in the creek, when you sat in that car, the upholstery which was still wet would go "*squish-squish*." You know what? My daddy never said a word to me about it. And all I could think about was that beautiful blonde boy Gary, looking down at me laughing as I rode around going "*squish-squish*" for him.

I tell that story for what might have been. I really liked him—Gary. He was from a real nice family—we had a lot in common. You never know; I could've married him. Instead, I married his roommate. Patrick. We met at the funeral. It was a relationship forged in grief and *doomed* from the start. We didn't have a single thing in common, save our sadness over Gary's death. I stayed with him for nine years, I don't know why. I really did try, 'cause my daddy used to say,

**DADDY**   Deb you don't just toss people aside 'cause they have problems.

**CLARINDA**   [*To the* STAGE MANAGER.] Hey_____, can you bring up the house lights a little so we can see who we got here tonight?

**STAGE MANAGER**   Sure, Clarinda.

[*HOUSE LIGHTS up.*]

[CLARINDA *crosses down, sits on the edge of the stage, and talks directly to the audience.*]

**CLARINDA**   Hey, y'all are pretty good looking! [*Singles out a spiffy patron*] Some people still dress up for the theatre, y'all give her some applause. Okay now. [*Scans the house.*]

If you're eighteen to thirty-five years old, and you *believe*, in your youthful exuberance, that you can *change* the person you're with, that through your *love* and *devotion*, you, and you alone, can heal their childhood scars and get them to *stop* smoking, *stop* drinking or any other destructive behavior . . . *leave* them now and save yourself *thousands and thousands of dollars in therapy and legal fees!*

[*She returns to stage.*]

My first husband was what you'd call a *functional* alcoholic, worked hard, never hit me, hardly ever raised his voice. He was just sort of *absent* from the proceedings. And no amount of my optimistic, "*Hey things are good, the glass is half-full!*" could rouse him from his profound, inner sadness. Try as I might, I could not wake him up. He did not like to *go*. So I *went* without him, *go*-ing on the road to *do* theatre, *go*-ing to *see* theatre, *go*-ing to acting class, *go*-ing to opening nights. There were plenty of men around. Many intelligent, beautiful, talented, fantastic, homosexual men of the *theatre!* But I knew something was not *right. Something's missing. Need something here. Maybe a baby would wake him up! I know I'll have a baby!*

It was a *planned* pregnancy. I *planned* it all. Planned and executed the cutest nursery, with a *Jungle Book* theme. Good for a boy—or a girl with *spirit*. I had a "birth *plan*," no drugs. I planned to have my baby *au naturale*. And, I did too. I had a baby without Tylenol! But, you can't *plan* everything.

July 1988, a month before Daddy died; a hot sticky night in Atlanta. Closing night of *Steel Magnolias*—a party, a celebration! I'm there in my "Shelby" costume—the pink Laura Ashley dress I wore in the show. Seven months pregnant and you couldn't even tell it. During the party Patrick *disappeared*; I couldn't find him *anywhere*. Finally, I went into the men's restroom and found him on his knees mopping up blood. He was so drunk he didn't realize the blood was gushing from his own face. He'd fallen and busted his chin on the porcelain sink.

Around midnight I rushed into the emergency room of Piedmont Hospital in midtown Atlanta looking for someone to sew him up. And, the nurses were incredibly *rude* to him. This middle-aged nurse jammed a wad of packing into his face and told us to . . .

**RUDE NURSE**   WAIT!

**CLARINDA**   I was outraged! How could they be so rude to *my* husband? And *then* it hit me. It hit me like a bucket of ice water being *dumped* right *over* my head. To them, he was nothing but a common *drunk* and they had seen him every Saturday night of their careers. *Oh my god, you're an alcoholic. What are we going to do?*

He *insisted* that it was just a hand-to-mouth thing and if *I* would only keep more *non*-alcoholic beverages around the home it wouldn't be a problem. For the next two *years*, I made more iced-tea than any *five* good southern women put together, bought cases of Cokes, and had bottled water delivered to the door *way* before that was vogue. And guess what?

[*She looks at audience, and shakes her head—as if to say—"how could I have been so stupid?"*]

August 1988, the day my daddy died to be exact.

[*She gets in the car, sits in the passenger seat.*]

Patrick is driving me to get a sonogram. I look over at him in the car and think to myself very clearly, "*My daddy is dead. You are not remotely capable of filling his shoes. You are not the man of my life.*" I knew it for sure.

[*She makes a notation in her new journal.*]

Mama said the last long drive they took together was through the beautiful mountains of West Virginia. Daddy bought two things on that trip: a present for Mama, a book, Joseph Campbell's *The Power of Myth*, and a great big stuffed rabbit with green overall britches and a hat, for his new grandbaby. Mama told me she walked in on Daddy, day before he died, and found him next to the fireplace having a *conversation* with Rabbit.

[*Picks up her own green journal and uses it as "the rabbit."*]

DADDY    You're a fine looking Jack-Rabbit! Yes, you are—a purty fine looking hare.

CLARINDA    September 16, 1988. Two weeks after Daddy died, I was sitting in the nursery rocking and I wrote this.

[*Singing*]

CLARA WAS A-COMING
BUT SHE HADN'T GOT HERE YET.
CLARA WAS A-COMING
BUT SHE HADN'T GOT HERE YET.
OH, GRANDDADDY, HE LEFT EARLY
JUST TO CHECK AND SEE
IF CLARA WAS A-COMING
AND HOW LONG THAT SHE MIGHT BE.
HE PASSED YOU ON THE WAY HERE
HE STOPPED TO HOLD YOUR HAND
HE SAID, "OH, IT'S CLARA THAT'S A-COMING."
BIG ROSS, HE STRETCHED OUT HIS HUGE HAND
AND PATTED YOUR SOFT RED HAIR
AND WHISPERED, "CLARA I'M-A-LEAVING
BUT I'LL WATCH YOU FROM OVER THERE."

[*She picks up her journal and writes.*]

September 29, 1988. My labor starts. Mama calls.

[*SOUND: Phone ring.*]

**MAMA**   Clarinda, what are you doing?

**CLARINDA**   Well, Mother, I've done twelve loads of laundry, finished the baby's curtains, organized the nursery. I've been vacuuming, and washing windows.

**MAMA**   Oh my, you're nesting! I'm on the way!

**CLARINDA**   Mother hops in her car and drives from Boone, North Carolina, to Atlanta, Georgia—normally a six-hour drive. She made it in four and half. She *flew* over South Carolina. Mama arrives at West Paces Ferry Hospital about 3 A.M., and walks into my "birthing suite."

[*SOUND: Kitarō—"Crystal Winds".*]

I'm in the bathtub with the lights turned out. My registered nurse-midwife is pouring water over my belly to soothe me, she has Kitarō music playing on the sound system.

**MAMA**   Well . . . things have certainly changed since I did this.

**CLARINDA**   Despite her grief, my mama was a trooper. She's in bed with me when the baby comes, her head right beside mine, making me laugh. The midwife is telling Mama to "*hush*," and me to "*breathe.*" She catches the baby as she comes into the world and hands her to Mother.

**MAMA**   Oh, Clarinda, what a beautiful girl-child. Welcome, Clara Tyler.

[CLARINDA *exits the hospital, crosses DS.*]

**CLARINDA**   I made such plans! But you can't plan your baby.

[*IMAGE: CLARA baby picture with a bow.*]

[*SOUND: VO Men and Women.*]

| MATURE WOMEN: | GAY MEN: |
|---|---|
| She's such a good baby. How old is she? Just precious. | I got her these shoes. Those eyes. Big blue eyes. Look at that outfit! This smocking is done by hand. |
| **MATURE WOMEN:** | **GAY MEN:** |
| She looks like your daddy. Look at that strawberry hair. She's not sitting yet? | Oh, if you take her picture next to this railing every year on her birthday, you can see how much she's grown! |

She's not sitting yet?

My wonderful *theatrical* family—the gay men with impeccable style; and my dear theatre mothers, the older actresses in my life—kept Clara in *swishy* ruffled outfits. She *never* appeared in public without a great big bow. Cosby was totally wrong about *hom-e-o-sexuals*. They weren't after me for sex. They just wanted to *dress* me and my baby.

For the next two years, I immerse myself in my baby and my career. Somebody has to make a living. Patrick gets fired for being *difficult*. I take any *union* acting job I can scrounge up. I'm mooooving fast. But, there are times when the universe just reaches out and says, *"Girl, you have got to make a change."*

January 1, 1991. I'm driving my dilapidated 1986 gunmetal grey Plymouth Horizon. The first car I bought myself and at this point it had seen better days, it bore the bumps, taps, and kisses of my careless youth.

[*She sits in driver's seat.*]

Clara and I are on the one straight stretch of road between Atlanta and my grandparents' farm in Murray County, Georgia.

[*IMAGE: Highway.*]

I'm zipping along US 411, clipping along about sixty miles an hour, and the hood of my car—flips up, *cracks* the windshield, wraps around, and *dents* in the roof over my head!

[*SOUND: Car crash. Baby crying. Sounds of the car pulling off and driving off during the following. Layering again as before.*]

[*To* CLARA] Clara! Hang on, baby! We're okay. Mama's gonna fix it.

[*To the audience.*]

My daddy taught me how to drive in *adverse* conditions. I know what to do. Don't panic. I *ease* my foot on the brake, *ease* off onto the shoulder, get out, check on Clara, tie the hood down with some twine and I *limp* this poor beat-up car the last few miles home.

[*She adjusts the rear view mirror, and sings to* CLARA.]

[*Singing*] IN A CABIN, IN THE WOODS
LITTLE MAN BY THE WINDOW STOOD
LONG CAME A RABBIT HOPPING BY
KNOCK, KNOCK ON MY DOOR.

You want your Rabbit? Here's Bunny.

[*SOUND: Fade out on crying baby.*]

[*Singing*] HELP ME, HELP ME, THE RABBIT CRIED
I JUST NEED A PLACE TO HIDE

[*SOUND: Car stopping.*]

COME LITTLE RABBIT, COME INSIDE

[*She gets out of the car, picks up* CLARA, *walks downstage rocking her.*]

I'LL TAKE CARE OF YOU.

We're here. We're okay now. We're home.

My granddaddy, ever dependable, was waiting on the front porch when we pulled up. He took one look at my car, one look at me and I *cried*, because I could.

The next morning, my granddaddy, Carl, takes Clara and me out and he buys *us* a brand new Chevrolet *Cavalier*. He pays *cash*, because he doesn't *believe* in credit. That Cavalier was a teal color and it was my favorite thing. I had that car for ten years and never once scratched it. Because, I knew for *sure*, it would be the one and only *free* car that I would ever receive.

[*She picks up a piece of chalk/red clay.*]

Every time I go home to see my grandparents, I stop by my father's grave and pick up a couple of rocks from there around the head stone . . . that good ol' red Georgia clay.

[*She kneels at her father's grave.*]

Daddy, I cannot save this man. But, I *can* raise Clara. Red, Georgia, clay. This is the same clay I used to draw hopscotch on my grandmother's sidewalk as a little girl.

[*She crosses back to the car.*]

I always keep a couple pieces of this clay in the ashtray of my car. It keeps me safe. It protects me. And it keeps me on the road to where I'm going.

[*BLACKOUT. IMAGE: Red clay road. SOUND: upbeat country music female artist such as Nanci Griffith. END OF ACT I.*]

# ACT II

[*Lights up.* CLARINDA *claps her hands.*]

**CLARINDA**    Come on Clara, it's time to brush teeth. We gotta do it baby. Open up.

[*She sings a song such as "If All The Raindrops" from Barney and Friends, something that ends with her making a wide mouth:*]

*Aah aah aaah aaah aaah aaah aannnh*
*Aanh aanh aannnh.*

Ppppppppppppbbbbbbbbbb. POP! Make a big MOUTH. BIG mouth like Mommy. Sip of water and spit. Try to SPIT. COME ON, baby—Spit Like A Big Girl!

I know, *spitting* is typically frowned on in polite society. But, for Clara and me, it became a thing of joy. It meant we had buckled down, done the hard work, and now it was playtime.

[*She sits on the platform, handing toy blocks to "Clara".*]

[*To* CLARA] Here, Clara, put it up. [*to audience*] Information comes dribbling in . . . [*To* CLARA] Let's make a tower. [*To audience*] It doesn't hit all at once, it's a gradual process. [*To* CLARA] Can you put it on top? [*To audience*] Clara was maybe eighteen months old. We were at a party. She was sitting up, but not very well. So, we're on the floor and I had pillows propped up all around her and she kept tipping over, without putting out her little hand to brace herself. This man laughed.

**MAN**   Whoa, the gravitational pull in this room is amazing.

**CLARINDA**   Once, in the grocery store, a cashier said:

**CASHIER**   What's wrong with her?

**CLARINDA**   For the first couple of years, to the outside world, I'd say, "She'll be fine; she's just a little slow to walk." But I was doing what I was raised to do: RESEARCH. Reading everything I could.

Sept. 30, 1991. Clara's third birthday! I take the cake out of the oven to cool, blow up balloons and hang streamers. Clara and I go out to the mailbox.

[*Walks upstage holding hands with* CLARA.]

Oh, look here's a card from Granddaddy, with a US Savings Bond! That'll be worth a lot by the time you go to college.

[*Returns to platform/house.*]

There was a thick envelope from Scottish Rite Children's Hospital. [*To* CLARA] Here you want this?

[*She hands* CLARA *a block, opens the envelope and reads.*]

A comprehensive assessment: genetics, neurology, speech, physical and occupational therapy reports.

Clara Tyler Cullen. Date of Birth: 9.30.88, age: 35 months. Current functioning: 6–12 months. Patient has already received high level of early intervention. "Significant motor, cognitive and developmental delays." IQ: 57. Twenty-five spoken words. Unlikely patient will progress past twenty-four months in most areas.

[CLARINDA *stands quickly, and slams the report closed. She knocks down the block tower with a CRASH!*]

I need to ice the cake. I should change her dress and put a bow in her hair; people will be coming over.

[*She crosses to the "hospital" area with file folder and knocks on the back of the platform.*]

[*IMAGE: Hospital corridor.*]

Ma'am, ma'am, here's her reports. Should we go back?

[*A pre-recorded voice of the* HOSPITAL NURSE *answers.*]

**NURSE**   [VO] Can't you see you are not my only patients? I'll get to you when I can.

**CLARINDA**   Well, our appointment was for over an hour ago, and she's not very good at waiting. [*To* CLARA] Okay Clara, this is the last cracker. [*To* NURSE] How much longer?

**NURSE**   [VO] I said, I'll GET TO YOU!

**CLARINDA**   Lady, lady—look at me. Yesterday was her third birthday and I got a letter in the mail from this hospital. It was not a card with puppies on it. It said this child will never drive a car, she will never go to college, she will never get married. We will be *lucky* if she gets to the cognitive level of a *two*-year-old. So . . . I really *need* you to be *nice* to me. *Okay? Please?*

**NURSE** [VO] Okay.

[*Leaves hospital, dropping file folder, crossing DSC.*]

**CLARINDA** My ol' daddy had a saying:

**DADDY** Deb, you've got to wake up every morning, strap on your armor, go out yonder, and *slay* the dragons!

**CLARINDA** My life with doctors had just begun. We saw doctor after doctor—neurologists, and genetics people. Some were kind, others had *God*-like attitudes, but all of them asked me these questions. They wanted every detail of pregnancy, birth, and development.

**DOCTOR** [*A condescending voice*] How does Clara compare with a "typically developing" child?

**CLARINDA** She's my only baby. So how would I know? You're the one with all the *initials* after your name—how 'bout you tell me?

And tests! They all ordered tests: blood tests, EEG, MRI, DNA, triple-banded chromosomal studies. Normal. All her tests were *normal*. But, she was not. No diagnosis, no number, no code for the insurance. This world is not an easy place for those who don't fit the mold. And the biggest minds I could find all stood around my baby and scratched their heads.

**MALE DOCTORS** [VO] Clara. Female. Patient ID 25067841. Normal gestation. No birth trauma. Neurological problems of unknown etiology.

**CLARINDA** Something's wrong with her brain. We don't know *what*. We don't know *where* it came from. We don't know *why*.

[*IMAGE: Clouds moving. SOUND: Wind, gentle.*]

[CLARINDA *climbs to the top of the platform.*]

I get a picture sometimes—in my mind—of angels hovering with Clara in their arms—ready to bring her into the world. Not sweet, fat, cherubs, these angels are big and fierce and they are *lifting* the roofs off houses . . . *searching* for a home for Clara.

**ANGELS** Oh no, don't give her to that one, she'll fall apart. No. No. No. Oh . . . look. See that big red-headed gal? She looks like she can *hang*. Give her to her!

**CLARINDA** The hardest thing about having a child with special needs is not the child. It's dealing with the doctors, the insurance companies, the *bureaucracy*. I could spend all day, *every* day, on the phone, or at the computer working on all things Clara. If I give up acting, I'm pretty positive I could get a job in a doctor's office. Every service, every activity comes with a mound of paperwork. A big chunk of my life is dealing with *bureaucrats*!

[*Walks upstage, gets in line, forms in her hand.*]

And, their *receptionists* . . .

[*She hands the* HOSPITAL NURSE *a form.*]

Here's her form.

**NURSE**  [VO] You didn't fill in this box. Do it again.

**CLARINDA**  I didn't fill in that box because she doesn't have a diagnosis.

**NURSE**  [VO] Do you have her Medicaid card?

**CLARINDA**  Yes, here's her Medicaid card. We also have private insurance. Do you want that card?

**NURSE**  [VO] You'll have to reschedule, we only see Medicaid on Tuesdays.

**CLARINDA**  What?

**NURSE**  [VO] You'll need to reschedule.

**CLARINDA**  [*Angry, but trying to keep it together.*] Look, I realize you see Medicaid cases today. The lady explained that to me when she made this appointment. And I told her we have the *other* coverage, and y'all scheduled us for today, and we're here. So, please, just see her today.

**NURSE**  [VO] We can't.

**CLARINDA**  Why not?

**NURSE**  [VO] It's not our policy.

[CLARINDA *reaches her breaking point.*]

**CLARINDA**  I don't care about your policy. I just care about her being *seen*. And yes, we have the other insurance coverage, but *she* has Medicaid. So you can see her, too! She has a special *kind* of Medicaid, named for a little girl who *DIED*, while her parents tried to get a bill passed through Congress, waiting around for someone like you to *stamp* the *form*! So, go get her chart, open that door, and take us back there to see the doctor. *NOW!!!!!!!!!!!!!!!*

[*She regains her composure, as she watches the* NURSE *walk away. The* NURSE *returns.*]

Thank you.

[*Drops file folder and calls to the* STAGE MANAGER'*s booth.*]

_____, can we have a little bit of house lights?

[*HOUSE LIGHTS to half. She sits at the edge of the stage.*]

I'd like to *apologize* to all the medical, dental, and hospital professionals I've screamed at over the years. I realize you were *just doing your jobs.*

[*Starts to go but stops and sits again.*]

But, see, that's the problem: you were *just* doing your job and not one jot *more* to make her life better. And, it's *my* job to be her strongest advocate, to get her the best there is, and to constantly *push* and *nudge* and *cajole* and ask *questions*; can't we do better? Isn't there another way? Surely, there is something more we could be doing for Clara?

I learned a lot from my southern upbringing but *nothing* prepared me for this fight. I don't enjoy being "Warrior Mommy." But the squeaky wheel gets the grease. Hollering and carrying on about the *Disabilities Act* and "*I will SUE you!*"—tends to get *results*. Nobody likes to see a normal-looking mother "flip-out" in public. So, sorry . . . thanks, just doin' my job.

[*HOUSE LIGHTS out. She returns to the stage.*]

So, *brushing* Clara's *teeth* has always been a huge ordeal because among her many symptoms is a thing called "*sensory integration dysfunction.*" Her senses are *intensified*. She is tactically defensive—sensitive to *touch* . . . Hey, you'd squirm too if someone tried to rub a bristly thing covered in goop all over your mouth. And in particular this sense of the "*vestibular*," that's the sense that tells us *where* our body is in space, where our feet are in relation to the ground.

[*Hangs a foot off the platform steps.*]

That vestibular . . . is just *off* in Clara.

The *job* of Clara can be daunting, but it's impossible to be depressed about Clara when you are in her physical presence. She's such a happy little soul. Like my daddy—Clara is . . . *just tickled* to be her.

**CLARA**  I eek! I nunch! I tidered. I good girl! Mmmore Juice! Shake. Shake. Shake. Kitty. Dog. Baby. Hug. Hug. Barney. WOW! I Bee-uu-ful. C-L-A-R-A. 450-6222. Yay, good job! Thumb up. I love you. Mama. Ok. Bye-Bye!

**CLARINDA**  She slows me down, and very often I have *perfect* days with my *imperfect* angel.

[*Picks up toy blocks and puts them away.*]

Years with top occupational therapists taught me to get *organized*, not an easy task for your [*Yogi Bear inflection*] *average* actress. These women taught me the importance of routine, consistency, using the same words, doing it the same way *every* day. And the three R's: repetition, repetition, repetition.

[*She sits with Clara in the "bathtub."*]

[*Miming the action.*] *Let's take a bath. Clara, wash. Face first. One—two—three.*

[*Points to underarm.*]

One—two—three. Switch hands. One—No. Big girl! Do you want to *live in a house with friends*? *Clara do it. Two—three. Yay! Good job!*

[*Leaves "bathtub" area, crossing DSC.*]

And they were right. It works! Now look, I don't go in much for organized religion, but, I am a *true* convert to the *church* of . . .

[*Throws hand in the air like a believer at a tent revival.*]

 . . . Occupational Therapy!

Clara is like a *glacier*. You can't *see* her *moving* in the water. But, through consistency, repetition, and sheer *will*, in two, three, or *ten* years her glacier has *moved*. And, though we now know she is only sixteen months old mentally, Clara is potty-trained—took *twelve* years. She can dress herself, bathe herself—and what is so amazing to me—after *years* of wrestling with her, sometimes, in the middle of the day, she'll say:

[*Returning to the bathroom area.*]

**CLARA**  Teeff. Teeff.

**CLARINDA**  She actually *wants* to brush her *teeth*.

[*Leaves bathroom area, crossing DS.*]

Clara and me, it was just the two of us. I HAD to get enough union acting jobs to keep the great Screen Actors Guild *health insurance plan*. [*secretively*] I have played a hooker on TV. Y'all, please don't judge me too harshly.

I beat the bushes and enlisted many great caregivers: Christine, the young actress who lived with us and took Clara to therapy appointments; Miss Darlene, the grandmother who took Clara overnight if I had, as actors often do, odd hours. And, Miss Vonzetta, who picked Clara up from the bus and got her addicted to

[*SOUND: "Wheel of Fortune Theme."*]

**CLARA**  Yay, R!

**CLARINDA**  I needed professionals. This is not a child who can be left with the teenager down the block. I got full custody of Clara in the divorce. Patrick got a visit every *other* weekend. So, every *other* weekend, I *dated*. Now I never really dated much in college, I just got engaged. After I got divorced, I started going out again. And I was having so much fun! This was the '90s. I was in my thirties—a time when most gals are looking to settle down, get married, have kids. Been there. Done that. I was looking for nothing but entertainment. I was pretty popular. Miss Charlotte said,

**CHARLOTTE**  Clarinda, being boy-crazy doesn't look quite so attractive at your age. You're not nineteen.

**CLARINDA**  But she also said,

**CHARLOTTE**  You never skip a stage in life.

**CLARINDA**  And I skipped dating in college. So, I decided to go back and pick that up. I date tall, pretty, self-absorbed young actors. Nobody serious, just FUN. A neighbor wanted to fix me up with an Italian chef.

**NEIGHBOR**  [*excited*] It's perfect. He is in town to do his internship with the Culinary Institute. He'll only be here for a few months. If it doesn't work out, you won't ever have to see him again.

**CLARINDA**   Okay. His name was Mario Giuseppe Phillipo Rosario Lamonto. Joey Lamonto! He was fun and outgoing. He cooked these fabulous meals! I think *once*, in everyone's life, you should have an *Italian* lover. But then . . . you've got to give them back, because, you might have *other* things you want to do with your life! We dated for a few months. I really liked him. I *never* introduce my every-*other*-weekend boyfriends to Clara. What is the point of introducing Clara to a leading man who wears eye cream? But I introduce Joey to Clara. Clara really likes him. But, Clara really likes *everybody*. He carries her around on his shoulders, plays with her. I never lift a grocery bag or open a door in his presence. One day, we were at my house watching TV, I got up to leave the room. I came back, he didn't see me, but I *saw* how he was looking at my child—like he absolutely HATED her. He turned, saw me see him, and he *knew* and I *knew* that it was *OVER*. So, back to dating boys. Harmless, fun, boys. I told all my friends:

[*She crosses to a local watering hole, chatting with girlfriends.*]

I'm never gonna get married again. I'm just gonna have boyfriends, drink wine, be mysterious, and write books.

[*Clinks a toast with girls. LIGHTS change. Leaves bar area, crossing downstage.*]

In the meantime—gotta keep working. My agent called me all excited. I had been cast in a small role in this movie with a prestigious Italian director, Carlo Carlei. But, they had done some switching and *now*, I was going to be playing the much bigger part of Matthew Modine's secretary. So, it was

**MAKE UP ARTIST**   [*Fey*] Rush, rush, rush!

**TEAMSTER**   [*Macho*] Get down to the set, lady.

**ITALIAN COSTUME DESIGNER**   [*Languid Italian accent*] Get coostumed.

**MAKE UP ARTIST**   Hurry. Hurry! Get made up.

**TEAMSTER**   We've got to get you to the set, lady.

**ITALIAN COSTUME DESIGNER**   CARLOooooo wants to speak to you.

**CLARINDA**   This little Italian man with curly hair and a beard, tells everyone else to . . .

**CARLO**   [*A thick Italian accent*] Clear de set! I muss a speak to Clareeenda alone.

**CLARINDA**   He holds my hands,

**CARLO**   Clareeenda, I must esxplain to you why there is so much confusion, and we are swish de parts. You see, we are re-write de part and she issa much bigger. So I say to dem for dese part I must have Clareenda, because, of all de girls we look at, you are my favorite. But, Clareenda, I'm a so sorry to tell you that now, we are CUT de part, and she is no so big. But I want to thank you for being inna my movie.

**CLARINDA**   So, we do my part and it's one tiny scene. Somebody, one of the producers, I think, whispered to me right before we roll—

**PRODUCER**   [*Authoritative*] You've secretly been in love with him all of your life.

[CLARINDA *nods knowingly.*]

**CLARINDA**   [*In a sexy voice*] So, I do the scene. CUT!

[*SOUND: Movie buzzer.*]

Carlo comes running over,

**CARLO**   No, no, no. Clareenda, that . . . is another movie. You are a con-cern for him only!

[*Nods apologetically.*]

**CLARINDA**   So, I do the scene. Cut!

[*SOUND: Movie buzzer.*]

**CARLO**   Clarinda that was a wonderful. Thank you for being inna my movie. Eh, you should come to Hollywooood!

**CLARINDA**   Well, bless your heart, that's awfully sweet of you. Tell you what, I'm doing a play right now, would you like to come?

**CARLO**   [*Amused*] Yes, Clarinda, tell me of a you play. I will come.

**CLARINDA**   Well, he *tried*. But Carlo never made it to my play. But my accountant, Ernie, came. Ernie may not be a big director, but he is a real fan of the theatre.

**ERNIE**   [*Overzealous, with a sibilance in his voice.*] I just love that Horizon Theatre because the actors are right there. They're so close to you. That play was great I'm telling you, you oughta take it to New York. To Broadway.

**CLARINDA**   That's very kind of you, Ernie. *Funny*, this Italian just told me I should go to Hollywood.

**ERNIE**   You had a good year. Let's get you a big refund so you can give it shot.

**CLARINDA**   And he did, he got me a huge refund. Well, it was huge to *me*. I couldn't move to L.A., *could I?* Funny thing, one of my theatre mothers ended up in Carlo's movie with a BIG part. The two of them really hit it off; they got together and decided it was time for me to . . .

**CARLO**   . . . go to Hollywoood.

**CLARINDA**   Carlo set me up interviews with Hollywood agents. Mother kept Clara. The plan was to scope it out, do the interviews and, if someone signed me, I'd come back with Clara in January for *pilot* season. So, I take my refund money and *fly* to L.A.—just to check it out.

[*Picks up a notebook, and reads from it.*]

November 24, 1994. Thanksgiving. Been in L.A. three weeks.

[*IMAGE: Venice Beach.*]

*Love* the weather. *Love* my Venice Beach sublet, but *missing* Clara. Got her the cutest outfit at Venice Beach with a matching *bow*. Found out best special ed services are in Beverly Hills, Malibu, and Santa Monica. Carlo let me use his Santa Monica address. [*secretively*] Had to pretend to be his mistress to get in to see Special Ed programs. Eh, if it helps find a good school for Clara. Think I'll open a *school* for phone manners. *Receptionists* at these talent agencies need my help. Once in to see the agents, they're perfectly nice, in a *slick* sort of way. Everyone here seems so happy to meet you and *eat lunch*. They just couldn't be sweeter or more supportive in that moment they're with you. But then they're on to the next person or thing. No one says "No," but they'll *maybe* you to death. Got invited to a dinner party. Don't much want to go.

[*Puts the journal down. Sits at dinner table.*]

But I did, and I had a good time. It was a great group: world travelers, writers, actors, a few scarves, and *nice* wine. But formal, place cards, no choice of seat-mates. I was seated across from a man in a starched, pink, button-down shirt. Very preppy. I figured him to be a stockbroker or an accountant. He's an actor! Fate? An actor named Googy Gress. That's his name, well it's not his real name, his real name is Francis Gress, Jr., but his whole family calls him by his nickname "Googy," and it's his stage-name with the union and it's on his American Express card. We talk. And he's nice.

**GOOGY**    What are you doing here?

**CLARINDA**    I'm here to interview with agents and I *might* come back for pilot season.

**GOOGY**    Do you have a commercial agent?

**CLARINDA**    No.

**GOOGY**    Tell you what, when you come back in January give me a call, I'll set you up an appointment with mine.

**CLARINDA**    And then . . . he did that thing that is so *rare* in Hollywood. He *actually* did what he said he would do. We became friends, no dating vibe, just friends. One night I was sitting across from him, and I was looking at him, *maybe* really looking *at* him for the first time. Not at the outside. Googy is a big guy. But I was looking *inside*, at his eyes. They're blue and sparkly. When he laughed he kind of . . .

[*Imitates GOOGY shaking his shoulders while laughing just like her daddy.*]

. . . I told him my daddy passed away. And he told me about his mama, from Alabama, who *died* when he was nineteen. Clarinda, slow down, this person is important. He asked me on a date. I showed up at his house, his roommate answered the door,

**ROOMMATE**   Googy is in Sarah's room playing.

**CLARINDA**   Huh? Sarah was the roommate's six-year-old child, exactly
Clara's age. Googy was on the floor coloring with Sarah. Beside them lay the
remnants of a tea party. Okay. So, he's great with kids. Is this a setup?

**GOOGY**   Well, Clarinda, what do you want to do on our first date?

**CLARINDA**   I don't know, Googy, whatever you want to do.

**GOOGY**   Okay, let's do my favorite thing.

[*She sits in passenger seat of the car.*]

**CLARINDA**   And he took me on a long *drive*. Up the coast, onto the curvy
roads of the Malibu Mountains. We stopped at a state park and went *wading*
in a creek. I think riding in his car was the first time I took a deep breath in
Los Angeles.

I didn't introduce him to Clara right away. Because, I was afraid. If he
rejected Clara then he rejected me and he was not just some every-*other*-
weekend boy. He mattered. I braced myself for inevitable rejection. Her
biological father couldn't even deal with her, but the day of reckoning
arrived. I take Clara to his house. There are stairs and she's having trouble
walking. Then a dog appears from nowhere and knocks her down and she
gets dirt all over her. She's a crying, drooling *mess*. Googy picks her up . . .

**GOOGY**   Well, hello. Your mom didn't tell me about your freckles. Piece of
cake, Clarinda. Can of corn.

**CLARINDA**   This is the man of my life. I knew it for *sure*. Clara found the
father she needed. We dated for a year, he asked me to marry him *three*
times. I kept stalling trying to give him an out in case Clara proved too
much. The third time he gave me this.

[*Shows off her ring.*]

And I said, yes. *Three* is my lucky number.

[*IMAGE: L.A. skyline. SOUND: An instrumental version of a song, such as "Night-swimming."*]

AUGUST 17, 1996. Googy and I were married on the top of the tallest
building in downtown L.A. with a 360-degree view all the way to the ocean.
Helicopters buzzed by throughout the ceremony. Clara called out
GOOOOGGGY, GOOOO . . . ggggeeee through the whole thing. I drank
champagne, kissed everybody, and danced slow.

For our honeymoon, we went to Europe for a whole month. I said, "Googy,
nobody takes a whole month of their life off to vacation."

**GOOGY**   We do.

**CLARINDA**   The last time I'd been away from home for that long was when I
went to Mexico with Daddy.

[*She picks up her journal. IMAGE: Piazza San Marco in Venice, Italy.*]

Aug. 30, 1996. Venice, Italy. Venezia! I love Venice. When we arrive the first thing we do is run down to look at the Piazza San Marco. It's two steps down from the sidewalk onto the Piazza through these arch things. The night we got there, there was an orchestra playing, and the second Googy and I step onto the Piazza . . .

[*SOUND: Movie Moment bell. SOUND: "Ode to Joy." The music, however, comes to a screeching halt.*]

Lest you think it was all roses—two-week mark of our trip—some internal mother alarm clock is going off. I have to speak to Clara. I have to hear her voice. This is 1996 and Europe is changing over to "touch-tone." While trying to use a calling card in a phone booth in Vienna, I *lost* it!

[*Steps up to SR side of the "car" as phone booth.*]

*Why* isn't this thing working? Aaah. I have to call Clara.

**GOOGY**   Clarinda, give it up. Relax. Be here with me.

**CLARINDA**   No! I have to speak to her.

**GOOGY**   Clarinda, she's fine. Let's go.

**CLARINDA**   Back up out of this phone booth right now or you and me are gonna have real trouble!

We had a huge fight. But, we did make up. It's not easy to be married to someone who is totally *awake, aware, engaged* in all aspects of your life. But, it is way more interesting and fun.

Googy is a rare man. He went from hanging out at swanky parties with movie stars to getting up early and watching *Barney* with Clara. When I'm working, Googy takes Clara on long drives and they eat breakfast in Palmdale or some such place, so I can sleep in.

Clara is so happy to be with whoever she's with, the only absent person she's ever *pined* for besides me is . . .

**CLARA**   Goooooooooooooooooooo-geeeeeeeeeeeeeeeee!

**CLARINDA**   It takes a village to raise any child. My *"Never say die! Won't take no for answer. Hey, we can work around your schedule!"* mentality reaps Clara many special teachers, therapists, and helpers. But Clara's most devout champion, her *second mother*, is a great, yet tiny, Chinese lady named Jeannie Cheung. Jeannie did not need to work for us. I dare say, Clara is the one of the few Special Olympic Athletes to arrive at practice in a *Porsche*. Jeannie is a marathoner with the L.A. Leggers. She won best in her age group once in the L.A. Marathon. Jeannie does all of Clara's physical therapy appointments.

**JEANNIE**   [*Heavy Chinese accent*] Come on Clara, you can do it!

**CLARINDA**   Jeannie and I are twelve years apart in age so we share the same sign in Chinese astrology, the Ox.

**JEANNIE**   The mothers, hauling the load and taking care of others.

**CLARINDA**   With Jeannie's own two daughters all grown-up and in college; Jeannie still had so much mother-love left to give. She never shies away from difficult tasks: attending Clara's doctors' appointments with me, helping to calm her fears while she undergoes procedures she cannot comprehend. Real moms can't be squeamish. And Jeannie, a great mother, understands. Very early after she started working with us, Clara was maybe nine, and Jeannie did the classic mom move.

**JEANNIE**   Okay, Clara, blow.

**CLARINDA**   Then she switched sides.

**JEANNIE**   Good girl, blow again.

[*Mimes wiping hands and tossing used tissue.*]

**CLARINDA**   It was then and there; I knew I had found a second mother for Clara. Jeannie gave Googy and me the gift of time.

We had a son, Frankie. Francis Gress, the *third*. Named for Googy and his daddy. I threatened just to call him "3." Frank was born July 24th, 2000. Jeannie was over the moon!

**JEANNIE**   A boy, a Golden Dragon. Clara, 1988, also Dragon. In Chinese astrology, Dragon is LUCK-y. Clarinda, if you have *three* Dragons you will be the most revered mother, the great mother, honored and cared for in old age.

**CLARINDA**   Jeannie, they're twelve years apart! If I have another Dragon, I'll be on the Oprah Winfrey show. No more Dragons.

So, I got busy, and in January 2003 I had my *third* child, a lucky little Horse, who I named for Daddy, Carl Au*gus*tus Ross Gress. Daddy used to say,

**DADDY**   You don't know what you know, 'til you know it.

**CLARINDA**   See, I thought I couldn't have other children until I got Clara a little further along, a little more therapy, a few more skills. And what I found out was—Frank and Gus did so much for Clara: here were two "*typically developing*" playmates. Jeannie and I discuss the boys often. We know that these little men will long outlive us both and eventually it will be the two of them who take over our *Oxen's* job of looking out for their sister.

Very few dentists will treat special needs kids, even with the good insurance. We take Clara to the UCLA Children's Dental Center because it's the only place that will see her—and it is such a *nightmare*. They put her in the *quiet* room— a sound proof room—so her screams won't frighten other children. She has to be restrained using a papoose—also known as a "straight-jacket," to prevent injury to herself and others. It's so stressful. I argue with the Dean of the School of Dentistry, "*Surely there is someone out there with a better plan? Someone who can do a better job with Clara's teeth?*"

No. No one had anything better than UCLA. So every six months like clockwork, we go. She bursts into tears when we turn onto Westwood Boulevard, and she doesn't stop screaming until it's over. Googy has to lift her into the chair and help hold her down and I lean over her, counting to ten, coaxing her to keep her mouth open.

[*Kneels over SL platform blowing on* CLARA's *face.*]

*Seven. Eight . . .* Clara is looking up at me, sweating, straining with terror in her eyes.

*Nine, you can do it. Ten. Good girl.*

[*Slowly, shakily, stands up.*]

The amazing rubber ball that is Clara bounces right back. After all the trauma and screaming, she hops up and goes to lunch with her Jeannie.

[*Sinks down to sit.*]

I go home and go to bed for the rest of the day. Years of *searching*, and asking, and *knowing* in my guts there had to be someone with a better plan. *Never say die!* I've found THE MAN, the *Holy Grail* of special needs dentists—Dr. Frank Enriquez in Torrance, California. Dr. Frank in his *wisdom* gives his special needs patients a low dose of *Valium* to calm them so he can do his work without a *straight jacket. Genius!* A kind, humane, understanding doctor.!

[*SOUND: "Ode to Joy." Instrumental. She picks up the journal.*]

November, 2006. Unbelievable! I have fired one or two therapists in my day who I deemed non Clara-worthy, but Amy, a top-notch occupational therapist who has worked for Clara for twelve years, fires us.

AMY  Clarinda, Clara has plateaued. In my professional opinion she is ready for group living.

CLARINDA  What? She may be eighteen on the outside but not on the inside!

AMY  It would be unethical of me to continue to treat her in your home. I don't feel it's the best environment for Clara.

CLARINDA  Wait a minute! How can you say our home is not the best place for Clara? Have I not spent the last eighteen years of my life working on behalf of this child?

AMY  Clarinda, for the past few years, our collective goal, yours, Jeannie's, and mine, has been to prepare Clara to "live in a house with friends." The repetition, and all these therapy hours have paid off. Clara's ready. I think she will flourish in a home with others like her.

CLARINDA  No! I am not ready. That's one day, *off* in the *future.* Even though I respect Amy, I completely ignore her advice. I tell Jeannie.

JEANNIE  Clarinda, think about it, maybe Clara is ready for "college." My girls go to college. Maybe this group home could be *Clara's* college.

**CLARINDA**   She had faith. It didn't frighten Jeannie. She saw it as a natural part of life.

**JEANNIE**   Things change, you move on.

**CLARINDA**   I remained unconvinced.

[*Drops the journal, mounts SR platform. IMAGE: Santa Monica house.*] December 2006. The Friday before Christmas. Pandemonium in the Gress household! Chocolate chip cookies, red striped pajamas, mayhem! Jeannie comes over with presents for the kids. [*To the kids*] "Look! Sponge Bob! You guys go play." [*To audience*] She looked awful, she'd been crying.

**JEANNIE**   Googy, Clarinda, I have stage four lung cancer.

**CLARINDA**   No! [*Sobbing, pleading.*] No, no, no. Jeannie never smoked; ate brown rice and fish. She ran *marathons*. The world is not fair. Our *luck* had run out. Jeannie is irreplaceable. I can't do the *job* without her. I am forced to face the next stage of Clara's care.

I start to look for a group home. And on the days she is able to—in between *grueling* chemo treatments—Jeannie comes with me. The laws in California only allow you to look at a group home with an opening, and, the client— Clara—must have an open file and must be ready to *move in*.

We find a place. Clara starts to do some weekends, spend-the-nights. A friend from Special Olympics Bowling, *Shirley*, already lives there full time. My *gut* tells me it is a great place. But . . . that niggling perfectionist, daughter of *two* college professors cannot "*compare and contrast*" this home with other homes. I can't make a *plan*. I have to go on *faith*.

[*IMAGE: CLARA graduation picture with* JEANNIE *and the family. SOUND: "Pomp and Circumstance."*]

June 27, 2007. Clara does her culmination walk and receives her "Certificate of Completion" with the graduating class of '07 at Santa Monica High. Jeannie *insisted* Clara participate in the ceremony: cap, gown, flowers, cake, balloons. Jeannie never does anything halfway. Secretly, I wonder, will Clara really know what is happening? Jeannie, in her wisdom, wants my boys Frank and Gus to see their sister is not so very different. She's one of all the other sisters and brothers on this day who will walk away from their families into their new lives of college or work.

**JEANNIE**   Clara will know this is important and she is a BIG GIRL.

**CLARINDA**   So, Clara walks the walk cheered on by me, Googy, the boys, and her Chinese mother. We whoop and holler so loudly they have to tell us to *sit down*. Jeannie pushes her girl over the finish line.

Clara *transitions* beautifully to group living—her *college*. Though she is disabled, *hormonally* she still has a strong desire to separate from me. She's . . .

**CLARA**   [*Signing in the International Sign Language.*] ALL DONE!

**CLARINDA**   . . . having me brush her *teeth*.

Jeannie visits Clara's college.

[CLARINDA *assists an ailing* JEANNIE *into* CLARA's *new "home."*]

She lets the staff at that group home know of our spiritual conversion to the . . .

[*"Praise Jesus" Tent Revival hand gesture.*]

*Church!* of Occupational Therapy.

**JEANNIE**   Clara is special. This child is loved. She have *two* mothers. We work too hard, too many years, to have her backslide now!

**CLARINDA**   When a dying woman talks, people listen.

The night Clara moved in for real: I unpack her suitcases and hang all her matching outfits together. I leave a headband for every outfit. No more bows, headbands are for Big Girls. Googy hooks up her TV and drives me home, where he sits in the car and *sobs.* [*To* GOOGY] "Honey, take your time. I'll go up and see the boys."

I make myself rise to the occasion, walk upstairs and I have a toast to our *Big Girl.* It's hard to be the sibling of a special person but even though she can be so difficult the boys love their Sissy fiercely. Frank Gress crawls into my bed that night . . .

**FRANK**   [*As a toddler, sad.*] Sissy's never coming home.

**CLARINDA**   Of course she is, she'll be home on weekends. She's just at *college.*

All the work, all the years, all of it moving towards this large *looming* goal when *"one day"* she would *"live in a house with friends."* It is so unbelievably, stunningly, amazing when *"one day"* arrives.

After the 30-day waiting period, I go to pick Clara up for a visit. She is standing at the door with her backpack. Her hair is *beautiful* in a French braid. Her pride shines in her beaming face. Oh, if she could've she'd've said . . .

**CLARA**   See, Mama, I am a BIG GIRL now; I'm at the BIG GIRL house, doing BIG GIRL things!

**CLARINDA**   I can die now. They *can* do it *without* me—and *don't you tell I said this*—but *maybe* they can do the *job* better than I can.

[*She picks up the journal.*]

Sunday, February 3, 2008. We got the call that they would start hospice on Monday for Jeannie. Knowing it would be Clara's last chance to see Jeannie, I was really hoping she'd behave.

We arrive. Clara runs around—I think she was looking for Jeannie's little dogs—but finally she settles down and comes up to Jeannie's bed and ever so gently she lay her head on Jeannie's chest.

**CLARA**  Thank you.

**CLARINDA**  From her small repertoire of spoken words, she picked the perfect two.

**CLARA**  Thank you.

**CLARINDA**  Jeannie kissed Clara softly on the top of her head. What a privilege it was for me to witness this perfect moment.
[*It is a new day.* CLARINDA *returns the journal to the SR cube.*]
April 30th, 2009. Gus Gress and I were doing arts and crafts in Clara's room. I was searching for colored paper and *look* what I found—
[*She kneels and retrieves a "Communication" notebook from SR cube same spot as Daddy's journal in the first act.*]
—one of Clara's old *communication* notebooks. We used notebooks like this to send notes between home and school and to Jeannie who often picked Clara up directly from school. After Clara *graduated* I *purged* years of contentious documents: pink parental rights booklets, and "out of compliance" forms. I was eager to take off my armor and put our battles with the school district behind us. I threw out *mounds* of stuff including several of these *communication* notebooks because they mostly have entries like: Send money for pizza. She needs wipes. Just quick, to the point notes, but Jeannie would sometimes *wander*—taking the time to write in amazing *historical* detail—about what she and Clara did together.
February 23, 2005.

**JEANNIE**  What a beautiful sunny day. Clara is lucky. We went to Petco. Clara greeted everyone.

**CLARA**  HI. HI. HI!

**JEANNIE**  Many people allowed Clara to pet their dogs and she said,

**CLARA**  THANK YOU.

**CLARINDA**  February 25th, 2005.

**GOOGY**  Dear Jeannie, we cannot thank you enough. You, my dear, are the most extraordinary piece of LUCK we have ever had. Thank you again and again.
Love, Googy.

**CLARINDA**  February 28th, 2005.

**JEANNIE**  My pleasure. You and Clarinda are the extra-ordinary ones. Clarinda believes Clara can function IF we are all on the same page. The teachers reinforce and reiterate what I do with therapists and I reinforce what they do in school. XOXOXO, Jeannie.
[*Holds up the notebook.*]

This notebook, which I found by *accident*, is a tangible reminder of a mother's devotion. I am glad to have it, because I never want to forget *her*.
[*Returns notebook to the SR cube/drawer.*]
There it was buried under construction paper, play-dough, coloring books, and dried up markers in the bottom of a dresser drawer in Clara's room. Actually, it was the same old 1970s Broyhill chest of drawers that used to be in my old room back home.
[*She takes down her hair, crossing DS. SOUND: Dance music.*]
Recently, Googy and I went to a fancy wedding for his buddy, who is a big Hollywood agent. The bride's family runs a vineyard about an hour outside of L.A. Catholic ceremony, full mass; lot of kneeling and standing, people took communion. It took *forever*! And there was this soloist in the balcony of the church. Older lady, singing, a tune I think you know . . .

**OLD LADY**    [*Singing badly*] SUNRISE, SUNSET, SUNRISE, SUNSET swiftly fly the yeeeaaaars.

**CLARINDA**    And *she* wasn't doing it nearly *that* well. I got the giggles. And a friend of ours, wicked [*3 fey air "snaps"*] sense of humor, got the giggles too. He looked at me and the same thought flashed through our brains: *This agent has no singers under contract*, or else this woman wouldn't be singing at his wedding.

But, we got to the reception and it was *fabulous*! A big tent in the middle of a vineyard, with flowers, linens, dinner, belly dancers, and a live band. My friend got happy and led a conga line! It came time for the official dances.
[*SOUND: Music. Waltz.*]
Googy and I watched the bride and groom's first dance and applauded. The bride began to dance with her father. I was standing there having a great time socializing, and suddenly . . . I burst into tears, and I really could *not* figure out why I was crying. But my *heart* knew what it saw; it just took my *head* a few moments to catch up. There are still times when the loss overwhelms me.
[*Crosses back to the car.*]
I am on this journey, and I don't always know whether I am to ride or to drive.
[*Holds an imaginary handle on the dashboard.*]
But, I'm a hanging, Daddy, I'm *hanging*.

[*LIGHTS: To black. IMAGE: Daddy with cowboy hat.*]
The End.

# girls. in boys pants.

Kato McNickle

# Kato McNickle

Kato McNickle is a Connecticut-based playwright, director, and artist. *Ariadne on the Island* is a 2015 participant in the New Works Festival at Gulfshore Playhouse in Naples, FL, 2010 Clauder Award recipient, and 2008 O'Neill National Theater Conference finalist. *girls. in boys pants.* was presented as part of the 2Cents Ink Fest and awarded Best Play in 2015. *Minotaurs. Toreros.* was presented by TalkStory Theater at Smith College in 2014. Recent playwriting awards include a 2008 Heideman Award finalist with Actors Theatre of Louisville for *About a Hundred Pancakes*; Theatre for Youth National Playwriting Award 2010 for *Chance of Rain: A Noah Riff*; a 2007 O'Neill National Theater Conference finalist for *Minotaurs. Toreros.*; and an Ensemble Studio Theatre New Voices Fellow for Fencers. She has studied playwriting with Paula Vogel, Bonnie Metzgar, Kia Corthron, and Donna DiNovelli. Plays and selections have been published by Smith & Kraus in a recent *Best Monologues for Women*; *The Lodestone Quarterly*; the *Brown Classical Journal*, and *Lemon Puppy Arts Journal*. She is Vice-President of the Mystic Paper Beasts, a Connecticut-based puppetry troupe, and partner of the Dragon's Egg Performance Space. She holds a BA from Brown University in Ancient Studies. She is a member of the Dramatists Guild and the Star Wars Fan Club.

# Production History

*girls. in boys pants.* was featured in the 2Cents Acting Out Ink Festival in spring 2015 in Los Angeles and was awarded Best Play, and Best Actress to Lindsay Lance for her portrayal of Danni. The play was developed through the National Theater Institute playwriting component led by Donna DiNovelli at the the O'Neill Theater Center. The play was workshopped at Vassar College in their experimental theater lab directed by Vanessa Soto, and by the Planning Stage in New London, CT.

*girls. in boys pants.* was produced as part of the 2Cents Acting Out Ink Festival at the Hudson Theatres in Hollywood. The show opened on Saturday, April 18, 2015, and was directed by Kitty Lindsay, and featured the following cast:

Lindsay Lantz as **DANNI**
Andrea Nelson as **SOPHIA**
Ashley Brown, Ted Greenly, Veronica Olah, and Arthur Solomon as **THE CHORUS**

The Vassar College Experimental Theater workshop took place in the Streep Studio on February 28, March 1 & 2, 2005.

Directed by Vanessa Soto
Julia Weldon as **DANNI**
Michelle Castro as **SOPHIA**
Hillary Lavin, Josh Luckens, Alison Matthews, and Elisha Schaefer as **THE CHORUS**

## Notes:

it's about art & politics. the world of art and the world of words. one woman, Sophia, is the artist. the other woman, Danni, is the political writer.

but really . it's about sex . and gender . and sexuality . and sensuality . and sexual politics . and rules . and a kiss [but that's later]

it begins with Sophia working in the college studio, painting. the chorus is her artwork. Danni interrupts because she is writing a story about the arts on campus for the college paper.

this is how they meet.

Sophia is infuriated by the story Danni writes.

## characters

**SOPHIA** an artist . visual . about beauty . art major
**DANNI** a writer . roguish . about control . dual major journalism/poli-sci
**CHORUS** 2 men . 2 women . they create the outer world . and are the voices & shapes of the inner-worlds that Sophia & Danni project

## requirements

an open space . occasional furniture . 2 microphones wt stands

## notes regarding language

words spoken by the chorus in cascading dialogue might move like water . other times it could riff and repeat like jazz . you're an artist in love with theater, you'll get there and make it your own .

the chorus speaks text from the following sources:
the 2004 spring eddie bauer catalog
"art a crash course" by julian freeman
the sidewalk at the university of connecticut some years ago
"cocktails a-go-go" by susan waggoner and robert markel
"histoire de france" by armand colin, première année
political buttons from my college days
"breathing together, quotations on the mysteries of love compiled by richard kehl
"third factory" by viktor shklovsky
brainstormed passages from my notebooks

• • •

[*an overture. of sorts. the* CHORUS. *The* CHORUS, *two men and two women in an open space that will be many things. As the* CHORUS *speaks the Litany of the Pants, a woman appears in silhouette behind a screen. She dresses, beginning with her pants—thus inspiring the Litany. She wears men's clothes, and concludes the dressing ritual by tying her tie. This is* DANNI.]

**CHORUS**     100% cotton * Relaxed fit * Sits at the natural waist * Roomy seat and thighs * Fuller leg with slight taper at the ankle * Hidden credit card pocket * Contrasting inside waist band * Twill tape hanger loop for easy hanging * All seams are double stitched for strength * Machine wash * Imported

[DANNI *appears. She observes from far away, behind. She breathes with the* CHORUS . . . In. Out. In . . . anticipation. right now it's a college art studio. after dark. The four members of the* CHORUS *are present. They will become the colors of the creation. They whisper.*]

**CHORUS**     crimson . canary . cobalt . fog . sienna . brown . sky . robin's egg . goldenrod . rainforest . turquoise . turtle shell . aqua . pearl

[*The light reveals* SOPHIA, *who stands in front of the* DANNI, *looking forward. At the canvas. She holds a palette and several brushes. She wears a tank-top sans bra and men's khaki trousers cinched at the waist with a wide leather belt. She speaks matter-of-factly.*]

**SOPHIA**     Art.

**CHORUS**     Art     Artsy     Artist     Artiste

**SOPHIA**     Making art.

[SOPHIA *dabs paint onto a brush.*]

**CHORUS**     Artisan     Artsy-fartsy     Artist     Art

**SOPHIA**     At its best—

[*She makes a broad stroke with the brush. Individuals in the* CHORUS *stretch and shape with each corresponding stroke.*]

**CHORUS**     Leonardo     Michelangelo     Picasso     O'Keeffe

[*stroke*]

**SOPHIA**  flows from the hands

[*stroke*]

**CHORUS**  Rubens   Raphael   Renoir   rar-rar-ren-rer-ro-   O'Keeffe

[*stroke . stroke*]

**SOPHIA**  without going thru the brain. without distillation thru active thought.

[*stroke*]

**CHORUS**  Manet

    [*stroke*]

    Monet

    [*stroke*]

    Delacroix

    [*stroke . stroke . stroke stroke stroke*]

    [*speaking with the above noted strokes*] oh—oh—o o O'Keeffe?

[*stroke.* SOPHIA *continues to paint, the* CHORUS *becoming the painting.* DANNI *appears. Her hair is cropped short, she wears khaki pants, a tucked-in button-down-shirt and a wide necktie, looking more like a journalist à la 1940 than the present day. She lights a cigarette as the light finds her. She has been watching* SOPHIA *work. The* CHORUS *whispers more colors as she speaks.*]

**DANNI**  Artists. Art. Artistes. Artsy-fartsy. If you ask me. Never much understood art. Fine art. Just not something I understand. Oh. Commercial Art. I understand that. But Fine Art? I took class. Art Appreciation. Ever had to write a paper about a woman artist? A non-twentieth-century woman artist? If you ever have, then you know the one. There's one everybody writes about. Just one. And she's an amazing story. Know who I mean? If you know art, then you know who I mean.

**CHORUS**  Artemisia

**DANNI**  Artemisia Gentileschi. That's her. Her father was an artist.

**CHORUS**  so that helped.

**DANNI**  A follower of Caravaggio.

**CHORUS**  That helped too.

**DANNI**  She was the first woman to ever be admitted to the Art School in Florence. She is most famous for having been raped by one of her teachers and later painting her master-work *Judith and the Head of Holofernes*, which depicted the death of a man who looked very much like her old art teacher. Now there's some art that means something. If you ask me.

    [*The light becomes inclusive. The* CHORUS *becomes still.*]

    So what is this?

**SOPHIA**  Are you smoking? You can't smoke—

**DANNI**  I know— it's bad for me.

**SOPHIA**  It's bad for the paintings. You can't smoke in here at all.

**DANNI**  Oh. Right. Public building.

[DANNI *snuffs out the cigarette against the sole of her shoe.*]

**SOPHIA**  These materials are flammable.

[DANNI *places the cigarette back in the pack.* SOPHIA *scowls.*]

**DANNI**  They're expensive.

**SOPHIA**  It's against the law.

**DANNI**  And expensive.

**SOPHIA**  Why are you here?

[DANNI *takes out a small tape recorder, clicking it on.*]

**DANNI**  Interview. For a story. About art on campus. The content of art. So what is this?

**SOPHIA**  It's my work.

**DANNI**  It's big.

**SOPHIA**  It isn't finished.

**DANNI**  But what's it going—what's the plan? Is there a plan?

**SOPHIA**  A general framework.

**DANNI**  A framework?

**SOPHIA**  I don't like to set limits. On my work. Predisposed limitations. The medium is limit enough.

**DANNI**  Huh.

**SOPHIA**  Color and two-dimensional canvas. That's already limiting.

**DANNI**  If it's limiting you, then why not do something else?

**SOPHIA**  Who are you?

**DANNI**  I'm from the paper.

**SOPHIA**  But who are you?

**DANNI**  Danni Buzz. From the "Danni Buzz Column." Read it?

**SOPHIA**  That can't be your real name.

**DANNI**  It's short. For "Danielle."

**SOPHIA**  Uh-huh.

**DANNI**  Really.

**SOPHIA**  I'm busy. I have to do this.

**DANNI**  And you are . . . ?

**SOPHIA**  Busy.

**DANNI**  Name?

**SOPHIA**  Why?

**DANNI**  The article.

**SOPHIA**  Sophia.

**DANNI**  And . . . ?

**SOPHIA**  Just put "Sophia."

**DANNI**  Very. Artsy.

**SOPHIA**  What?

**DANNI**  Your artwork—

**SOPHIA**  I'm working—

**DANNI**  I mean, what is it?

**SOPHIA**  It's beautiful. I create beauty.

**DANNI**  Uh-huh.

**SOPHIA**  Look. It isn't finished.

**DANNI**  What about content? What's your art about?

**SOPHIA**  It's about—me, I guess.

**DANNI**  Are you that interesting?

**SOPHIA**  Why are you here?

**DANNI**  The article.

**SOPHIA**  I'm learning. I'm a student.

**DANNI**  Art major?

**SOPHIA**  Of course.

**DANNI**  Year?

**SOPHIA**  Fourth.

**DANNI**  You cold?

**SOPHIA**  What?

**DANNI**  You look—cold.

[DANNI *grins. just a little.* SOPHIA *realizes that she is wearing only an undershirt and grabs up an overshirt and puts it on as she speaks.*]

**SOPHIA**  Working keeps me warm.

**DANNI**  Let me ask you more about your art.

**SOPHIA**   I have to finish.

**DANNI**   It's for the article. Here. I'll buy you something warm. Coffee?

**SOPHIA**   Coffee?

**DANNI**   Talk over coffee? Down the road? Take forty minutes? Make you famous.

**SOPHIA**   Forty minutes.

[SOPHIA *and* DANNI *sit at a cafe table, the tape recorder between them. The* CHORUS *reads aloud from a newspaper, alternating lines of speech, occasionally speaking together.*]

| | |
|---|---|
| **SOPHIA**   Art is everywhere | **CHORUS** |
| | For the first time |
| Try not to see art. Right now | |
| | I have realized |
| You can't. | |
| | It's not art I don't understand |
| Not with your eyes open anyway. | |
| | It's artists. |
| Art. Artistry. | |
| | I don't understand artists |
| It isn't always obvious. | |
| | who create art |
| I'm an artist | |
| | only concerned with themselves |
| I make art for me. To please me. | |
| | Unaware |
| to please me and hope | |
| | that art, the best art |
| hope it connects | |
| | is bigger than the artist |
| hope that others see | |
| | and not just painted on an oversized canvas |
| see some of themselves | |
| | Recently I met an artist she's pretty     and so's her art    pretty . . . |

[SOPHIA *goes to her painting, looking at her art, not quite touching its surface.*]

in the thing that I make     that
pleases me     pleases them          please
please     pleases me.   pah-leeze . . .

[DANNI *clicks off the tape recorder. The* CHORUS *slaps the paper to* SOPHIA. *She looks at the story, pleasant at first, but growing darker as she continues to read.* DANNI *is served a coffee by one of the* CHORUS. *The rest of the* CHORUS *gets coffee too, one of them plays guitar.* SOPHIA *storms past the coffee shop, sees* DANNI *and moves in, shaking the newspaper. Occasionally, but not too often, the guitar might act as a voice accentuating some of the spoken moments during the following dialogue.*]

**SOPHIA**  What—what—what—?!

**DANNI**  You read the article?

**SOPHIA**  It's—it's—it's—!

**DANNI**  Wanna coffee?

**SOPHIA**  No—no—no.

**DANNI**  I'll buy—

**SOPHIA**  What makes you think—what gives you the right—why are you doing this to me? Why did you do this?

**DANNI**  I wrote what I saw.

**SOPHIA**  You totally misrepresented everything I said to you. Everything I said—

**DANNI**  Were you misquoted?

**SOPHIA**  Context.

**DANNI**  Context?

**SOPHIA**  You made me sound—I made it sound—you twisted everything!

**DANNI**  I didn't change the context. That's what you said. You said—

**SOPHIA**  But you twisted it. You twisted in—those points. Those other things. *Your* points! You made me sound—

**DANNI**  Trivial.

**SOPHIA**  Yeah. Yeah. Yes. Trivial. My art is not trivial.

**DANNI**  It's not?

**SOPHIA**  No. It means something.

**DANNI**  What?

**SOPHIA**  What?

**DANNI**  What does it mean?

**SOPHIA**  It means—it means—it's—me. It's me.

**DANNI**  Yeah. Well. That's my point. That's trivial.

**SOPHIA**  A human being is trivial?

**DANNI**  Context. Why don't you sit. Have a coffee.

**SOPHIA**  I'm not—I wouldn't—I'm not going to sit with you.

**DANNI**  Suit yourself.

**SOPHIA**  Maybe I'll—maybe I'll—write a letter—to the editor. Or something.

**DANNI**  Make a statement. Take a stand. Cool. You like martinis?

**SOPHIA**  I don't know—what?

**DANNI**  I like martinis and was thinking. I know this place and we could—

**SOPHIA**  I'm not talking to you.

**DANNI**  Well. You. Are.

**SOPHIA**  Stop talking.

**DANNI**  You could leave—

**SOPHIA**  Stop talking.

[DANNI *sips her coffee.* SOPHIA *doesn't move.* DANNI *finishes her coffee and leaves.* SOPHIA *watches her go.* DANNI *doesn't. She doesn't even wave. Just leaves. Purposefully not watching. The guitar continues and becomes something intricate . very Windham Hill . a table laden with grapes, wine glasses, and cheese arrives in the center.*]

**CURATOR**  Everything set? Here? Everything? Sophia? Sophia? Wine? Have we wine?

[SOPHIA *enters with the wine.*]

**SOPHIA**  Here. Wine. I was dressing.

**CURATOR**  Look. People. Pour.

[SOPHIA *fills several glasses with merlot, careful not to spill or set anything out of place. The* CURATOR *takes the first glass.* SOPHIA *dutifully fills another. Two* PATRONS *enter. They examine the grapes and the cheese. They each take a glass.*]

**PATRONS**  I love art. Look at these. . . . Are these grapes? . . . These are good grapes. . . . oooh—cheese. . . . Mmmm. Cheese . . . I love art. . . . Art openings. Mmm hmmm.  Fun.  Very fun.  These are grapes.  Mmm hmmm.

**SOPHIA**  More wine?

**PATRONS**  That'd be great. Thanks, hon. Merlot.  Merlot.  It's the grape.  It's the region.  The region?  The region and the grape.  I think that's Burgundy.  Burgundy?

The region and the grape. Ahhh. The region and the grape. I love art. I love art openings. These are good grapes. Mmm hmmm. Mmmm. Hmmm.

**SOPHIA**  More wine?

**PATRONS**  That'd be great.  I love these grapes!  Thanks, hon.  So where's this artist from?

[SOPHIA *tries to answer—can't get in edgewise.*]

Is he here? He's gotta be here. Let's look. Let's look. Look over there. Let me get a few grapes. Thanks, hon. Look at these? Will you? Where's the artist? The artist? The artist. Is he here? Should be. Where? Should be? Hmmm. Let's look. Look here. Mmmm. Uh huh. Mmmm. Huh.

[DANNI *enters. The guitar continues.* SOPHIA *is arranging grapes and cheese.* DANNI *approaches.*]

**DANNI**  This the opening?

[SOPHIA *turns. Sees* DANNI. *Turns away.*]

**SOPHIA**  What are you—why are you—why are you here?

**DANNI**  Danni Buzz. From the paper. This is an art opening, right?

**SOPHIA**  Yeah. Yes.

**DANNI**  Thought I'd cover it. For the paper.

**CURATOR**  Wine? Sophia? People?

[SOPHIA *pours more wine.*]

**SOPHIA**  Wine?

**DANNI**  Naw. Thanks.

**SOPHIA**  It's complimentary. For the opening. Free.

**DANNI**  I know. Yeah. Of course. One. Okay? One.

[DANNI *takes a glass. The* CURATOR *goes to the* PATRONS. *They admire the art.*]

**SOPHIA**  The cheese too. And the grapes. No smoking.

**DANNI**  These are good grapes.

**SOPHIA**  Anything for a supporter of the arts.

| | | | |
|---|---|---|---|
| **PATRONS &** | So? | **DANNI** | So. |
| **CURATOR** | So? | **SOPHIA** | So? |
| | It's | **DANNI** | This art—it's I'm looking |
| | Color | | There's color |
| | Full | **SOPHIA** | It is "colorful" |
| | Lots | **DANNI** | Lots of color. |
| | and lines lines and | **SOPHIA** | Color. You review art a lot? |
| | curves curving spirals | | I mean, Your command |
| | I like the colors I enjoy | | over the language and |
| | the line | | concepts — |
| | almost sculpted almost | **DANNI** | It's for an article Is this |
| | Is this paint? | | paint? |
| | yes. Huh. Oil Ahhh. | **SOPHIA** | Of course. They're |
| | Oil. | | paintings. |
| | Wine? Wine? Oh. Wine. | | Paintings by Miguel  Soto |

Yes Yes yes Yes Thank
you. Yes. Of course.

**CURATOR**  Sophia? Wine?

Sophia? Wine?

He paints in oil. Intense
color in oil. He paints the
colors of home his home
Tropical tropics heat. Hot
color heat.

Wine. Yes. Here.

[SOPHIA *pours the* PATRONS *more wine. The* CURATOR *takes them to look at other works. The guitar continues.*]

**SOPHIA**  Look. I've got a job—I work here—I'm working. If you're here for the wine or the cheese or whatever go ahead and take some and just go but I've got things I'm doing I'm very busy right now and I've got things to do. This is an opening.

**DANNI**  That's what I'm here about. The opening.

**SOPHIA**  You don't like art—

**DANNI**  I like art—

**SOPHIA**  You like to attack art—

**DANNI**  I don't attack art—

**SOPHIA**  You don't.

**DANNI**  I don't.

**SOPHIA**  You don't?

**DANNI**  No. I don't.

**SOPHIA**  What're you here for?

**DANNI**  To see—to see—see—art.

**SOPHIA**  Go look then.

**DANNI**  Is the artist here?

**SOPHIA**  Of course he's here.

**DANNI**  Where?

**SOPHIA**  He's here.

**DANNI**  You can't tell me? You won't tell me. I can't believe you won't—

**SOPHIA**  I—he's—shy. He likes to listen.

**DANNI**  You can't tell me?

**SOPHIA**  I can't tell you.

**DANNI**  Come on, tell me.

**SOPHIA**  No.

**DANNI**  Come on—

**SOPHIA**   I can't—

**DANNI**   Aww—just a hint. How 'bout a hint?

**SOPHIA**   I'm not supposed—

[DANNI *looks to the* GUITAR PLAYER.]

**DANNI**   Does he know?

**SOPHIA**   Yes he knows.

**DANNI**   Everyone knows but me.

**SOPHIA**   They don't know.

**DANNI**   But you're getting them liquored up to buy him though.

**SOPHIA**   Loosened up.

**CURATOR**   Sophia? Wine?

[SOPHIA *pours more wine for the* PATRONS.]

**PATRONS**   These are beautiful.   Look at these.   What color.   Look at that color. Everywhere.   Beautiful.   Inspiring really.   And that one matches my couch.

[*The* GUITAR PLAYER *stops.* DANNI *looks at the guitar player and takes out her note pad—can't write it fast enough.*]

**CURATOR**   Keep playing. Music? Wine? Sophia? Wine?

**PATRONS**   You're right.   These colors are fabulous.   Rich.   Vibrant.   And this one matches my couch.

[*Again, the music stops. The* CURATOR *speaks quietly to the* GUITAR PLAYER. DANNI *goes to the* PATRONS.]

**DANNI**   Color is important to you?

**SOPHIA**   Uh—wine?

**PATRONS**   [*to* DANNI] Yes. [*about wine*] Yes!

**DANNI**   The right colors, of course?

**PATRONS**   Of course.   Color is so   colorful.

[*The guitar playing resumes. The* CURATOR *speaks quietly to* SOPHIA.]

**DANNI**   And what matters the most?

**PATRONS**   How the piece makes you feel.   You should love it.   Really love it. Want to bring it home.   Be in your home.   Right.   Exactly right.   Love it.

**DANNI**   Even if it doesn't go with the couch?

**PATRONS**   Oh.   Well.   It has to go with the couch.   Like that one.   That one goes with the couch.   It'll look great with the couch.

[*The* GUITAR PLAYER *stops playing and approaches the* PATRONS, *saying something rude in Spanish, then*]

**GUITAR PLAYER**   You cannot have it.   It was not made   I did not make it to go with   YOUR COUCH!   You can not have it   It is not yours   Go home

[*The* GUITAR PLAYER *flies away. The* CURATOR *rushes to the* PATRONS.]

**CURATOR**   Excuse. Please. Ladies. Excuse. He's. You can see. Shy. He's very. Shy. An artist.

**PATRONS**   That was   That was   He was   He was   insulting   very insulting   Was that him?   The artist?   What does he mean   I can't have it?   If I buy it   If she buys it   I can have it   It's hers   I can have it   Do you want it?   I don't want it.   She doesn't want it.

**SOPHIA**   More wine . . . ?

**CURATOR**   He's. Very. An artist. You understand.

[*The* CURATOR *runs off after the* GUITAR PLAYER.]

**PATRONS**   No more wine.   What time?   Oh.   We should go.   We should go. We're going.

**DANNI**   Not buying?

**PATRONS**   No. Not. No.

[*The* PATRONS *leave.*]

**DANNI**   No sale.

**SOPHIA**   Would you just go.

**DANNI**   So the artist—He's a good guitar player.

**SOPHIA**   Don't write about this—

**DANNI**   Are you kidding?

**SOPHIA**   Please. Don't.

[*The* CHORUS *enters.*]

**CHORUS**   I met an artist the other day.

**DANNI**   An artist chases away two buying customers because he doesn't like their reason for buying the work?

**CHORUS**   He's a good guitar player

**SOPHIA**   It's his work.

**CHORUS**   and an artist.

**DANNI**   He wants to sell it. They want to buy it—

**CHORUS**   He cares about his art—

**SOPHIA**   It's his work—

**CHORUS**   Cares about it so much—

**DANNI**  It's his business—

**CHORUS**  He has trouble letting go—

**SOPHIA**  It's his work. It's the gallery's business.

**CHORUS**  Letting it go to the highest bidder—

**DANNI**  Still. He sells it—

**CHORUS**  Letting it go to the uncouth—

**SOPHIA**  He makes it.

**CHORUS**  Letting it go to his head.

**DANNI**  To sell it.

**SOPHIA**  Sometimes—

**DANNI**  To sell it.

**SOPHIA**  Okay! To sell it.

**CHORUS**  When he would be better off—

**SOPHIA**  They're like his children—

**CHORUS**  Getting it into his head from the get-go—

**DANNI**  Children? That's just, that's just, that's a ridiculous term.

**CHORUS**  That he created this art—

**SOPHIA**  They are.

**CHORUS**  for others—

**DANNI**  They're paintings.

**SOPHIA**  They're his paintings.

**CHORUS**  in the first place.

**SOPHIA**  You're never going to understand.

**CHORUS**  I really enjoyed the grapes.

**DANNI**  You mind if I take some more of those grapes?

[SOPHIA *glares at* DANNI. DANNI *leaves. The table is removed.* SOPHIA *sits, staring at her work, the* CHORUS *behind her, breathing—*SOPHIA *breathes with them . . . In. Out . . . in. Three of the* CHORUS *fade behind. One moves forward and speaks, a friend of* SOPHIA's.]

**FRIEND**  It's looking—

**SOPHIA**  Oh . . . !

**FRIEND**  Sorry.

**SOPHIA**  Didn't know you were there.

**FRIEND**  It's looking good. Shaping up. Ship shape, so to say . . .

**SOPHIA**   It's big.

**FRIEND**   It's beautiful. You've got delicate color and balance—

**SOPHIA**   See these?

> [SOPHIA *takes several swatches of cloth from her pocket. She stands and holds them forward, toward her painting.*]
>
> This one matches. Here. And this one. Here. And look. This one goes here.

**FRIEND**   You thinking about collage? Multimedia?

**SOPHIA**   Living rooms.

**FRIEND**   A comment on consumerism? On domestic bliss? On Americana?

**SOPHIA**   No. Look at these. Did you know that they just give these to you, if you ask. they just give them to you and you can match them up with wall colors and drapes and and—See? They match. They match! And this. This. This would totally match your parents' sofa, wouldn't it?

**CHORUS**   Now that you mention it . . .

**SOPHIA**   Beautiful.

> [*Crazy drums and excited sounds fill the air. The* CHORUS *in silhouette shakes cans of non-existent spray paint and faux paints words on the ground. They gather as a crowd around the words, wondering where the words came from and who could've painted them and what do the mean?* SOPHIA *approaches the crowd and stares at the ground ahead of her, shocked by what she sees. A chorus member takes pictures of the ground and of* SOPHIA. *She blinks at him.* DANNI *approaches from behind. She looks at the ground and then to* SOPHIA.]

**DANNI**   So you're The "Sophia." "Sophia" of the Sidewalk.

**CHORUS**   Sophia. U. R. Hot-ta-taaa.

**DANNI**   "Sssoooooopppphhhhhiiiiiiaaaaaaaaaaa—" It's big. See? You're famous. And you have a potential stalker or umm admirer.

> [*The camera clicks again.* SOPHIA *pushes the camera away. The crowd moves on. The camera guy leaves.*]

**SOPHIA**   I don't need this.

> [DANNI *writes in a spiral-bound pad*]

**DANNI**   Not much of a poet, though. "Sophia U R hot" I do like the letter "U" instead of the word "you" and just the "R" for the whole unnecessary clutter of the overused verbiage. Cuts right to the chase. You have a boyfriend?

**SOPHIA**   I do not know who did this. And what are you—what are you—why are you here?

**DANNI**   Danni Buzz. I'm with the paper and you are today's news, baby.

**SOPHIA**   Haven't you done enough to me already?

**DANNI**  So what's the—what is the term?—medium. Yeah. That's it. Medium. Seems to be "spray paint." A regular Picasso this stalker slash admirer of yours. Do you have a boyfriend? Seeing anyone?

**SOPHIA**  Are you putting that in the paper too?

**DANNI**  Maybe he's got a rival. Maybe he'd know something.

**SOPHIA**  Why do you want to ruin my life?

**DANNI**  Background for the story. I'd wanna get him. For a comment. For the story. It's thorough journalism. My job. I'm a reporter. An observer of facts. You have a boyfriend?

**SOPHIA**  You ever wear a dress?

**DANNI**  That's not part of the story. You have a boyfriend? That is.

**SOPHIA**  No.

[DANNI *writes it down. Looks at* SOPHIA.]

**DANNI**  "No." And. No. You drink martinis? I'll buy.

**SOPHIA**  I've never. I don't. Know.

**DANNI**  Is that "no" "N" "O," or "know" you don't "know," you know, with a "k," if you like them?

**SOPHIA**  I don't. "*Know*"

[DANNI *tries to decide. Whatever. Tears off a leaf of paper from the pad.*]

**DANNI**  Here. That's the place. That's the time. Be there. I'll be there. So if it's "no" "N" "O," then, I'll see you around maybe sometime around campus or something maybe at a football game or something sometime or alumni reunion or something like that ten years from now or so. But if it's "know" not "knowing" but wanna try . . . then I'll see you there. Tonight. At eight. O'clock. 'kay?

**SOPHIA**  Why?

**DANNI**  I. Want to learn your content. For. Context. The story.

**SOPHIA**  The story.

**DANNI**  We can discuss. We'll talk about. Ever hear of Artemisia Gentileschi?

**SOPHIA**  Oh! I. Wrote. A paper about her. For—

**SOPHIA/DANNI/CHORUS**  —Art Appreciation.

**DANNI**  Art. Appreciation.

**SOPHIA**  Yeah. Art. Appreciation. It was a pre-major requirement.

[DANNI *and* SOPHIA *leave. then. a reprise. of sorts. the* CHORUS *storms in carried on a wave of crazy jazz sound. The two women are stand-up comics, sharing a microphone.*]

CHORUS  [*the men whispering into a microphone*]

| | |
|---|---|
| 100% cotton | CHORUS  [*comic women—trading lines*] |
| *Relaxed fit | Ever notice |
| *Sits at the natural waist | women's pants    have such |
| *Roomy seat and thighs | shitty pockets    Yeah. |
| *Fuller leg with slight taper | No room in 'em. Ever notice |
| at the ankle | women's pockets tend to come all |
| | sewn shut |
| *Hidden credit card pocket | like women don't need pockets? |
| | Like women can't use pockets? |
| *Contrasting inside waist band | That's why women don't pay |
| | for dinner. |
| *Twill tape hanger loop | |
| for easy hanging | Why. |
| *All seams are double stitched | No pockets. |
| for strength | |
| *Machine was Imported | I think it's just a scam to keep |
| | the pocketbook industry |
| | in business |
| [*The men laugh, sit on stools to | Ever notice how plus size women's |
| watch the rest of the act.*] | pants the waist comes up to here |
| | Up to here! |
| | I'm an ample woman. |
| | I just don't need a pair a pants. |
| | I gotta belt around my brassiere! |
| | They could make a brassiere belt. |
| | They could. |
| | And you know what? |
| | Women would buy it. |
| [*The men laugh.*] | How? No pockets. |

[*The men howl. The women go to them. One sits with them, the other takes their order. A jazz quintet plays. The microphones are left in their stands, one to each side of the playing area.* DANNI *sidles up to a microphone. Sighs into. Looks around furtively.* SOPHIA *tentatively approaches the other microphone, nervous. She wears "a little black dress."* DANNI *sees her and clears her throat. They both speak softly into the microphones, looking and facing forward as though the other were directly across. Everyone in the bar can only speak thru a microphone, up close, quietly, being mightily amplified.*]

**DANNI**  You. Wow. You're. Here. And. You. Wow. Changed.

**SOPHIA**  We were going out, so I thought.

**DANNI**  Wow. I'm. Glad.

**SOPHIA**  Do you always wear a tie?

**DANNI**  Not always. Sometimes I sleep. Or shower.

**SOPHIA**  Ahhh.

**DANNI**  It's vintage.

**SOPHIA**  Vintage?

**DANNI**  Old.

**SOPHIA**  I know—I know what "vintage" means.

**DANNI**  Yeah. Oh. Sorry. I'm. Wrong foot.

**SOPHIA**  I'm looking forward to martinis.

**DANNI**  I like martinis insteada one-a those sweet ruby-red drinks.

**SOPHIA**  What's wrong with sweet ruby-red drinks?

**DANNI**  Is this that foot again? Just I don't take to that much sweet all at once. I never liked Kool-Aid as a kid or anya that either.

**SOPHIA**  Ahh. I had a question about —well—about—

**DANNI**  Martinis?

**SOPHIA**  Your story.

**DANNI**  Oh. That. Well.

**SOPHIA**  I was wondering—I was hoping—do you ever change them?

**DANNI**  I spell check.

**SOPHIA**  Change them, like rewrite them?

**DANNI**  I usually write a couple of drafts, when there's time—

**SOPHIA**  I mean, would you maybe could you write another take a look at my art and write another what I'm saying is just look at my art more of my art and just think about it would you think about it—?

**DANNI**  Drinks are here.

[*Their drinks are served.*]

[*to the* WAITRESS] Thanks.

**SOPHIA**  Could you do that?

[*The* WAITRESS *pushes her way to speak into* DANNI'S *mic. It's rather awkward for everyone, but them's the rules.*]

**WAITRESS**  Anything else?

[DANNI *pushes in.*]

**DANNI**  No. Thanks.

[WAITRESS *pushes to the mic.*]

**WAITRESS**  You let me know.

[DANNI *pays. Tips. Well.*]

**SOPHIA**  Thanks.

**DANNI**  Yep.

**SOPHIA**  So . . . ?

**DANNI**  Try it. I'm dying to know . . .

[SOPHIA *sips her drink.*]

You like it?

**SOPHIA**  It's. Mmm. Sharp.

**DANNI**  Martinis take time. And skill.

**SOPHIA**  You didn't answer.

**DANNI**  I like to come here. You like jazz?

**SOPHIA**  You still haven't—What is a martini?

**DANNI**  Sophistication. Content.

**SOPHIA**  What's in them?

**DANNI**  Vermouth and jazz.

**SOPHIA**  Really—what's in them?

[*A* MAN *from the* CHORUS *pushes his head in to speak into* SOPHIA's *mic. Again. Awkward.* SOPHIA *is surprised. Yields.*]

**MAN**  two and a half ounces gin   one tablespoon dry vermouth   mix with cracked ice in a mixing glass, then strain into a chilled cocktail glass. Garnish with a stuffed olive or a twist of lemon peel.   I couldn't help hearing—hope you don't mind—pardon me—[*to* SOPHIA] can I buy you a drink?

[SOPHIA *can't get back to the mic, therefore, she's mute.*]

**DANNI**  We're all set.

[*The* MAN *signals the* WAITRESS.]

**MAN**  Wanna dance?

**DANNI**  We're talking.

**MAN**  [*to* SOPHIA] What's your name?

**DANNI**  We're trying to talk.

[SOPHIA *can't get to the mic, she whispers to the man, inaudible.*]

**MAN**  That's a beautiful name. "Sophia."

**DANNI**  Beautiful. Let me tell you about beautiful. America the Beautiful, right? America the Beautiful. Yeah. She's the girl everyone talks about dreams about goes ga-ga for. She's the girl everyone wants to take to the prom, the American wet dream. But here's the thing. You take her to the prom, you dream about her in youth, but then you get older, and you start seeing, you start realizing, "hey, this broad is high maintenance. She's a whole lotta work." So you start looking around. Your eye wanders, and who do you find? Who do you settle for and move in with, get a mortgage and a two-car garage? Convenience. That's right. Convenience becomes the beauty. Ease and comfort and who cares about style. America the Convenient. paved. easy. strip mall. internet. That's the girl we marry.

[*The* MAN *and* SOPHIA *stare blankly at* DANNI, *not quite sure what to make of the speech.*]

**MAN**  Let's dance. You dance?

[SOPHIA *can't answer, so, unable to do anything else, she goes with the* MAN. DANNI *lights a cigarette. The* MAN *takes* SOPHIA *to the dance floor. They dance. A martini arrives. The* WAITRESS *pushes to* DANNI's *mic.*]

**WAITRESS**  It's on him.

[*She indicates a man seated at the bar. He waves. Eerily, he is dressed like* DANNI. DANNI *nods, grins, thumbs up, turns forward frowning, downing the martini.* SOPHIA *looks to* DANNI *from the dance floor, but* DANNI *doesn't look at her, so* SOPHIA *continues to dance. The* WAITRESS *goes to the other microphone.*]

**DANNI**  I dreamed it was nineteen-forty-four in France and I was a war correspondent reporting on the progress of the Allied invasion.

[*The* WAITRESS *speaks low into the mic while* DANNI *tells her story into her microphone.*]

| **WAITRESS**  Non seulement la guerre devint | **DANNI**  I was in a little watering hole outside of Paris as the Allies approached |
|---|---|
| de plus en plus atroce, mais elle s'étendit dans le Monde entier. | and I met with my source about the upcoming events and vowed I would do anything to get my story. And then I saw her. |

[*The jazz music stops. The* WAITRESS *sings a French cabaret song.* DANNI *continues, the role of* DANNI *will be played by the other man from the bar. The one who sent over the drinks. He wears the same shirt & tie as* DANNI. *The enactors simply act. They do not pretend to talk. sings a French cabaret song, or perhaps plays a concertina. or small accordion . . . something French.*]

**DANNI**  She was dancing with a GI an officer by the look of him. She saw me
  [SOPHIA *sees the man playing* DANNI.]
  and she knew what I was there for. I lit a cigarette and waited. She liked to make me wait. She was that kinda dame. She stopped dancing with the guy and comes over. and she knew what I was there for. I lit a cigarette and waited. She liked to make me wait. She was that kinda dame. She stopped dancing with the guy and comes over.

[SOPHIA *goes to the man playing* DANNI.]

"You shouldn't smoke." she says. It's bad for you." "Honey" says I. "Smoking is the only tangible evidence I got that I'm still breathing." "You're breathing. I can feel it." And she kisses me. Long and deep. Breathing in the smoke left in my lungs. My breath in her now. Why you gotta go? Cuz that's where the story is, baby. Why you gotta be out front? Cuz that's where the story— stay   can't   can't? Won't.   Gotta. It's the story. and this story's bigger than me or us or anything. Tomorrow, I'll be in Paris. "See ya." she says. Yeah. See ya. Paris.

[*The man playing* DANNI *leaves, blowing a kiss. The song ends.* SOPHIA, *crying, leaves.* DANNI *is alone.*]

And I'm in Paris the next day with the bombs and the blood and the crash . . . And I never see that little girl again. Until today.

[DANNI. *Sulks. two* CHORUS *members remove the microphones and stands. A woman* CHORUS *member stands near the back. She sings ardently. skillfully. beautifully. to the universe.* DANNI *listens from the bar.*]

**WOMAN SINGING**   [*a cappella*]
WHAT IF I COULD
SWALLOW THE OCEAN
WHAT IF I COULD
WALK THRU A FIRE
WHAT IF I COULD
FLY IN THE MOONLIGHT
WOULD I BE DESIRED?
WHAT IF I COULD
BUST DOWN A MOUNTAIN
WHAT IF I COULD
SEE THRU YOUR HEART
WOULD IT MAKE ME
JUST A LITTLE WISER
COULD THAT BE A START?

[DANNI *throws a few dollars to the woman and is gone. The* CHORUS *begins tacking up pieces of paper—securing them to the walls, to the floor, to each other . . .* DANNI *enters with a fistful of papers in hand. She approaches each of the pinned-up notices and pulls them down, taking a moment to check what is written on each. Once they are all gathered,* DANNI *continues on her search for the next paper. a large bench appears. The space becomes a museum gallery, and most of the* CHORUS *becomes the art. One* CHORUS *member is a spectator and carefully takes in the displays.*]

**CHORUS**   [*whisper chants*] Leonardo * Michelangelo * Picasso * Caravaggio * Rubens * Raphael * * Renoir * Manet * Monet * Delacroix * Artemisia * O'Keeffe?

[*As he is about to move on to the next gallery* SOPHIA *enters with a drawing pad and charcoal. He notices her, and then continues on. the* CHORUS *continues its whisper . . .* SOPHIA *takes in the art, and is eventually drawn to the unseen work hanging in front of the bench. She sits on the bench, concentrating hard on the image in front of her. She doesn't like what she has drawn and turns to a new leaf. She begins again. The space is quiet.* DANNI *enters from behind, with the fist-full of papers, also looking at the art. She sees* SOPHIA. *Hesitates. Thinks about leaving. Approaches, papers crackling.* SOPHIA *turns, sees* DANNI, *continues to sketch.*]

**SOPHIA**   You got my message.

**DANNI**   Your message?

**SOPHIA**   In your hand.

**DANNI**   You did this?

**SOPHIA**   I thought of it as an artistic installation. Environmental collage.

**DANNI**   What was the point?

**SOPHIA**   You complain a lot.

**DANNI**   Pinning up my columns all over campus is art now?

**SOPHIA**   They're not all over campus.

**DANNI**   I found them—

**SOPHIA**   You found them between the newspaper office and the museum. A deliberate pattern between two points.

**DANNI**   Why bring me here?

**SOPHIA**   To see some art. Really take the time to look.

**DANNI**   I'm looking—

**SOPHIA**   Without talking.

**DANNI**   I can't talk—?

**SOPHIA**   Try just to look.

**DANNI**   Okay—

**SOPHIA**   Shhhh.

**DANNI**   Ahhhh.

**SOPHIA**   Hmmm?

[DANNI *puts her finger to her lip for "shhhh" followed by a thumbs up and takes in some of the art. She returns to the painting engaged by* SOPHIA.]

**SOPHIA**   Art should make you stop. Make you stop and look and be with it and stick with you, even after you've moved on, you think?

**DANNI**   You like this one?

**SOPHIA**  It made me stop.

**DANNI**  Who's this?

**SOPHIA**  Who?

**DANNI**  Who's it by?

**SOPHIA**  There's a placard.

**DANNI**  There is.

[DANNI *reads the placard. Looks again at the painting. Looks at* SOPHIA.]
What were these for?

**SOPHIA**  Stop.

**DANNI**  I can't talk at all?

**SOPHIA**  Stop being so cynical. Stop complaining. These are all complaints—

**DANNI**  Rants.

**SOPHIA**  Rants?

**DANNI**  It's the "Weekly Rant." That's my column. I write other stories too. People like the "Rant." It's very popular. It gets people thinking—and talking—

**SOPHIA**  What do you do?

**DANNI**  I write.

**SOPHIA**  Besides writing. Do you do anything?

**DANNI**  I have classes. I listen to jazz. And I write.

**SOPHIA**  But you don't do anything.

**DANNI**  I don't have time. I'm busy writing.

**SOPHIA**  Complaining—

**DANNI**  Reporting. I'm a reporter.

**SOPHIA**  You're a student.

**DANNI**  A student reporting. And reporters don't get involved.

**SOPHIA**  They don't?

**DANNI**  Observers of fact.

**SOPHIA**  Uh-huh.

**DANNI**  Yeah "uh-huh."

**SOPHIA**  Just so you know, spray paint, when you hold down the nozzle, these little speckles of paint collect on the corners of your index finger.

**DANNI**  Huh.

**SOPHIA**  Just so you know.

**DANNI**   You're working. I'm interrupting.

**SOPHIA**   Interrupting is your primary occupation.

**DANNI**   Am I stopping you?

**SOPHIA**   I uh think yes perhaps I don't probably.

**DANNI**   What is that? You're doing.

**SOPHIA**   This?

**DANNI**   That.

**SOPHIA**   Work.

**DANNI**   Ahh.

**SOPHIA**   Observation.

**DANNI**   Oh.

**SOPHIA**   For class. Studying—the masters. Noticing, noting, how they handle, handled, the work, the structure. I'm drawing. Drawing the paintings. Trying to draw. Anyway.

**DANNI**   Like reading Hemingway.

**SOPHIA**   Right. I guess. I've never read Hemingway.

**DANNI**   Ahhh. I have.

**SOPHIA**   Oh.

**DANNI**   May I see it?

**SOPHIA**   What?

**DANNI**   Your drawing, may I see it?

**SOPHIA**   No no.

**DANNI**   Why?

**SOPHIA**   It's figures, people, and I don't, no.

**DANNI**   Why not?

**SOPHIA**   No. No.

**DANNI**   You're drawing that? Her?

**SOPHIA**   Yeah. Yes.

**DANNI**   And I can't see it?

**SOPHIA**   In front of you. The real one. It's much better.

**DANNI**   What made you choose this one?

**SOPHIA**   It's well she's beautiful.

**DANNI**   Yes.

**SOPHIA**  Ethereal even.

**DANNI**  Yes.

**SOPHIA**  Even though she's not real.

**DANNI**  Yes.

**SOPHIA**  She's impossibly tall.

**DANNI**  Yes.

**SOPHIA**  But still—

**DANNI**  Yes?

**SOPHIA**  Real. Unreal real.

**DANNI**  Yes.

**SOPHIA**  Is that anything like Hemingway?

**DANNI**  Yes.

**SOPHIA**  Have you ever copied Hemingway?

**DANNI**  [*laughs. then.*] Yes.

**SOPHIA**  Would you let me read it?

**DANNI**  [*laughs. then.*] Yes.

[SOPHIA *opens her pad.*]

**SOPHIA**  See?

**DANNI**  Yes.

[SOPHIA *continues her study.* DANNI *sits next to* SOPHIA *on the bench.*]
That guy . . . the other night . . .

**SOPHIA**  Where did you go?

**DANNI**  You went dancing.

**SOPHIA**  One dance.

**DANNI**  That guy.

**SOPHIA**  Where did you go?

**DANNI**  I just figured.

**SOPHIA**  He asked me to dance. I wanted to dance.

**DANNI**  Ahh.

**SOPHIA**  Does it matter?

**DANNI**  No.

**SOPHIA**  "No."

**DANNI**  Did you stay long?

**SOPHIA**  No.

**DANNI**  Go with him?

**SOPHIA**  [*laughs. then.*] No.

**DANNI**  Am I bothering you?

**SOPHIA**  No.

**DANNI**  Do you want me to rewrite the article?

**SOPHIA**  [*laughs. then.*] No.

**DANNI**  No?

**SOPHIA**  You were right.

**DANNI**  I was just writing. Being clever, I think, more than thinking, seeing, really.

**SOPHIA**  Why do you think I'm here? Doing this?

**DANNI**  You're practicing. You're learning. You want to be an artist.

**SOPHIA**  Because you were right.

**DANNI**  Yeah?

**SOPHIA**  Yes. Let me show you something . . .
[*Everything changes. The* CHORUS *sits cutting fabric and placing bits on the wall.*]
Here it is.

**DANNI**  What is it?

**SOPHIA**  An art installation. A real art installation. A bunch of us are doing it.

**DANNI**  What's all this?

**SOPHIA**  Couches. Fabric for couches. We're making a collage from the fabrics and then—
[SOPHIA *dips her fingers in some pigment.*]
We paint. See?
[*She swirls some color around the wall. Some of the* CHORUS *members do the same, leaving handprints and swirls of color.*]
I'm calling it "Matching the Couch."

**DANNI**  Your idea?

**SOPHIA**  Yeah. After I read your "Rant" about the gallery opening, I started thinking.

**DANNI**  See?

**SOPHIA**  Then I started doing something. Here. You do something. Try this.
[SOPHIA *offers* DANNI *some paint.*]
Leave your mark.

**DANNI**  I'm not an artist. I wouldn't know what to make.

**SOPHIA**  Writing's not art?

**DANNI**  Journalism is more craft.

**SOPHIA**  What do you write for fun?

**DANNI**  What do you mean?

**SOPHIA**  You must just write something for fun?

**DANNI**  I'm a journalist.

**SOPHIA**  How about a poem? Ever write a poem?

**DANNI**  Poetry! You've gotta be kidding. I do not write poetry.

**SOPHIA**  Never?

**DANNI**  Not of my own volition.

**SOPHIA**  Really.

**DANNI**  A waste of time.

**SOPHIA**  Huh.

[SOPHIA *puts the paint away and cleans her hands. It dawns on* DANNI *that she has put her foot in it. Again. Back peddling.*]

**DANNI**  Not that there aren't good poets I mean there are there can be there are some good poets—

**SOPHIA**  I really like poetry.

**DANNI**  Reading its okay. I mean yeah people read it I read it I've read some I have read poems.

**SOPHIA**  I was just hoping you liked poetry, that's all.

**DANNI**  It's just that it can be so so so nihilistic and strange and you have to read it so so slow—

**SOPHIA**  Or it can be personal and probing and honest.

**DANNI**  I guess—

**SOPHIA**  I can't believe you're a writer not interested in poetry.

**DANNI**  I don't have time. I'm busy writing stories. News stories.

**SOPHIA**  Yeah. Okay.

**DANNI**  Thanks for showing me your installation.

**SOPHIA**  Yeah. Thought. Art. On campus. Your article.

**DANNI**  Hey. Uh. Do something with me?

[*The* CHORUS *collects and becomes a college courtyard, late at night. The* CHORUS *becomes the structures: a WALL, a DOOR, the CORNER of the building and a*

BENCH *in front of the wall. They breathe as one, slowly, carefully, their mouths gaping.* In. Out. In. Out. In . . .]

**WALL**   silence

**DOOR**   silence

**CORNER**   silence

**BENCH**   silence

**CHORUS**   [*as a unit*] silence is the voice of complicity.

[DANNI *pulls some chalk from a pocket.*]

**DANNI**   Chalk.

**SOPHIA**   Chalk?

[DANNI *scrawls words across the* WALL. *The sound of chalk on a hard surface squeaks along with her hand-strokes.*]

**DANNI**   We—can—not

                              **CHORUS**   we cannot change

    change—un—less—we—

                                        unless we survive

    sur—vive

                                        but we will not survive
                                        unless

    but—we—will—not

                                        we change

    sur—vive—un—less

                                        unless unless unless

    we—change.

**DANNI**   Parents are gonna freak, huh?

**SOPHIA**   So you're the person who does this?

**DANNI**   See? I do something.

**SOPHIA**   Why am I here?

**DANNI**   I thought . . . if you don't want . . . I just thought you'd . . .

**SOPHIA**   What should I do?

**DANNI**   You're artistic. Think of something. Make a statement.

**SOPHIA**   You hate my art. Remember?

**DANNI**   I don't hate your art.

**SOPHIA**   I hate my art.

**DANNI**   Content. Think about content. I am an observer of fact; you are an observer of line. Both require content. You with me?

**SOPHIA**  Content.

[SOPHIA *settles on the sidewalk. She begins to draw a large shape.* DANNI *scrawls on the door.*]

**DANNI**  Ask—

| | **CHORUS** | Ask ask ask ask ask ask ask |
|---|---|---|
| your—self | | yourself self self self |
| ques—tions | | ask yourself ask yourself ask |

**DANNI**  I wonder how many times these walls have been marked up? Parent's Day happens every year, right? Always got lots a people got lots to say. . .

| **WALL** | **DOOR** | **CORNER** | **BENCH** |
|---|---|---|---|
| fear fuels hatred | | | |
| feeds war | we still have | | |
| breeds fear | a dream | minds are like | suck off |
| fuels hatred | we still | parachutes | suck suck |
| feeds war | have a | they only function | suck off |
| fear breeds | dream | when open | suck suck |
| fuels hatred | we | minds are like | suck off |
| feeds war | still have a | parachutes they | suck off |
| | dream | only function | suck off |
| fuels hatred . . . | we still have . . . | when open . . . | suck off! |

[DANNI *moves to the corner and scrawls.*]

**CHORUS**  We are not amused.

**DANNI**  "We are not amused." That's a good one. That's a good one all right. What'dyou got?

[DANNI *looks at* SOPHIA's *work.*]

What do you got?

**SOPHIA**  It's not finished. It's—it'll be—

**DANNI**  What is it?

**SOPHIA**  —a flower.

**DANNI**  But what'sits say?

**SOPHIA**  "Flower"?

**DANNI**  Is that a joke? Are you joking?

**SOPHIA**  No.

**DANNI**  But you're joking, right?

**SOPHIA**  It's a flower.

**DANNI**  I can—yeah. It's a flower. But what's it mean? What'sit say?

**SOPHIA**  It says—"flower." I made it for you.

**DANNI**  This is political. We're making a statement. Come'on! What kinda statement does "flower" make?

**SOPHIA**  I thought it'd be nice.

**DANNI**  We're not trying to be nice. It's not supposed to be nice. It's supposed to be a wake-up call! It's supposed to make 'em think! It's supposed to MEAN SOMETHING!

**SOPHIA**  It means something to me. A hopeful sentiment.

| WALL | DOOR | CORNER | BENCH |
|------|------|--------|-------|
| civil disobedience | | | |
| is civil | He's pretty | | |
| defense | but can he type | avoid Freud | |
| | | | suck off |

**DANNI**  Here. Look. Watch me.

[DANNI *goes to the bench and grinds the words into the surface with a vengeance.*]
See?

[SOPHIA *looks.*]

**SOPHIA**  Yeah.

**DANNI**  It says something.

**SOPHIA**  Yeah.

**DANNI**  "Art is more than a pretty sentiment." That says something.

**SOPHIA**  Yeah.

**DANNI**  So what's yours gonna say?

**SOPHIA**  It's a real quiet flower.

**DANNI**  It's stupid. A flower is stupid! Worse than stupid! Cliché. And I'm outta chalk. Gimme sa'more chalk!

**SOPHIA**  You should have brought more then.

**DANNI**  Not for more stupid flowers.

**SOPHIA**  Yeah, for more stupid flowers.

**DANNI**  I'm doing all the work here. Give me the chalk.

**SOPHIA**  You go get more.

**DANNI**  Now! While no one's around!

**SOPHIA**  I'm making flowers. Beautiful, truthful, flowers. For Parent's Day. That's my statement. My gift to the school. Something beautiful. People will be sad when they wash away. They'll be missed—not like yours. People will be glad when they're gone because they're ugly and rude and and—Is this what you write? Is this all you are? This is didactic rhetoric! When are you gonna put yourself on the wall? When are you gonna leave a piece of you—something personal—something that really matters—something from deep down that isn't just a slogan or a gimmick or a a a rant!?

**DANNI**   Give me the chalk—I'm done asking nice.

**SOPHIA**   Look at your "message"! You're all over the place! It reads like the back of an '84 Pinto!

[DANNI *moves in fast. They grapple for possession of the chalk as the* CHORUS *speaks.*]

| WALL | DOOR | CORNER | BENCH |
|------|------|--------|-------|
| Join the army | | | |
| travel to | lobotomies | | |
| exotic lands | for republicans | is there life | |
| meet exciting | it's the law | after college | suck off |
| unusual people | lobotomies for | is there | suck suck |
| and kill them | republicans | life after | suck off |
| join the army | it's the law | college is there | suck suck |
| travel to exotic . . . | lobotomies . . . | life after . . . | suck off! |

[*The grappling has become a brawl, and* DANNI *hurts* SOPHIA. *Everything stops. Silence.* DANNI *steps back.* SOPHIA *takes the chalk and smashes it into dust by any means possible, under foot, by breaking it into bits, by throwing—all except one piece.* SOPHIA *takes the piece and writes boldly on the back wall.*]

**SOPHIA**   [*writes*] "—I   am—   —   my   —   a r t"

[*She puts the chalk in* DANNI'S *hand.* SOPHIA *leaves.* DANNI *stands. Silent.*]

**CHORUS**   silence

**CHORUS**   silence

**CHORUS**   silence

**CHORUS**   silence

**CHORUS**   [*as a unit, whispered*] silence.

[DANNI *goes to the board and writes the letters "h" and "e" changing "art" to "heart."* DANNI *goes to the flower and touches it, lies on the ground beside it. on her side. slightly curved. a half moon. with her feet tucked behind. The* CHORUS *breathes. In. Out. In. Days pass.* DANNI *does not move. A woman from the* CHORUS *goes to* DANNI, *takes the piece of chalk, and finishes* SOPHIA's *flower while she speaks.*]

**WOMAN**   [*drawing*] The only regret   I will have in dying   is if it is not for love. —Gabriel Garcia Marquez

[*The woman remains, kneeling beside* DANNI *as a man from the* CHORUS *approaches, also kneels, takes the chalk, and continues with more flowers as he speaks.*]

**MAN**   [*drawing*] There are   worse occupations in this world   than feeling a woman's pulse —Laurence Sterne

[*The chalk is passed to the next* CHORUS *member, who continues creating the garden, kneeling.*]

CHORUS    [*drawing*] When my desire grows to fierce    I wear my bed clothes inside out. —Ono No Najera

[*The chalk is passed to the fourth* CHORUS *member, and the drawing continues . . .*]

CHORUS    [*drawing*] Love probably doesn't exist. It is not a thing, but a landscape,    consisting of a series of objects unconnected to each other, but seen as a whole. —Viktor Shklovsky

[*The* CHORUS *is now all kneeling around* DANNI. *They look at one another. Speak to one another. And. React. Respond. Flattered. Or. Impressed. Or. Moved. At some point, they gently remove* DANNI's *shoes and socks. The garden grows . . .*]

CHORUS    I came upon no wine so wonderful as thirst.—Edna St. Vincent Millay

CHORUS    You're beautiful. Like a May Fly. —Ernest Hemingway

CHORUS    Being kissed on the back of the knee is a moth at the window screen. —Anne Sexton

CHORUS    I teach my sighs to lengthen into songs. —Theodore Roethke

CHORUS    It is for love that I live all alone. Because the lovers I imagine are safer than the ones I have known. —Anonymous

CHORUS    If you wish to drown, do not torture yourself with shallow water. —Bulgarian Proverb

CHORUS    Passion is sweeter split strand by strand.    Divided and re-divided like mercury    then gathered up only at the last moment. —Jeanette Winterson

CHORUS    Love is made by two people, in different kinds of solitude. —Louis Aragon

CHORUS    Love's a fire. But whether it's going to warm your heart or burn your house down, you can never tell. —Joan Crawford

CHORUS    At the touch of love everyone becomes a poet. —Plato

[*Each* CHORUS *member flies away as they speak.* SOPHIA *enters.*]

CHORUS    Sophia enters

CHORUS    Sophia returns

CHORUS    Sophia sees Danni

CHORUS    Sophia isn't sure about anything at all.

CHORUS    Oh, she's sure.

CHORUS    She's not.

CHORUS    Shhhhh. She's trying to say something.

**CHORUS**  She is?

**CHORUS**  What?

**CHORUS**  Shhh!

**SOPHIA**  Danni? Danni? Danielle?

**DANNI**  Ooooooooooohhhhhh . . . I hate that. Don't call me that.

**SOPHIA**  I had to see you.

**DANNI**  Go away.

**SOPHIA**  I. Want to show you something. Prove something.

**DANNI**  Don't look at me, okay? Don't even look at me.

**SOPHIA**  Sit up.

**DANNI**  No.

**SOPHIA**  Just sit up. Are you hurt? Did someone hurt you?

**DANNI**  I'm going to die.

**SOPHIA**  Sit up.

**DANNI**  No.

[SOPHIA *sits next to* DANNI.]

**SOPHIA**  I want to prove something. To you. About me. My point. The other night. I was trying. With the flower. To make a point. Well. To piss you off. It was supposed to piss you off and yeah so it did and you pissed me off and I've been pissed off for a few days now but the thing is the thing is. I can't stop thinking about you, see? So there it is. I can't and, are you all right?

**DANNI**  My feet are freezing.

**SOPHIA**  Where are your shoes?

**DANNI**  I. I. I. Took them off. Or someone stole them. Someone's walking around sweating in my shoes. It doesn't matter. Anyway. Your point?

**SOPHIA**  My point?

**DANNI**  You said you had a point?

**SOPHIA**  I'm sorry your feet are cold.

**DANNI**  That's your point?

**SOPHIA**  My point? No. Would you like my shoes?

**DANNI**  Your point?

**SOPHIA**  My point. First. First. Let me say. Let me tell you. Let me say. I'll tell you. I. Last night. I had. This. I had a dream. I had a dream about us. It was about us and the thing is, see? We were forty. Forty years old, the two of us. I had a dream that we were forty years old and we lived somewhere I guess

I guess it was somewhere it must've been somewhere, except I'm not sure where, but that doesn't matter. There wasn't any ocean. It was just land with hills and grass and trees, and there were mountains over that way, when we looked West or North I think, but anyway. There were horses. We had a barn with our horses and I would get up mornings and feed them. And we had a kitchen and it smelled like apples. Isn't that funny to smell in a dream? But I could smell them. Apples. And we were forty. A whole lifetime away.

**DANNI**  Is that your point?

**SOPHIA**  No. No. No. That's not my point, that was just a dream I had, that's all. I just wanted to tell you it. But my point. My point. This. This is my point.

[SOPHIA *unfolds her little black dress.*]

I want. I would like. I want you. To wear this. To put this on. I want. To see it on you. To see if it fits to see how it fits to see if this is ever going to work and then . . .

**CHORUS**  Then . . . ?

**DANNI**  Then . . . ?

**SOPHIA**  Then. Let me. Draw you. I want to draw you. In it. See? I've never drawn a person before, people. Still-lifes and abstracts and gardens and flowers. But no people. And I and I think maybe, it's time to try. Even though I won't be good at it, but I want it to be you. You Danni. Will you? Will you? For me?

**DANNI**  I don't wear dresses. I don't wanna wear a dress. It doesn't hang right. I don't feel like me anymore. I feel like a fool and I can't just wear one like that. I wear men's pants. Cuz they suit me. I like the pockets. 100% cotton. relaxed fit. sits at the natural waist. fuller leg with slight taper at the ankle. hidden credit card pocket. all seams are double stitched for strength. machine wash. imported. But a dress? It isn't me.

**SOPHIA**  No. It isn't you. It's a dress. And that. That isn't you either. It's a shirt. And your tie? I love your tie, Danni, your vintage tie, but even that isn't you and those pants aren't your legs either. What I want to draw what I need to see. Is content, Danni. I want to know your content. I want to see it in this context. And I want to draw it, I need to draw it, so I can understand every line. And then. We'll see. We'll go. slow.

**DANNI**  I. Uh. Have. I wrote. Here.

[DANNI *takes a paper from her pocket and hands it to* SOPHIA. SOPHIA *unfolds it and begins to read.*]

**SOPHIA**  Roses are red     violets are blue—

[SOPHIA *looks at* DANNI.]

are you making fun of me?

**DANNI**  It's a poem.

**SOPHIA**  Yeah.

**DANNI**  Read it. Just . . . okay . . . ?

**SOPHIA**  Roses are red violets are blue and all I see is your . . . All I see is your . . .

[SOPHIA *continues to read. The* CHORUS *reiterates* . . .]

**CHORUS**  roses are red    violets are blue    all I see is    your hand drawing lines    the way you'd draw them    in chalk    over blacktop    impossibly tall    whole gardens    I dreamed red    roses    from your hands    only yours would be    scarlet or crimson or sunset    and I could breathe them in

[*The* CHORUS *breathes in.*]

out

[*The* CHORUS *breathes out.*]

in

[*The* CHORUS *breathes in.*]

unreal real    roses on my breath.    did I ever tell you    you are beautiful when you paint?

**SOPHIA**  Can I keep this?

**DANNI**  I wrote it for you.

[SOPHIA *folds the paper and puts it in her pocket.*]

**SOPHIA**  See? I'm always afraid of getting lost. Going someplace new and just getting lost. So I always bring a map. That's what we need. Right now. That's what we'll do. A map. So. Lie down.

**DANNI**  Lie down?

**SOPHIA**  Over here. On your back. I'll have to get close to the bone.

[*Simple music, chimes, woodwinds, lyre. Something ancient.* DANNI *removes her tie. Gives it to* SOPHIA. *She then unbuttons her shirt. Removes it. A tank-tee underneath, looking very much like* SOPHIA *did that first time.* DANNI *rolls her pant legs up too, while* SOPHIA *folds her discarded clothing.* DANNI *lies down, surrendering control.* SOPHIA *positions* DANNI's *hands and legs, just so, on the ground, spread from one another. even her fingers.* SOPHIA *takes up the chalk and draws a careful outline of* DANNI's *body on the ground while she speaks.*]

**SOPHIA**  Where have I never been?

a coal mine

a salt mine

in medieval France

in modern France

or Greece or Italy or Russia

i have never been to the moon
  or Mexico

**CHORUS**  i have never ridden a Greyhound Bus
i have never been to a pro boxing match
or boxed in a pro ring
i have never fought a duel
or been in a brawl
looted a store
never been to Mardi Gras
never been to an opera
never been to jail

**DANNI**  never been dead
been close though
never been to a rodeo
never seen the Alamo
never seen a volcano
went once to Ohio
but not Cincinnati

**CHORUS**  never been in a courtroom
or been to a race track
or a rocket launch
or a fencing match
never seen Mount Rushmore
or all five Oscar Best Picture Nominees

**SOPHIA**  never been to China or Tibet
although Tibet is sometimes in my dreams

**CHORUS**  never been to Cairo
or with Jane Goodall
studying chimpanzees in Gombe
never worked in a sweatshop
never worked in an office building
never been on a submarine gone to sea
never been inside someone else's brain
or in their blood

**SOPHIA & DANNI & CHORUS**  [*hushed*] I've never heard another person's
thoughts while they were thinking

[*The map is complete.* SOPHIA *helps* DANNI *to her feet.*]

**SOPHIA**  And here.
[SOPHIA *kneels and draws.*]
is her heart.

**DANNI**  She needs a brain?

**SOPHIA**  Brain. Of course. You know,

[SOPHIA *draws a brain.*]

the ancient Egyptians believed that thought emanated from the heart and the brain was an organ that only produced mucus. Which is why they entombed the heart, but threw away the brain. And here

[SOPHIA *draws*]

Her eyes. And here

[SOPHIA *draws*]

Her mouth.

**DANNI**  Gets her into trouble.

**SOPHIA**  And lips. Still. Something . . . ?

[SOPHIA *gets the little black dress and spreads it over the figure.* DANNI *frowns.*]

Beautiful, isn't she.

**DANNI**  Aww, I don't—

**SOPHIA**  Mouth, gets her into trouble.

[*They look at each other.*]

And her eyes, and lips.

[*Slowly.* SOPHIA *kisses* DANNI.]

**DANNI**  Sophia.

[SOPHIA *has at last heard* DANNI *speak her name.*]

**SOPHIA**  Mmm-hm.

**DANNI**  Dance with me.

[*They prepare to dance, as does the* CHORUS, *taking partners.* ALL *breathe, clasping hands. In. Out. In. about to begin. then. dark. music continues. maybe voices. simple. supple. beautiful*]

END OF PLAY

# SCHOOLED

Lisa Lewis

# Lisa Lewis

Lisa Lewis's play *SCHOOLED* (*Time Out New York* Critics' Pick, Four Stars) had a critically acclaimed sold-out run at the 2015 New York International Fringe Festival, was awarded the Festival's Overall Excellence Award for Playwriting, and was chosen for an extension at the Fringe Encore Series at Soho Playhouse. Her plays have been developed by Naked Angels, Davenport Theatricals, the New Ohio Theatre, Core Artist Ensemble, and New Helvetia Theatre's Sacramento New Works Festival, where she was an artist in residence. A *New York Times*–published essayist and acclaimed storyteller, her work has appeared in the *New York Times, ELLE Magazine, Kirkus Reviews, New York Theatre Magazine,* and *New York Press.* A graduate of NYU's Tisch School of the Arts, Dramatic Writing Program, Lisa spent six years as a story analyst for New Line Cinema, Tribeca Film, and the Weinstein Company.

# Production History

*SCHOOLED* made its world premiere as part of the New York International Fringe Festival. It was produced by the Present Theatre company, presented by the All-Americans, directed by James Kautz, and featured the following cast and creative team:

LILLI STEIN* as Claire
QUENTIN MARÉ* as Andrew
STEPHEN FRIEDRICH as Jake
Tyler M. Perry (Set Design & Props)
Christopher Metzger (Costume Design)
Evan Roby (Lighting Design)
Jeanne Travis* (Sound Design & Production Stage Manager)
Judy Bowman, CSA (Casting)
Matthew Schneider (Original Dramaturg)
David Gibbs/DARR Publicity (Press Rep)
Form Theatricals—Anthony Francavilla & Zach Laks (General Management)

*Denotes Actors Equity Association

It was extended as part of the Fringe Encore Series at the Soho Playhouse.

Winner of the 2015 NY International Fringe Festival Overall Excellence Award for Playwriting.

For more info on the show visit SCHOOLEDThePlay.com.

## Characters

**Andrew** (50s) A b-list screenwriter who had a handful of major hits in the '90s with dark cop and psychological thrillers, but hasn't put out a good movie in 10 years. On his second marriage with two small children. Teaching at his alma mater because an old friend runs the program. A truly heartfelt guy, who has grown bitter and disappointed over the years.

**Claire** (23) Born in Atlantic City, New Jersey. A scholarship student who has forced her way along by sheer will and some talent. She's scrappy, but unsure, her vulnerability covered by a tough attitude. She's trying hard to be successful, but she's not always the best judge of character.

**Jake** (24) A young Gatsby with a heart. Feels the pressure to be successful like his family. He has the confidence and sense of stability that privilege brings and doesn't like his security being threatened.

## Synopsis

*SCHOOLED* explores the widening chasm between privilege, economic class, and the opportunities for success. Two students vie for a competitive grant from their roguish professor in a taut threesome that tests their romantic relationship and their ethics. A biting drama with surprising humor, *SCHOOLED* is an examination of the lies we tell ourselves, and the truths we refuse to believe.

## Setting

The action takes place in New York City. August to May of the present school year. The stage should be divided into three spaces: a dive bar, a dorm room, and a teacher's office at a university. Other locations can be imagined through lighting and sound.

# PROLOGUE

[ANDREW *stands downstage before a classroom. He makes eye contact with his students, enjoying the moment, rolling along on the sound of his own voice.*]

**ANDREW**    I know you're all nervous, who's the best, who's your competition? I've sat right where you are now. Back when real people could afford this place. No offense. If you're here, you got money or talent, hopefully both. Money, mostly. Here's the deal. I can't show you how to have vision, I can't make you more talented, but I can teach you how to give up those things to get your movie made. You think I'm kidding?

My greatest moment? Just before *Devil's Daughter* came out. The golden hour. When your movie opens and it's panned, or it's a big success and it doesn't change anything. The high lasts ten minutes and then you want more. You can eat the greatest meal of your life, but you're still gonna be hungry the next day.

So, what do you wanna know? Anyone? Here's a trick. When you're in a pitch meeting, doesn't matter what you're pitching, could be a story about Pol Pot and the Killing Fields, tell them it's a story about hope. They'll love that.

## SCENE ONE

[ANDREW's *office at the university. The desk covered with scripts. A poster for the movie* Devil's Daughter *on the wall. A photo of his daughters on his desk.* ANDREW *sits at his desk, script in hand.* CLAIRE *knocks hesitantly on the open door.*]

**CLAIRE**    Excuse me, Professor Owens? I'm Claire, Film 202, Dirty Realism on Wednesdays.

**ANDREW**    I know who you are.

[ANDREW *looks up from his work.* CLAIRE *steps in, just barely.*]

**CLAIRE**    Is now a good time? I just wanted to say I love your class, and your movies. *Hard Crime* is amazing.

**ANDREW**    How come you know *Hard Crime*? Everyone here just watches *Devil's Daughter*.

**CLAIRE**    Come on. That scene where the gangster beats up his buddy who ratted on him, then buys him a drink. Like they can still be friends. Floored me. *Means to an End*, great too. And *Bloodsoaked*. When they said you'd be teaching, I was the first to sign up for your class.

**ANDREW**    Really? Wow.

**CLAIRE**    My dad was a huge fan.

[ANDREW *is insulted.* CLAIRE *doesn't notice.*]

**ANDREW**  Your dad, huh?

**CLAIRE**  So how come you don't write good guys?

**ANDREW**  'Cause they don't exist. If someone's doing something nice for you, it's because it coincides with what they want.

**CLAIRE**  That's depressing.

**ANDREW**  Nah. That's how things get done.

**CLAIRE**  Your movies are dark. I like that.

**ANDREW**  I'm doing a romantic comedy next.

**CLAIRE**  Really?

**ANDREW**  No. But I'd do whatever they give me. I didn't think I had fans. I have producers who blow hot air up my ass—everyone in Hollywood tells ya you're great, not because you are. In case you become great. They're covering their ass.

[JAKE *knocks on the door and enters.*]

**JAKE**  Hey babe. I didn't know you were in here. I hope I'm not interrupting.

[ANDREW *reaches out to shake* JAKE's *hand.*]

**ANDREW**  Not at all, guy. Nice work on your first draft.

**JAKE**  Thanks so much, man.

**ANDREW**  I was really impressed. How'd you finish it so fast? What are you guys on these days?

**JAKE**  It's just been flowing. When you're in the zone, right?

**ANDREW**  If you're lucky. We should sit down sometime. Talk about what your plans for the future are.

**JAKE**  That would be awesome.

[CLAIRE *watches as* JAKE *steals her moment with the professor.*]

**ANDREW**  You ever seen *The Third Man*?

**JAKE**  Maybe . . .

**ANDREW**  Orson Wells.

[CLAIRE *jumps in.*]

**CLAIRE**  [*Quoting*] "In Italy under the Borgias they had warfare, terror, and bloodshed, but they produced the Renaissance. In Switzerland they had brotherly love, democracy, and peace. What did that produce?"

**CLAIRE**  [*Together*] "The cuckoo clock."

**ANDREW**  [*Together*] "The cuckoo clock."

[ANDREW *grins.*]

**ANDREW**  She knows it.

**CLAIRE**  Orson Wells ad-libbed that. It wasn't in Graham Greene's original script.

**JAKE**  I'll have to check it out.

**ANDREW**  I think it'll give you some ideas.

**JAKE**  Awesome. Listen. Speaking of the future. I was wondering if I could get your okay to miss a couple of classes. David Singer is doing research for his new movie in New Orleans—he invited me to assist, but I have to get your approval. It's a great opportunity.

**ANDREW**  How many classes?

**JAKE**  Just three. I'd love to work with him. We have a really similar aesthetic.

**ANDREW**  You don't like *my* movies?

[CLAIRE *looks at her feet, embarrassed.*]

**JAKE**  No, I do. *Devil's Daughter* is great, but it's a thriller. I'm trying to do something a little more . . . realistic. You know?

**ANDREW**  You can learn a lot from a thriller. Action defines character. What someone does tells us who they are.

**JAKE**  Absolutely. You're so right. [*Beat*] If it's too much to miss, I could drop yours and take it next semester. Singer said he might not be teaching then. He's doing a half New York, half LA thing. Apparently his film just got greenlit.

**ANDREW**  Ah.

**JAKE**  You'll probably be here though, right?

[*A beat.* ANDREW *stews.*]

**ANDREW**  Do whatever you want, guy. It's your education.

**JAKE**  Thanks. I really appreciate it. I'll definitely check out *Third Man*.

[*He reaches to shake* ANDREW's *hand.* ANDREW *hesitates before taking it.* JAKE *turns to* CLAIRE.]

**JAKE**  I'll see you later?

[CLAIRE *nods.* JAKE *kisses her demonstratively.*]

**JAKE**  Oh hey, you left your keys at my place.

[*He pulls them from his pocket and hands them to her.* CLAIRE *shoves them in her bag, embarrassed.* JAKE *exits. A beat.*]

**ANDREW**  I thought teaching would be fun. Pass on my hard-earned wisdom. But you guys think you know more than I do.

[CLAIRE *winces.*]

**ANDREW**   You're all so serious.

**CLAIRE**   We're not supposed to be?

**ANDREW**   Oh god, the collective ego in this class, it's inspiring. Make a B movie. You don't have to do it forever. The money's in franchises. I'd love to do some quirky little relationship drama like you guys, there's just not the time.

**CLAIRE**   Everyone in class would love to have your career.

**ANDREW**   Everyone in class is twenty. They would also love a popsicle and a nap.

**CLAIRE**   Come on.

**ANDREW**   Students want careers, guys like me wanna start over. Journalists want to be screenwriters. Screenwriters want to direct. Playwrights want to write for TV-

**CLAIRE**   What do you wanna do?

**ANDREW**   Musical theatre.

[*She laughs.*]

**CLAIRE**   Most of the time, I'm scared I'm gonna end up writing cat blogs in New Jersey. But then I think, what if I do make it, win the Oscar, and I'm still not satisfied?

**ANDREW**   Let's get a little perspective here, you're already disappointed with the career you don't have?

[CLAIRE *holds out her script.*]

**CLAIRE**   Why did you give me a B?

**ANDREW**   It means there's room for improvement. If I give you an "A," call the Coen brothers. It's not a criticism of your talent.

[CLAIRE *points to a page.*]

**CLAIRE**   You wrote "spider puke" here? What's that even mean?

[*He takes the script.*]

**ANDREW**   That's says "spell check."

[*She takes it back.*]

**ANDREW**   Spider puke, I'll have to steal that.

**CLAIRE**   I worked so hard on this and it's just trash—

**ANDREW**   I didn't say it was trash. Good writing takes time. Actually, bad writing takes time too.

**CLAIRE**   —I know we're supposed to be, like, immune to criticism and insecurity—

**ANDREW**  —Oh god, who said that?

**CLAIRE**  You know how in *The Artist's Way*, she tells you to embrace your spiritual journey—

**ANDREW**  —Stop reading *The Artist's Way*. That's how you end up writing cat blogs. You want to make great movies, watch Truffaut, Goddard, Brian De Palma. Make friends with actors, editors. School is a place to meet people.

**CLAIRE**  You went here, didn't you?

**ANDREW**  They kicked me out. But as soon as *Devil's Daughter* made seven figures, they couldn't wait to get me back.

**CLAIRE**  Why'd they kick you out?

**ANDREW**  I wasn't serious like your boyfriend there. Had my son when I was in college. He's your age. Lives in L.A., near his mom.

**CLAIRE**  I'm twenty-two.

**ANDREW**  I thought you were older.

**CLAIRE**  You telling me I look old?

[ANDREW *laughs.*]

**ANDREW**  There's a lot of authentic detail in your script. Is your father a gambler?

**CLAIRE**  He was a salesman.

[ANDREW *gives her a long look.*]

**CLAIRE**  It's a *little* autobiographical.

**ANDREW**  *Devil's Daughter* is about my first wife.

**CLAIRE**  Your wife's a transsexual serial killer who castrates people?

**ANDREW**  Ex-wife. I told her it was a metaphor for our relationship.

**CLAIRE**  How many wives have you had?

**ANDREW**  Just two. [*Beat*] Hey listen. If you want to work on your script, I'm happy to help. I can meet you after class, as a thank-you for knowing the rest of my movies.

**CLAIRE**  Really?

**ANDREW**  That's what I'm here for. If you want my advice. Free Friday night?

**CLAIRE**  Perfect.

**ANDREW**  The White Horse Tavern on Hudson, seven-thirty?

**CLAIRE**  The bar?

**ANDREW**  Booths, cheap drinks, and they don't bother you. That okay?

**CLAIRE**   Of course. Yeah. It's very . . . male. You guys drink hard liquor and write about your phallus. My generation drinks coffee and writes about wanting to cuddle.

**ANDREW**   I drink beer actually. I'll buy you one.

**CLAIRE**   Amazing. Thank you. It's a date.

[*He tips the stroller at* CLAIRE, *dismissing her.*]

# SCENE TWO

[CLAIRE'*s tiny dorm room, a bed, a desk, a mini fridge. She rushes as she gets ready to go out. She tucks in a tight button-down shirt. Then zips on high-heeled boots. She checks the mirror again. Nervous, she untucks her shirt, fluffs her hair and adjusts her boobs.* JAKE *enters, startling* CLAIRE.]

**CLAIRE**   Oh my god, you scared the shit out of me.

**JAKE**   We gave each other keys. Am I still supposed to knock before I enter?

**CLAIRE**   I'm not used to you letting yourself in. It doesn't give me a chance to hide my midget love slave.

**JAKE**   If that's what you're into. I'm cool. You look amazing. Where are we going?

[*He kisses her hello. She's delighted, but distracted.*]

**CLAIRE**   I'm meeting Andrew.

**JAKE**   Oh, you're still doing that? It's Friday night. I wanted to take you to that fancy Thai place you like.

**CLAIRE**   That's sweet, but I can't cancel.

**JAKE**   You're wearing *that* to meet Andrew?

**CLAIRE**   What do you mean, why not?

**JAKE**   You look like you're going on a date.

[*She looks in the mirror again.*]

**CLAIRE**   I do not.

**JAKE**   Your hair is all silky.

**CLAIRE**   Fine. How's this?

[*She puts her hair in a messy bun.*]

**JAKE**   You look more serious when you wear your glasses.

[*She digs in her purse to find her glasses. She puts them on and looks at herself in the mirror.*]

**CLAIRE**   Better?

[JAKE *gives her a looking-over.*]

**CLAIRE**   Stop. You're making me self-conscious.

**JAKE**   What exactly did he say to you?

**CLAIRE**   That he'll help me with my script. As a thank-you for knowing his body of work.

**JAKE**   [*Teasing*] Sounds like a sex thing.

**CLAIRE**   Shut up. I can't believe he's even taking time to talk to me.

**JAKE**   This is a business meeting, you need to look more professional.

**CLAIRE**   Putting your tongue in my mouth in front of a teacher wasn't what I'd call professional.

**JAKE**   [*Sheepishly*] You told me to be more affectionate.

[JAKE *sifts through a pile of clothes on the bed.*]

**JAKE**   What about this?

[*He hands her a bulky blazer. She puts it on, it's ugly. He reaches over and buttons the jacket.*]

**JAKE**   There you go.

**CLAIRE**   Are you sure? It's very *Working Girl.*

**JAKE**   What's wrong with that? I wake up every morning and aspire to be Melanie Griffith.

[*She takes it off. He sifts through the other clothes.*]

**CLAIRE**   Would you like me to wear a burka?

**JAKE**   What about a sweater?

**CLAIRE**   It's eighty degrees outside.

**JAKE**   The school is air-conditioned.

**CLAIRE**   [*A beat.*] We're meeting at the White Horse.

**JAKE**   [*Surprised*] What's wrong with his office?

**CLAIRE**   Your dad does his meetings at the Yale club. I don't think you should call Professors Owens "man." That's not very respectful.

**JAKE**   He calls me guy. Hey guy. Like he's about to sell me a Buick.

[CLAIRE *rolls her eyes.*]

**JAKE**   I wish you had taken Singer's class with me. Now *he's* a genius.

**CLAIRE**   Andrew's my favorite professor.

**JAKE**   I guess you made that pretty clear.

**CLAIRE**   I'm not allowed to compliment my teacher?

**JAKE**   Does he think you're hitting on him?

**CLAIRE**  You told Thelma Schoonmaker you loved her "oeuvre." Were you hitting on her?

**JAKE**  She's 75.

**CLAIRE**  Well, I can tell a 50-year-old man "I like your movies" without it meaning "I want to sleep with you."

**JAKE**  You are 100% right.

**CLAIRE**  Thank you.

**JAKE**  But that's what men hear.

**CLAIRE**  That's not my problem.

**JAKE**  Were you flirting with him?

**CLAIRE**  You flirt all the time. With that poetry major at the copy shop so she'll give you a discount. Oh, you think I didn't see that? Like you really need 80 cents off your order. What about your boss at Sony? Don't you laugh at his jokes, act like he's fascinating?

**JAKE**  He doesn't *want* to sleep with me.

**CLAIRE**  Lucky you.

**JAKE**  As long as you know the message you're sending.

**CLAIRE**  What message? I brushed my hair. Shame on me.

[*A beat.*]

**JAKE**  Are you wearing a push-up bra?

[*A beat.*]

**CLAIRE**  Fuck you. Someone I respect has taken an interest in my work. Tonight is a big deal for me.

**JAKE**  [*Defensive*] Andrew hasn't written a decent movie in ten years. He probably doesn't have any connections.

**CLAIRE**  He's on the grant committee. Don't you want me to be successful?

**JAKE**  Andrew is on the grant committee?

**CLAIRE**  This is my chance to impress someone who could really help me. Everyone already knows *you're* amazing.

**JAKE**  Claire, you're very good. Very perceptive. Your characters are truthful and funny—

**CLAIRE**  But your stuff is *really* smart.

**JAKE**  —Your stuff is smart too.

**CLAIRE**  But you're like Aaron Sorkin smart.

[JAKE *is pleased.* CLAIRE *rolls her eyes at how easy he was to appease.*]

**JAKE**  Actually, my internship is paying off. My boss read *Nightrunners*. I think he liked it.

**CLAIRE**  That's incredible.

**JAKE**  Usually when I get him Starbucks in the morning, it's just for him, but today he said I should get one for myself too.

**CLAIRE**  I'm sure you'll have the Oscar in no time.

[*She kisses him, then pulls away and looks in the mirror.*]

**JAKE**  I can look at your script, if you want help. I got an A on my first draft.

**CLAIRE**  Andrew gave you an A?

[*He shrugs, playing it down.*]

**JAKE**  He wrote "great stuff" at the top.

[CLAIRE *holds up a different shirt, then throws it down. She's lost her confidence.*]

**CLAIRE**  Fuck.

[*He takes her hand.*]

**JAKE**  Hey, hey, it's great you're going after the grant.

**CLAIRE**  You want Singer's nom, right? That's why you're so keen on going on the trip with him.

**JAKE**  We'll see. He's bringing four of us to assist.

**CLAIRE**  Will it be weird if we're both nominated?

**JAKE**  Not at all. [*Beat*] I just wish you weren't going to meet another guy in a bar.

**CLAIRE**  He's not another guy. He's my teacher.

**JAKE**  Look, I know there's a double standard. I know I sound like an asshole. I just want him to take you seriously. Trust your talent. [*Beat*] Maybe you should bring the sweater? For me? [*He hands her the cardigan.*] In case it's cold there?

[*She puts on the sweater, gazing one more time in the mirror, she pulls it across her chest, nervous. JAKE rubs her shoulders.*]

**JAKE**  If he doesn't think you're brilliant, he's an idiot.

## SCENE THREE

[*The White Horse Tavern. ANDREW is hunched in a booth, yellow manila notepads and pens around him. He Pauses his scribbling to chug from one of the four pint beer glasses on the table. He carefully lines the empty glasses in a row, then goes back to writing. A moment later, he angrily rips off a page, and stuffs it into an empty glass. CLAIRE enters, the cardigan wrapped around her. She spots ANDREW, who doesn't notice her.*]

**CLAIRE**  Mr. Owens?

[ANDREW *looks up from his work.*]

**ANDREW**   *Miz Freeman.*

**CLAIRE**   You said to be here at 7:30? Am I interrupting?

**ANDREW**   No, no.

**CLAIRE**   You look deep in thought.

[*He stands up out of the booth and awkwardly hugs her.* CLAIRE *puts down her bag.* ANDREW *looks her over, noticing her cleavage.* CLAIRE *notices the many empty beer pints.*]

**CLAIRE**   Sure I'm not interrupting? Did you get the draft I emailed? I printed you a copy just in case.

[*She pulls her script from her bag and hands it to* ANDREW. *He puts it aside.* CLAIRE *rattles on.*]

**CLAIRE**   I had a version of the second act where she doesn't get on the bus, but then I remembered to raise the stakes like in *Devil's Daughter* when the detective tells her she's a suspect—

**ANDREW**   Hey, whoa . . .

**CLAIRE**   Did you think when she stays with him it's believable? Or maybe I should do it where at first she says no, but . . .

**ANDREW**   Claire. Take a breath. Take a breath.

**CLAIRE**   [*Embarrassed*] Oh. Sorry.

**ANDREW**   No, actually take a breath.

[*She actually does.*]

**ANDREW**   You look nice.

**CLAIRE**   Thanks.

**ANDREW**   Can I get you a drink?

**CLAIRE**   Coffee?

**ANDREW**   Really? I thought you'd be a drinker.

**CLAIRE**   Why?

**ANDREW**   I can tell a lot about a person from their writing.

**CLAIRE**   Huh. I woulda thought you'd be taller, *from your movies.*

[ANDREW *stares at her.*]

**CLAIRE**   Sorry. I drink coffee, mostly.

**ANDREW**   Nothing romantic about coffee.

[CLAIRE *slides into the booth with her feet curled under her. She wraps the cardigan across her chest.*]

**CLAIRE**   So were you able to look at the new draft?

[CLAIRE *takes her laptop out of her backpack and sets it up on the table.* ANDREW *reaches over and slams the laptop shut, getting into her space. She's startled.*]

**ANDREW**   Fuck the laptop! Wrap your hand around a fucking pen.

**CLAIRE**   Sorry. I—

**ANDREW**   Where's your notepad?

**ANDREW**   I'm so used to typing.

[ANDREW *gives her a fresh notepad.*]

**ANDREW**   Use this. You should have stacks of these. You should have walls built out of them.

[CLAIRE *puts the computer away and digs in her bag.*]

**CLAIRE**   [*Embarrassed*] No pen.

[ANDREW *sighs. He gives her one of his.*]

**CLAIRE**   I think I've forgotten how to write by hand.

[ANDREW *folds her hand around the pen.*]

**ANDREW**   Put the date at the top.

[CLAIRE *does.*]

**ANDREW**   Now tear that page off and crumple it up.

**CLAIRE**   What?

**ANDREW**   Come on. It's satisfying.

[ANDREW *rips off a page, crumples it, and jams it into an empty glass. He nods at her to do the same. She does.*]

**ANDREW**   You can't do that with a computer.

[CLAIRE *does one more, with gusto.*]

**ANDREW**   Hey! Don't waste paper.

**CLAIRE**   Oh! I . . .

**ANDREW**   It's a joke. You sure you don't want a drink?

**CLAIRE**   No thank you. [*making up an excuse*] Beer calories.

[ANDREW *finishes his beer and starts another already on the table.*]

**ANDREW**   I swim laps. You work out?

**CLAIRE**   I substitute anxiety for exercise.

**ANDREW**   Ever try meditating?

**CLAIRE**   It's not my thing.

**ANDREW**   I do it every time I sit down to write. Gets the bullshit outta my system. Try it with me.

**CLAIRE**  That's okay.

**ANDREW**  Meditating. Marty taught me this.

**CLAIRE**  Marty?

**ANDREW**  Marty Scorse . . .

**CLAIRE**  Scorsese, right. Oh.

**ANDREW**  Incorporates the magical experience. The "now." That's about really being in this moment. Say it with me. Now.

**CLAIRE**  Is *this* a joke?

**ANDREW**  Say *Now*.

**CLAIRE**  No thank you.

**ANDREW**  This is meditation. Say *Now*. [*Beat*] Come on. Say it.

**CLAIRE**  Now?

**ANDREW**  Now.

**CLAIRE**  Now?

[ANDREW *takes a deep breath. It's a little sensual. He gestures at* CLAIRE *to do the same. She does, hurriedly.*]

**ANDREW**  [*a slow exhale*] Now.

**CLAIRE**  Now?

[*He takes her hands.*]

**ANDREW**  Now . . .

**CLAIRE**  Now . . .

**ANDREW**  Now . . .

**CLAIRE**  Now . . .

**ANDREW**  See that. *Now* you're in the moment. Good. That's a magical experience. Meditation is great. After my divorce, it was like—whoa—why haven't I been doing this all my life? [*Beat*] Now.

**CLAIRE**  Now.

**ANDREW**  [*Together*] Now . . .

**CLAIRE**  [*Together*] Now . . .

[*A Beat.*]

**ANDREW**  How do you feel?

**CLAIRE**  Good?

**ANDREW**  Really?

**CLAIRE**  I don't know.

**ANDREW**  [*He points at his head.*] Everything I need is all right here. Sure I can't buy you a drink? My treat.

**CLAIRE**  What kind of beer is that?

**ANDREW**  Sam Adams. Can't do hard liquor. *Have to remain a functioning alcoholic.*

**CLAIRE**  It's a little weird to drink with my teacher.

**ANDREW**  I'm just another struggling writer.

**CLAIRE**  Yeah right.

**ANDREW**  Hanging out and talking about our work, getting to know each other. Where you, uh, where ya from Claire?

**CLAIRE**  Atlantic City.

**ANDREW**  People are actually from Atlantic City? What's that like? Taffy, the boardwalk, summers in the ocean?

**CLAIRE**  Only tourists eat the taffy.

**ANDREW**  You like growing up there?

**CLAIRE**  It wasn't like cool or anything.

**ANDREW**  But you snuck into the casinos?

**CLAIRE**  My ma was a blackjack dealer. I basically grew up in the break room. Started working as a cocktail waitress at Harrah's when I was fifteen. Ma got me a fake ID.

**ANDREW**  Wow.

**CLAIRE**  I play a good hand of Texas Hold 'Em.

**ANDREW**  Maybe you could teach me some tricks.

**CLAIRE**  I could make you a winner.

**ANDREW**  Whew! A cocktail waitress? In the little outfit? You sure you don't want a drink?

[CLAIRE *shakes her head no.*]

**CLAIRE**  Mr. Owens, Atlantic City is a scratch-off ticket floating in a sewer. So if I seem a little intense, and by the way, I prefer *motivated*, it's 'cause I'm trying to do something with my life that doesn't involve being a cocktail waitress.

**ANDREW**  You can call me Andrew. I'm gonna take you up on that poker lesson.

[*She pushes her script toward him.*]

**CLAIRE**  After you help with my script.

[ANDREW *laughs.*]

**ANDREW**   Your parents still live in Atlantic City?

**CLAIRE**   My ma's still there.

**ANDREW**   What about your pops?

**CLAIRE**   He died.

**ANDREW**   Oh. I'm sorry.

**CLAIRE**   Yeah.

**ANDREW**   I was never close to my dad.

**CLAIRE**   I was close to mine.

[*A beat.*]

**ANDREW**   So this story about the gambling father in Atlantic City, it's very personal?

**CLAIRE**   All right, yeah. It is.

**ANDREW**   Then don't write it.

**CLAIRE**   Wait. Are you saying it sucks?

**ANDREW**   Nobody cares about your little life story and getting it right. Nobody but you.

[*A beat.* CLAIRE *is stung.*]

**ANDREW**   [*Feeling a little contrite.*] What I'm telling you is as an act of mercy. To save you some pain. You put your life in there, you don't own it. After the producers cut everything you love, the director and actors rewrite it, it's been focus-grouped and fucked by the market research guys. You won't recognize it. If you care, write a novel. Don't take it to Hollywood unless you want to get your heart broken. And you can do that in New York and this city has better food.

**CLAIRE**   Is that what happened to you?

**ANDREW**   To everybody. Imagine Fitzgerald's producers' notes, "let's not call him Gatsby, what if we call him Bob. The Great Bob—isn't that more relatable?" *That* shit is screenwriting.

**CLAIRE**   So why do you do it?

**ANDREW**   If I wrote you a check for half a mil and asked you to change some words. You'd say no?

**CLAIRE**   Half a mil? That much?

**ANDREW**   *Or*, you can be piss poor with integrity and argue every edit, but it still won't tell the story you want, because nothing on this page will ever capture the actual complicated bullshit of life.

**CLAIRE**   Jesus. So you hate it?

**ANDREW**   Nah, I fucking love making movies. I just don't take it personally. I live in the city, I have kids. Costs a fortune. You just gotta know why you're doing it.

**CLAIRE**   You *sound* bitter.

**ANDREW**   I'm strawberry syrup compared to some guys in this business. [*Beat*] But if I were you, right now, I would get as far away from Hollywood as you can. You're young, you're beautiful. You should be traveling, making love, talking to everyone. The world is full of characters. Have you been to Nigeria?

**CLAIRE**   No. Have *you* been to Nigeria?

**ANDREW**   I've had a life. Tried the wrong drugs. Scored with the wrong women. Watched my friends get boring, my parents get old and seen the sun set over this city for fifty fucking years. So *I* have enough to write about.

**CLAIRE**   Yeah I get it. I can't afford to go to Nigeria. Jake has an internship with Sony.

**ANDREW**   Fuck internships. You want to spend a year picking up sushi for some producer who's most creative idea is ordering the spicy tuna? Buy a camera. Start shooting. Meet people.

**CLAIRE**   I met you. What's that gonna do for me?

[*She points to her script.*]

**ANDREW**   Good. That's good. You gotta hustle. I never had an internship. My pops was a union carpenter, snuck me into Silver Cup. I handed my first script to an AD on the set.

**CLAIRE**   That's cool.

**ANDREW**   Your pal Jake. He's got some polish on him, right? I can tell.

**CLAIRE**   Jake's a good guy.

**ANDREW**   Beware the golden boys. They tarnish.

**CLAIRE**   You're giving me dating advice?

**ANDREW**   I'm an all-around guru. I didn't think he'd be your type.

**CLAIRE**   Why not?

**ANDREW**   A fucking cocktail waitress. Your dad didn't mind?

**CLAIRE**   I told you. He was dead.

**ANDREW**   Right. Sorry. Can I say something?

**CLAIRE**   Yes.

[CLAIRE *readies her pen and paper.* ANDREW *puts his hand on top of* CLAIRE'*s. A long Beat.*]

**ANDREW**   I'm sorry about your dad.

**CLAIRE**  Thanks.

[CLAIRE *stares at their hands intertwined on the table. After a Beat,* CLAIRE *withdraws her hand from his.*]

**CLAIRE**  We can reschedule.

**ANDREW**  You just got here.

**CLAIRE**  It just seems like. Maybe when you're not . . .
[*She gestures to all the empty glasses.*]
I should go. Jake was right.

**ANDREW**  You think I'm drunk?

**CLAIRE**  No, I . . . I don't know . . . Are you? I'm sorry I guess that's none of my . . . I'll just.

[CLAIRE *grabs her backpack and swings it over the table knocking over the beer glasses* ANDREW *had carefully aligned.*]

**CLAIRE**  Shit. I'm sorry.

[*They rush to mop up the mess.*]

**CLAIRE**  Your notepads.

**ANDREW**  They'll dry. Imagine if this was a computer.

**CLAIRE**  I should go.

[CLAIRE *is up and out of the booth.*]

**ANDREW**  Relax. Sit down. We'll talk about your script.

[ANDREW *pulls a copy from his backpack. He scans his notes.*]

**ANDREW**  There's no inciting incident. The first act blows. Act two you have me. When she gets off the bus to go back to her dad, move that to the first ten pages. Get there faster.

[CLAIRE *Pauses, intrigued.*]

**CLAIRE**  How?

**ANDREW**  She has to *choose* to stay. It's gotta be her decision.

**CLAIRE**  She doesn't think she has a choice.

[CLAIRE *slides back into the booth.*]

**ANDREW**  What does she want? Her dad's a fuck-up and the game is dangerous, but she wants to win, right? Everyone's got a choice. You can get anything, if you're willing to live with the consequences.

[CLAIRE *thinks hard on this.*]

**ANDREW**  Do a wide shot of her back on the boardwalk looking up at the casino, silhouetted in the sunset, just her, and we'll know.

**CLAIRE**  Wow. Okay. Anything else?

**ANDREW**  You sure you don't want a drink? [*Beat*] *Unless* you'd feel more comfortable working on this in class.

[*He holds up his empty pint glass. CLAIRE hesitates. ANDREW starts to put away the script with his notes on it.*]

**CLAIRE**  Wait.

[CLAIRE *is curled up in the corner of the booth. She slowly sits up, puts her feet on the floor, pulls her hair out of the bun. She takes off her cardigan and leans over the table toward ANDREW.*]

**CLAIRE**  Maker's and Seven.

**ANDREW**  That's my girl.

# SCENE FOUR

[*One month later. The dorm room. CLAIRE sits on the bed in tee-shirt that says FUCK YOUR DAY JOB, WRITE A SCREENPLAY. ANDREW's yellow manila notepad on her lap. JAKE is beside her in his boxers and tee-shirt working on his laptop.*]

**CLAIRE**  Now. Now. Now. Now . . . Now . . .

[JAKE *glares at her annoyed.* CLAIRE *continues "nowing" but softer now. Still,* JAKE *can't concentrate.*]

**JAKE**  All that *Way of the Peaceful Warrior* shit. You used to make fun of that.

**CLAIRE**  It's really helped me. It's about being in the moment.

**JAKE**  Gross.

**CLAIRE**  Try it. It'll relax you.

**JAKE**  No thanks.

[*She puts her notebook down and starts to kiss him, his arms, chest, legs, lifting his shirt.*]

**CLAIRE**  [*"Nowing" after each kiss.*] How 'bout now? Now?

**JAKE**  The last thing I want to think about when you're putting your mouth on my body is Andrew.

[CLAIRE *stops with the kissing.*]

**JAKE**  All he does in class is listen to himself talk. [*Mimicking Andrew*] "The plot is a car. Characters are the gasoline."

**CLAIRE**  I like that analogy.

**JAKE**  It's a ridiculous analogy. Who talks like that?

**CLAIRE**  That's his thing. He's the wise, embittered screenwriter guy.

**JAKE**  No, he's the self-important hack.

CLAIRE  Why'd you take his class, then?

JAKE  'Cause *you* did.

CLAIRE  Cute.

JAKE  Yeah, I am cute.

CLAIRE  Check it out.

[*She hands him* ANDREW's *latest script.*]

JAKE  He gave you his script?

CLAIRE  Cool right?

JAKE  But why did he give it to you?

CLAIRE  Wants to know what I think.

JAKE  *He's* the teacher.

CLAIRE  He's a writer like everyone else. He respects my opinion. *Haunted Desert.* A horror movie set in the Wild West.

JAKE  I don't know why he hasn't won an Oscar.

CLAIRE  I think his movies are deeply psychological. There's like, real pathos.

JAKE  Pathos?

CLAIRE  Yes.

JAKE  I never noticed.

CLAIRE  You've only seen *one* of Andy's movies.

JAKE  You're calling him Andy now?

CLAIRE  I don't call you Jacob.

JAKE  You're sleeping with me.

[*A beat.*]

CLAIRE  Do you think Andrew is happy?

JAKE  You're the one who spends all your time with him. [*With a forced lightness*] No one in class gets that kind of attention.

CLAIRE  Not everyone can be Jake and get an A on the first draft. [*Beat*] Andrew's not making the films he wants. He has to support his family. He has two little girls and thirty-year-old son. He doesn't have time to *explore his art.*

JAKE  I bet he wants to explore your art.

[CLAIRE *goes quiet.*]

JAKE  [*Feeling remorseful.*] My dad got me a membership to MOMA. They're doing a retrospective on Yoko Ono this month.

CLAIRE   I saw a video once where she let people cut chunks of her clothes off while she just sat there. It was so weird. So vulnerable and lonely.

JAKE   I know you love that stuff. We could go with my parents in a couple of weeks. I want them to get to know you better.

CLAIRE   Another chance to impress Bunny and Ray Ray.

JAKE   They don't actually call themselves that.

CLAIRE   Yeah, but their friends do. I aspire to have cutesy names for us someday. What do you think of Chinchilla and Mr. Crow?

JAKE   Crows are creepy. What if we were Chinchilla and Chihuahua?

CLAIRE   That sounds like we're strippers for a Mexican drug cartel.

JAKE   What about Kiki and Bobo.

[*She laughs.*]

JAKE   So can I plan the museum thing with my parents?

CLAIRE   I love that they're so into art. It's not really my mom's thing.

JAKE   Yeah sort of. They're just not into *me* doing it.

CLAIRE   I know. They don't understand how good you are.

[JAKE *grins. He takes her hand, snuggles closer.*]

CLAIRE   You know, Andrew thinks you're really talented.

JAKE   He said that?

CLAIRE   He said you're polished.

JAKE   Well, he's got good taste.

CLAIRE   Oh, now you like him.

[CLAIRE *leans back on the bed, lost in thought. She taps her pen on her manila pad.*]

CLAIRE   I think he's like . . . poignant, you know?

JAKE   Poignant? I guess that's better than hot.

CLAIRE   He's an alcoholic. He drinks like four beers an hour.

JAKE   And this is the guy you want to be your mentor? [*Beat*] Andrew's got a career, a family, a three-million-dollar Brooklyn brownstone. I know you, Claire. He doesn't need you to take care of him. Trust me. He's supposed to be helping you.

CLAIRE   He is.

JAKE   Has he gotten you an internship? Is he gonna introduce you to his agent? Has he even looked at your script?

CLAIRE   He reads my pages, he's a great editor, really rough.

**JAKE**   When are you going to let me read it?

**CLAIRE**   When it's ready.

**JAKE**   Don't you want to read mine?

[*He hands her a copy of his script. When she tries to take it, he holds it out of her reach.*]

**JAKE**   Quid pro quo. I have ideas if you need a fix. The lovers discover they're siblings, the mom's a spy, the dad gets a sex change.

**CLAIRE**   I'm gonna use all of those.

**JAKE**   See, we work so well together. I miss reading each other's stuff. But I guess you'll be busy with Andy's script now. [*Beat, a realization*] Oh wait, are you writing about me?

**CLAIRE**   I just need to do this for myself okay?

**JAKE**   With Andy.

[*A long beat. He grabs her script and ruffles through it.*]

**CLAIRE**   Don't. I would *never* read your stuff without permission.

**JAKE**   You read my journal when we first started dating.

**CLAIRE**   I thought you left it out on purpose!

[*She holds her hand out for the script. He hesitates.*]

**CLAIRE**   Give it to me *now*!

**JAKE**   Oh? *Now*? You want it *now*?

**CLAIRE**   Come on.

[*A Beat.*]

**CLAIRE**   Give me back my script, please.

[JAKE *tosses the script on the bedside table. He pushes her down on the bed.*]

**CLAIRE**   Just stop.

[*He pins her arms over her head.*]

**JAKE**   I thought this was what you wanted.

**CLAIRE**   I'm not in the mood.

[*He presses against her.*]

**JAKE**   What does Andy say when he's being *rough*?

[*They stare at each other, surprised by* JAKE's *ferocity.* CLAIRE *hesitates, then gets into it.*]

**CLAIRE**   He says, "Do it the way I tell you."

[*He kisses her hard. She kisses him back. She turns out the bedside lamp. Her script falls to the floor.*]

# SCENE FIVE

[ANDREW, *downstage, lectures to his class.*]

**ANDREW**  How do you show a love story on screen? Anyone know? It isn't sex. A montage? No. I hate motherfucking montages. They're everywhere. You can't get through a chick flick today without eight shots of people holding hands and lip-flapping over an iTunes commercial. That's lazy folks. You're letting the soundtrack do all the work.

Raymond Chandler used to tell a story about a writer who couldn't figure out how to show a man falling in love. Then one day the guy's in an elevator and a man with a hat gets on. At the next floor, a bunch of women get in and the man doesn't take his hat off. They go up another floor and a woman gets on, and she gives the man the *slightest hint of a smile*, and this time, this time, *the man takes off his hat.* [*Beat*]

Now, how do you show a man falling out of love? Same scene. But you put him in the elevator with his wife.

# SCENE SIX

[*The White Horse Tavern.* CLAIRE *and* ANDREW. ANDREW *is a bit more fired up than usual.*]

**ANDREW**  Cameras are masculine and aggressive. They're invasive. How would you like something right up in your face like that.

[*He puts his hand uncomfortably close to her face.*]

**CLAIRE**  They even look phallic.

**ANDREW**  It's a big dick shooting out of a guy's head.

**CLAIRE**  This is your analogy? Filmmaking is consensual, the actors want to be there. You're not raping them.

**ANDREW**  Ask an actor what it feels like.

**CLAIRE**  That's why there aren't more women directors? Because the medium is aggressive?

**ANDREW**  No. It's because the money men in charge won't trust a hundred million dollar budget to a chick and the teamsters who make up 90 percent of every crew won't take orders from one. It's the most obvious kind of misogyny.

**CLAIRE**  [*Suspicious*] Oh, so you're a feminist?

**ANDREW**  There's a lot about me that might surprise you.

**CLAIRE**  Why didn't you ever want to direct?

**ANDREW**  I can't get up that early in the morning.

**CLAIRE**   Singer's only taking guys to New Orleans.

**ANDREW**   It's New Orleans.

**CLAIRE**   So?

**ANDREW**   Have you ever been there? Bourbon Street?

[*She shakes her head no.*]

**ANDREW**   You can't bring female students if you want to have a good time, unless you want to have a *really* good time.

**CLAIRE**   That's totally unfair.

**ANDREW**   You say sexist, I say felony. You're going into a hard biz, what can I tell you.

**CLAIRE**   Why aren't you worried about hanging out with a girl?

[*A beat.*]

**ANDREW**   We're friends.

**CLAIRE**   Your wife doesn't care we're here so late?

**ANDREW**   She knows I'm working. Three nights a week. [*Beat*] She doesn't get jealous anymore. Hasn't for a long time.

**CLAIRE**   I doubt that.

**ANDREW**   She's occupied with the girls. And work. *Anyway.*

[*A beat.*]

**ANDREW**   Do you realize you've had my script for two weeks? I don't give that to just anyone. I don't litter the world with my creative seed. You didn't read it? You lost it? You hated it?

**CLAIRE**   Hey! Take a breath. [*Beat*] I took my time with it. I was really honored that you gave it to me.

[*She pulls ANDREW's script from her bag.*]

**ANDREW**   You had this on you the whole night and you didn't say a word? You let me go on for an hour about cameras?

**CLAIRE**   You like to talk.

**ANDREW**   Well?

**CLAIRE**   Do you actually want my opinion or am I just supposed to adore you and tell you how great it is?

**ANDREW**   So you didn't like it? [*Beat*] I gave it to you. I want to know what you thought.

**CLAIRE**   It's good.

**ANDREW**   Yeah?

**CLAIRE** Really good. It's . . . sad.

**ANDREW** It's a horror movie.

**CLAIRE** Well. It's sad. You write really sad stuff.

**ANDREW** You got that from the part where he kills the guy with the giant axe, or where he smothers the guy with the saddle.

**CLAIRE** The guy loses his family and they come back to haunt him for the rest of his life. That's devastating.

[ANDREW *shrugs, playing it off.*]

**ANDREW** Even horror characters need believable motivations.

**CLAIRE** How come you don't want to write a real person movie? Not an apocalypse, or a haunted house, or a Wild West serial killer.

**ANDREW** [*Joking but defensive.*] Hey, that's not bad. What about an apocalyptic virus ravages the west, while a serial killer rampages and the only place to hide is a haunted house.

**CLAIRE** Okay. [*A long beat.*] You're better than your screenplays.

**ANDREW** That's a crap thing to say.

**CLAIRE** Actually, it's a compliment.

[*She finally hands him the script. He flips through it, quietly annoyed.*]

**CLAIRE** They're just some notes. I wasn't saying it's not good.

[CLAIRE *opens her notebook and begins writing.* ANDREW *leans back in the booth, thumbing through his script. He looks closer at her notes. They're good. He takes his time reading them.*]

**ANDREW** Thanks.

[*They continue to work quietly on their own.*]

**ANDREW** What you have to say, it's important to me. It is.

**CLAIRE** Really?

**ANDREW** Yes. Thank you for taking it so seriously.

[*He signals for another drink.*]

**ANDREW** Maker's and Seven.

**CLAIRE** Cool.

[*They write.* ANDREW *takes notes on her notes. After a while,* ANDREW *reaches across the table and puts his hand on* CLAIRE's, *stroking it as they work. Eventually,* CLAIRE *shifts, gently, but deliberately, drawing her hand out from* ANDREW's. *She covers her move by reaching for her drink. A long Beat.*]

# SCENE SEVEN

[CLAIRE *enters the dorm room followed by* JAKE, *who slams the door. They both look a little depleted.* CLAIRE *rattles on, aware* JAKE *is upset but not sure how to help.*]

**CLAIRE**   I didn't know Yoko Ono was so . . . all those close-up videos of women's vaginas. Seeing vaginas with your boyfriend's dad . . . and then eating oysters. [*She shudders.*] Your mom was surprisingly into it though.

[JAKE *is sulking, lost in thought.*]

What's wrong?

**JAKE**   Fuck him. When is he gonna get it in his head that I'm not his little protégé? He has my sister for that.

**CLAIRE**   Sometimes I think your dad doesn't really see you as a separate person.

**JAKE**   It's all about him, you know? *Dr. Corbin.*

[JAKE *paces the small room.* CLAIRE *leads him to the bed and settles him against her so she can give him a shoulder massage.*]

**CLAIRE**   Your dad is very controlling. He ordered everyone's food, like we'd just want what he wanted. Steak tartare is gross. It's a pile of raw meat with a raw egg on top. It doesn't make any sense.

**JAKE**   He was trying to impress you.

**CLAIRE**   He isn't going to be satisfied until you're a mini version of him.

**JAKE**   You think he's your best friend, and then bam, he hits you with disappointment. You know what he said when I got into school here? "Congratulations, *but no one's life has ever been saved by a screenplay.*"

**CLAIRE**   He's probably jealous you're doing something creative. He's so competitive with you.

**JAKE**   Or, he's afraid I'm going to be a giant failure.

**CLAIRE**   You'll never be a failure. It's not in your genes.

**JAKE**   I have to do something really great though. To show him. Like really impressive.

**CLAIRE**   Try not to let him get in your head. If you're happy, he should be happy.

**JAKE**   Ahhhh! You're right. I know you're right. [*Beat*] I wish I could drop everything and live off the grid.

**CLAIRE**   We could go to Nigeria.

**JAKE**   Nigeria?

**CLAIRE**   You know what would really piss them off? You should make super arty installation pieces like Yoko. If they're worried about you doing movies, wait 'til you film fifteen minutes of someone's thigh.

**JAKE**   Sometimes I think my dad is cool and then—

**CLAIRE**   Yeah, parents are like that.

**JAKE**   I'm sorry. I shouldn't be complaining.

**CLAIRE**   No, you totally should. You're allowed.

[JAKE *drums his foot against the side of the bed, more nervous than we've ever seen him.*]

**CLAIRE**   Screenplays actually saved my life. Growing up, all I did was watch movies. Even when my dad was at his darkest, we could put on a movie. I'd lay my head on his shoulder. And he was happy for a couple of hours. We could watch a—

**JAKE**   [*cutting her off*] You know what my dad said when you were in the bathroom? He said you were messed up because of what happened with your father.

[CLAIRE *turns red.*]

**CLAIRE**   Is that what *you* think?

**JAKE**   No. Never. Of course not.

**CLAIRE**   [*Getting worked up*] I thought your parents liked me. Your mom's always so nice. She got me that gift certificate to Bloomingdale's.

**JAKE**   [*Backtracking*] Oh no, no, they do.

**CLAIRE**   What did he mean, messed up? Like I'm gonna . . . what? Explode? Did I do something weird in front of them?

**JAKE**   [*Trying to fix it*] I think he meant you've been through a lot. You're a survivor. That's a good thing. Hey, they like you. They do.

**CLAIRE**   But I'm messed up? Did your mother say something about me?

**JAKE**   No. Never.

**CLAIRE**   Not a compliment or anything?

**JAKE**   She says you're really unique.

**CLAIRE**   That's a euphemism for messed up.

[*An epiphany.* JAKE *jumps up.*]

**JAKE**   You know what? We should move in together.

**CLAIRE**   What? Where did that come from?

**JAKE**   Yes! That's exactly what we should do.

**CLAIRE**   But we haven't talked about it.

**JAKE**   Don't you want to?

[CLAIRE *waivers, put on the spot.*]

**CLAIRE**   Well, yeah. I'm just. That's pretty serious.

**JAKE**   I thought this was serious. We've been together a year. Once we graduate we have to decide what we want. We're a team, right? I want to make plans, *with you.*

**CLAIRE**   I know.

**JAKE**   I don't want to be with someone if it's not real you know. I guess we'd date other people? Is that what you want?

**CLAIRE**   [*Panicking*] What? No.

**JAKE**   But if you're not ready . . .

**CLAIRE**   I was just, surprised. [*Beat*] Where would we live?

**JAKE**   We can live where I am now. It's big enough.

**CLAIRE**   It's a two bedroom in the village. There's no way I could afford to be your roommate. It's gotta be like $3000 a month.

**JAKE**   My parents own it. They're gonna give it to me.

**CLAIRE**   Wow. They'd let me move in, with all my stuff? Feels weird.

**JAKE**   They're never even in the city. Just come live with me.

**CLAIRE**   Would you tell them I'm living there? It wouldn't be mine, they could kick me out any time.

**JAKE**   I wouldn't let that happen.

**CLAIRE**   Maybe we could get our own place? Crown Heights is cool now. *Time Out* said it's the next frontier.

**JAKE**   You don't really want to live in some shithole in Crown Heights do you? It's not safe. Be serious. This is an opportunity, Clairebear. We can be artists in the village. Focus on our writing. Sit in a coffee shop all day. We could have three scripts done by the end of the year.

**CLAIRE**   Aren't you gonna get a job?

**JAKE**   [*Starting to get annoyed*] *Writing is working.* Don't worry so much.

**CLAIRE**   Easy for you to say.

**JAKE**   This is the dream, Claire. Fuck everyone who tells us what we should be doing. You could save money to make a film.

[CLAIRE *thinks hard, trying to look at the long game.*]

**CLAIRE**   I guess, maybe if I get a better job, *and get the grant.*

**JAKE**   Has Andrew said anything about it?

**CLAIRE**   Not yet. [*Beat*] You really want to move in together?

**JAKE**   Yes! What do I have to say? Forget about the rent, I'll deal with my parents. Will you move in with me?

**CLAIRE**  You really like me that much?

[*A beat.*]

**JAKE**  I'm in love with you.

**CLAIRE**  You are?

[*A grin spreads across* CLAIRE'*s face. They kiss, emphatically.*]

# SCENE EIGHT

[*The White Horse Tavern. Scripts, yellow manila pads, pens and drinks cover the table.* CLAIRE *is throwing darts. Most of her attempts bounce off the target and roll on the floor.* ANDREW *is nodding through a cell phone conversation. He finishes.*]

**ANDREW**  Fuck yeah!

[*He spins* CLAIRE, *then tosses back a beer.*]

**ANDREW**  They bought the horror script. They're calling it Clint Eastwood meets *The Ring.*

**CLAIRE**  Congratulations!

**ANDREW**  Whew. Yeah.

[ANDREW *is thrilled with himself.* CLAIRE *is mesmerized.*]

**CLAIRE**  God. What's that like?

[*He laughs.*]

**ANDREW**  Feels good.

**CLAIRE**  I want that.

**ANDREW**  I just sold a fucking script! You gonna buy me a drink?

**CLAIRE**  You're the one with the money.

**ANDREW**  Yeah, I am!

**CLAIRE**  Does that . . . cover you for a while?

**ANDREW**  The money? Well, the agent, the manager, the IRS gets a cut.

[CLAIRE *starts packing her stuff.*]

**ANDREW**  What are you doing?

**CLAIRE**  Don't you want to go home and celebrate?

**ANDREW**  With you. You deserve credit. Your notes helped, you should know that.

**CLAIRE**  Did they?

**ANDREW**  They were good. I mean, you were tough. I thought I was an asshole, but you're . . . My agent was impressed.

**CLAIRE**   He was? At CAA?

**ANDREW**   I'm flying out to L.A. for the shoot.

**CLAIRE**   You should take me with you. I'm a great assistant.

**ANDREW**   Maybe I should.

**CLAIRE**   I could take notes. Get you snacks. Tell everyone you're writing when you're taking a nap. But seriously. I hope it's a huge success.

**ANDREW**   Nice to get what you want for a change.

**CLAIRE**   I'm so happy for you.

**ANDREW**   Yeah? Thanks. You know, Laura didn't even read it.

**CLAIRE**   Why not?

**ANDREW**   She doesn't like screenplays. It took her a month to read the last one and she didn't say one word about it. When I asked, she said it was *nice*.

**CLAIRE**   Ouch.

**ANDREW**   She thinks movies are low culture. She reads the Jonathans. Lethem, Franzen, Foer. That's what a Queens guy gets for marrying a chick from Brooklyn.

[*An uncomfortable beat.*]

**ANDREW**   So when are you gonna sell a script and buy *me* a drink?

**CLAIRE**   Show my stuff to your agent, I'll buy you more than a drink.

**ANDREW**   What kind of thank you ya got in mind?

[CLAIRE *misses another shot. The dart sticks in the wall behind the board.*]

**ANDREW**   Here. Come here. Look.

[*He takes her hand with the dart and tries to guide her into a good throw. This time she hits the dart board.*]

**ANDREW**   There you go. [*Beat*] My agent's gonna tell you the same as me, you can't have a two-page voice-over.

**CLAIRE**   But if the words are good.

**ANDREW**   Nah. Nah. Too precious.

**CLAIRE**   What if I cut it and no one gets what I'm trying to say?

**ANDREW**   Don't try to say something, that's so obnoxious. Give your audience a break. They're bored, ordinary people. [*Beat*] One of my first screenplays was 280 pages long. At a minute a page that's like four and half hours and change. Every word was brilliant, god's gift. My agent, he held it upside down, he used to bang it against his desk. I said, "What the fuck are you doing?" He said, "I'm trying to get your ego to fall out of it." Every time I cut ten pages, I went back, he banged it again. The same fucking thing. Bang! Bang!

[ANDREW *grabs the darts and starts shooting, he's not bad, on target, aggressive.* CLAIRE*'s next throw hits the backboard and bounces onto the floor. She picks it up, embarrassed.*]

**CLAIRE**   Was he right? Did it make your script better?

**ANDREW**   It sold. If that's what good means to you.

**CLAIRE**   Sold is good. Was it the story you wanted to tell?

**ANDREW**   That story was *street smart, and gutsy and beautiful.*

[ANDREW *takes a shot.*]

**ANDREW**   That version's still sitting in a drawer, though.

**CLAIRE**   So you did want to make an art film?

[ANDREW *laughs at her naiveté.*]

**ANDREW**   I had a producer once ask me could I put more crotch in a shot. A woman, her words. Can we get more crotch in there? This ain't art. It's a down payment on your first apartment.

**CLAIRE**   That much?

**ANDREW**   You know who makes art, retarded people. Really. It's called outsider art. People who have extreme mental disabilities, they draw because they can't help themselves. Everything else is about fame, getting paid, and getting laid.

**CLAIRE**   People were telling stories on the wall of a cave 30,000 years ago. The Greeks invented the Gods of Olympus to make sense of the chaos. So they could feel less alone.

[*He cuts her off.*]

**ANDREW**   Eh. I hate this *I'm an artist* bullshit. The mysticism. It's a calling, don't do it unless you can't do anything else. Poor me and my artistic calling. Uhhhhhh.

[*He pretends to flagellate himself over his shoulders.*]

**ANDREW**   Wanna be impressive? Raise kids that don't hate you. Have a sex life that's not so boring you'd rather watch the news. I love my girls, without them, I'd be here all day.

[ANDREW *takes out his cell phone and shows* CLAIRE *pictures of his daughters.*]

**ANDREW**   That's Nora picking flowers upstate.

**CLAIRE**   Cute.

[*He grabs her empty glass.*]

**ANDREW**   Hey, you want another? Maker's and Seven?

**CLAIRE**   It's 3 p.m. on a Wednesday.

**ANDREW**   It's brunch. You know, I'd drink more if I could. I'd do more drugs if they weren't so bad for you. Trouble is, well, I'm such a health fanatic.

**CLAIRE**   They should put you on a Wheaties box.

**ANDREW**   Is that a no? [*He puts her glass down.*] I was working with Liz here the other day, from class. Now she can drink. Have you read her script? Fucking terrific.

**CLAIRE**   [*Uncertainly*] Have you been working with her a lot?

**ANDREW**   Sure. She's a hoot. Very talented.

[*A beat.* CLAIRE *picks up the darts.*]

**CLAIRE**   You know what I like about darts. It's not about chance. But a hair off, a tiny misjudgment and the whole game changes. That's how a good player loses.

[*She easily makes three bull's-eyes.*]

**ANDREW**   You're shitting me? A minute ago you were about to put someone's eye out.

**CLAIRE**   You're terrible at darts.

**ANDREW**   What the fuck's going on here? How'd you do that?

[CLAIRE *walks behind him and puts the dart in his hand, then, with her hand on his, she teaches him how to throw.*]

**CLAIRE**   The weight of the arrow in your palm, the pull of your wrist, the friction between your fingers and the dart. Let your shoulders settle into your back, then . . .

[*The dart sails out of his hand and hits the board.*]

**CLAIRE**   Practice.

[*She leans back against the wall.* ANDREW *glances at her as he shoots. He hits the backboard.*]

**ANDREW**   Now you're making *me* nervous.

**CLAIRE**   Good.

[*A beat.*]

**ANDREW**   Why didn't I meet you ten years ago?

**CLAIRE**   I was twelve.

**ANDREW**   Oh, you're, nah, you're an old soul.

**CLAIRE**   That's what older men say when they want to sleep with you.

**ANDREW**   Is that what you think I want?

**CLAIRE**   Jake says you do.

[ANDREW *grins at the thought of* JAKE *being jealous.*]

**ANDREW**   You get a lotta older guys hitting on you?

**CLAIRE**   My mom's boyfriends. My high school history teacher.

**ANDREW**   Did you always say no?

[CLAIRE *lets another shot fly.*]

**ANDREW**   Okay. Once the semester's over, we're gonna talk about this assistant job. 'Cause it's not a bad idea, having you on set, bounce notes off you. You'd meet some good people. [*Beat*] Uh, you're gonna have to bring some shorts though, hot in L.A.

**CLAIRE**   Are you telling me what to wear? You can't do that.

**ANDREW**   So slap me on the wrist.

[ANDREW *holds out his wrist.* CLAIRE *doesn't move. He takes her hand and smacks his. They playfully slap at each other, leaning in and laughing.* ANDREW *pulls her close. Holding her too long.*]

**CLAIRE**   What are you doing?

**ANDREW**   What do you want me to be doing, Claire?

[*He runs his hand over her hair and leans in, slowly, for a kiss. At the last moment,* CLAIRE *ducks her head away and pulls gently out of his embrace.*]

**CLAIRE**   I'm keeping the voice-over.

[ANDREW *steps back, frustrated. Shaking the moment off.*]

**ANDREW**   Three lines. Five max.

**CLAIRE**   You can't sum up a life in five lines.

**ANDREW**   You can do it in six words. Hemingway did. Here's mine. [*counting on his fingers*] "I should have owned a bar."

[CLAIRE *rolls her eyes.*]

**ANDREW**   Lot of good men came up in this establishment. Dylan Thomas, Delmore Schwartz. Sitting in these booths, scribbling on cocktail napkins, bedding undergraduate poets. *Admirable men.*

**CLAIRE**   Dylan Thomas drank himself to death here.

**ANDREW**   Fuck that. I'm celebrating. Sell a movie to Hollywood you deserve to get drunk. You know how many women have tried to fix me?

**CLAIRE**   Are you proud of that?

**ANDREW**   Sure.

**CLAIRE**   What about your family?

**ANDREW**   Hey. I just made tuition for my kids. I'm not hurting anyone.

**CLAIRE**  Why aren't you with your daughters now?

**ANDREW**  I'm working.

[*She looks at the darts, the drinks.*]

**ANDREW**  Why aren't you with your boyfriend? [*Beat*] Laura's with the girls at her parents'. They're taking a break from the city. Okay? [*Beat*] What are you busting my balls for? I already got a wife.

**CLAIRE**  My dad thought he wasn't hurting anyone either.

**ANDREW**  I'm not your father.

[CLAIRE *picks up the darts and shoots, one, two, three. They hit the dartboard with satisfying smacks.* ANDREW *watches her, feeling a little remorseful.*]

**ANDREW**  What was he like? Your old man?

**CLAIRE**  Nobody cares about my little life story, right? Nobody but me.

[*She pulls the darts from the board and shoots again.*]

**ANDREW**  My old man was an asshole. I told myself he was trying to teach me something, but he was just a son of a bitch.

[CLAIRE *pulls the darts out of the board. She offers them to* ANDREW *but he gestures for her to shoot again.*]

**CLAIRE**  My dad lived for the movies. Ask him anything about old actors. He knew all the stories, James Dean, Burt Lancaster, Steve McQueen, *the tragic flaws of beautiful leading men.*

**ANDREW**  He was a salesman? What did he sell?

**CLAIRE**  He did everything. Sold carpets, waitered, drove a limo. Once he invested in a ferret farm. The ferrets escaped and mated and the state of New Jersey sued him. [*Beat*] His game was poker. The next hand was always gonna change his life.

**ANDREW**  That must have been tough on you.

[CLAIRE *shrugs.*]

**CLAIRE**  I felt sorry for *him*. He was the kinda guy who would look in the mirror and see what he wasn't. He loved me though. He really wanted me to do all right.

[ANDREW *nods.*]

**CLAIRE**  When he died I put five bucks in his casket, a picture of James Dean, and a bottle of Maker's. That was my dad.

[*A Beat.*]

**ANDREW**  You're not gonna get him back by putting him in a movie.

**CLAIRE**  [*Sharply*] I'm not trying to.

**ANDREW**   A two-page voice-over won't do it. What do you want? An apology? An explanation? You'll waste your fucking life waiting for some epiphany. And when it doesn't come you'll be even more pissed off.

[*A Beat.* CLAIRE *turns away, tearing up. He puts his hand on her shoulder.*]

**ANDREW**   Claire?

[*She doesn't turn around.*]

**ANDREW**   Hey, I'm sorry. Come here.

[*She turns toward him. He gently hugs her. She puts her head on his chest, crying herself out.*]

**ANDREW**   Can I buy you dinner?

[*She steps back and wipes her eyes.*]

**CLAIRE**   I've never seen you eat. I thought you subsisted on beer.

**ANDREW**   There's a sushi place around the corner.

**CLAIRE**   I'm not hungry.

**ANDREW**   You know what always makes me feel better? We should see a movie. I feel like I haven't seen a fucking movie in years. Isn't that crazy? I love sitting in theatres. You know? When the lights go down and *you don't know where you're headed.*

[CLAIRE *nods. A Beat.* ANDREW's *cell phone rings. He glances at it, torn.*]

**ANDREW**   I'm sorry, I have to take this.

[*He steps aside to take the call.*]

**ANDREW**   Hi, Bethy. Daddy's working. Mmmm . . . you did, did you help? Sprinkles? Yeah, sprinkles. That's my girl. Hello? Hello?

[ANDREW *puts the phone away.*]

**ANDREW**   Are you ready?

## SCENE NINE

[ANDREW's *office.* ANDREW *is working at his desk, a little hung over. He tosses back a handful of Excedrin with a cup of coffee. Yellow manila pads and stacks of scripts on the desk and floor.* JAKE *knocks on the open door and enters.*]

**JAKE**   Hey?

**ANDREW**   Hey, guy.

**JAKE**   You got a minute?

**ANDREW**   Just a minute.

**JAKE**   I wanted to say congrats. I heard you got a new movie in the chute.

**ANDREW**   Claire tell you that?

**JAKE**   She talks about you a lot. Says you been a big help on her script.

**ANDREW**   Glad to hear that.

**JAKE**   She's always doing that now thing.

[ANDREW *laughs.*]

**ANDREW**   Homeless guy taught me that. Told me his hands were lethal weapons. The "now" kept him from killing people. Coulda been bullshit.

**JAKE**   So it's not real meditation?

**ANDREW**   It's real if it works.

**JAKE**   Do you do it?

[ANDREW *just smiles.*]

**JAKE**   Congrats about the movie. So cool, man. It's got great buzz.

**ANDREW**   There's always a buzz before you get stung.

**JAKE**   Yeah, I hear ya.

**ANDREW**   So what can I do for you?

**JAKE**   I was wondering if I could buy you a drink, maybe pick your brain on a couple things. I know you're a beer drinker. I know a place that's got great microbrews . . .

**ANDREW**   Are you asking me out?

**JAKE**   Oh, no, I . . . you're joking.

[ANDREW *nods.*]

**ANDREW**   Can't. I gotta pick my daughter up and the traffic on the bridge is gonna be nuts.

**JAKE**   You have a car in the city?

**ANDREW**   It's a minivan, but I listen to Zeppelin in it so that's gotta count for something.

[JAKE *jumps on this connection.*]

**JAKE**   I love Zep! John Bonham, quite simply, the most badass drummer to ever get behind a kit.

[ANDREW *nods. He glances at his watch.*]

**ANDREW**   So what's up?

[JAKE *grabs a chair across from* ANDREW.]

**JAKE**   I wanted to ask you . . . How do I get an agent?

**ANDREW**   You're probably gonna have to sleep with one.

[JAKE *is taken aback. A beat.*]

**ANDREW**   I'm kidding. [*Beat*] You think you're ready for an agent?

**JAKE**   I want to take it to that next level, you know.

**ANDREW**   What level is that?

**JAKE**   Have you thought about the production grant?

**ANDREW**   [*Laughing*] Have *I* thought about it?

**JAKE**   I assume you're throwing in for Claire, which is cool, Claire is amazing, but if not, can I submit anything to you? My project is really strong and I'm prepared to start shooting immediately. I could write up a treatment, or if you need more information, whatever it takes? Unless you've already made up your mind . . .

**ANDREW**   Ah. [*Beat*] Wow. That's a pretty slick pitch.

**JAKE**   I just want you to know I'm interested. I think I have a great script and—

**ANDREW**   Does Claire know you're going after the grant?

**JAKE**   Sure.

**ANDREW**   Does she know you're coming to me for the nomination?

[JAKE *shifts uncomfortably.*]

**ANDREW**   Envy will suck the air out of any relationship.

**JAKE**   I'll be very happy for her if she wins.

**ANDREW**   Oh, that's good. Well said. Claire told me you were good. [ANDREW *nods to himself, smirks.*] You ever think about moving to L.A.? You'd do great in L.A.

**JAKE**   You think I should?

**ANDREW**   With that hair, definitely.

**JAKE**   Why aren't you there?

**ANDREW**   I'm not an L.A. type. Hollywood is full of Jakes, guys like you who got all the chicks in high school. Except in TV, TV's, you know, a buncha nerds.

[JAKE *laughs.*]

**JAKE**   I didn't get all the chicks.

**ANDREW**   Oh, yeah?

**JAKE**   I did all right. You didn't?

**ANDREW**   I got one. She had my son when I was 19.

**JAKE**   Oh, right. Claire told me that.

**ANDREW**   New York is for guys who look better over forty. Anyway, my kids are in school here and I can't move 'em.

**JAKE**   I hear ya.

**ANDREW**   Jake, why'd you take my class?

**JAKE**   I've always been a fan of your movies.

**ANDREW**   What do you like about them?

[*A beat.*]

**JAKE**   I think they have real *pathos*. They're deeply psychological.

[ANDREW *senses* CLAIRE's *line.*]

**ANDREW**   Which is your favorite?

**JAKE**   *Devil's Daughter.*

[ANDREW *studies* JAKE.]

**ANDREW**   What's your second favorite?

**JAKE**   I prefer to look at an artist's *body of work*. The ways in which he subverts his genre. You're so good at pacing.

**ANDREW**   Pacing.

**JAKE**   Yeah. Yeah.

[ANDREW *laughs to himself.*]

**ANDREW**   Jake, I gotta tell you something. You have a gift.

**JAKE**   Really?

**ANDREW**   That's very impressive what you did just now. You're an A-game schmoozer. I'm not. It's a talent I've always been jealous of. I could see it right away in you. A fucking gift.

**JAKE**   I wasn't schmoozing you . . .

**ANDREW**   Since you walked in the door. It's not an insult. It shows hunger, which I appreciate. Claire *isn't* hungry, *she's starving*. Now I find that really interesting, 'cause you never know what someone like that will do.

**JAKE**   I want the grant as much as Claire does.

**ANDREW**   Then stop blowing smoke up my ass.

[*A beat.*]

**JAKE**   Fine. Singer's nominating the science fiction dork. What do I got to do to get the nomination from you?

**ANDREW**   Ah. You think you deserve it more than Claire?

[JAKE's *not gonna answer that. A beat.*]

**ANDREW**   Lemme tell you something. *The plot is a car, Jake*—the protagonist is the driver of that car. That person's gotta be lead on the pedal, a master at sharp turns. And most of all, guy, most of all, they've got to be someone I want to *spend time with*. You know what I'm saying?

[JAKE *takes this in.*]

**JAKE**   So it's great you like Claire's writing. You've been working with her a lot.

**ANDREW**   She's very passionate.

**JAKE**   Isn't it distracting writing at a bar?

**ANDREW**   Hemingway did it.

**JAKE**   Hemingway?

**ANDREW**   You want my advice? Go where the buzz is. Everything's happening in L.A.

**JAKE**   Claire and I have to talk about it. We're moving in together.

**ANDREW**   Claire didn't mention that.

**JAKE**   You think she tells you everything?

**ANDREW**   Hey it's cool. But if I were you, kiddo, I'd take it slow. I see these twentysomething guys in my neighborhood, trust me. Pushing strollers, three kids and a puppy pulling them in different directions, looking like they have no idea how they got there.

**JAKE**   You know what's really hilarious, what cracks me up? These guys in their fifties, with little kids, on their second marriage and heading for a third. Looking like assholes and they don't even know it.

[*A long beat. They glare at each other.*]

**ANDREW**   You're gonna do fine, guy. You've got Hollywood written all over you.

## SCENE TEN

[CLAIRE'*s tiny undergraduate dorm. A loud, insistent knock on the door.* CLAIRE *is startled. She jumps up to open it.* ANDREW *stands in the doorway, grinning, drunk.*]

**CLAIRE**   What are you doing here?

**ANDREW**   You haven't been at the bar in a while. I brought you a birthday present.

[CLAIRE *is stunned.*]

**ANDREW**   Are you gonna let me in?

**CLAIRE**   How did you know where I live?

**ANDREW**   Course rosters. Jake's in New Orleans right?

**CLAIRE**   Yeah, but it's really late.

**ANDREW**  I took a chance. I wanted to surprise you. Boo!

**CLAIRE**  I'm working on a paper.

**ANDREW**  Just for a minute. To give you the present.

[CLAIRE *opens the door wider. He steps into the claustrophobic space.*]

**ANDREW**  Wow. Is this it? It's not what I imagined.

**CLAIRE**  This is what an undergraduate dorm looks like.

[CLAIRE *grabs at a bra hanging from the desk chair and shoves it under a book.* ANDREW *sits down on the bed.*]

**ANDREW**  Tiny bed. Can two people sleep in this?

**CLAIRE**  Not really.

**ANDREW**  So this is all your stuff.

[*He picks up a teddy bear from the bed and stares at it.* CLAIRE *takes the bear from him. Smooths down its fur and puts it back on the bed. She stands over him, arms crossed. He pats the bed next to him.*]

**CLAIRE**  Why don't we go to the bar?

**ANDREW**  I just came from there. Come on. I won't bite.

[CLAIRE *sits on the end of the bed, as far as she can from him.*]

**ANDREW**  I brought you these.

[*He hands her a stack of DVDs out of his worn black backpack. Then scoots over next to her and looks over her shoulder as he explains each movie.*]

**ANDREW**  You're gonna love *Sullivan's Travels* with Veronica Lake. It's really great. In fact there are moments in your writing that remind me of Preston Sturges. *Double Indemnity* and *Lady Eve* with Barbara Stanwyck. Classics, study these. And a remastered version of *The Third Man*, because you said you loved it.

**CLAIRE**  Wow.

**ANDREW**  This is the stuff you gotta be watching. And all of Billy Wilder, I'll get you those next. We can watch them together. Did I tell you I met Billy? It was at this crazy party and the guy was 90 years old. Hey do you have anything to drink?

[CLAIRE *stands up.*]

**CLAIRE**  [*re: the DVDs*] These are really great. Thank you.

[ANDREW *lies down on the bed. He sees the teddy bear again, facing him. He hands it to her.*]

**ANDREW**  Can we put this somewhere else?

**CLAIRE**  Andrew get up.

[*She grabs his hand to pull him out of the bed. He sits up for a moment then slumps back down pulling her on top of him.*]

**ANDREW**   Can we kiss for a second?

**CLAIRE**   No.

[CLAIRE *gets up.*]

**CLAIRE**   I'll walk you out.

**ANDREW**   You know, I never got to do that. Make out in a dorm. I was already married. I always thought it would be great.

[*He stumbles over a box on the floor.*]

**ANDREW**   What's with all the boxes?

**CLAIRE**   I'm moving.

**ANDREW**   Oh right, shacking up with the Jakester. He told me. Stopped by my office.

[CLAIRE *stops.*]

**CLAIRE**   He did? When?

**ANDREW**   Did he tell you he's not getting Singer's nomination?

[*She shakes her head no.*]

**ANDREW**   Gave me a hard pitch for the grant, actually.

**CLAIRE**   [*defensive*] There's nothing wrong with him pitching you.

**ANDREW**   I guess he doesn't see you as competition. [*He lets this land.*] I told him how great you are.

**CLAIRE**   So do you like his script?

**ANDREW**   You and I have been working a lot together, but I have to consider everybody. Jake's project is good.

[CLAIRE *sits back down on the bed.*]

**CLAIRE**   So is mine. Thanks to you. Is it down to me and Jake?

**ANDREW**   He thinks he deserves it. You shoulda heard his pitch.

**CLAIRE**   Jake's good at getting what he wants.

**ANDREW**   Sure he is. He's got you. [*He kicks the box.*] Jake's a smart guy from a smart family. Imagine what they expect from him. After the tutors and tennis lessons. *The pressure.* But with you he can relax. With you he can feel superior, he doesn't have to try.

**CLAIRE**   Jake doesn't need me to feel superior.

[ANDREW *grins. She slipped.*]

**CLAIRE**   He works hard. He's really talented. He's gonna be famous someday.

**ANDREW**   If you think Jake is so brilliant and wonderful, why don't I nominate him?

**CLAIRE**   Are you going to?

**ANDREW**   Well, who do *you* think should get it?

[*She's incredulous, caught off guard.*]

**CLAIRE**   It's not my decision.

**ANDREW**   Oh, you want to leave it up to the gods?

**CLAIRE**   Do you think I have the best script?

**ANDREW**   I'm very invested in you, Claire. Your progress, your career.

**ANDREW**   *But* I look at Jake and think, *he's* really got it together.

**CLAIRE**   I think these grants should go to the people that actually need them.

**ANDREW**   Not to the best script?

**CLAIRE**   You think *he* has the best script?

**ANDREW**   Hypothetically.

**CLAIRE**   The script is important. But in whose life is the grant gonna make a difference? [*Carefully*] Jake has a lot of opportunities.

**ANDREW**   Exactly, I have to give it to someone who is really going to use it. Someone who's going places. Who's got a future.

**CLAIRE**   He'll have a future because his parents will buy him one. It's like rock, paper, scissors, *Jake.*

[*She exhales, she's been waiting a long time to say this.* ANDREW *grins.*]

**ANDREW**   Wow. All right. I hope his mother's at least bipolar.

**CLAIRE**   Unfortunately not. She's a psychiatrist though.

**ANDREW**   You'd think that woulda fucked him up.

**CLAIRE**   Nope.

[*They laugh a little.*]

**ANDREW**   You should be with someone who respects you.

**CLAIRE**   Do you really think I write like Preston Sturges?

[ANDREW *steps toward her. He takes her chin gently in his hand, pulling her to him. They kiss. Gently, tentatively at first, then passionately.* ANDREW *moves from her lips, kissing her earlobe, her jaw, her neck. Finally,* CLAIRE *pulls away. They stare at each other. He leans toward her again. She gently pushes him back.*]

**ANDREW**   I'll see you tomorrow?

**CLAIRE**   I can't. Jake's coming by with the truck to pack.

**ANDREW**   Come by the bar tomorrow. One drink. We'll talk about the nomination.

[*He waits until she finally, nods yes.* ANDREW *exits.* CLAIRE *slumps down on the bed, head in her hands.*]

# SCENE ELEVEN

[ANDREW *is at the bar, surrounded by beer pints and eating sushi.* CLAIRE *enters.*]

**ANDREW**   I've been here all day. I wasn't sure you were gonna show. Let me get you a drink.

**CLAIRE**   I can't stay. Someone could have seen you last night.

**ANDREW**   Let 'em. I don't care.

**CLAIRE**   Well, I do. What about Jake?

**ANDREW**   Claire, you know I used to love writing in this bar *alone. Now* I'm always staring at the door, hoping you'll come in.

**CLAIRE**   You get sentimental when you've had . . . five beers.

**ANDREW**   We could go to dinner. There's a great Italian spot next door. The gnocchi melts.

**CLAIRE**   You said you wanted to talk about the nomination.

[*Her phone buzzes with a text. She glances at it but doesn't answer.*]

**ANDREW**   My buddy has this cabin upstate. I go every August. You should come up. A writing retreat.

**CLAIRE**   Let me think about it.

**ANDREW**   It's on a lake. You can see the mountains. No competition. No reading *Variety.* It would give us time together. Outside the city.

**CLAIRE**   I have to apply for jobs. Start working.

**ANDREW**   [*A flash of anger.*] You think Jake can't spare you for a couple weeks? [*He backtracks, a new tactic.*] A little career advice. You need another script. People are gonna ask what else you're working on.

[*Her phone buzzes again.*]

**ANDREW**   Is that him?

**CLAIRE**   I'm sorry. I should go.

**ANDREW**   Why did you even come by then?

**CLAIRE**   Because you said you wanted to talk about the nomination.

[CLAIRE *heads for the door.*]

**ANDREW**   Fine. Go ahead. Tell Jake you won.

[*She stops.*]

**ANDREW**  That's right. The nomination is yours.

**CLAIRE**  I really have it?

**ANDREW**  It's what you want right? Congratulations.

[*He raises his glass to her.*]

**CLAIRE**  Andrew, *thank you.*

[*He takes a long chug of his beer. It takes her a moment to process.*]

**ANDREW**  It'll mean we really get to work together.

**CLAIRE**  But you're giving it to me because you love my script, right? I took all your advice.

[JAKE *enters.*]

**JAKE**  I knew you would be here. We're supposed to be moving. The truck is double parked outside the dorm. Why aren't you answering my texts?

[CLAIRE *stands up out of the booth.*]

**CLAIRE**  I was just leaving. Andrew, we can talk later. [*With meaning*] Thank you.

**ANDREW**  Hey guy, we're celebrating. Claire's got my nomination.

[JAKE *looks at the two of them.*]

**ANDREW**  You know what that means, the grant's hers.

**JAKE**  What are you talking about? I didn't see it posted.

**ANDREW**  It's my decision. You didn't know that?

**JAKE**  It's not up to you. There's a committee.

**ANDREW**  You sure about that, guy? A bunch of ICM adjuncts with one foot in L.A. The grant's in the bag, Claire. Don't you worry.

**JAKE**  He's lying to you.

**ANDREW**  Poor Jake. Have a drink? I hear they've got some great microbrews.

**JAKE**  She doesn't need your grant.

**CLAIRE**  Yes, I do!

**JAKE**  He's giving it to you because he wants to sleep with you.

**ANDREW**  Whoa. Listen.

**JAKE**  Don't whoa me you schleppy-looking motherfucker!

**CLAIRE**  Jake, stop.

**JAKE**  Are you seriously doing this on the day we're supposed to move in together?

ANDREW   I gave the grant to Claire because she worked hard—

JAKE   I worked hard too, but you're not buying me drinks. You write shitty movies, you hit on girls half your age.

CLAIRE   I'm getting his nomination because my project is good.

JAKE   You don't have the best script.

——

CLAIRE   How would you know?

[JAKE *looks away.*]

CLAIRE   You read it? After I asked you not to.

ANDREW   I told you the golden boys tarnish.

JAKE   You're too close to the story. It's not a screenplay—it's therapy.

CLAIRE   Maybe you just don't understand it.

JAKE   You're winning because you're hot.

CLAIRE   Is it so hard to believe he thinks I have potential?

JAKE   The potential to sleep with him. Why didn't he nominate you a month ago? He's stringing you along to see if he can get in your pants.

ANDREW   He's a sore loser, Claire. A silver-spooned pissant who's always gonna make you feel inferior.

JAKE   [*To* ANDREW] just trying to get back at me because I have more talent now then you ever will.

CLAIRE   You think he gave me his nomination because I flirted a little? Welcome to being a woman in film.

JAKE   So you're using him?

CLAIRE   Flirting isn't fucking. Nothing happened.

ANDREW   Nothing happened? Felt like something in your dorm room last night. Tiny room. Tiny bed.

CLAIRE   Jake? He came by. Drunk. I told him to leave.

ANDREW   That's right. Blame the drunk.

CLAIRE   [*Insistent*] Shut up Andrew. Nothing happened.

JAKE   You have no idea how humiliating this has been.

CLAIRE   I'm sorry.

JAKE   I'm going to the dean.

CLAIRE   Why? To take the grant away from me?

JAKE   It isn't earned.

**CLAIRE**   Earned? Who pays for your apartment, for the eighty grand education?

**JAKE**   That grant is prestigious. It's not the money.

**CLAIRE**   For some people, it's the money that makes a difference.

**JAKE**   You think I don't deserve it?

**CLAIRE**   I think you don't realize how lucky you are.

**JAKE**   When you say lucky, you mean spoiled. I have to climb the ladder like everyone else.

**CLAIRE**   But you started out on a higher rung.

**JAKE**   It doesn't mean I don't work my ass off.

**CLAIRE**   Try collecting cans so you have lunch money and watch your parents put your dimes in a slot machine.

**JAKE**   You're not poor. That may be the story you tell yourself, but you live in one of the most expensive cities in America and you go to fucking *art* school. People who worry about money don't become screenwriters.

**CLAIRE**   Right, 'cause only kids with money get to make art these days.

**ANDREW**   He'll never get it babe. You two are in the same school, not the same class.

**JAKE**   [*re: babe*] You had the advantage here, Claire. Not me.

[*A long beat, a standoff.*]

**CLAIRE**   You have everything.

**JAKE**   Maybe my dad was right.

[JAKE *turns toward the door.*]

**JAKE**   [*To* ANDREW] And you're not fucking Hemingway.

[JAKE *storms out of the bar, the door swinging shut behind him. A beat.* CLAIRE *stands by the table, shell-shocked.*]

**ANDREW**   You knew that was gonna happen. Guy like that, can't bear losing. Shocks the system, happens so rarely. Course they never really lose. And people like us never really win.

**CLAIRE**   How could you do that?

**ANDREW**   I know it hurts now, but that was never gonna last. Sit down. We were discussing your triumphant victory. You're gonna get the grant.

**CLAIRE**   Jake said he was going to go to the dean.

**ANDREW**   The dean and I are friends.

[CLAIRE *slumps into the booth.*]

**ANDREW**   Get another drink. Let's celebrate. You have a favorite restaurant?

[CLAIRE *looks up, a deer in headlights. She shakes her head.*]

**ANDREW**   You're scared? Getting what you want can be terrifying.

[*He reaches out and takes her hand gently pulling her toward him.*]

**ANDREW**   I was thinking, you'll come out to California and work with me on the set. It'll be great. You'll see what a real shoot's like and when it's over we'll drive up the coast. There's a little Mexican place in Santa Barbara that sells fish tacos right on the beach.

**CLAIRE**   I can't do that.

[CLAIRE *pulls her hand away.*]

**ANDREW**   Tell me you've walked past this bar and not thought of me.

**CLAIRE**   Because you're always here.

**ANDREW**   How many hours have we spent together? Why do you keep coming back?

**CLAIRE**   I love writing with you.

**ANDREW**   Is that all?

**CLAIRE**   *I'm* here because this is the only place where I can actually get your attention.

**ANDREW**   You can't sit in a bar with a man until 2 a.m. every night and pretend nothing is going on. The way we talk, *the way that you kissed me.*

**CLAIRE**   That was a mistake.

**ANDREW**   It didn't feel like one to me.

**CLAIRE**   I just needed help on my screenplay, Andrew. That's all.

**ANDREW**   Well you're a better actress than you are a writer.

**CLAIRE**   It's not like I don't care about you.

**ANDREW**   Says the spider to the fly.

**CLAIRE**   You came on to me!

**ANDREW**   No I didn't.

**CLAIRE**   Why did you wanna buy me a drink so badly that first night?

**ANDREW**   I want everyone to drink. I'm an alcoholic.

**CLAIRE**   That's bullshit.

**ANDREW**   You coulda said no, if you were so happy with your boyfriend, if you were so goddamn uninterested.

**CLAIRE**   If I said no would you be giving the grant to Liz right now or Jake?

**ANDREW**   This isn't a game to me. You came into *my bar*! The single place in my life where I have some dignity.

CLAIRE   Because you said you were gonna help me.

ANDREW   People have feelings, Claire.

CLAIRE   You're married.

ANDREW   *Married people* have feelings.

CLAIRE   Did you really think we would run off together? You're gonna hide in some cabin and pretend you don't have a family. I can't bail you out of your life, Andrew.

ANDREW   [*Defensive*] Too bad we didn't meet when you were a cocktail waitress. I coulda had you then.

[*A beat.* CLAIRE *is crushed.*]

CLAIRE   You need to get yourself some help.

ANDREW   Get out of my bar.

CLAIRE   I don't want to lose you.

ANDREW   Me or the grant? I'm such a fucking idiot.

CLAIRE   Look, about the grant—

ANDREW   Get the fuck out of my bar. Get out!

[*She hesitates. Then exits.* ANDREW *watches the door swing shut. He raises his glass and drains it.*]

## SCENE TWELVE

[*Six years later. The Tribeca Film Festival. A screening. The sound of polite applause.* CLAIRE *stands in front of a movie screen. She looks good, more mature . . . nervous but poised.*]

CLAIRE   Hello Tribeca Film Festival. Welcome to the world premiere of *The Gamble.* I'm Claire Freeman, the writer and director, it's an honor to get to introduce this film. It's taken six years to make this. Thank you to everyone who supported our Kickstarter campaign, we wouldn't be here without you.

For those that are about to see it for the first time, thank you. I know you're taking a risk. Will I like it, will I be entertained, will I feel something? Will Jake Gyllenhaal be at the after party? I'm worried too. It's crazy what we do, isn't it? Art . . . Uh oh, that's a scary word. A bunch of scouts for Warner Brothers just got up and left. Something is commercial when it makes money, right? Well, I've made $43,000 in credit card debt. So it must be art.

But seriously, this story is very personal to me. It's dedicated to someone I lost. I know you can't bring a person back by writing a movie about them. But you can tell the story of how they changed you.

At the end of the day, this is a story about hope.

# SCENE THIRTEEN

[*People mingle in the theater lobby after the screening.* ANDREW *is milling around with a bottle of water. He looks good, thinner, better dressed. He takes a deep breath and comes closer. It's awkward.*]

**ANDREW**   Nice work in there. You kept the voice-over though.

**CLAIRE**   It was the story I wanted to tell. I didn't think you'd come to my screening.

**ANDREW**   I have a film in the festival.

**CLAIRE**   I know. [*Beat*] When *Haunted Desert* came out I thought of calling but . . .

**ANDREW**   Yeah, they panned it. You coulda said. "*Hey, I heard your movie sucked, I hope you're okay.*"

[CLAIRE *looks away.*]

I hate these things. The mingling. Why does everyone look so shiny?

**CLAIRE**   People are getting these cosmetic glazes on their face now, gives them that Thanksgiving turkey look.

[ANDREW *smirks.*]

**CLAIRE**   I love it. That's the actor from . . .

**ANDREW**   Where he played the albino lifeguard.

**CLAIRE**   *All he ever wanted was his place in the sun.*

[*They laugh.*]

**CLAIRE**   So, you finally made—

**ANDREW**   Yeah, my *art film.* I had fun doing it. No budget. One camera, out there totally in the dirt. It was . . . it was awesome.

**CLAIRE**   That's great.

**ANDREW**   Did you see it?

**CLAIRE**   It was *street smart and gutsy and beautiful.*

[*He laughs softly, remembering.*]

**CLAIRE**   It really was.

**ANDREW**   After *Haunted Desert* flopped my agent dropped me. Probably good. You know, gave me a chance to—[*He holds up his water.*] Try something different. Sober. Five hundred and forty-seven days.

**CLAIRE**   [*Totally shocked*] Wow. Congratulations.

**ANDREW**   Thanks.

**CLAIRE**   I've been gluten-free for about a week. And I've never been more depressed.

[ANDREW *laughs.*]

**ANDREW**  You look different. What is it?

**CLAIRE**  I breathe more.

[*He laughs.*]

**ANDREW**  You would have hated the shoot for *Haunted Desert*. It was a shit show. Director was a prick, rewrote the whole fucking thing. Out there in the Mojave, 108 degrees. [*Beat*] Anyway, you were right. I was better than that.

[*A beat.*]

**CLAIRE**  Still got a little crotch in there.

**ANDREW**  You know I like a little crotch.

[*They laugh, embarrassed to have fallen so easily back into their pattern.*]

**CLAIRE**  I'm really happy for you.

**ANDREW**  Thanks. I'm happy for me too. I mean, I'm actually happy.

**CLAIRE**  How are your kids?

**ANDREW**  Great. Smarter than me. You, uh, still with?

**CLAIRE**  Jake? *Oh*, no. He went out to L.A. I keep in touch with Phillip Moskowitz though.

**ANDREW**  Giant robot women who use his thoughts against him.

**CLAIRE**  He used the grant to make a sci fi . . .

[*She trails off.*]

**ANDREW**  I'm here with my wife.

[*He looks into the crowd but doesn't wave.* CLAIRE *tries to follow his gaze.*]

**CLAIRE**  [*Too enthusiastic*] Ohh. Cool. That's great. I thought you guys might have—

**ANDREW**  Split? Nope. We're working on it. We have the kids . . . *You just gotta know why you're doing it.*

**CLAIRE**  Good for you. You really . . . that's . . .

[CLAIRE *nods vigorously, trying to hide a rush of feelings.*]

**CLAIRE**  I walked by the bar the other day.

**ANDREW**  Oh yeah?

**CLAIRE**  It's a cell phone store.

**ANDREW**  Even places move on.

**CLAIRE**  I guess you found a new office.

**ANDREW**  Yup, got a desk and everything.

[*A beat.*]

**CLAIRE**  Do you miss the bar?

**ANDREW**  I spent twenty years of my life in there. Sometimes you don't realize you're in a rut until someone pulls you out of it.

**CLAIRE**  I wish things had ended differently.

**ANDREW**  [*Sharply*] Why? You've done well for yourself.

[CLAIRE *is taken aback by his tone.*]

**CLAIRE**  I wish we were friends, I mean. I miss talking about movies with you. [*Beat*] Maybe we could go to a coffee shop, sometime. Here's my card—

[*She holds it out. He doesn't take it.*]

**ANDREW**  I don't think that's a good idea.

[*A beat as she realizes he's saying no.*]

**CLAIRE**  [*Embarrassed*] Oh. No, you're right . . . I'm, I'm sorry.

**ANDREW**  It's not that I don't—

**CLAIRE**  No. Sure. I understand. [*Beat*] I never wanted to hurt you.

**ANDREW**  [*Not meanly*] You knew exactly what you were doing.

**CLAIRE**  [*Calmly*] You make me sound like a mercenary. I was your student. I was twenty-two. You had all the power.

**ANDREW**  You let me sit there and make a fool of myself. You knew I had feelings for you and you didn't care.

**CLAIRE**  That's a line every woman walks until she's backed into a corner.

[*He moves to leave.*]

**ANDREW**  I hope you got what you wanted, Claire.

[*He turns away from her. A beat.*]

**CLAIRE**  You know to get in here, your name had to be on the list? The guy ran his finger down the page, and there it was. My name. I wish my dad coulda seen it. It's a nice feeling, isn't it? When the doors finally open for you.

[*A beat as he takes her in one last time. He nods and exits into the crowd. CLAIRE takes a deep breath and a sip of her drink. She stands up a little straighter. The sounds of the party rise as the lights fade on CLAIRE, alone, looking out at the party, out at her future.*]

END OF PLAY

# St. Francis

Miranda Jonte

# Miranda Jonte

Miranda Jonte, a Bay Area native, is an actor, playwright, and producer. Her first play, *Greasemonkey*, received its world premiere in New York City in 2013. Her ten-minute romp, *All in a White Trash Pie*, debuted at the Amphitheater Space at Lincoln Center in 2014. Her next full-length play, *St. Francis*, began as a one-woman show in 2013, and was produced as an ensemble piece at the New York International Fringe Festival in 2015. She is a two-time semi-finalist for the Princess Grace Award in playwriting for *Greasemonkey* and *St. Francis*. She received her BA in Acting from Chico State in California, and her MFA in Acting at the Actors Studio Drama School (now New School for Drama) in New York. She resides in New York City.

# Production History

*St. Francis* was produced by Hey Jonte! Productions in association with Michael Bitalvo as part of the New York International Fringe Festival in August 2015. The production was directed by Stephen Brotebeck at 440 Studios in the Robert Moss Theater with the following cast and creative team:

**TESSA**   Miranda Jonte*
**MOLLY MATTIE**   Meghan Rose Tonery
**WILL/ TYLER**   John Whitney
**NICK/ JOEY/ YOUNG MAN**   Frank Mayers
**MADELEINE/ GWEN/ COUNCILWOMAN PORTER**   Valerie Lonigro*
**BILL/ COUNCILMAN STACEY**   John Moss*

*Denotes Actors Equity Association

Director   Stephen Brotebeck
Associate Director   Kerry Flanagan
Stage Manager   Kyrie McCormick
Lighting   Jason Fok
Set Design   Andrew Mannion
Props   Cali Anne Mills, Julia Fishenfeld

*ST. FRANCIS*

*Takes place in Arcata, a coastal town of Humboldt County in Northern California, over six weeks. There is no intermission.*

## Characters

**TESSA**—34, veterinarian turned rescue worker
**MOLLY MATTIE**—18, Tessa's right-hand gal. Smart, sweet, clever, indispensable.
**WILL**—34, lawyer. Tessa's childhood sweetheart

## Ensemble

**NICK**—30s, local sheriff
**BILL**—60s, regular walker at the shelter
**MADELEINE**—30s, entitled mom
**GWEN**—40s, Molly's aunt
**YOUNG MAN**—20s
**COUNCILMAN STACEY**—50s
**COUNCILWOMAN PORTER**—40s/50s
**JOEY**—8 yrs old
**TYLER**—8 yrs old

The cast can be six actors. The ensemble should comprise two men, one woman. They each play several roles.

One actor should play the first ensemble track of NICK, YOUNG MAN, and JOEY.

One actor should play the second ensemble track of BILL and COUNCILMAN STACEY.

One actor should play the third ensemble track of MADELEINE, GWEN, and COUNCIL-WOMAN PORTER.

The actor playing WILL also plays TYLER in the second scene.

## Playwright's note

*There is a large chalkboard, which reflects that month's adoptions, fosters, and intake, and tracks progress for some of the dogs. This board will be altered throughout the play. It should be the heart of the set.*

*[Board setup for top of show: April Adoptions. Date. Two Categories of Adoptions/Fosters, and Newbies. Date is 4/8. Under Adoptions/Fosters [A/F] are MOOSE, JELLY BELLY, BANDO. Under Newbies are ROSIE, POPPY, ROO.]*

# SCENE ONE

*[The shelter. TESSA has been picked up by NICK, local cop. She is dead drunk, but starts off presenting more sober than she should. TESSA is on a mission. She swings wildly in this monologue; it is dead serious, but darkly comic. NICK is very much part of the action. Their arguing precedes their entrance.]*

**TESSA**   No I didn't!

**NICK**   Tessa! People saw you!

**TESSA**   Who saw me?

**NICK**   Everybody in the bar.

**TESSA**   I was in the parking lot.

**NICK**   You're drunk, Tessa.

**TESSA**   You're drunk!

*[She goes to chalkboard and writes "MY DOG" in big letters across board.]*

**NICK**   You picked a fight with Randy—you had a run-in—look Tessa—this is bad. Everyone—

**TESSA**   Nicky! I did not have a run in with Randy Warren. You were my best friend in high school. Remember? My bosom buddy. I did not pick a fight. I said— . . . I'm gonna cut off his ears.

**NICK**   What?!

**TESSA**   Well, he cut off his dog's ears, so survey says he'll like it.

**NICK**   Please tell me that's not why you had bolt cutters in your truck.

**TESSA**   No! Those aren't my bolt cutters. *[Goes offstage, returns with beer.]* I found his dog lying on 'em, bleeding all over 'em. I picked her up and put her in my truck, and I grabbed the cutters too, 'cause they were rusty and someone could get hurt.

**NICK**   Wait. Tessa, you drove?

**TESSA**   That was like five hours ago, OHMIGOD. Yes. I drove. So I went to the clinic—and here I am again because I am always at the clinic—and those cutters were rusty, so I sewed her up and gave her anti-toxins for tetanus.

[*Indignant*] I would never use bolt cutters on someone. That's so barbaric. [*Fishes in her pocket, pulls out her prize, satisfied.*] Scissors. That's gonna hurt. [TESSA *opens her jacket. She is covered in blood.*] Shit. No, I'm good. This is not my blood, this is dog blood.

[*Seeing the gore on her,* NICK *begins to help her out of her shirt, and during the following, helps her don a clean scrub shirt. Her torso should be bloody.*]

**NICK**  This looks really bad, Tessa. No, not that. [*He means the blood.*] Oh, Tess. Tessa, you were waiting for him.

**TESSA**  [*Explains*] Randy's an asshole. Remember how mean he was to you in high school?

[NICK *has found* TESSA's *phone in her pocket. He begins to scroll through her contacts.*]

Why are you calling Julie? Don't call Julie; she's at home with her kids. C'mon Nicky. I did not lie in wait. I went to Maxine's after I sewed up his dog that's not Randy's dog anymore, BY THE WAY. I don't think so. You can totally commandeer a dog.

[*Nausea from the booze kicks in.* NICK *gives her aspirin and water.*]

What was I talking about?

**NICK**  Cutting off Randy's extremities.

**TESSA**  Yeah, no. It wasn't pre-medicated. Mediated. I'm not Ted Bundy. [*She builds her case.*] I mean, who brings scissors to a fight? [*She has been smart about this.*] I went to Maxine's to hang out and say hi to people. Randy just happened to come in after work. Like fate.

[*He has her phone again.*]

Don't call my dad. My dad—[*She sits on the floor.*]—I'm sitting down—my dad—everybody knows my dad hates me. My dad is an asshole. This town has a lot of assholes in it.

**NICK**  Yep.

**TESSA**  So, you're black, right? You're the only black person in town. And in high school—you were black in high school—and now you're the sheriff. That's just, it's prophetic justice. It is, it's prophetic. Nick, remember how mean Randy was to you? We should go to Maxine's—and—do you have your gun on you? No—I'm kidding—oh, but you can hold him for me.

[TESSA *curls up on the dog bed she has sat in, and passes out.* NICK *looks at her a moment, puts her coat over her.*]

[*Lights change.*]

[*Board transition: setup remains the same.*]

# SCENE TWO

[*The shelter.* TESSA *wakes with a start, sees her mess, and gathers herself, wiping "MY DOG" off the board.* MOLLY *enters, goes to board, changes date to 4/9.* TESSA *picks up a ringing phone.*]

**TESSA**  This is Tessa. Hey Ro. What? OK, lemme look. [*She goes to her laptop, clicks, looks.*] Oh God. Wha—

**MOLLY MATTIE**  What happened to his neck?

**TESSA**  OK. Yes. We'll take him. Take him to Julie for vetting and emergency, bring him here for rehabbing. Oh, you're at Julie's? Good. [*looks at laptop again*] Jesus Christ, I can't even tell what kind of dog this is. He's really skinny—is he Husky—he should be at least 60lbs. [*She goes to board, writes KINGSTON, 31lbs.*]

[*A third grade class has assembled for a field trip, along with an adult chaperone. It is late morning. A woman is with the kids as their chaperone. She has a baby strapped to her. She looks like a hippie earth mother, but by design. A rich hippie. She carries a large Starbucks cup. She will spend most of this scene looking at her bejeweled phone.* TESSA *is with her helper,* MOLLY MATTIE. *The kids are played by the other cast members.*]

Hey kiddos. What are you doing here?

**JOEY**  Story time! Hi Tessa!

**TESSA**  Story time's tomorrow! Hi Joey. Today is field trip day! My name is Tessa, and we're going to talk to you about animals.

**JOEY**  I'm an animal!

**TESSA**  You are, but! I'm talking about the kind with four legs. Do you know what kind?

**CHILDREN**  Cats! / Monkeys! / Dogs! / Hippos! / Dinosaurs. [*The mother with them joins in.*]

**TESSA**  Who said dogs? [*Points*] Was that you? Now, how many of you have pets at home? [*More than half raise their hands.*] What kind of pet do you have?

**JOEY**  I have a goldfish!

**TESSA**  Does he have a name?

**JOEY**  Popeye!

**TESSA**  That's a good name!

**JOEY**  I have a cat too! He's Popeye too!

**TESSA**  [*Calling on another*] You have a pet?

**TYLER**  I have a guinea pig! He squeaks.

**MOLLY MATTIE**   They do squeak! Isn't it a funny noise?

**MADELEINE**   Especially when he squeezes him.

**MOLLY MATTIE**   Yeah I wouldn't do that. [MADELEINE *shrugs.*]

**JOEY**   I have a pet! My little sister! [*Giggles ensue.*]

**TESSA**   OK, how many of you know what a shelter pet is?

[*Little hands raise.*]

**JOEY**   Um . . . I forgot.

**TESSA**   That's okay. A pet is an animal that lives at home with you and your families. But a shelter pet is waiting for a family to take him home with them.

**TYLER**   Like adopting?

**TESSA**   [*Pleasantly surprised*] Yes! It is adopting.

**TYLER**   My brother is adopted.

**MOLLY MATTIE**   That's really cool. My aunt and uncle adopted me.

**TYLER**   He's my little brother. He's Chinese. I didn't know you could adopt animals! Can you adopt dogs?

**TESSA**   Oh, you can adopt dogs, and people—and rabbits—you can adopt anything!

**MADELEINE**   I might not want to use that word. Children who are adopted may feel as if they're being diminished if we start using "adopt" for everything.

**MOLLY MATTIE**   If you're taking an animal into your home, your household, your family, and caring for them—

**MADELEINE**   Adopt a highway, adopt a tree, a whale—it reduces the importance of a child. Just a little something to snack on.

**MOLLY MATTIE**   You can also adopt an idea, or a stance—

[TESSA *puts her hand on* MOLLY'*s arm. They resume with the kids.*]

**TESSA**   Every animal that is in a shelter needs a family.

**JOEY**   Even horses?

**TESSA**   Even horses.

**JOEY**   He could sleep in my bathtub.

**MOLLY MATTIE**   Coooool.

**TESSA**   What's my job?

**JOEY**   You're a shelter pet!

**TESSA**   Close. I have, with me right now, a shelter dog. You want to meet him?

[*This is met with a chorus of cheers.*]

**MADELEINE**  That's why we're here.

**TESSA**  Molly, my helper, is going to bring him in. [MOLLY *leaves.*] I run an animal shelter. This is a rescue shelter, because it's full of dogs that we've rescued.

**JOEY**  Do you live here?

**TESSA**  No, but sometimes, if the dogs are sick, or really scared, I sleep here to make sure they're OK.

**JOEY**  My mom does that with me.

**TYLER**  My family all sleeps together!

**MADELEINE**  We have a communal bed.

**TYLER**  Are you an animal doctor?

**JOEY**  You're a vegan?

**TESSA**  I'm a veterinarian. Oh, someone's ready to meet you. He's a very nice doggie, and he loves kids, and we don't want to startle him. We're going to be nice and gentle.

**TYLER**  Do you have a family?

[MOLLY *walks downstage to* TESSA *with George. The* KIDS *ooh and aah.*]

**MOLLY MATTIE**  Everybody, this is George.

[*The* KIDS *echo "Hi George!"*]

**TESSA**  George is one of my favorite people.

**TYLER**  He's not a person! Can I pet him?

**MOLLY MATTIE**  Sure! You can say, "Hi George," then let him smell your hands, and then go ahead! He loves it when you scratch him right here. [*Indicates under her chin*]

**JOEY**  He's soft! He likes it!

**MOLLY MATTIE**  Does anyone else want to say hi to George?

**TYLER**  I have a dog at home.

**MOLLY MATTIE**  Oh, what's its name?

**TYLER**  It's a *boy*. And my dad bought him for me for my birthday. He cost $7,000.

**MADELEINE**  I wanted to get two, a boy and a girl, but no. "We can't afford it." We can totally afford it.

**TESSA**  [*To the kids*] George knows some cool tricks. Want to see?

**TYLER**  My dog knows tricks. He's a purebred.

**JOEY**  What kind of dog is George?

**TYLER**  George is a mutt.

**JOEY**  What's a mutt?

**TESSA**  A mutt is my favorite kind of dog.

**TYLER**  My dog is a purebred Samoyed. He came from Siberia. His name is Vlad.

**TESSA**  Who here knows what a superhero is? [*They all say, "I do!"*] Okay. A superhero has different powers, right? A mutt is made of lots of different kinds of dogs. Some mutts have bloodhound in them: they have a really good sense of smell and they help the police solve crimes. And some dogs have border collie in them, which means they can jump really high, and because they herd cows and sheep, they know where everyone in your family is in the house at all times.

**TYLER**  My dog can pull sleds and herd reindeer.

**TESSA**  California's got a big reindeer problem.

**MADELEINE**  Did you just patronize my son? [TESSA *looks at her. A tense moment, then*] Sorry, I just go all mama bear sometimes. Continue. [TESSA *resumes with the kids.*]

**TESSA**  Now George—he has German Shepherd in him, so he's strong and really smart. He's also part cattle dog, so he is loyal, and brave. Which means a mutt is kind of like a superhero, because they have all these really cool qualities rolled into one—like mixing Superman with Spiderman and Batman.

**TYLER**  Batman doesn't have any superpowers, stupid. He's a self-made billionaire who makes his own gadgets.

**JOEY**  I thought he inherited his money.

**TYLER**  Vlad is the best dog there is. He's purebred Samoyed.

**JOEY**  [*Quietly to* TESSA] I like mutts, too.

**TYLER**  My dog was $7,000. He's Siberian.

**TESSA**  OK, well you named him after a Romanian despot.

**MOLLY MATTIE**  Transylvanian.

**TESSA**  [*Nods*] If we're getting all nuts and bolts.

**MOLLY MATTIE**  And that is nowhere near Siberia.

**TESSA**  Different continent.

**MOLLY MATTIE**  Unless it's way Western Siberia.

**TESSA**  This is true.

**MOLLY MATTIE**   Then it's arguable.

**TESSA**   But. It's like naming your Indonesian elephant "Hitler."

**MOLLY MATTIE**   Those are endangered.

**TESSA**   I love that you know your geography.

**MADELEINE**   We don't talk about Hitler.

**TYLER**   You can't even sell your dog on eBay.

**TESSA**   How do you even know what eBay is? You're eight.

**MADELEINE**   I buy and sell on eBay. I craft.

**JOEY**   Can I bring my sister to story time tomorrow?

**TESSA**   That would be great!

**JOEY**   Can she meet George?

**MOLLY MATTIE**   Yes! You guys can read to George, he loves it.

**TESSA**   Who wants to meet our workers? They're giving the dogs baths right now.

**TYLER**   I bet you my dad makes more money than you do!

**TESSA**   I bet he does, too.

**TYLER**   A LOT of money.

**TESSA**   Samoyeds are really nice dogs.

**MADELEINE**   [*Taking* TYLER *and leaving*] Thanks Trish.

**TESSA**   But they're prone to renal failure, known as Samoyed hereditary glomerulopathy. Plus diabetes, dysplasia, and progressive retinal atrophy. That means they go blind. Your dad's gonna need it.

**JOEY**   Bye, Tyler!

[*End of scene*]

[*Board transition: Change date to 4/17, Kingston weight to 33, move* ROO *to A/F, add* BLUE *to Newbies.*]

## SCENE THREE

[*Shelter.* MOLLY MATTIE *and* TESSA *are busy at the desk, going in and out.* BILL *comes through the back, post-walk.*]

**BILL**   Thanks, Tessa. Gracie's happy as a clam.

**TESSA**   When are you gonna make an honest woman out of that dog, Bill?

**BILL**   In time, Doc. Wife's got to say yes.

[*The rich hippie from the field trip has returned. She has the baby in a papoose, and a stroller, which is also full. She carries a Starbucks cup.*]

**MOLLY MATTIE** [*To* TESSA] Adopt a highway adopt a tree.

[*She exits quickly.*]

**TESSA** What? HI! Madeleine. Hi.

**MADELEINE** Tricia! Hello! How are you?

**TESSA** Tessa. I'm fine, thanks. How are you?

**MADELEINE** Great! I need a dog.

**BILL** I'm gonna take Gracie out again.

[*Does a 180, exits through kennel door.*]

**TESSA** [*Eyeing her load*] You sure don't need a drink? [*Falls flat*] You need a dog.

**MADELEINE** Well, my widdle men do! [*In a talking-to-children voice.*] I just had a baby! Number five! And my widdle men missed it! They don't allow children in the delivery room. Oh! I'm sorry—you probably don't have kids—[TESSA *just watches her, says nothing.*] So, if the mountain won't come to Mohammed—[*She smiles, but* TESSA *remains silent.*] then Mohammed will come to the mountain! We would like to buy a girl dog for our dog. Well, I would. Mommy brain! We'd like to put puppies in the mommy's belly and have the boys watch the birth. Well, I would. I think the cycle of life is important. So—I need a dog. [*There is no reaction. Explains*] The Little Red Farm in Garberville lets kids watch goat births and cow births.

**TESSA** They're an environmental education center.

**MADELEINE** Well see, I want to educate my boys! They're home-schooled. And what better way than real-time gestation and delivery? You can't get that in public school science class. [TESSA *is simmering.*] Oh! You're worried about the litter of puppies! Of course! We'll give them back to you.

**TESSA** You'll give them back.

**MADELEINE** Yes.

**TESSA** You'll give them back to me.

**MADELEINE** I promise. Girl Scout's honor! I can sign a contract [TESSA *turns and leaves through the exam room.* MADELEINE *follows.*] Tricia? [*To* MOLLY MATTIE, *who comes back in*] Her energy is a little combative.

**MOLLY MATTIE** [*Stepping in, with unfailing good cheer, which lasts throughout the entire exchange.*] Hi! We met at field trip day. I'm Molly Mattie. You were a Girl Scout?

**MADELEINE** No, I was never a Girl Scout.

**MOLLY MATTIE** [*To stroller*] Hi fellas! Wow, you've got your hands full!

**MADELEINE** I'm Madeleine. Maddy—you're another Maddy!

**MOLLY MATTIE**   No, it's different. So, what's goin' on?

**MADELEINE**   Well, I'd like to get a dog for my boys—

**MOLLY MATTIE**   Right, OK—you want a dog to bring home to your boys, inseminate her—it's the professional term—with your Samoyed and let the little ones experience the miracle of a live birth. Is that right?

**MADELEINE**   Yes! Oh, you get me. Thank you.

**MOLLY MATTIE**   Well, Madeleine—

**MADELEINE**   [*Corrects her*] Maddy, Maddy. [*She is so completely obsequious and transparent.*]

**MOLLY MATTIE**   Mattie. Like a boy. The thing is, Maddy, once a girl dog is brought to the shelter, we spay her. Every dog. We neuter the males.

**MADELEINE**   Every dog.

**MOLLY MATTIE**   Yep.

**MADELEINE**   You're telling me every single dog back there—every single one—is spayed.

**MOLLY MATTIE**   Yep. See, we're obligated by law, and our contract with the city; there are no unspayed bitches allowed on the premises.

**MADELEINE**   How dare you. [MOLLY MATTIE *is unswayed.*]

**MOLLY MATTIE**   Tessa's in the back. I think she's got an eleven o'clock.

**MADELEINE**   I'm glad they're shutting you down. [*Leaves*]

**TESSA**   [TESSA *enters.*] Molly Mattie. You can't do that.

**MOLLY MATTIE**   I just asked myself, "What would Tessa do?" And you were gonna hit her, so . . .

[TESSA *puts her face in her hands, then after a moment, is unable to contain herself.*]

**TESSA**   What do you think she's driving?

**MOLLY MATTIE**   Mercedes minivan.

[*They run over to the window together and peek out. It is indeed a Mercedes minivan.* TESSA *goes back to the desk.* MOLLY MATTIE *has spotted something outside, and goes to retrieve it.* TESSA *picks up the phone.*]

**TESSA**   Hey Jerry, those Kurunda beds—we're here all day today if you want to swing by. Thanks Jerry. I've got a six-pack here with your name on it. [MOLLY MATTIE *has come back in with a box. She knows* TESSA *will not be happy.*] Jerry's dropping off the beds later—what's the box?

**MOLLY MATTIE**   Someone left it out front. [*She says no more.*]

**TESSA**   Is it another dead animal? [MOLLY *shakes her head.*] What's in it?

**MOLLY MATTIE**   Um.

**TESSA**  What's in the box, Mol? [*Quoting that oh so famous movie*] AH, WHAT'S IN THE BOX? [TESSA *walks over, looks, sighs.*] Oh, no. No no no no no. Take 'em in the back, check 'em out, write it up. [MOLLY MATTIE *goes.*] Fucking cats.

[*Lights change.*]

## SCENE THREE-POINT-FIVE

[*Downstage.* BILL *and* TESSA *sit opposite each other in chairs with headphones on. A small table with a recording device sits between them.*]

**BILL**  And all these middle-aged men in their underwear are running screaming through the campsite. Their bellies looked like glow-in-the-dark bowling balls.

**TESSA**  Where were you during all this?

**BILL**  Watching from my truck. Folks, once again, we're coming to you live from the top floor of Aaron Bros Lumber and Hardware here in the Arcata Square, and this is the Hard Hat Hour with Bill Taylor. Stop and by, say hello, bring us some donuts if you're so inclined. [*To* TESSA] Say, I saw your dad at the VA last week.

**TESSA**  Oh.

**BILL**  He had Hank with him. I gotta say, the meanest SOBs they got there turn into marshmallows when Hank comes around.

**TESSA**  Hank's a good dog.

**BILL**  He's your dad's shadow. Your dad rescued Hank, is that right?

**TESSA**  Yeah. Nice segue.

**BILL**  I do like the radio. Your dad—we're talking about Walter Bartlett here for those living under a rock, or you tourists driving through on your way up to Ashland. Your rescue is One Paw Two Paw, and you're on McMorrow Road right now—and folks, that's what we're here to talk about today— Doc Bartlett needs your help. She'll be at the city council meeting two weeks from tomorrow, let's get on out and support her. If you can pass flyers, bring some blankets by the shelter— [*To* TESSA] any requests?

**TESSA**  We're always looking for fosters for our pups, long or short term.

**BILL**  And for the love of Pete, I expect to see your cars in front of Bear Claw Bakery, and support not only the Doc here but your local mom and pops, not that Starbucks eyesore they're so hot-to-trot to get in here. [*Phone buzzes.*] And I've just gotten a text from my wife telling me, "Norma Rae, could you mow the lawn when you get home?" Tessa, thanks for coming by. Is there anything you'd like to tell the folks listening in?

**TESSA**  You going to come by and walk Gracie later?

**BILL**  You know it.

**TESSA**  She's a good match for you Bill. [BILL's *phone buzzes.*]

**BILL**  [*Reading from phone*] "Over my dead body." Hey—before we wrap things up—how do you know a dog will be a good match for someone?

**TESSA**  Sometimes it's a feeling. You just know. Often it's just common sense. Not going to put a working dog with a sedentary owner, or a lapdog with an active one. It's just logistics, and a little bit of chemistry. Like you with Gracie.

**BILL**  Folks, if I'm not on the air tomorrow, it's because my wife has done me in/murdered me. How did you know Hank was the right dog for your dad? How'd you match them up?

**TESSA**  I didn't—he didn't get Hank from me. [*Beat*] I'm glad they found each other.

[*Lights change.*]

[*Board transition: add* BOOMER *to A/F.*]

## SCENE FOUR

[TESSA *and* MOLLY MATTIE *are stationed in the town square, holding a spay/neuter clinic and adoption event.* GWEN, MOLLY's *aunt, jogs or power walks across the stage with earphones in.*]

**TESSA**  Hey Gwen!

[GWEN *doesn't hear, continues 'til offstage.*]

HEY GWEN!

**GWEN**  [*Jogs back on, laughing*] Hi Tessa. Hi sweetie. I was in the zone.

**MOLLY MATTIE**  Hi Aunt Gwen!

**TESSA**  You in the market?

**GWEN**  Sorry ladies. We're good with three. You forgot your lunch. [*Hands it to* MOLLY MATTIE]

**MOLLY MATTIE**  I did! I left it in the fridge! Thanks Aunt G.

[GWEN *hands* TESSA *a second bag.*]

**GWEN**  Makes sure she eats it.

**TESSA**  Oh I will.

**MOLLY MATTIE**  She's talking about you.

**TESSA**  You made me lunch?

**GWEN**  Molly says you don't eat.

**MOLLY MATTIE**   Coffee and licorice.

**TESSA**   I like licorice.

**GWEN**   This is turkey on sourdough, an apple, string cheese, and cookies.

**TESSA**   I love sourdough. It's my favorite.

**GWEN**   We know.

**TESSA**   You made me lunch. [*She is touched by the gesture.*]

**GWEN**   Yeah.

[TESSA *exits.*]

**MOLLY MATTIE**   That means she likes it.

**GWEN**   I know. All right sweetie, I'll see you at home. Spay dogs!

**MOLLY MATTIE**   We will. Bye Aunt G.

> [MOLLY MATTIE *is left onstage, in charge.* WILL *approaches. The following is charming.*]
>
> Hi! Are you looking to adopt? Or do you have a dog that needs to be spayed?

**WILL**   Hi. Neither, actually—

**MOLLY MATTIE**   Or foster? We're looking for fosters, too, which is great practice for when you do become a dog parent.

**WILL**   Uh—

**MOLLY MATTIE**   You know, a lot of people don't realize how much they need a dog in their lives until they get one.

**WILL**   Are you hard-selling me?

**MOLLY MATTIE**   You seem like a hard sell. [*He indicates she should continue.*] A dog won't hog the blankets, or borrow your clothes, like your stupid sister does, or [*Sussing out the situation*] like a girlfriend who's trying to stake her claim. A dog is always happy to see you, *and* [*Appealing to his age*] if you need to stay active to fight off that weight that creeps on as we get older, you've got a built-in running partner, AND—a dog is the only thing on earth that loves you more than he loves himself.

**WILL**   You didn't know my mom.

**MOLLY MATTIE**   Past tense?

**WILL**   She passed.

**MOLLY MATTIE**   You definitely need a dog.

**WILL**   It's been seven years.

**MOLLY MATTIE**   [*She won't be deterred.*] PTSD.

**WILL** [*Amused and charmed*] Is this operation your baby? [*Referring to the whole shebang*]

**MOLLY MATTIE** Oh no. I mean, yes, but no. Tessa owns it—do you know Tessa? It's hers, she runs it, she's my boss, but she's more like my older sister, or my aunt.

**WILL** You're clearly not a silent partner—

**MOLLY MATTIE** No, I'm 18! I started as a volunteer, when I was 14? I was in 4-H. But I've been a real, like on-the-books employee since I was 16. And it looks good on the college application—I'm gonna be a vet—so, really good—but I like it. I love it. [*Sees her opening*] Do you like dogs? [*Hands him a puppy*]

**WILL** [*Appreciating her tactic*] Nice. A vet, huh?

**MOLLY MATTIE** Yeah. I mean, Tessa went to Davis—she's a vet—and it's a really good school, like one of the best, and so I'm looking at Davis, but there's also Oklahoma (I have family there)—

[TESSA *enters, and is finishing setting up. She doesn't see* WILL.]

**TESSA** Molly. I could hear you talking nonstop from a block away. You're not going to Oklahoma. It's not even in the top twenty, and, it's Oklahoma.

**MOLLY MATTIE** But—

**TESSA** C'mon Mol, earthquake or tornado? [*Age-old discussion*] You want to go to a top three school—MAYBE a top five—but that's only—

**MOLLY MATTIE** Because Cornell dropped to number five. And Ivy League is Ivy League even if it's number five.

**TESSA** Give me the top three. Current top three.

**MOLLY MATTIE** Davis, Colorado, A&M.

**TESSA** Good girl. Davis & Colorado have been in the top three for a long time kiddo. And Texas? [TESSA *indicates "no." She turns to introduce herself to* WILL.] Hi, sorry about the hard sell, she's usually much more subtle than that. [*The words stop as she registers him.*]

**MOLLY MATTIE** This is Tessa!

**WILL** Hi. [TESSA *is dumbstruck.*] What's the matter, Tam Tam, cat got your tongue?

**MOLLY MATTIE** Tam Tam?

**TESSA** [*To* WILL] Don't.

**MOLLY MATTIE** Yeah, she hates cats.

**WILL** Can I call ya "Doc"?

**MOLLY MATTIE** Oh, I wouldn't.

**WILL**   Wow, she hates a lot of things.

**TESSA**   [*Finding her voice*] What are you doing here?

**WILL**   Seeing my dad.

**MOLLY MATTIE**   You're visiting?

**WILL**   I'm moving back. [*Grinning*] How 'bout that, Tam Tam?

**MOLLY MATTIE**   Back?

**WILL**   I grew up here.

**MOLLY MATTIE**   WHY are you moving BACK?

**TESSA**   Molly Mattie!

**WILL**   My dad's retiring and I'll be taking over for him.

**MOLLY MATTIE**   A family business? That's so sweet, like Norman Rockwell! [*Explaining*] My grandparents love Norman Rockwell. How do you guys know each other?

**TESSA/WILL**   [*In unison*] We grew up together. / Tessa was my girlfriend.

[*They look at each other, then back at* MOLLY, *and try again.*]

**TESSA/WILL**   He was my boyfriend. / We grew up together.

**MOLLY MATTIE**   No way!

**WILL**   Yep. All through high school and college.

**MOLLY MATTIE**   Really?? Oh my God, that's so romantic! Like *Dirty Dancing*! High school sweethearts—[*Gasps; to* TESSA] Was he your first kiss?

**WILL**   I was not. But what do you want to bet I was her best kiss?

**MOLLY MATTIE**   Oh my God you guuuyyyys!

**TESSA**   Great. [*To* WILL] Look what you did.

**MOLLY MATTIE**   I had my first kiss last year, but I didn't really like him, so it doesn't really count.

**TESSA**   Will, Molly, Molly, Will.

**MOLLY MATTIE**   You're really handsome.

**WILL**   I like her.

**MOLLY MATTIE**   Tessa doesn't have a boyfriend right now.

**TESSA**   [*To* WILL] Have you had lunch?

**WILL**   No—

**TESSA**   Go eat lunch.

**WILL**   Wow Tam Tam, you're wound a little tight.

**TESSA**   Don't—

**MOLLY MATTIE**   Where was your guys' first kiss?

[TESSA *indicates she either can't remember or can't be bothered to remember.*]

**WILL**   It was on her front porch after homecoming.

**MOLLY MATTIE**   [*Rapturous*] Tessa had me watch all of John Hughes's films, we had a movie marathon—do you know who John Hughes is?—And— [*She is swooning at the romance of it all.*]

**WILL**   [*Playing along, referencing* Pretty in Pink] Ducky or Blaine?

**MOLLY MATTIE/TESSA**   [*In unison*] Blaine! / Ducky.

**MOLLY MATTIE**   Why do you call her Tam Tam?

**WILL**   Well, the good doctor here used to get carsick. And on a field trip to Mt. Tamalpais—

**MOLLY MATTIE**   I know Mount Tam! My parents take me to see the mountain play there every year!

**WILL**   So, you know how you park your car, then they bus you up to the top? [*She nods. He points to* TESSA.] This poor kid got so bus sick they had to pull over so she could throw up all over the side of Mount Tam. She was GREEN. And she slept the rest of the trip with her head in my lap.

**MOLLY MATTIE**   What about when you got out?

**WILL**   We never got out. Stayed in the bus. She puked her poor guts out, then just sacked out on me and slept. Sixteen, sick as a dog, and fast asleep like a baby. We were stuck like glue ever since.

**MOLLY MATTIE**   Metaphors and similes! I love English.

**TESSA**   [*This has been niggling at her.*] Our first kiss was in the cab of your truck after we had to put our Setter down.

**WILL**   Yes it was.

[*She's been had.*]

**TESSA**   That was sneaky.

**WILL**   It was crafty.

**TESSA**   Underhanded.

**WILL**   Shrewd.

**TESSA**   You married someone else.

**WILL**   Only after you did.

**MOLLY MATTIE**   This is like the Lifetime Movie Network! [*Stops short*] No! [*Finds it*] This is a Hallmark movie.

**WILL**   So, you think you'll get into Davis?

**TESSA**  [*A fact, not a push*] She'll get in.

**MOLLY MATTIE**  I think I have a pretty good chance—and I'm really hoping I get a scholarship, or something. They're wicked expensive. Did you know that Germany is tuition free?

**WILL**  I did know that.

**MOLLY MATTIE**  That's pretty cool. I wish they did that here. My friend Chloe told me that you can sell your eggs? For like, a lot of money? And I'm eighteen—and I heard that you do it more than once?

**TESSA**  You're not selling your eggs. Just get into Davis first.

[MOLLY MATTIE *skips off stage.*]

That kid.

**WILL**  She likes you.

**TESSA**  Well, there's no accounting for taste.

**WILL**  So, no boyfriend?

**TESSA**  You're married.

**WILL**  Divorced.

**TESSA**  In my spare time, I like to macramé, and go for walks on the beach, and have a glass of wine while looking at the sunset while I macramé.

[MOLLY MATTIE *comes tearing back onstage, talking as she enters.*]

**MOLLY MATTIE**  I think you should take Rhett Butler—do you know the real Rhett Butler? Not like know him know him, that was Clark Gable, and he's dead. I love that movie—THIS Rhett Butler is a Bassett Hound/ Shepherd mix, and he's kinda funny lookin', but he's super smart and he sleeps at the foot of your bed. You'll have to pick him up and put him on it though, 'cause he's got those Bassett legs. Oh! You should get those doggie steps up to the bed, so they can go up and down—what kind of bed do you have? [WILL *looks at* TESSA, *who ignores him.*] You should totally take him.

**TESSA**  Yeah Will, you should totally take him.

**MOLLY MATTIE**  Seriously, when I take him out, the women start talking to him in these really stupid baby voices. It's so obnoxious—Rhett Butler is a total chick magnet.

**WILL**  [*Looking at* TESSA] Sold.

[*Lights change.*]

[*Board transition: 4/27, Kingston weight now 39, erase BOOMER, add CHICKEN to Newbies, add MAX and RHETT BUTLER to A/F.*]

# SCENE FIVE

[*The shelter.* MOLLY MATTIE *is in her usual spot, standing and manning the phone, and directing any traffic that comes through.*]

**MOLLY MATTIE**  Mrs. Randall—we're not that kind of shelter. You can't bring us wildlife—we're not the Lindsey Museum. It's what? It's hissing? OK, that's a possum, and I wouldn't go near it. Bye Mrs. Randall.

[TESSA *has come in with coffee. Phone rings again.*]

One Paw, Two Paw. Mrs. Randall—what do you mean it doesn't have any fur? [*puts hand over receiver, to* TESSA] She says there's an animal she wants to bring us, it's hissing, and it doesn't have any fur.

**TESSA**  Ask her if it has legs.

**MOLLY MATTIE**  Mrs. Randall, does it have any legs? She says no.

[TESSA *reaches for phone.*]

**TESSA**  Mrs. Randall, hi. That's a snake. [*Noticing*] Why is Boomer's name gone?

**MOLLY MATTIE**  They returned him.

**TESSA**  What? After a day? Is he okay?

**MOLLY MATTIE**  He bit their cat.

**TESSA**  They don't have a cat.

**MOLLY MATTIE**  They do. They lied. [*Shrugs*] They just really wanted a dog.

**TESSA**  Boomer: good with kids over eight, no cats.

**MOLLY MATTIE**  They didn't believe us.

**TESSA**  We vet all the dogs! We color code their personalities! We test them on cats, kids, and other dogs! Wait a minute—we did a home visit. There was no cat.

**MOLLY MATTIE**  They put him in the closet.

**TESSA**  No. Good. I don't want one our dogs with them, ever. No. Put them on the no-fly list. And call the other shelters too, and let them know. [MOLLY *does.*] In a closet?! Careless. Fucking. Assholes. Do not repeat that. OK.

[BILL *walks in. He is wearing a ball cap and colorful sweatshirt. He keeps moving as he talks.*]

**BILL**  Hey Tessa, morning Molly. Here to see my girl.

**TESSA**  Heya Bill, she's waiting for you. Have a good walk. [*He goes through kennel door. To* MOLLY] Good news, good news—a woman's been following Kingston's rescue on the website and brought in a ton of dog sweaters to keep him warm. We got video of the meeting; can you post it to—

**MOLLY MATTIE**  YouTube, Twitter, Facebook, yep, I'm on it.

**TESSA**  And pull out a thank-you card. Did you fill out your financial aid for Davis?

**MOLLY MATTIE**  Uh, yeah. [*Her demeanor has changed.*]

**TESSA**  Do you want me to drive you to your interview? What's wrong?

**MOLLY MATTIE**  It's just really expensive.

**TESSA**  I can always call the dean.

**MOLLY MATTIE**  Do not call the dean. That's embarrassing.

**TESSA**  OK. Julie's sending us a Rottie who just had puppies, we'll give them their own kennel, just do some shuffling—story time is in an hour—and the foster tree?

**MOLLY MATTIE**  We have three new foster moms and dads. Carlos interviewed them over the weekend. They're good to go.

**TESSA**  Good.

**MOLLY MATTIE**  The Andersons will take the bullies, Ricky and Eck.

**TESSA**  Together?

**MOLLY MATTIE**  Yes.

**TESSA**  Great.

[*Writes RICKY and ECK on the board, adding asterisks to denote they are fosters.*]

**MOLLY MATTIE**  The Rileys are new to fostering, so we're placing TunaFace with them, [TESSA *writes TUNAFACE under A/F with asterisk.*] and the Glenns have fostered for years—they just moved here—Carlos thinks either Lola or Salami would be good for them.

**TESSA**  Have they done food guarding before?

**MOLLY MATTIE**  Yes.

**TESSA**  Then Salami.

[*Writes SALAMI with asterisk under A/F.*]

**MOLLY MATTIE**  My mom saw Bob White in the supermarket. He said he's thinking about another dog for Peanut. He wants to get a puppy.

**TESSA**  Peanut is 9 years old. She's not gonna want a puppy in her space. OK.

[*Lights change: TESSA is on the phone.*]

**TESSA**  Bob, hey, it's Tessa. I'm good, thanks, how are you? Listen, I heard you're looking for another dog. Yeah . . . I've got your dog. She's a great animal. She's two. She's spayed, she's housebroken—[*The question she doesn't want to be asked; hedging*] Uh, we've had her two years. It is a long time, you're right. Well, she's not the prettiest of dogs, but you don't want a beauty queen, you want a dog who'll go on your runs with you. No, she's not a Staffie, she's a Dogo. People mix 'em up all the time. Oh, Dogos are great dogs, they're smart, loyal, great with kids—and she loves other dogs, so she and Peanut will be friends for life. We call her Elsa Lanchester. Well, like I said, she's not gonna win any beauty contests, so people have been a little shy about taking her home . . . she was—you know what a bait dog is? Bait dogs are used in dogfight—no, she . . . —yes! It's what it sounds like. Actually! Aggressive traits are deliberately bred OUT of Dogos, so she was just a sitting duck, poor thing. We found her, and we fixed her up, and the staff here loves her. Well, her left eye, the left side of her face, is, it's just a slope, actually, but she's got full mobility, great guard dog, very protective of her people . . . right. Uh huh. Bob, I promise you, you couldn't ask for a better pet.

Right. Got it. [*Can't help herself*] It's just, funny, you know. Just funny. I think it's funny.

Because you married a woman with no tits and no chin. [*Hangs up*]

[*Lights change.*]

## SCENE SIX

[WILL's *office. It is done in rich woods and greens. Deck, glass desk lamp. Oriental rug, bookcases, diplomas and a photo or two. It is both homey and professional.* WILL *sits as his desk.* TESSA *opens door and pokes her head in.*]

**TESSA**  Hi.

**WILL**  Well, hello.

**TESSA**  Hi. [*Cutting to the chase*] I need legal advice.

**WILL**  I'm well, thanks.

**TESSA**  Can you help me?

**WILL**  How are you? Not really, I hate all that social etiquette crap, especially when it's with someone you've shared bodily fluids with.

**TESSA**  I just have a question.

**WILL**  God Tessie, you used to be so fun. [*She gives up, turns to go.*] Tam Tam—come back. What's your question? [*She hesitates, comes back into room.*] Just move that stick out of the way, and sit down. [*She looks for a stick, realizes he's teasing her.*] Really. Have a seat. What's up?

**TESSA**  Can I [*Searches for words*] cash in my life insurance?

**WILL**  Why? What's going on?

**TESSA**  Can I? I can do that, can't I?

**WILL**  Uh . . . well I'd have to look at the documents, and the reasons why—

**TESSA**  I don't want to talk about why. Oh—and I know I should talk to the bank about this, could I mortgage my house? Put a second mortgage on it, I mean? The first was one for the shelter—but—could I?

**WILL**  *Is* this about the shelter?

**TESSA**  Yes, it's about the shelter. OK. So—my mom started a trust for me— [*Checking in with him*] can I just talk? [*He indicates that she's already on a roll.*] I've been wondering if I should ask my dad for early access to the trust that my mom left. I want to put Molly through school. She's talking about selling her eggs—

**WILL**  A lot of women do it, I've heard—

**TESSA**  I know. I don't want her to feel she has to. I did it a few years ago, and it was awful—

**WILL**  Why?

**TESSA**  Why was it awful or why did I do it?

**WILL**  The latter.

**TESSA**  That's irrelevant. I needed a cargo van and a mobile X-ray machine.

**WILL**  Did you get them?

**TESSA**  Yeah. Someone ended up donating their old van. It looks like a murder van, but it works. I got the X-ray machine, and gave everyone else a check.

**WILL**  Aren't they volunteers?

**TESSA**  Yeah.

**WILL**  How much do you make?

**TESSA**  We rely on donations, fiscal and material, and on sponsors, and anything extra isn't really extra, and I put it right back in. A "salary" is pointless.

**WILL**  Can you sell your eggs again?

**TESSA**  No.

**WILL**  Was it really so bad?

**TESSA**  [*Mocking*] Oh, you are such a boy. The drugs you take make you feel like shit, and the injections—

**WILL**  [*He looks stricken and sick.*] Shots?

**TESSA**  [*She knows he hates needles.*] Shots. Every day.

**WILL**  [*Stops her*] OK. [*Fascinated*] You can't do it again?

**TESSA**  No. One, I've only just aged out of it—which is too bad, because this is prime real estate. And even if I hadn't, they won't do it again, they're worried about the long-term effect.

**WILL**   How many times have you donated?

**TESSA**   Six. [*Back to business*] I need a way to make this money—what? Stop looking at me. Like that. Stop. Don't feel sorry for me.

**WILL**   I don't.

**TESSA**   Look—I'm just—I'm sure you're still a super-nice guy. But—I need to find this money. Molly is so smart, and her skills—she'll skyrocket at Davis. She deserves a top-notch education.

**WILL**   You love Molly.

**TESSA**   Don't get all sensitive.

**WILL**   [*Enjoying himself*] I've seen you naked.

**TESSA**   OK. Borderline inappropriate.

**WILL**   Is it though?

**TESSA**   I have to get ready for my appeal.

**WILL**   For what?

**TESSA**   The city denied me the sale of a bigger shelter for us. Meanwhile, they're shutting me down because they sold my building to a Starbucks!

**WILL**   Is this the city council meeting on Thursday?

**TESSA**   Yeah. Me versus them. I need a place to put these dogs. Plus Molly. Whether I win the appeal or not, every contingency plan I have—[*She's out of options. Shrugs. The truth*] I'm out of eggs.
[WILL *pulls whiskey out of his bottom drawer, pours her some. She slugs it, and his too.*]
Thank you. [*Beat*] You saw me naked a long time ago. Things aren't where they used to be.

**WILL**   Can I see? OK. OK, all right, this is what we're gonna do. I am going to refer you to Mel, an associate of ours.

**TESSA**   Why?

**WILL**   Because this is a conflict of interest. For me.

**TESSA**   What are you talking about, conflict of interest? [*He hesitates. She jibes him.*] Because we used to go together?

**WILL**   Don't belittle me, Tessa. [*She says nothing.*] Ok Tam Tam, look. My father is your father's lawyer, he's in charge of all his accounts, estate, will, trust, everything. I'm taking over for my dad, and I'm inheriting all of his clients—your dad, too. I can't counsel you with regard to him. I can only counsel HIM with regard to YOU.

**TESSA**   That is so unfair.

**WILL**   I know.

**TESSA**   Can you offer me advice as a friend? A peer?

**WILL**   Tessa, I've had access to all your father's documents, legal and otherwise—

**TESSA**   What's otherwise?

**WILL**   His personal statements—

**TESSA**   Personal st—[*A moment of clarity. She is unsettled.*] About what?

**WILL**   Riders he included as to why certain things should be carried out certain ways—

**TESSA**   About me?

[*He shakes his head to indicate he can't comment.*]

Like why the trust was changed? [*He won't look at her.*] What did he say about me? What did you read about me? Do you know why he hates me? 'Cause I sure as fuck don't know why.

**WILL**   Tessa—

**TESSA**   Thank you for meeting with me.

[*He comes out from behind his desk and goes to her. He is truthful and genuine.*]

**WILL**   My hands are tied here, Tessa. Even if I gave you little bits of casual advice, it just wouldn't be aboveboard—I'm going to send you to Mel—he's the best attorney around when it comes to estates, trusts, and assets—he's better than I am. Do you believe me? [*She nods.*] I want to help, and this is the best way I can. For now. Are you OK? [*She nods.*] Tessa. We'll figure it out.

[*She exits.*]

[*Lights change.*]

[*Board transition: Change date to 4/30, Kingston weight to 40lbs. Add* FOSSE *to A/F, and* ROOSTER *to Newbies.*]

## SCENE SEVEN

[*The shelter.* TESSA *is on the phone,* MOLLY *works on the computer, office phone on her shoulder.*]

**TESSA**   Is that so? After two days? [*To* MOLLY]

**MOLLY**   Tessa, can you—[*Points to computer.* TESSA *looks.*]

**TESSA**   Tell them to put him in a Bailey Chair, he should be fine. [*back to phone*] Well. Congratulations, you are officially a foster failure. It tends to happen with first timers. It's a good thing. OK, we'll be in touch. The Rileys would like to adopt Ricky and Eck. [*She erases the asterisk next to* RICKY *and* ECK.] What do Ro and Nelson have for us?

**MOLLY MATTIE** [*As this goes on,* TESSA *comments here and there.*] There's a litter of puppies—looks like they might have parvo—that's Julie. There are two senior dogs, 10 and 12—they're bonded—

**TESSA** Yes.

**MOLLY MATTIE** [*Moving down the list*] 11-year-old lab with congestive heart failure and a really big tumor on his spine. Can't walk. It's inoperable. End stage.

**TESSA** Call . . . call . . . Vanessa. She'll take him for hospice.

**MOLLY MATTIE** [*Beat*] Oh my God. Someone bought our wish list on Amazon.

**TESSA** What? [*Keeps writing on the board*]

**MOLLY MATTIE** Someone bought everything we've been asking for on Amazon. Oh my God. William Landry? Do you know a William Lan— ohmigod! Is that Will? He bought one of everything. He's courting you! It's so romantic! It's a "big gesture"! He's wooing you! [TESSA *has come behind her to look.*] Will and Tessa sittin' in a tree—k-i-s-s-

[*A* YOUNG MAN *rushes in carrying a heavy cardboard box leaking blood/a bloody, blanketed bundle.*]

Tessa—

[*Stepping forward, she takes bundle. He says nothing for a moment, realizes it's expected of him. Then—*]

**YOUNG MAN** He was—hit by a car—

[TESSA *takes the dog box into the exam/operating room door, which is very distinctly separate from the kennel door. She is in vet mode. It has gone quiet in the room. The* YOUNG MAN *is standing, waiting.* MOLLY MATTIE *continues to do her job.*]

**MOLLY MATTIE** Are you OK?

[*He nods. The phone rings.*]

One Paw, Two Paw. We're open 'til five. [*Hangs up*] Do you want to sit down? [*He doesn't answer. Phone rings again.* MOLLY MATTIE *watches him.*] One Paw, Two Paw. We have three Chihuahua mixes here, would you like to come by? All three are good with kids—10 to 5. [*Hangs up; to* YOUNG MAN] Hey— weren't you here like a month ago? [*Phone rings*] One Paw, Two Paw. Uh huh. OK. Got it.

[*Takes her phone and goes out front door, gone a second, comes back in and continues conversation. She stays in front of the exit.*]

Like maybe six weeks ago or something?

[*At this moment,* TESSA *bursts out of the exam room, bloody and murderous. The* YOUNG MAN *takes off, slamming through the exit, shoving* MOLLY MATTIE *aside.* TESSA *follows him outside, comes back a moment later.*]

**TESSA** Call Nick. Give him the plate number. Don't EVER block the door when someone like that is around! That piece of shit is the kid who brought his dog in last summer; he'd been fighting her? He's Randy Warren's cousin. Call Julie to do a necropsy. The dog is dead.

[*Exits through the vet door, swings back through.*]

I have the city council meeting.

[*Looks down at her bloody shirt.*]

[*Lights change.*]

# SCENE EIGHT

[*City council meeting.* TESSA *faces the audience, where the* COUNCIL MEMBERS *are peppered. When she addresses them, she addresses audience, too. Unbeknownst to* TESSA, WILL *watches the proceedings.*]

**COUNCILMAN STACEY** Next is Tessa Bartlett, appealing the Arcata Council decision of March 1st to deny the right of sale to One Paw, Two Paw. Tessa, whenever you're ready.

**TESSA** Doctor.

**COUNCILWOMAN PORTER** Excuse me?

**TESSA** I said "doctor." I am a doctor of veterinary medicine. I went to UC Davis, I was a specialist in emergency and critical care, and was head of surgery at 29. I then began what was my clearly ignominious retreat into the far less noble world of rescue work, it is the hardest thing I've ever done—it is so hard, it is, it is, it is ugly, the things I see, the people I deal with— the Randy Warrens—who is the greatest example of a coastal redneck this town has ever seen. Please address me as doctor. I will be a vet for the rest of my days in our great state of California, because it is an ineluctable need.

I offer spay and neuter services—a service I insist on providing to this city for free—I stay a vet so that when I get a phone call on a Sunday to please make a house call to put down a 14-year-old German Shepherd who is blind and incontinent, and who is the love of her owner's life, Stu, I do it. I'm a doctor. I field offers to this day to run emergency rooms. I got a call from Burlington, Vermont, this morning, to head their teaching hospital. I know you wish I were there right now. But this is my home.

And right now I'm the only no-kill shelter in the county, and you— everyone here—you're going to have to go home and tell your kids why there's no more story time at One Paw, Two Paw. You're going to have to tell your kids AND your parents what happened to all those dogs they love to read to, and walk with. And then once you tell them the "what," you'll have to tell them "why."

You don't know what to do with me. I got that—I get it—I'm loud, I'm not polite, but you don't need to know what to do with me. Just give me the place on Harkness—sell it to me—*I* know what to do.

Thank you to the council for your time and attention. I'm just going to end with this: The world is a dangerous place to live, not because of the people who are evil, but because of the people who don't do anything about it.

**COUNCILMAN STACEY**    Thank you Dr. Bartlett. We will take this into consideration and vote once the meeting has adjourned. You set, Liz? Meeting adjourned.

**WILL**    [WILL *approaches her.*] Hey, you OK?

**TESSA**    [*Softens*] You came. That's very nice of you.

**WILL**    You did good, Tam Tam. [*A lawyerly assurance*] It's in their best interest to vote for you.

**TESSA**    You bought Amazon.

[*There's a pause full of excitement and friction; it's not unpleasant.*]

**WILL**    Well, not all of it. So, Doctor. [*She laughs.*] I have a question for you.

**TESSA**    Is it Rhett Butler? Does he hog the covers?

**WILL**    Oh no, he and I have got a system all worked out. [*A moment, then*] Do you remember our last kiss?

[*Her phone buzzes. She looks at it.*]

**TESSA**    Oh shit. I have to go.

[*She exits.*]

[*Lights change.*]

[*Board setup remains same.*]

## SCENE NINE

[*The shelter. Nighttime. It is empty but the lights are on, or partially on. There is a knock at the door. WILL is outside.*]

**WILL**    Tessa? You there? [*More knocking*] Tessa?

[TESSA *comes out from the kennel portion of the shelter, book in hand. She opens the door.*]

Hi. The door was open.

**TESSA**    Oh shit. Hi.

**WILL**    Molly told me where you were.

**TESSA**    Molly's at my house.

**WILL**    Yeah, I know—

**TESSA**   Oh! Sorry—yeah, she stays with George whenever I stay here. Is everything OK?

**WILL**   Yeah—

**TESSA**   Sorry. Gimme a sec, I'll be right back.

[*Hands him the book, goes back into the kennel for a moment. He peruses book. She returns.*]

Sorry I ditched you earlier. Someone dumped a dog out in front—they don't care if we're closed—and she's really skittish, she needed a bath and grooming. But now she's all clean, and perfect—[*Writes* LUCKY *on board during this*]

**WILL**   Are you staying the night?

**TESSA**   Yeah, she's got an infection on her back leg. It'll be fine, but I'm changing the bandage every four hours and keeping her company.

[*He holds up the book. It's a kids' book.*]

I read to them.

**WILL**   That's unexpected. It's sweet.

**TESSA**   Yes. I'm so sweet. It's ten o'clock. What are you doing here? Where's Rhett Butler?

**WILL**   He's having a slumber party with Molly and George. You won, Tam Tam.

**TESSA**   Won what?

**WILL**   They voted in your favor. You got the sale.

**TESSA**   What?! Really?! Oh my God! You came over here to tell me that?

**WILL**   I did. Now, the second part.

**TESSA**   Oh God.

**WILL**   It's not bad. They're giving you a week to move. From tomorrow.

**TESSA**   WHAT?

**WILL**   Don't panic—

[*She begins to go into work mode.*]

**TESSA**   That building needs renovations! Is that a seven business day week? And I'll get the weekend too? Or—

**WILL**   Hey. Hey hey hey—it's OK. It's ten o'clock. You're not going to get much done right now other than work yourself into a lather.

**TESSA**   Are you going to tell me to relax?

**WILL**   Ohhh no. I value my life. But . . . I just thought you'd want to know. And celebrate. You were great today.

[*He pulls out a bottle of wine, and grabs two mugs from the desk, too. He picks one up, reads from it.*]

"I like big mutts and I cannot lie."

[*He looks around and takes in the shelter. He notices the bookcase full of children's and pre-teen books. Goes over and squats in front of it.*]

Story time?

TESSA   Yeah. People donate books all the time, and Tuesdays one of the volunteers reads to the kids. But the kids come in all the time to do their homework and read to the dogs. It sounds silly, but it's actually great for both of them. [*She is suddenly taken with the idea of more space, more opportunity, and begins to see it.*]

WILL   [*Picking up on her thoughts*] What'll you do with your new digs?

TESSA   Well. The building is 4,000 square feet, plus the acre of land next to it—[*panics*] oh God, how am I going to get the money together in a week?

WILL   Breathe Tessie. Drink your nine-dollar wine.

TESSA   You spent nine dollars on me? People will say we're in love.

WILL   Tell me what you see for your new place.

TESSA   Oh, we can have a whole room for the readers—with benches, and pillows—and shelves on the wall—at different heights for the different ages of the kids who come?—and dog beds. Maybe artwork by a local artist for the walls? Or photos of the kids' pets, and family pets, on the walls? [*Has an epiphany*] I can call Bill! You remember Taylor Construction?

WILL   Yeah, Bill Taylor.

TESSA   Bill is totally in love with Gracie, she's one of our dogs. He walks her all the time. He's retired, but Taylor Construction was his. His sons run it now. I wonder if he'd be foreman for the build.

WILL   You should ask the Aaron Bros. to donate the materials.

TESSA   That's a great idea. OK.

WILL   Breathe, Tessie.

TESSA   [*She takes a deep breath and a big drink of wine.*] This is the best nine-dollar wine I've ever had.

WILL   Did you really break a guy's nose last year?

TESSA   He's lucky I didn't pull his spine through his dick.

WILL   Why?

TESSA   He deserved it.

WILL   You just walked up to him and hit him.

**TESSA**   He was sitting on his porch talking to a friend. I walked up, he turned, and I hit him.

[*She demonstrates a downward punch.*]

**WILL**   What if he'd hit you back?

**TESSA**   No. I had two things going for me. Surprise, and [he was sitting on a bucket]—gravity.

**WILL**   C'mon Tam Tam—show me a punch.

**TESSA**   You want me to hit you.

**WILL**   No—I just want to see how you handle yourself.

**TESSA**   If you expected a punch, I'd just kick you in the nuts.
[*He gestures "c'mon."*]
You're—really?

**WILL**   I know you're going to do what you want. I can at least help you be effective.

[*They put down their mugs, slowly circle each other, her with her fists up.*]

**TESSA**   Are you sure?

**WILL**   Guard your face, Tessie. [*She goes to hit him, he blocks her easily.*] Saw it coming a mile away.

**TESSA**   Well, I'm afraid of hurting you.

**WILL**   With your soft little girl hands?

[*She attacks him fully; she's clearly a better fighter.*]

**TESSA**   Wow. You make middle age look really good.

**WILL**   Fuck you, Tam Tam.

**TESSA**   Your language is atrocious.

**WILL**   Yes, you're such a delicate little flower.

**TESSA**   I am delicate.

**WILL**   [*Giving it back to her*] Eh. You're looking a little tired there, Tessie. Gotta take better care of yourself. Do some yoga.

**TESSA**   Fuck you, counselor. Be right back
[*She disappears again to check on the pup.* WILL *pulls a book out of the little bookcase and looks at it.* TESSA *comes back.*]
She's good. I put her in with Petey. He's really good with the little ones.

**WILL**   Why do you say your dad hates you?

**TESSA**   Jesus. [*Honestly*] Because he does.

**WILL**   Why?

**TESSA**  I don't know.

**WILL**  You don't know. Nothing?

**TESSA**  Nothing. I have no idea.

[WILL *holds up the book.* TESSA *smiles.*]

**WILL**  Miss J read this to our sixth grade class, and you cried and cried.

**TESSA**  I did. It's a great book. So.

[*The following is awkward, sweet courting.*]

**WILL**  So.

**TESSA**  . . . You hang your shingle out?

**WILL**  Next week.

**TESSA**  Why are you being so nice to me?

**WILL**  Why not?

**TESSA**  You want to take your pants off? Jacket! Your jacket! Do you want to take your jacket off? [*Floundering*] I have cookies!

[*She goes again, and* WILL *cobbles together a comfy spot for them on the floor out of dog beds, his jacket, and hers. She returns without cookies.*]

I don't have cookies.

**WILL**  Where's your husband?

**TESSA**  I am not leaving this room again. Ex-husband. He's in Sausalito, with his wife. She's very blond. She's nice. Uh . . . both vets. They raise Goldens. Which are break-your-heart dogs. They send a Christmas card every year, and a check for the shelter. It's very sweet. They're good for each other. Where's your wife?

**WILL**  Ex-wife. France. Where do you sleep here?

**TESSA**  There's a cot, but I usually do this—sleeping bag on a couple of dog beds.

**WILL**  Do you miss emergency medicine?

**TESSA**  I miss the money—

**WILL**  Vets don't make that much—

**TESSA**  If you're a specialist—double it—but, no, I don't. This makes more sense to me. It sucks- but—and don't laugh—but it's like I found the right puzzle piece.

**WILL**  I get it. [*He picks up the book.*] Read?

**TESSA**  You want me to read to you?

**WILL**  Yeah.

[*She takes the book, and he settles in.* TESSA *begins to read from* Where the Red Fern Grows, *or* The Art of Racing in the Rain. *She gets halfway through the page, and begins to cry.*]

**TESSA**  Sorry. [*She tries to compose herself.*] This is—[*Indicates him, the company, the closeness*] It's just really nice.
[*He brushes her hair off her face, and hands her his wine.*]
You give me booze whenever I get upset.

**WILL**  Yes, ma'am. [*A moment, then*] What happened to you, Tam Tam? What happened to make you so angry/ferocious/provoked all the time? [*She doesn't answer.*]

**TESSA**  This wine is really terrible.

**WILL**  [*He laughs. A moment, then*] Molly idolizes you.

**TESSA**  Isn't it frightening?

**WILL**  She's a great kid.

**TESSA**  I heard her say "twat" yesterday. Twat! She called someone a "twat"!

**WILL**  [*Feigning horror*] Where would she hear such a word?

**TESSA**  It's a great word, Will. People are twats! They're twats, Will, they're twats. People are twats. And assholes. Twat and asshole—those are my favorite.

**WILL**  Mine too.

**TESSA**  You, sir, are no lady.

**WILL**  Neither are you.

**TESSA**  Why'd you move back here?

**WILL**  My dad's getting older. Be nice to be closer to my nieces and nephews. And it's pretty.

**TESSA**  You glad to see your dad?

**WILL**  Yeah. He wants to fish. He and his lady friend want to travel across the US in their airstream. It's nice to come home.

**TESSA**  You won't get bored?

**WILL**  Nah. You can get bored anywhere, Tessie. But no, I don't think so. Maybe have a kid or two.

**TESSA**  Let's hope your boys can swim at your age.

**WILL**  My boys can swim.

**TESSA**  Every man is so certain—

**WILL**  My boys are fine.

**TESSA**  You might want to ease up on that wine then—

**WILL**   Why?

**TESSA**   Alcohol can lead to infertility and impotency, and given your age—

**WILL**   Is there a reason I need to be potent in the next couple of hours?

**TESSA**   No! No! No, I—[*Beat. She addresses his earlier question.*] It's—it's um, the callousness I see. Every day. The lack of care, I think? It's not the dogs who get beaten, it's the dogs people neglect, that are tied up and forgotten about, that are starved, that—people talk about man's inhumanity to man, but it's people's total indifference to animals—the most gentle of souls, who are made purely of trust, and love, who would lay down their life for you— these loving beings, their fate is in our hands—and a dog can be bleeding out on a street, and people will walk right on by, and I don't—I don't get it, Will. I can't comprehend—and this [*Referring to her anguish*], it won't turn off. I can't turn it off. I wish I could. I wish I didn't care. Because this—what I see—this is all the time.

[*He hands her more wine.*]

"The more I learn about people, the more I like my dog." Mark Twain said that. Now this is where you say, "A dog is not a child."

**WILL**   You can't compare 'em. You also can't prove they're different. I can leave my dog and go to the store, but I can't leave a newborn. It's just logistics. It's the only measurable thing. People are twats. I'll read?

[*She assents. He picks up the book and begins to read aloud. A few sentences in, she moves so she is now settled between his legs, his back against the desk. He continues reading. They are two perfect puzzle pieces. He takes another drink of wine. Halfway through the next sentence when she stops him:*]

**TESSA**   Will.

**WILL**   What's up?

**TESSA**   Thank you for the wine.

**WILL**   I'm afraid we just drank the last of it.

**TESSA**   You make it taste like twenty-dollar wine.

[*She settles in again, and he resumes aloud with the book. After several sentences, TESSA breaks in.*]

Will.

**WILL**   Yeah?

**TESSA**   I'm sorry I married someone else.

[*He puts the book down. It is what he's been waiting for. They kiss and wrap around each other, sinking into the makeshift bed.*]

[*Lights change.*]

[*Morning.* WILL *and* TESSA *are curled around each other, fast asleep on the floor.* MOLLY MATTIE *lets herself in, and finding them there, tiptoes to them. She places an open envelope on the floor next to them, and leaves. A moment later, they stir, see each other, and kiss.* TESSA *spots the envelope on the ground, reaches for it, and reads it contents.*]

**TESSA**   Molly got into Davis.

[*Lights down.*]

# SCENE TEN

[*Afternoon. Outdoors. The backyard of* TESSA'*s father. She has stopped for a visit. There is minor evidence of a project, i.e., a shovel on the ground, bag of potting soil, a cinderblock, or a couple of bricks. Just enough to suggest the place and activity.*]

**TESSA**   [*Offstage*] Dad?

[*She enters and finds him, somewhere out in the audience. She attempts to get his attention.*]

Dad? Hey, Dad! Hey. [*Leans against fence*] Hi. [*Surveys backyard*] What is all this, what are you doing? A pond? You're building a pond? Digging—a koi pond. You want some help? [*Making conversation*] I heard that Hank's hips are getting stiff. Julie told me. She said she gave him Rimadyl, and Julie's a great vet, but I brought you glucosamine.

I don't know if you heard, but I won my appeal, and the city is selling me the plot over on Harkness. It's a great place for us. The thing is, I've only been given a week to make the transition. Crazy, right? There's construction that has to be done. There are codes. Plus, we're at capacity, and the dogs keep coming. I'm the only no-kill shelter in the county; these dogs have nowhere else to go. If I could give them away, I would. But people want to pay $7,000 for a fucking over-bred piece of—sorry. Language. I love that you rescued Hank. Hank is a great dog.

[*Her big pitch*] The trust that Mom left—I'd like to access it—not all of it, just enough to make the sale and cut a check so we can begin making the facility battle ready for the dogs. I've got the Aaron Bros. in town who will do the labor for free if I pay for the materials. Which is amazing, but I've only got seven days to make this happen, and it would kill me to have to turn down their offer. Starbucks takes over next week—I need quick cash. So, I'm asking you if you'll grant me access. [*Corrects herself*] Early access. Dad, I know. I know it says when I'm thirty-five, but this can't wait until November.

Even if I went back to work at the hospital, I wouldn't get my first check for a month. I opened a shelter so I could be the on-site vet and put that money elsewhere.

So. Business proposition. You lend me the money, and in November I'll repay you from the trust. We can write up a contract and have it notarized and everything—and with interest. I'm not money-focused—

Why won't you help me? I know things have been not good since Mom died. And lately people say you don't answer the phone or the door. What's going on? And don't tell me it's in my head. What did I do to you? [*Realization*] The ring. Mom's ring. This is about Mom's ring. No. No. Dad, when you gave me that ring, you said, if you ever get into a tight spot and have to sell it, that's OK. You gave me the papers it came with! [*Stops herself*] You cannot be mad at me for this. I know it was an heirloom. I offered to let you keep that ring twice. And you said no both times. Do you think that was fun for me? Do you think I wanted to do it? I was sleeping on the floor at the shelter. I had to replace my surgical equipment.

[*Gathers herself*] I didn't do it to upset you or to spite you—and I understand that you're angry. I'm sorry, Dad. [*Baffled*] Dad? Dad? Walter!

Okay. See you around, Walter. [*Leaves, comes back*] Am I not an heirloom?

[*Lights change.*]

[*Board transition: board is wiped clean. Change April Adoptions to May Adoptions. Date is 5/3. Change Kingston weight to 42. Add* WILKE *to A/F, add* SPIKE *to Newbies.*]

## SCENE ELEVEN

[*The shelter. May 3rd. Busy as usual.* MOLLY MATTIE *opens mail.*]

**MOLLY MATTIE**   Tessa! C'mere!

[TESSA *enters from the back.*]

Look—the couple that adopted Cinnamon? They sent an update.

**TESSA**   I love updates! She looks so happy! I love it—put it on the board.

[MOLLY *goes over to a big corkboard which has letters and photos from dogs' adoptive families. She tacks it to the board.*]

**MOLLY MATTIE**   I love happy endings.

[BILL *enters. It is not his usual non-stop visit.*]

**BILL**   Hi Tessa.

**TESSA**   Hi Bill. Oh! You need the keys for Harkness.

**BILL**   Yes, but that's not why I'm here. [*He takes off his cap.*] I uh—I'd like to make it official.

[TESSA *grins.*]

I'd like to adopt Gracie.

[TESSA *is very happy, comes out to hug him.*]

**TESSA**   Yes! Congratulations.

[*Writes* GRACIE *under A/F.*]

**BILL**   Gracie—she uh, she's awfully friendly with that little dog.

**TESSA**  Pax.

**BILL**  Pax. You think she'll be sad when we take her home?

**TESSA**  I think she'll be very happy when you take her home. [*helping him along*] I think Pax might be sad. I think he'll miss her.

[*He nods, taking this in.*]

**BILL**  Tessa. I'd like to adopt Pax, too.

[TESSA *adds* PAX *to* A/F.]

**TESSA**  You think your wife will be OK with that?

**BILL**  I bought her a car.

**TESSA**  You want to take them tonight? Tomorrow?

**BILL**  Tonight.

**TESSA**  I'll get you all set.

**BILL**  Big day tomorrow—

**TESSA**  Yeah, for both of us. Thank you for helping.

**BILL**  I hope you adopt 'em all out.

**TESSA**  So do I.

[BILL *heads back to the kennel. Phone rings,* TESSA *answers.*]

One Paw, Two Paw. Hi Julie. Goddammit. All right. I know. OK, thanks for letting us know. Me too. Bye. [*Hangs up*] We lost the parvo puppies.

**MOLLY MATTIE**  All of them?

[TESSA *nods.*]

Poor things.

**TESSA**  Yeah. OK. Well—we've got six vacancies. That's good.

**MOLLY MATTIE**  Yeah. I'll get the vans ready for tomorrow.

**TESSA**  Great. Let's make sure to take adults and seniors, no puppies this time. Finn, Brody, Willie Nelson, Elsa.

**MOLLY MATTIE**  [*She is texting someone.*] It's the parking lot at Pitchford's— [*Explaining*] my aunt and uncle are coming tomorrow, I think.

**TESSA**  They're getting a dog?

**MOLLY MATTIE**  I think so. They keep talking about empty nest syndrome.

[GWEN *walks in.*]

Hi Aunt Gwen!

**GWEN**  Hi sweetie.

**MOLLY MATTIE**  You're here! Where's Uncle Jim?

**GWEN**  He's helping the guys load the vans. Hi Tessa.

**TESSA**   Hey Gwen, nice to see you. How are you? A very loud little bird told me you're thinking about a dog.

**MOLLY MATTIE**   Ohmigod! I'm gonna show Uncle J Elsa Lanchester.

[*She dashes outside.*]

**GWEN**   We are.

**TESSA**   I think Molly will choose well for you.

**GWEN**   She adores you, you know.

**TESSA**   I'm sorry. I keep telling her to aim higher.

**GWEN**   Tessa. I don't—[*She finds the words.*] thank you. Thank you for helping with Molly.

**TESSA**   Gwen, Molly is like my kid sister. I would be lost without her. So thank *you.*

[MOLLY *bursts back in.*]

**MOLLY MATTIE**   Aunt G! You have to meet Elsa! And tonight you can sleep on it and then when you come tomorrow you'll totally want to take her home! (You'll see. It works every time).

**GWEN**   She's hard to say no to.

**TESSA**   [*Takes off her Davis sweatshirt*] Mol, this is for you, and I'm going to go get Pax and Gracie ready for Bill. He's adopting them.

**MOLLY MATTIE**   Ohmigod!

**GWEN**   Put it on! Ohmigod.

[BILL *enters.*]

**BILL**   Gwen!

**MOLLY MATTIE**   Bill! You're taking the dogs!! You're adopting Gracie!

**BILL**   I am. Gwen, I'm meeting the Aaron Bros. tomorrow morning at Harkness. They're donating the lumber and materials. We're gonna start on the construction around 8 a.m. Can you still be available to run errands for us?

**GWEN**   Oh yeah—I'm all set, and I'll take care of lunch, too. When should we plan to paint?

**MOLLY MATTIE**   We got the 4-H to paint.

**BILL**   Terrific. Give it a few days, there's going to be a lot of sawdust and stuff floating around, so maybe mid-week. Sound good?

**GWEN**   Sounds great. I was thinking about putting planters out front, window boxes, and . . . you're pouring the walk last?

[BILL *nods.*]

I've got some great old mosaic pots we can line the walk with.

**BILL**   I think she'd love that.

[*He begins to talk about his plans for the place as the lights fade.*]

So, we're going to create an open plan for the lobby—

[*Lights change.*]

# SCENE TWELVE

[TESSA *and* WILL *are at his place. It is late, they are sleeping.* TESSA's *phone rings. And rings. And rings. She rolls over into* WILL, *who wraps his arm around her. Her phone rings again.* WILL *hears it, leans over her, and picks it up.*]

**WILL**   Tessa. [*Rousing her*] Tessa. It's Molly.

**TESSA**   What?

**WILL**   Molly just called. [*Looks at phone*] She's called four times. You have ten missed calls.

**TESSA**   [*Fully awake now*] What? Is she OK? Was there an accident?

[WILL's *phone rings, and there's a banging on the door.*]

**WILL**   [*Answering phone*] Hello? Molly? Are you OK? What? She's here with me—where are you? Wait—there's someone at the door.

[*He exits.* TESSA *has begun to listen to her messages.* WILL *comes back. The following is somber and careful.*]

Tessa. Nick's here. There's been a fire.

**TESSA**   [*She goes very still.*] Where.

**WILL**   At the shelter. [*Stops her*] No—wait. Nick—[*Calling for him*] Nick?

**TESSA**   Nick?

[NICK *fills the doorway. He is in plainclothes but with badge and gun visible.*]

**NICK**   Tessie. Sit down?

[*She shakes her head. He sits her down and kneels in front of her.*]

There was a fire at the shelter, Tessa.

**TESSA**   Is it bad?

**NICK**   Yes honey. It was bad.

**TESSA**   Is it out?

**NICK**   Yes.

**TESSA**   Can I go down there? I have to go down there—I have to find—I'll just take them to my place, I'll bring them all to my house, and—

**NICK**   Tessa. [*He shakes his head.*]—It burned to the ground, Tessie.

**TESSA**   But—the dogs—

**NICK**    [*Shakes his head*] There's nothing, Tessa. There's nothing left.

**TESSA**    George—

**WILL**    George is here, Tessa. He's in the garage with Rhett Butler.

**NICK**    Tessa. Listen to me. I'm going to drive you down to the shelter, and Will's going to follow us, OK?

**TESSA**    I don't—how—

**WILL**    Honey. They think Randy Warren set the fire. Nick's got him at the jail now.

**TESSA**    Take me down there right now.

**NICK**    [*Turns so* WILL *can't hear him*] I promise you Randy will be not be able to walk tomorrow.

[*Lights change.*]

## SCENE THIRTEEN

[*Bare stage. It is early morning.* BILL *is front and center, ostensibly in front of the new place on Harkness. He is there to send everyone home, all while fielding phone calls.*]

**BILL**    [*He addresses the audience as his workers.*] I know you've all heard about what happened last night, and I know you got up early to be here, and I thank you for doing that. I know Tessa would appreciate it, but there's no building today, guys. Go on home. [*Answers phone*] Hi Dan. I know. We're not moving on this today. Thanks. [*As soon as he hangs up it rings again.*] Mike, hi. You heard. Yeah. Just hold off on delivery. Ok. I'll tell her. [*Ends call.*]

[WILL *enters.*]

Hey. How is she?

**WILL**    [*He shakes his head.*] Have you seen her?

**BILL**    No—is she OK? I thought she was with you.

**WILL**    I can't find her. She was at the shelter with Nick and me around 1 a.m., and now she's gone. [*His phone rings.*] It's my dad. If you see her, please call me.

**BILL**    I will.

## SCENE FOURTEEN

[*Two days later.* TESSA *has a shovel, a small pile of black garbage bags, which she is carrying to the back one by one. She is filthy.*]

**WILL**    Tessa. I've been looking for you for two days.

[*She keeps working.*]

I'm so sorry Tessa. I'm so sorry. Tessa. I need to talk to you.

[*She takes a bag to the back.*]

Honey—[*Fully takes in the situation*] what are you doing?

[*He goes to look. She doesn't stop him.*]

Are you allowed to do this? How did you get them—I'll help you.

[*She stops him.*]

Tessa. I need to talk to you about your dad. Your dad—

**TESSA**   Walter.

**WILL**   What?

**TESSA**   His name is Walter.

**WILL**   Your da—Walter—he died yesterday, Tessa. Yesterday morning. You don't have your phone, Tessa, and my dad was listed as his emergency contact. Honey, let me help you.

[*She won't let him.*]

Tessa, I need you—will you come with me? Tessie, your—Walter—was very sick. He had cancer, and it was very bad. Did you know he was sick? [*Walking her through it*] The first time, he did chemo, and it worked. The second time, he did chemo again, and it worked. It came back pretty fast a third time.

**TESSA**   Cancer?

**WILL**   He didn't tell anyone, Tessa.

**TESSA**   He didn't look sick.

**WILL**   He died yesterday morning.

**TESSA**   Why isn't your dad telling me this?

**WILL**   He's up north in Trinidad. There are—some things we need to talk about.

**TESSA**   It's a conflict of interest.

**WILL**   He said to go ahead. Walter put his affairs in order a year ago in October. He'd finished his second round of chemo. His estate and assets were sizable. He was worth 8 million—that doesn't include the house and the land, which is just about 30 acres. Originally he left 1/20 of his estate to you. He came in on Friday and amended some things, Tessa. Tessa.

**TESSA**   He froze the trust.

**WILL**   The trust isn't mentioned. Just listen. Your dad left everything to Hank.

[*She has sunk to the ground.*]

Tessa. Your dad left Hank to you.

[*She looks up.*]

[*Blackout.*]

END OF PLAY

# Hamlet-Mobile

An exploration of grief using Shakespeare's *Hamlet*, 4 actors, and a van

Lauren Ludwig

# Lauren Ludwig

Lauren Ludwig is a multimedia director and writer who grew up outside of Syracuse, NY. She is the founder of the Los Angeles immersive theater company Capital W, with whom she wrote and directed *Hamlet-Mobile* and *And The Drum*. Her past work has earned a Hollywood Fringe Festival "Best of Comedy" Award, an *LA Weekly* "Best of the Fringe" Award, and a *Chicago Reader* "Critics Choice" distinction. She regularly directs the comedy show Lost Moon Radio, with whom she has several television projects in development. Lauren also founded the filmmaking collective Darty Hall; with them she wrote and directed her first feature film, *5 Pilgrims*, which is currently in festivals. She is a graduate of the AFI Directing Workshop for Women and Northwestern University.

# Production History

*Hamlet-Mobile* was originally produced by Capital W in Los Angeles, CA, as part of the Hollywood Fringe Festival 2015. It starred JB Waterman, Lizzie Prestel, Hunter Seagroves, and Heather Gottlieb. It was directed by Lauren Ludwig and produced by Monica Miklas, with production design by Shing Yin Khor, costumes by Rachel Weir, sound design by Dave McKeever, lighting design by Brandon Baruch, and stage management by Will Holt.

## A NOTE ON THE SHOW

*Hamlet-Mobile* is an immersive, site-specific experience. It lives in the blurry line between fiction and truth. In this script, the characters are named after the actors who originally played them; they should be changed for future productions to suit each cast. We must believe the cast are truly in The Moving Shadow. We must believe they have lived and performed in the van together for years.

The eight pieces are meant to be performed in any order, as many times as you like. In the original production, the Hamlet-Mobile would park in a location and perform one of the eight plays on a loop for two hours. They next day, it would perform another one.

Most of the pieces are intended for audiences of one or two people. Whatever else changes in each production, don't change that. Intimacy is the currency of *Hamlet-Mobile*.

## CHARACTERS

The cast are the remaining members of The Moving Shadow, an experimental theater company of some repute, though always living on the edge of poverty.

**MARLON PINE**   The recently deceased founder and artistic director of the theater company. *Hamlet-Mobile* was his unfinished magnum opus.

**JAMES**   Principal actor in the company for 10 years. Looked up to Marlon Pine as a surrogate father. Believes himself the natural heir to the theater company. He has "directed" this production of *Hamlet-Mobile*.

**HUNTER**   Actor. Marlon Pine's semi-distant relative. In the company for 3 years. Knows Pine didn't like or respect him that much. Stayed in the company out of bull-headedness and pride. Naturally at odds with James.

**LIZZIE**   Principal actress. In the company longer than anyone else; knew Pine the longest. Many in the company assume they were romantically involved at various points. Quietly pulls the strings, but isn't interested in power. Less den mother, more lone wolf.

**HEATHER ANN**   Young actress. Joined the company 5 years ago when they came to her town for a 3-month residency. Never speaks about her past or her family. Pine treated her like an adopted daughter.

## THE LOCATION

The "Hamlet-Mobile" is a converted cargo van that's seen multiple owners and over 200,000 miles. It runs with the steady determination of an old horse out-walking death. It was bought at a bargain and remade into a stage, a home, a shrine, and a safe harbor for the company. The outside of the van is covered in tapestries, paint, and signage announcing "Hamlet-Mobile," quotes from the group's late mentor, show times, rules, etc.; it is a *useful* space above all else. The dominant motifs are flowers and skulls.

On the inside, the Hamlet-Mobile features several areas:

**A Shrine to Marlon Pine**    A large photo of the group's late mentor hangs on the wall. Surrounding it are crosses, flowers, candles, etc. One of the windows nearby may look like stained glass.

**The Sleeping Area**    pillows, sleeping bag or hammock, family photos.

The Kitchen/Bathroom    mirror, first aid, an assortment of fake moustaches and stage make-up, an old coffee pot used for pissing in case of emergencies, huge jars of trail mix, a chore wheel.

**The Props Closet**    fake swords, masks, a cape.

**The Library**    The library features dozens of copies of *Hamlet* and Shakespeare's complete works. The wall has a map of Denmark marked like a road-trip map. Maybe a globe is there.

**The Cab**    multiple Buddhas and St. Christopher tokens, air fresheners, postcards from past destinations shoved in the visor.

**The Van Supplies**    A peg board with hooks holds tools, flash lights, jumper cables, a folded blue tarp, snow chains, maybe a spare tire.

### Other Stray Observations

There are cushions for the audience to sit on and a rug on the floor.

Many items are spray-painted with the company's logo. Other items are labeled according to which actor uses them.

Ophelia has covered multiple surfaces with hundreds of small origami flowers.

The space feels truly *used*.

## AS THE AUDIENCE COMES IN . . .

*Audiences approaching the van encounter a House Manager. She checks them in and offers them The Company History, a small zine that describes the company's backstory (see below).*

*She also encourages them to sign the Guest Book, a book on a podium that asks audiences to "Summarize Hamlet in 6 words." Audience members are encouraged to peruse past entries as they wait.*

*Some of* MARLON PINE'*s lectures play on a wireless speaker where audiences are waiting on the street.*

*Here is the text found in the zine:*

*The Moving Shadow: A History*

*The Moving Shadow was founded in 1998 by world-renowned theatre auteur Marlon Pine. After a life lived on the stage, performing and studying with the greatest theatre artists of his time and of times not his own, Pine had a dream. In the dream he was an owl. He followed the owl, which was himself, into the forest. The owl, which was himself, led him to a clearing. In the clearing he saw a one-third-scale replica of Shakespeare's Globe. He alone was the audience and he witnessed what he later called "a work of theatre that transcended sight and language, that spoke directly to the shadow inside of me." Awaking from his dream, Pine abandoned the theatre that he'd known. He founded The Moving Shadow. "Micro Theatre" was born.*

*The Moving Shadow is renowned throughout North American and Eastern European experimental theatre circles. The company members are exemplars at the top of their field, donating their best years to enact Pine's visions, eschewing a comfortable life in the gleaming theatrical institutions dotted across our country for a life of practice, discipline, and movement. The Moving Shadow is currently touring its production Hamlet-Mobile.*

*What Is "Micro Theatre"?*

*Micro Theatre is the brain-fruit of Marlon Pine. It is a branch of "Total Theatre" that is performed for audiences of 10 or fewer. It regularly, but not exclusively, includes site-specific locations, music, dance, intellectual texts, philosophy, art history, live poetry, dream recitation and interpretation, architectural analysis, spirit walks, revelatory visions, and animal guides.*

*What is Hamlet-Mobile?*

*Hamlet-Mobile is the magnum opus of Marlon Pine, though he was not able to complete it before his untimely death. It is 8 short plays inspired by Shakespeare's Hamlet, all performed in and around a van. Hamlet-Mobile is the first step in a revolution. It is mobile, it is micro, it is yours. It is currently driving, parking, and performing at the Hollywood Fringe Festival.*

## PIECE / CAST BREAKDOWN

Family Feud   James, Hunter, Heather Ann, Lizzie
The Body   James, Hunter, Heather Ann, Lizzie
Crown | Ambition | Queen   Hunter, Lizzie
Girl with Flowers   James, Hunter, Heather Ann, Lizzie
Interior. Kitchen. Night.   Lizzie, Heather Ann
The Break-Up   Heather Ann, James
The Gravedigger Hot Boxes the Van   Hunter, Lizzie
An Orgy of Blood and Ashes!   James, Hunter, Heather Ann, Lizzie

## AUDIENCE BREAKDOWN

*Number of intended audience members in each piece:*
Family Feud: performed on the street for as many people as are gathered
The Body: audience of 1
Crown | Ambition | Queen: audience of 2
Girl with Flowers: audience of 1 (or 2)
Interior. Kitchen. Night.: audience of 1
The Break-Up: audience of 2
The Gravedigger Hot Boxes the Van: audience of 1
An Orgy of Blood and Ashes!: performed on the street for as many people as are
  gathered

# FAMILY FEUD

*[Daytime. Audience members are not collected for this piece, but are rather accosted by the van while they wait on the street. On the street corner, HEATHER ANN waits, hidden amongst the audience, seeming like a street performer. She has a bucket of roses and a wireless speaker. The van screeches up to the curb. We hear muffled shouting inside. The side door bursts open. JAMES as HAMLET comes tumbling angrily out.]*

**HAMLET**   A little more than kin and less than kind!!!

[HUNTER *as* CLAUDIUS *and* LIZZIE *as* GERTRUDE *come out after* HAMLET. *They try to get him back into the van. They are aware of the audience. This is a public family fight.*]

**CLAUDIUS**   How is it that the clouds still hang on you?

**HAMLET**   Not so, my lord; I am too much in the sun.

**GERTRUDE**   Good Hamlet, cast thy knighted color off,
And let thine eye look like a friend on Denmark.
Do not forever with thy vailèd lids
Seek for thy noble father in the dust.
Thou know'st tis common; all that lives must die,
Passing through nature to eternity.

**HAMLET**   Ay, madam, it is common.

**GERTRUDE**   If it be,
Why seems it so particular with thee?

[HAMLET *is offended. He strips down to his underwear during the following speech to make his point.*]

**HAMLET**   "Seems," madam? Nay, it is. I know not "seems."
'Tis not alone my inky cloak, good mother,
Nor customary suits of solemn black,
Nor windy suspiration of forced breath,
No, nor the fruitful river in the eye,
Nor the dejected havior of the visage,
Together with all moods, forms, shapes of grief,
That can denote me truly. These indeed "seem."
For they are actions that a man might play;
But I have that within that passes show,
These but the trappings and the suits of woe.

**CLAUDIUS**   'Tis sweet and commendable in your nature, Hamlet,
To give these mourning duties to your father.
But you must know your father lost a father,
That his father lost, lost his, and the survivor bound
In filial obligation for some term
To do obsequious sorrow. But to persever
In obstinate condolement is a course
Of impious stubbornness.

**GERTRUDE**   'Tis unmanly grief.

**CLAUDIUS**   It shows a will most incorrect to heaven,
A heart unfortified, a mind impatient,
An understanding simple and unschooled.

For what we know must be and is as common
As any the most vulgar thing to sense,
Why should we in our peevish opposition
Take it to heart?

**GERTRUDE**   Fie, 'tis a fault to heaven . . .

**CLAUDIUS**   A fault against the dead, a fault to nature,
To reason most absurd, whose common theme
Is death of fathers, and who still hath cried,
From corse till he that died today,
"This must be so." We pray you, throw to earth
This unprevailing woe and think of us
As of a father; for let the world take note,
You are the most immediate to our throne,
And with no less nobility of love
Than that which dearest father bears his son
Do I impart toward you. For your intent
In going back to school in Wittenberg,
It is most retrograde to our desire,
And we beseech you, bend you to remain
Here in the cheer and comfort of our eye,
Our chiefest courtier, cousin, and our son.

**GERTRUDE**   Let not thy mother lose her prayers, Hamlet.
I pray thee, stay with us. Go not to Wittenberg. [*Beat*]
Come on. Get in the van.

[HAMLET *does not get in the van.* CLAUDIUS *and* GERTRUDE *aren't sure what to do. Finally* CLAUDIUS *breaks the silence and turns to* GERTRUDE.]

**CLAUDIUS**   I shall in all my best obey you, madam.

[*They walk back to the van and close the door behind them. We hear muffled fighting between* CLAUDIUS *and* GERTRUDE *as the van drives off.*]

[HAMLET *turns to the crowd on the street. He is still in his underwear. During the following speech,* HEATHER ANN *plays musical accompaniment from her wireless speaker and passes out long-stem roses to the audience members.*]

**HAMLET**   Oh that this too too solid flesh would melt,
Thaw, and resolve itself into a dew,
Or that the Everlasting had not fixed
His canon 'gainst self-slaughter! O God, God,
How weary, stale, flat, and unprofitable
Seem to me all the uses of this world!
Fie on 't, ah fie! 'Tis an unweeded garden,
That grows to seed. Things rank and gross in nature
Possess it merely. That it should come to this:

But two months dead—nay, not so much, not two.
So excellent a king, that was to this
Hyperion to a satyr; so loving to my mother
That he might not beteem the winds of heaven
Visit her face too roughly. Heaven and earth,
Must I remember? Why, she should hang on him
As if increase of appetite had grown
By what it fed on. And yet, within a month
Let me not think on 't; frailty, thy name is woman!
A little month, or ere those shoes were old
With which she followed my poor father's body,
Like Niobe, all tears—why she, even she
O God, a beast that wants discourse of reason
Would have mourned longer!, married with my uncle,
My father's brother, but no more like my father
Than I to Hercules. Within a month,
Ere yet the salt of most unrighteous tears
Had left the flushing of her galled eyes,
She married. O, most wicked speed, to post
With such dexterity to incestuous sheets!
It is not, nor cannot come to good.
But break, my heart, for I must hold my tongue.

[JAMES *wanders off or exits dramatically.*]

**HEATHER ANN**   [*To the audience*] Look for the van!!!

[*She runs off in the other direction.*]

## THE BODY

[JAMES *as* HAMLET *is in the driver's seat. He turns off the van. He waits. He's clearly torn about something. From the back of the van (which we cannot see) we hear quiet music and chanting.* HAMLET *looks back there. Then back at the audience.*]

**HAMLET**   Can you come with me?

[*They exit the car.* HAMLET *leads the audience around back. They open the back doors of the van . . . . . . to reveal the half-undressed body of* KING HAMLET (*played by* HUNTER). *The women wash his body, preparing it for burial.*]

[HAMLET *and the audience member crawl inside.*]

**HAMLET**   My father—methinks I see my father.

See, what a grace was seated on this brow;
Hyperion's curls; the front of Jove himself;
An eye like Mars, to threaten and command;

He was a man, take him for all in all,
I shall not look upon his like again.

[HAMLET *does something like finally touch his body—and it speaks:*]

**DEAD KING**   Mark me.

**HAMLET**   What?

**DEAD KING**   MARK ME

**HAMLET**   I will.

**DEAD KING**   My hour is almost come,
When I to sulphurous and tormenting flames
Must render up myself.

**HAMLET**   Alas, poor ghost!

**DEAD KING**   Pity me not, but lend thy serious hearing
To what I shall unfold.

**HAMLET**   Speak; I am bound to hear.

**DEAD KING**   So art thou to revenge, when thou shalt hear.

**HAMLET**   What?

**DEAD KING**   If thou didst ever thy dear father love
Revenge his foul and most unnatural murder.

**HAMLET**   Murder!

[*The dead body writhes, upset. The women try to contain it and calm it.*]

**DEAD KING**   Murder most foul, as in the best it is;
But this most foul, strange and unnatural.

**HAMLET**   Haste me to know't, that I, with wings as swift
As meditation or the thoughts of love,
May sweep to my revenge.

**DEAD KING**   'Tis given out that, sleeping in my orchard,
A serpent stung me; so the whole ear of Denmark
Is by a forged process of my death
Rankly abused: but know, thou noble youth,
The serpent that did sting thy father's life
Now wears his crown.

**HAMLET**   O my prophetic soul! My uncle!

**DEAD KING**   Ay, that incestuous, that adulterate beast,
With witchcraft of his wit, with traitorous gifts,—
O wicked wit and gifts, that have the power
So to seduce!—won to his shameful lust
The will of my most seeming-virtuous queen:
O Hamlet, what a falling-off was there!
From me, whose love was of that dignity
That it went hand in hand even with the vow

I made to her in marriage, and to decline
Upon a wretch whose natural gifts were poor
To those of mine!
But virtue, as it never will be moved,
Though lewdness court it in a shape of heaven,
So lust, though to a radiant angel link'd,
Will sate itself in a celestial bed,
And prey on garbage.
But, soft! methinks I scent the morning air;
Brief let me be. Sleeping within my orchard,
My custom always of the afternoon,
Upon my secure hour thy uncle stole,
With juice of cursed hebenon in a vial,
And in the porches of my ears did pour
The leperous distilment; whose effect
Holds such an enmity with blood of man
That swift as quicksilver it courses through
The natural gates and alleys of the body,
And with a sudden vigour doth posset
And curd, like eager droppings into milk,
The thin and wholesome blood: so did it mine;
And a most instant tetter bark'd about,
Most lazar-like, with vile and loathsome crust,
All my smooth body.
Thus was I, sleeping, by a brother's hand
Of life, of crown, of queen, at once dispatch'd:
Cut off even in the blossoms of my sin,
Unhousel'd, disappointed, unanel'd,
No reckoning made, but sent to my account
With all my imperfections on my head:
O, horrible! O, horrible! most horrible!
[*The women wrap the body, binding it and mummifying it.*]

If thou hast nature in thee, bear it not;
Let not the royal bed of Denmark be
A couch for luxury and damned incest.
But, howsoever thou pursuest this act,
Taint not thy mind, nor let thy soul contrive
Against thy mother aught: leave her to heaven
And to those thorns that in her bosom lodge,
To prick and sting her. Fare thee well at once!
The glow-worm shows the matin to be near,
And 'gins to pale his uneffectual fire:
Adieu, adieu! Hamlet, remember me.

[*The body stops talking. It is just a body again.*]

**HAMLET**  Father!

[*He grapples for his father. The women stop him, holding him off, protecting the body.*]

**WOMAN 1**  My lord, my lord,—

**WOMAN 2**  Lord Hamlet,—

**HAMLET**  Father!

**WOMAN 1**  Heaven secure him!

**HAMLET**  So be it!

[HAMLET *leaves the van. Outside the van, he turns back to the audience member.*]

**HAMLET**  O all you host of heaven! O earth! what else?
  And shall I couple hell? O, fie! Hold, hold, my heart;
  And you, my sinews, grow not instant old,
  But bear me stiffly up. Remember thee!
  Ay, thou poor ghost, while memory holds a seat
  In this distracted globe. Remember thee!
  Yea, from the table of my memory
  I'll wipe away all trivial fond records,
  All saws of books, all forms, all pressures past,
  That youth and observation copied there;
  And thy commandment all alone shall live
  Within the book and volume of my brain,
  Unmix'd with baser matter: yes, by heaven!
  O most pernicious woman!
  O villain, villain, smiling, damned villain!
  My tables,—meet it is I set it down,
  That one may smile, and smile, and be a villain;
  At least I'm sure it may be so in Denmark:
  So, uncle, there you are. Now to my word;
  It is "Adieu, adieu! remember me."
  I have sworn 't.

[HAMLET *sprints off. The audience member is led off by the Stage Manager.*]

## CROWN | AMBITION | QUEEN

[NOTE: *This piece involves action taking place at two different locations in the van at the same time.*]

**WITH GERTRUDE:**

[*The front seat of the van. When the audience enters,* GERTRUDE *hands them her phone.*]

**GERTRUDE**  Can you help me do a text? The buttons are just so small.

[*The audience member will see on the phone that the text is going to "Hamlet."*]

[*Dictating*] "Dear Hamlet. I hope you're well.

You probably don't understand what I've done." [*Beat. She's at a loss.*]

My friend Carol—no don't write this part—my friend Carol is divorced. She read that you're not supposed to introduce your kids to someone you're dating until you know it's serious. But then she also said you have to tell your kids before it gets too serious or else they'll feel betrayed. [*Beat*] What do we have?

[*The audience member reads back the text.*]

"You probably don't understand what I've done."

"I loved your father. Believe that if you believe nothing else." [*Beat*]

"The plight of women . . ." No erase that. [*Beat*]

"The choices of a Queen . . ." No erase that. [*Beat*] Shit shit shit.

[*She gets overwhelmed. She flips down the van sun visor to reveal an image of St. Christopher. She prays. She continues in silence for a few moments longer. She gives up.*]

My words fly up, my thoughts remain below:
Words without thoughts never to heaven go.

[*Beat*]

You know what? Just delete that.

[*She gets out of the car and indicates the audience member is to follow.*]

**WITH CLAUDIUS:**

[*Outside the van at the rear bumper.*]

[*At the same time as what we just read,* CLAUDIUS *is outside, working on a speech. He's got a pen and paper in his hands. The audience member approaches.*]

**CLAUDIUS**     [*to the audience member*] How does this sound? [*reads*]
Though yet of Hamlet our dear brother's death
The memory be fresh—maybe "green" is better. More visual. [*He amends it.*]
Though yet of Hamlet our dear brother's death
The memory be green, and that it us befitted
To bear our hearts in grief and our whole kingdom
To be contracted in one brow of woe . . .
[*Reads*]
Listen to that image. "One brow of woe." I'm killing this. [*reads again*]
Yet so far hath discretion fought with nature
That we with wisest sorrow think on him,
Together with remembrance of ourselves.
[*Beat*]
Does that sound too selfish?
[*Makes a note, moves on:*]

Therefore our sometime sister, now our queen,
The imperial jointress to this warlike state,
Have we, as 'twere with a defeated joy,—
With an auspicious and a dropping eye,
With joy in funeral—
No, I just used that.

[*Changes it*]
With *mirth* in funeral and with dirge in marriage,
In equal scale weighing delight and dole,—
Taken to wife: nor have we herein barr'd
Your better wisdoms, which have freely gone
With this affair along. For all, our thanks.

[*A bell summons him. He's instantly nervous, gathering his things together. He goes in the van.*]

## IN THE VAN TOGETHER:

[CLAUDIUS *and* GERTRUDE *run into each other in the van. They are both clearly nervous.*]

**GERTRUDE**   Hey.

**CLAUDIUS**   Hey. How are you?

**GERTRUDE**   Good, good.

**CLAUDIUS**   So, Polonius tells me he hath found
The head and source of all your son's distemper.

**GERTRUDE**   O!
I doubt it is no other but the main—
His father's death and our o'erhasty marriage.

**CLAUDIUS**   Well. We shall sift him. [*Beat*]
So, I'll see you at the play later?

**GERTRUDE**   Of course.

[*They both exit.*]

**GERTRUDE ALONE:**

[*Outside the van.* GERTRUDE *gets out her phone again.*]

**GERTRUDE**   [*To the audience member*] Can you type for me again? [*Audience member takes the phone.*] "Hamlet. We need to talk. You're in a lot of trouble. You really should not have killed Polonius" . . . [*Beat*] You can just type "P." [*Beat*] "I know you blame me, but I'm doing my best . . ."
[*She hesitates, overcome by her situation.*]
Such an act

That blurs the grace and blush of modesty,
Calls virtue hypocrite, takes off the rose
From the fair forehead of an innocent love
And sets a blister there, makes marriage-vows
As false as dicers' oaths: O, such a deed
As from the body of contraction plucks
The very soul, and sweet religion makes
A rhapsody of words: heaven's face doth glow:
Yea, this solidity and compound mass,
With tristful visage, as against the doom,
Is thought-sick at the act.
This was your husband.
See, what a grace was seated on this brow;
Hyperion's curls; the front of Jove himself;
An eye like Mars, to threaten and command;
A station like the herald Mercury
New-lighted on a heaven-kissing hill;
A combination and a form indeed,
Where every god did seem to set his seal,
To give the world assurance of a man:
This was your husband. Look you now what follows.
Here is your husband, like a mildewed ear
Blasting his wholesome brother. Have you eyes?
Could you on this fair mountain leave to feed
And batten on this moor? Ha! Have you eyes?
What devil was't
That thus hath cozen'd me at hoodman-blind?
A murderer and a villain;
A slave that is not twentieth part the tithe
Of my precedent lord; a vice of kings;
A cutpurse of the empire and the rule,
That from a shelf the precious diadem stole,
And put it in his pocket!

[GERTRUDE *springs up and tears open the van door, running inside* . . .]

**CLAUDIUS ALONE:**

[*While that was happening, in the front seat of the van,* CLAUDIUS *pulls out a stash of trail mix or some other road trip food. He starts stuffing his face as he speaks.*]

CLAUDIUS    O my offence is rank, it smells to heaven;
It hath the primal eldest curse upon't,
A brother's murder. Pray can I not,
Though inclination be as sharp as will:
My stronger guilt defeats my strong intent;

And, like a man to double business bound,
I stand in pause where I shall first begin,
And both neglect. What if this cursed hand
Were thicker than itself with brother's blood,
Is there not rain enough in the sweet heavens
To wash it white as snow? Whereto serves mercy
But to confront the visage of offence?
My fault is past. But, O, what form of prayer
Can serve my turn? "Forgive me my foul murder"?
That cannot be; since I am still possess'd
Of those effects for which I did the murder,
My crown, mine own ambition and my queen.
May one be pardon'd and retain the offence?
In the corrupted currents of this world
Offence's gilded hand may shove by justice,
And oft 'tis seen the wicked prize itself
Buys out the law: but 'tis not so above;
There is no shuffling, there the action lies
In his true nature; and we ourselves compell'd,
Even to the teeth and forehead of our faults,
To give in evidence. What then? what rests?
Try what repentance can: what can it not?
Yet what can it when one can not repent?
O wretched state! O bosom black as death!
O limed soul, that, struggling to be free,
Art more engaged! Help, angels! Make assay!

## BACK TOGETHER:

[GERTRUDE *flies into the back of the van, interrupting* CLAUDIUS'*s speech.*]

**GERTRUDE**    Ah, my good lord, what have I seen to-night!

**CLAUDIUS**    What, Gertrude? How does Hamlet?

**GERTRUDE**    Mad as the sea and wind, when both contend
Which is the mightier: in his lawless fit,
Behind the arras hearing something stir,
Whips out his rapier, cries, "A rat, a rat!"
And, in this brainish apprehension, kills
The unseen good old man.

**CLAUDIUS**    O heavy deed!
It had been so with us, had we been there:
His liberty is full of threats to all;
To you yourself, to us, to every one.

Alas, how shall this bloody deed be answer'd?
It will be laid to us, whose providence
Should have kept short, restrain'd and out of haunt,
This mad young man: but so much was our love,
We would not understand what was most fit;
But, like the owner of a foul disease,
To keep it from divulging, let it feed
Even on the pith of Life. Where is he gone?

**GERTRUDE**    To draw apart the body he hath kill'd:
O'er whom his very madness, like some ore
Among a mineral of metals base,
Shows itself pure; he weeps for what is done.

**CLAUDIUS**    O Gertrude, come away!
The sun no sooner shall the mountains touch,
But we will ship him hence: and this vile deed
We must, with all our majesty and skill,
Both countenance and excuse.

**GERTRUDE**    To England?

**CLAUDIUS**    Yes.

**GERTRUDE**    And he'll be safe?

**CLAUDIUS**    Of course. [*He kisses her.*] I love you. And your family.

[*She nods, not believing him, but not knowing how to take power back for herself.*]

**CLAUDIUS**    I'll see you in bed tonight?

**GERTRUDE**    Of course.

[*They separate.*]

**GERTRUDE ALONE:**

[*The front seat of the van.* GERTRUDE *mulls over her situation.*]

**GERTRUDE**    Sorry—can you do one more text for me? [*The audience member takes the phone*] "Hamlet. I'm not going to see you for a while." [*Beat*] "You are a beam of light that came out of me and into the world. Every breathe I take is to protect you. I will hold you in my arms, rocking you forever . . ." [*Beat*] Delete that. [*Beat*] Just say: "I'll miss you. Be safe in England. Love, Mom."

[*She flips down the visor. Tries to pray again. The audience member is taken out of the van by the Stage Manager.*]

**CLAUDIUS ALONE:**

[*At the back of the van, outside.* CLAUDIUS *looks up and sees a cross hanging from the roof of the van. He tries to pray.*]

**CLAUDIUS** Brother . . .
    If thou hast any sound, or use of voice,
    Speak to me.
    If there be any good thing to be done,
    That may to thee do ease and grace to me,
    Speak to me.
    If thou art privy to thy country's fate,
    Which, happily, foreknowing may avoid, O, speak!
    Or if thou hast uphoarded in thy life
    Extorted treasure in the womb of earth,
    For which, they say, you spirits oft walk in death,
    Speak of it: stay, and speak!

[*He looks out into nothingness. No one speaks. After a moment, the audience member is lead off by the Stage Manager.*]

## GIRL WITH FLOWERS

[*It is daytime.* HEATHER ANN *as* OPHELIA *sits in the back of the van. In the corner sits* JAMES *as* HAMLET.

*She repeats the following action:*

*1. Writes something on paper. 2. Folds it into an origami tulip. 3. Performs a little prayer. 4. Makes a tally mark on the wall.*

*We watch her do this three times with the following lines written on the papers:*]

**OPHELIA** "Wore a black shirt every day."
    "Yelled in rehearsals."
    "Let me sleep on his couch for a year."

[*After the third line,* HUNTER *as* POLONIUS *appears up in the front of the van.* OPHELIA *fights not to have her ritual interrupted, but it's clearly hard to concentrate with his voice.*]

**POLONIUS** My blessing with thee!
    And these few precepts in thy memory
    See thou character. Give thy thoughts no tongue,
    Nor any unproportioned thought his act.
    Be thou familiar, but by no means vulgar.
    Those friends thou hast, and their adoption tried,
    Grapple them to thy soul with hoops of steel;
    But do not dull thy palm with entertainment
    Of each new-hatch'd, unfledged comrade. Beware
    Of entrance to a quarrel, but being in,
    Bear't that the opposed may beware of thee.
    Give every man thy ear, but few thy voice;
    Take each man's censure, but reserve thy judgment.

Costly thy habit as thy purse can buy,
But not express'd in fancy; rich, not gaudy;
For the apparel oft proclaims the man,
And they in France of the best rank and station
Are of a most select and generous chief in that.
Neither a borrower nor a lender be;
For loan oft loses both itself and friend,
And borrowing dulls the edge of husbandry.
This above all: to thine own self be true,
And it must follow, as the night the day,
Thou canst not then be false to any man.
Farewell: my blessing season this in thee!

[*Over the course of the speech* OPHELIA *attempts to shut off the voice with various gestures and shapes.* HAMLET *joined in too. Finally,* POLONIUS *disappears.* OPHELIA *looks at the audience member for the first time.*]

**OPHELIA** What's your name? [*They answer.*]
Wanna make a fortune teller? You know, the paper thing?
[*She gets out paper, demonstrates one of those four-cornered fortune tellers.*]
You fold it like this . . . then this way. Then you write numbers on these sides. [*She gives them a pen.*] You have to do it.
[*The audience member writes the numbers on. Then she takes it back.*]
Then we ask it a question. The founder of our theater company, Marlon Pine, died 6 months ago while we were working on this show. His car ran off the road into a cement pylon. He was drunk. Fortune Teller, was his death an accident or a suicide?
[*To the audience*] Pick a number. [*They do, she moves the fortune teller.*] Now pick one of these numbers. [*They do and she lifts that flap, reads:*] "To be or not to be. Ha. Ha." [*Beat*] Well, this is not helpful. [*Beat*]
Let's do another one. Marlon was the abusive genius that held our theater family together. Fortune Teller, what will happen to our company now that he is gone?
Pick a number . . .
[*They do.*] Pick one of these numbers.
[*They do, she lifts the flap and reads:*]
"Carnal, bloody, and unnatural acts,
Accidental judgments, casual slaughters,
Deaths put on by cunning and forced cause,
And, in this upshot, purposes mistook
Fall'n on the inventors' heads: all this can I
Truly deliver."
[*Beat*] Fuck. [*Beat*]

Okay, one more. I joined the company when I was 16. My parents didn't even notice I left. Marlon made sure I ate dinner every night. Fortune Teller, what will happen to me now that he is gone?

Pick a number . . .

[*They do.*] Pick one of these numbers.

[*They do, she lifts the flap and reads:*]
And will he not come again?
And will he not come again?
No, no, he is dead:
Go to thy death-bed:
He never will come again.

His beard was as white as snow,
All flaxen was his poll:
He is gone, he is gone,
And we cast away moan:
God ha' mercy on his soul.

[*She considers this, unnerved. She picks up the pen and goes back to her flower-making ritual.* HAMLET *helps her fold too now. Write. Fold. Gesture. Tally mark.* GERTRUDE *and a* DOCTOR *enter.*]

**GERTRUDE**   Alas, sweet lady, what imports this song?

**DOCTOR**   Conceit upon her father.

**GERTRUDE**   Ophelia . . .

[OPHELIA *won't be interrupted or stopped now. She and* HAMLET *continue their flower-making.*]

**GERTRUDE**   I hoped thou shouldst have been my Hamlet's wife;
I thought thy bride-bed to have deck'd, sweet maid,
And not have strew'd thy grave.

[*The* DOCTOR *notices once of the flowers. He takes it.*]

**DOCTOR**   A document in madness: thoughts and remembrance fitted.

**GERTRUDE**   To my sick [*as sin's true nature is*]
Each toy seems prologue to some great amiss.
[*She notices the audience member and decides it's time for them to leave.*]
I'm so sorry about this. Thank you so much for coming . . .

[*She and the* DOCTOR *lead people out.*]

INTERIOR. KITCHEN. NIGHT.

[*The audience is led into the van.* HEATHER ANN *is sleeping in the hammock or in a corner. A radio softly plays local news in the corner.* LIZZIE (*as herself*) *comes in. She sees the audience. She clicks off the radio.*]

**LIZZIE**  Sorry . . . I thought you'd both be asleep. Am I bothering you? [*waits for answer*] I just wanted to make some noodles.

[*She starts making instant noodles in the kitchen nook. As she waits for them to boil she looks at the portrait of Pine. She notices some dust on it. Brushes it off. A long Beat.*]

To be, or not to be: that is the question:
Whether 'tis nobler in the mind to suffer
The slings and arrows of outrageous fortune,
Or to take arms against a sea of troubles,
And by opposing end them? To die: to sleep;
No more; and by a sleep to say we end
The heart-ache and the thousand natural shocks
That flesh is heir to, 'tis a consummation
Devoutly to be wish'd. To die, to sleep;
To sleep: perchance to dream: ay, there's the rub;
For in that sleep of death what dreams may come
When we have shuffled off this mortal coil,
Must give us pause: there's the respect
That makes calamity of so long life;
For who would bear the whips and scorns of time,
The oppressor's wrong, the proud man's contumely,
The pangs of despised love, the law's delay,
The insolence of office and the spurns
That patient merit of the unworthy takes,
When he himself might his quietus make
With a bare bodkin? Who would fardels bear,
To grunt and sweat under a weary life,
But that the dread of something after death,
The undiscover'd country from whose bourn
No traveler returns, puzzles the will
And makes us rather bear those ills we have
Than fly to others that we know not of?
Thus conscience does make cowards of us all;
And thus the native hue of resolution
Is sicklied o'er with the pale cast of thought,
And enterprises of great pith and moment
With this regard their currents turn awry,
And lose the name of action.

[*Beat, points at Pine's portrait*]

He hated that speech. Well, no—he didn't hate it, he just thought it was impossible. He refused to direct it. [*Looks at the noodles*] I don't even want these. Do you want them?

[*The audience member takes them or doesn't.* LIZZIE *kisses* HEATHER ANN *on the head. Turns the radio back on.*]

It helps her sleep.

[LIZZIE *leaves. The audience member leaves when they want.*]

## THE BREAK-UP

[*Nighttime.* JB *as* HAMLET *is somewhere in the van. He looks at the audience.*]

**JB**   I've broken up with 42 women.

That number sounds bigger to me now that I said it out loud.

I don't remember every one. Some of them are more like hunches. Like, "Oh I think I dated a girl that month on the Vineyard." But maybe I didn't. Some are vivid. I can feel the physical pressure of them in my arms if I think about it.

All of them: I broke up with.

That sounds like I'm bragging.

"I broke 42 hearts. 42 intelligent beautiful women weren't good enough for me." I'm not bragging.

I actually feel terrible. That word is dumb.

I feel . . . dark.

Like there's a thing in me . . . something that doesn't want it to work. Something I'm not aware of.

That's my worst fear—that I'm somehow sabotaging things. That after 12 years of therapy, 3 rounds of couple's therapy, 2 meditation retreats, 26 hikes alone into the wilderness . . . what if I'm secretly sabotaging everything? And I still can't see it?

It's hard to be present in something when you're so aware of how it looks from the outside. I know what I seem like:

"Fear of commitment"

But it's really really really not "Fear of commitment." I've been in love.

More than once. But then I fall out.

And most times, I don't get close at all.

The most disconcerting thing is that She always seems to get there. How can She be falling in love when I'm not?

The moment I realize it's happening . . . I feel sick. Like when I snuck out of the house in high school and I drove my friend Greg's car and crashed it. The moment the car hit the tree I wished I could close my eyes and undo every choice of the night.

It's sickening immediate regret.

"Oh no. It's happening. Again. She's falling in love. Stop, Stop."

But we usually keep dating a little while longer. Because I want to fall too. I don't want to die alone.

So I stick it out another few weeks, by which time she's talking about meeting my parents and I'm realizing she doesn't laugh at my jokes and that's a deal-breaker.

I've seen so many women hate me.

It's an unmistakable look.

[*The noises of nighttime increase. Crickets grow louder. The lighting shifts. A spray of stars on the roof of the van.* HAMLET *turns the dome light on and off a few times, trying to get the mood right.* HAMLET *pulls out a beer from a small cooler. There's a knock on the back of the van. It's* HEATHER ANN *as* OPHELIA.]

**OPHELIA**  Sorry I'm late.

**HAMLET**  It's okay. [*Beat*] How are you?

**OPHELIA**  Okay.

**HAMLET**  You want to come in?

[*She does.*]

You want a beer?

**OPHELIA**  No.

**HAMLET**  Did you take your parents' car?

**OPHELIA**  My dad dropped me off.

**HAMLET**  [*Scoffs*] He let you see me?

**OPHELIA**  He dropped me at Katie's and I walked.

**HAMLET**  Are you sure he didn't follow you?

**OPHELIA**  *Stop.*

[*Awkward beat. She puts down a paper bag of his stuff. It's labeled "Remembrances." He pulls out a few objects—a photo of them, a stuffed animal—then he finds a book.*]

**HAMLET**  I never gave you aught.

**OPHELIA**  You know right well you did.

[*She takes the book and shows him the inscription on the front cover.*]

**OPHELIA**  And with them words of so sweet breath composed
    As made the things more rich.
    Their perfume lost,
    Take these again, for to the noble mind
    Rich gifts wax poor when givers prove unkind.

[HAMLET *comes over to her. He kisses her. She responds. Then she stops him.*]

**OPHELIA**  There my lord.

**HAMLET**   When's your dad coming back?

**OPHELIA**   Why do you care?

[*He kisses her again. She gets frustrated, stops him, asks:*]

**OPHELIA**   Are you honest?

**HAMLET**   My lord?

**OPHELIA**   Are you fair?

**HAMLET**   What means your lordship?

**OPHELIA**   That if you be honest and fair, your honesty should admit no discourse to your beauty. For the power of beauty will sooner transform honesty form what it is to a bawd than the force of honesty can translate beauty to his likeness. This was sometime a paradox, but now the time gives it proof.

[*She angrily starts to leave. He stops her.*]

**HAMLET**   I did love you once.

**OPHELIA**   I was the more deceived.

[*He pulls her back toward him. Finally getting her to really listen.*]

**HAMLET**   [*Tender*] Get thee to a nunnery. Why wouldst thou be a breeder of sinners? I am myself indifferent honest, but yet I could accuse me of such things that it were better my mother had not borne me: I am very proud, revengeful, ambitious, with more offences at my beck than I have thoughts to put them in, imagination to give them shape or time to act them in. What should such fellows as I do crawling between earth and heaven? We are arrant knaves all; believe none of us.

[*She rushes in and kisses him. As they kiss each other:*]

**OPHELIA**   Get thee to a nunnery. If thou dost marry, I'll give thee this plague for thy dowry: be thou chaste as ice, as pure as snow, thou shalt not escape calumny.

**HAMLET**   If thou will marry, marry a fool, for wise men know well enough what monsters you make of them. To a nunnery, go, and quickly too.

**OPHELIA**   I have heard of your paintings too, well enough. God hath given you one face, and you make yourself another.

**HAMLET**   You jig and amble, and you lisp; you nickname God's creatures and make your wantonness your ignorance.

**OPHELIA**   Go to, I'll no more on 't. It hath made me mad!

**HAMLET**   It hath made me mad! Farewell!

**OPHELIA**   Farewell!

**HAMLET**   Farewell!

**OPHELIA**   Farewell!

[*The kissing has died down. They are really saying good-bye now.*]

**HAMLET**   Farewell.

**OPHELIA**   Farwell. To a nunnery, go.

[*She rushes out of the van.* HAMLET *finally turns back to the audience again.*]

**HAMLET**   O, what a noble mind is here o'erthrown.
   [*Beat*] Sorry you had to see that.

[*He reaches over to the radio and clicks it on. A sad song in Spanish plays. He takes the book and remembrances and holds them to him. The audience is led out by the Stage Manager.*]

## THE GRAVEDIGGER HOT BOXES THE VAN

[*There's music playing inside the van. The audience member waits outside. Like a long time. Eventually* HUNTER *as the* GRAVEDIGGER *emerges. He is dressed in dirty mechanic's coveralls. Smokes pours out of the back of the van.*]

**GRAVEDIGGER**   Oh shit, sorry friend. I didn't know you were waiting.

[HUNTER *walks to the front of the van. He opens the door and reaches into a cooler that's between the seats.*]

You want a Gatorade?

[*If they say no*] Are you sure, bro? It's super important to get electrolytes in there.

[*If they say yes*] Excellent. Good choice.

[*Either way, he continues into this story:*] I had a friend break down in the desert. Clutch cable snapped. No one came by for hours. He crawled under the car—did the whole bit, staying out of the sun. When a car finally picked him up—he's seeing triple. Talking to his dead aunt and shit—full-on hallucinating. Guy that picked him up had a case of Gatorade. My pal drank *sixteen*. He was *fine in half an hour*. Didn't even go to the hospital. This shit is magic.

[*He takes a drink.*]

My pal moved to Oregon after that. Died a few months later. Unrelated thing.

[*He turns back into the van, pulls out a tool box, hands it to the audience member.*]
You mind? Thanks.

[*He closes the door, guides them around the van to the hood.*]
All right. Let's see what we've got.

[*He lifts the hood, revealing a glowing green light in the engine. Perhaps there is a large image of a saint painted on the inside of the hood.*]
Fuck, dude. You got a problem here.

[*He goes to work on it. As he works he makes idle chatter. The tone is improvisational and should invite real audience response.*]

When I was younger I did a little traveling. I ended up in Turkey with this weird guy . . . And we went to this crazy palace. Huge. Back in the day there, the oldest brother got everything. The palace, the throne, the whole deal. The younger sisters got to marry and go away and be queen somewhere else. But the younger brothers got nothing . . . unless their older brother died and they moved up in the line . . . So murder became like a huge problem. Younger brothers killing older brothers. It got so bad they made this room in the palace called "The Brother's Room" and that's where the younger ones were kept. Locked up their whole lives.

Sometimes I fantasize a little about murder. But only for a good cause. Like maybe killing Clarence Thomas. He's the craziest one, he vote consistently. Obama would get to elect another liberal justice. Though, maybe John Roberts is a better choice—he's got a plan that scares me, man. Yeah, but anyway, one of them'd be dead and the court would swing liberal and history would *literally* be changed. One death—the world gets better.

But, fuck, I don't really think I could take another life. You gotta watch it drain out of them . . . I watched my Great Uncle die. He was scared shitless. It scared *me* shitless. Made me think death was this train barreling toward us—this unstoppable, just gonna slam right into me. BAM.

[LIZZIE *as the* OTHER MECHANIC *shoots out on a dolly from under the car, holding a tool.*]

**OTHER MECHANIC**   What is he that builds stronger than either the mason, the shipwright, or the carpenter?

**GRAVEDIGGER**   I don't know.

**OTHER MECHANIC**   The gallows-maker; for that frame outlives a thousand tenants.

**GRAVEDIGGER**   Thanks, Tom.

**OTHER MECHANIC**   Or—a grave-maker. The houses he makes lasts til doomsday.

[TOM *disappears.* GRAVEDIGGER *turns back to the audience member.*]

**GRAVEDIGGER**   Is that Gatorade okay?

[*Or:*] Are you sure you don't want a Gatorade?

[*He goes back to working on the engine.*]

How old are you? [*They answer.*] You got a death plan? [*Whatever they answer*]

Oh man, you gotta do a death plan. It's this thing where you tell the hospital what to do with you so they don't spend a bunch of money keeping you alive if you don't wanna be. 80% of health care spending goes into the last two weeks of life in this country. That's not the exact number, but it's close. People get scared talking about that shit. It's too surreal. We, like, cannot process that we're going back to dust. Some ancient evolutionary thing shuts it down. But you gotta fight past that, man.

My pal—the one who drank all the Gatorades—Yeah, when he found out he had cancer . . .

Fuck, dude, he was ready. It was like "Undiscovered Country—let's do this." It was a totally different mindset then my uncle, ya know? Made me realize: you can't treat it special. Death is like air. Alexander the Great was conquering all this shit and now he's asphalt.

[TOM *appears again with a new tool.*]

OTHER MECHANIC   Imperious Caesar, dead and turned to clay
Might stop a hole to keep the wind away.
O' that that earth which kept the world in awe
Should patch a wall t' expel the winter's flaw!

[*He holds out the tool.*]

GRAVEDIGGER   Thanks, Tom.

OTHER MECHANIC   Can I go on break?

GRAVEDIGGER   Can you test the bucket first?

OTHER MECHANIC   Yes.

[TOM *zips off again.*]

GRAVEDIGGER   You see a wrench over there, brother?

[*The audience member finds a wrench. The* GRAVEDIGGER *smacks the engine a few times with the wrench. Then he closes the hood, satisfied.*]

My point is: the value of every human life is absolute. It doesn't matter if you made Warren Buffet money or lived on welfare or killed someone or birthed a thousand kings. Whatever you gave or took, we end up in the same place. And people remembering your name later doesn't make you not-dead. The longest-lived and those who die soonest all lose the same thing. The present is all that they can give up, since that is all you have, and what you don't have, you cannot lose.

[*He turns on the car's engine. It turns over and works. If the van has a cherry picker or lift,* TOM *starts to rise in it. (If the van doesn't have this, he can be testing something else.)*]

OTHER MECHANIC   Hey, boss!

GRAVEDIGGER   Yeah?

OTHER MECHANIC   Age with his stealing steps
Hath clawed me in his clutch,
And hath shipped me into the land
As if I had never been such.

**GRAVEDIGGER**   Bucket looks good!

**OTHER MECHANIC**   Yeah!

[TOM *disappears. The* GRAVEDIGGER *turns off the van. To the audience again:*]

**GRAVEDIGGER**   Death's coming, brother. It's already here.

[*hugs the audience member, whispers in their ear:*]
The rest is silence. [*He ends the hug.*] You're all set here. Monica will get you set up with the bill. Should be about $210 for the parts and $30 an hour for the labor. You have any questions, tell Monica. She'll work it out. Have a good one, brother.

[*They shake hands. He gets back in the van and turns the music back on. The audience member leaves.*]

## AN ORGY OF BLOOD AND ASHES!

[*Outside the van. A podium is set up. Next to it, the founder Marlon Pine's photo has been moved from the van's shrine out to an easel. Flowers are around it.* HEATHER ANN *sits on some road cases, folds something in origami.* HUNTER *leans against the van, in thought. The actors are all themselves in this piece.*]

**HUNTER**   What do you think he'll ask for?

**HEATHER ANN**   I don't know.

**HUNTER**   Maybe like a full Catholic mass? He loves theatrical shit. Does that sounds good, Pine?

[*He stares at the photo.*]
I think wailing women. Hundreds of them. And maybe a chorus of children holding flowers. Singing hymns. Maybe some bagpipes.

[JAMES *comes in, harried.*]

**JAMES**   Is she here yet?

**HEATHER ANN**   No.

[*He leaves.* HUNTER *continues.*]

**HUNTER**   In Chinese funerals they burn paper versions of the stuff you'll need in Heaven. Like giant flat screen TVs and these tiny version of mansions. We should burn a flat screen for Pine. Would you like that, buddy?

**HEATHER ANN**   He would hate that.

**HUNTER**   Yeah, I know.

[*She finally looks up at him.*]

**HEATHER ANN**   Pine will want us to bury his ashes on a hillside under a giant boulder. And then we'll perform *Macbeth* from sunset to midnight and there will be no applause afterward. Our words will just hang in the air for eternity.

**HUNTER** That's not a bad guess.

[*They are interrupted by* JAMES *again. He comes out, goes to the podium.*]

**JAMES** We should start. Has she texted?

**HEATHER ANN** She'll be here.

[JAMES *looks at* HUNTER, *who's eyeing him.*]

**JAMES** What?

**HUNTER** Nice tie.

**JAMES** Is that what you're wearing?

**HUNTER** Yeah.

[JAMES *pulls out some papers and studies them.*]

**HUNTER** What is that?

**JAMES** Just . . . some thoughts I wanted to share.

**HUNTER** Is it a eulogy?

**JAMES** Not officially.

**HUNTER** How can you have a eulogy when we haven't read the funeral instructions? What if he doesn't want you to speak?

**JAMES** I think he'd want me to speak . . .

**HUNTER** We'll see when we open the instructions.

[JAMES *decides not to argue further.* LIZZIE *enters carrying an urn of ashes and an envelope.*]

**JAMES** You're super late.

[*She ignores him. He shuts up. She places the urn in front of the podium. Then looks at* JAMES, *waiting for him to move out of the way.*]

You want to open it?

[*Again, she ignores him. He moves away.*]

**LIZZIE** Thank you for coming to this reading of the burial wishes of Marlon Pine, founder of our theater company, The Moving Shadow. Sorry I kept you waiting.

[*She opens the envelope. Reads.*]

"My collaborators. My children.

The end has come. I have passed through the great veil and am beyond your help now. I don't know what it was that got me."

[HEATHER *clarifies to the audience:*]

**HEATHER ANN** He got in a car accident.

**HUNTER** He was drunk.

**JAMES** Shhhh.

**LIZZIE** "But I know it was Death's great plan and I honor her plan. Without destruction, creation means nothing."

[HUNTER *snorts.*]

**LIZZIE** "I heard that, Hunter."

**HUNTER** Fuck, does it really say that?

[*She ignores him, continues.*]

**LIZZIE** "As you may suspect, I have very specific wishes for my funeral. If they are not followed to my exact specifications, I will never know. But you will know. And you will not be able to live with yourselves. I know because I know. Each and every one of you.

We met before we lived, we lived until we died. We worked together side by side, creating life and art from nothing. We have been as gods, hurling thunderbolts at mountains and molding them into castles.

I will miss none of you. Because I am dead. But I know you will miss me because we were family. Not in the sense of blood connection but rather in blood spent. With that in mind, I direct you to perform the following actions:

One. The Moving Shadow must complete and tour my magnum opus, *Hamlet-Mobile.*"

**HUNTER** Done. Check.

**LIZZIE** "Two. In a funeral ceremony, each member of The Moving Shadow must share their true feelings in the moment they heard of my passing. The others will judge if you are lying."

**HUNTER** What the fuck . . .

**JAMES** Shut up.

**LIZZIE** "Three. My ashes must be mixed with a bucket of stage blood and utilized in the final duel scene of *Hamlet* within your production of *Hamlet-Mobile.*"

[HEATHER *gets up and goes in the van.*]

**LIZZIE** "That is all. And as you complete these tasks, remember what I always said, 'Enjoy the process. Demand the product.'

Yours here and everywhere,

Marlon Pine"

**JAMES** That's it? Nothing about eulogies, or who should say eulogies . . . ?

**LIZZIE** That's it.

**HUNTER** No bagpipes. No pomp. I'm shocked.

[HEATHER *reappears with a bucket of blood, heads towards the ashes.*]

**JAMES** Whoa, whoa, whoa. Wait a second.

[*She stops.* JAMES *inspects the letter.* LIZZIE *stays at the podium.*]

**LIZZIE** I'll go first: when I heard Marlon had died—

**JAMES** Wait. This can't be it.

**LIZZIE** This is it.

**JAMES** It's not enough. It's too small.

**LIZZIE** It's what he wanted. Are you going to disobey his last request?

[*She looks at* JAMES. *She looks over at* HUNTER *and* HEATHER. *No one responds.* JAMES *gives, goes and takes a spot in the crowd.*]

When I found out I was eating breakfast at that shitty theater lobby cafe. James came running in and told me. I started to cry hysterically but I felt nothing. It wasn't until I saw his body later at the hospital that I felt . . . devastated and hopeless and empty. I realized I'd left Heather Ann back at the theater and I hoped she wasn't slitting her wrists.

**HEATHER ANN** [*Meaning it*] Thank you.

**LIZZIE** I realized I didn't want her to be alone. I didn't want any of us to be alone. Marlon was the air, the sun, the stars and our guide through them. [*to the ashes*] Thank you.

[*She steps back. It's not clear who'll go next.* JAMES *finally steps up. He starts by reading from what he wrote.*]

**JAMES** "When I was eleven—"

**HUNTER** No. No way, man.

**JAMES** It answers the question.

**HUNTER** This isn't about you—

**JAMES** But it's okay it's about you?

**LIZZIE** HEY.

[LIZZIE *steps over to* JAMES. *She says something we can't hear. He gives up his speech to her and speaks from his heart.*]

**JAMES** I was standing outside the theater. I was rolling this tire toward the stage door because Marlon had asked me to. He said we needed it. I didn't know why. Then I heard a WOOP WOOP of a siren and thought, "I'm being pulled over." Which makes no sense because I was walking. Then the officer comes over and asks if I'm in the theater troupe, do I know Marlon Pine.

He tells me the news. And then I feel wetness coming through my jeans and I realize I'm on my knees.

I don't know what I felt.

He was a genius. The loss . . . His greatest ideas are now lost to the world forever. Whatever was trapped up there in his mind that could have brought audiences closer to that common burning thread of human experience—

**HUNTER**   Are you quoting your speech? You didn't just make that up.

**JAMES**   Fuck. You.

**HUNTER**   Okay, my turn: when I found out Pine was dead I felt relief. It meant no one was going to shame me or question my talent.

**JAMES**   What talent?

[*They go at each other to fight.* LIZZIE *tries to separate them. She can't.*]

You don't even deserve to be here!

**HUNTER**   I gave as much time to his art as anyone! And he threw it in my face!

**JAMES**   He knew you never loved him.

**HUNTER**   I did love him!

**JAMES**   I will fight with him upon this theme until my eyelids will no longer wag!

[*They wrestle. It's an ugly fight.*]

**HUNTER**   I prithee take thy fingers from my throat,
For though I am not splenitive and rash,
Yet I have something dangerous,
Which let they wisdom fear.

**JAMES**   Does thou come here to whine?
To outface me with leaping in his grave?

**HEATHER ANN**   HEY!

[*Everyone stops.*]

We need a duel.

**LIZZIE**   No.

**JAMES**   Yes!

**HUNTER**   Where's my sword?

[*They run off into the van.*]

**LIZZIE**   [*Turning to* HEATHER] No duels.

**HEATHER ANN**   That is but foolery; but it is such a kind of gain-giving, as would perhaps trouble a woman.

**LIZZIE**   That's sexist, Heather Ann.

[HEATHER ANN *ignores her and takes the ashes and stage blood. Someone hands* LIZZIE *a cup.*]

**HUNTER**   [*Inside the van*] Dude, don't even—that's my sword.

**JAMES** [*Inside the van*] You can't beat me without this sword?

[*The men reappear as* HEATHER ANN *is climbing onto the roof of the van to be* OSRIC.]

**HEATHER ANN**   Let the kettle to the trumpet speak,
The trumpet to the cannoneer without,
The cannons to the heavens, the heavens to earth,
"Now the king dunks to Hamlet." Come, begin!

[*The duel begins.*]

**JAMES**   One.

**HUNTER**   No.

**JAMES**   Judgment!

**HEATHER ANN**   A hit, a very palpable hit!

**HUNTER**   Well, again.

[*Sword fight.*]

**JAMES**   Another hit. What say you?

**HUNTER**   A touch, a touch. I do confess 't.

**LIZZIE**   Here, Hamlet, take my napkin; rub thy brows.

**JAMES**   Good madam.

**LIZZIE**   The Queen carouses to thy fortune, Hamlet.

**HUNTER**   Gertrude, do not drink.

**HEATHER ANN**   I will, my lord; I pray you pardon me.

**HUNTER**   [*to the audience*] It is the poisoned cup. I am too late.

**JAMES**   Come, for the third. You do but dally.
I pray you pass with you best violence.
I am afeard you make a wanton of me.

**HUNTER**   Say you so? Come on.

[*They fight more.* GERTRUDE *starts choking. Only* HEATHER *notices. The boys look up for judgement. She staggers forward.*]

**LIZZIE**   The drink, the drink!

[*They duel around her.*]

The drink!!! The driiiiiiiiiiiiink.

[HUNTER *breaks free.* GERTRUDE *turns to* HAMLET.]

O my dear Hamlet! THHHHEEEEE DRRRRRIIIINK!!!!!!

**JAMES**   O wretched queen!

[JAMES *crosses to* GERTRUDE *to care for her.* HUNTER *stabs* JAMES *when his back is turned.* JAMES *stabs* HUNTER *back. They each remain skewered on each other's sword.*]

**HEATHER ANN**   O proud death,
What feast is toward in thine eternal cell,
That thou so many princes at a shot
So bloodily hast struck?!?!

**LIZZIE**   GOOD NIGHT SWEET PRINCE!

[LIZZIE *goes running at the swords and impales herself. Now all three are locked together.* HEATHER ANN *takes the stage blood mixed with Pine's ashes and throws it at the three of them.*]

**HEATHER ANN**   If it be now,
'tis not to come; if it be not to come, it will
be now; if it be not now, yet it will come:

[*She dumps the remaining blood on herself.*]

The readiness is all!!!

[*And hurls herself on the sword too. They all stagger slowly to their deaths, one giant pile of blood and swords. The death takes a clownishly long time. As they hit the ground, they tumble off the swords, near death. But* HEATHER's *not done. She gets a Katana out of the van, and as she kills them all one by one:*]

**HEATHER ANN**   [*To the audience*] You that look pale and tremble at this chance,
That are but mutes or audience to this act,
Had I but time [as this fell sergeant, death,
Is strict in his arrest], O, I could tell you—

[*She stabs herself.*]

But let it be.

[*All are dead. Just the sound of the actors panting. Everyone catches their breath. Then they all sit up and look around. The actors quietly stand.*]

**HEATHER ANN**   [*To the audience*] Come on.

[*They get the audience to make a circle. Music plays. Or someone hums a song.* HEATHER ANN *speaks:*]

When I heard Marlon died, the first thing I thought of was this poem he
read me a long time ago:
Nature's first green is gold,
Her hardest hue to hold.
Her early leaf's a flower;
But only so an hour.
Then leaf subsides to leaf.
So Eden sank to grief,
So dawn goes down to day.
Nothing gold can stay.

[*The actors bow. The audience leaves.*]

# (becoming) Hue Man

T. Anthony Marotta

# T. Anthony Marotta

T. Anthony Marotta completed his Master of Fine Arts degree at the University of Tennessee, and achieved an advanced studies certificate of Lecoq Physical Theatre/Mask Pedagogy through the London International School of Performing Arts. Marotta is a director, performer, and fight choreographer, as well as mask and puppet sculptor. He studied with mask legend Donato Sartori in Padua, Italy, in the art of leather, papier-mâché, and clay mask creation and performance. As an assistant professor of theatre at the University of Georgia, he focuses his research on the physical expressivity of the performer and performances, with an emphasis on masks and object theatre. Marotta's work has appeared at regional and international venues, including Atlanta's Center for Puppetry Arts, Edinburgh Fringe Festival, Avignon OFF, and many other international festivals. He is a member of Actors' Equity and has recently served as fight director for the Utah Shakespeare Festival's summer seasons and tours.

# Production History

*(becoming) Hue Man* made its World Premiere at Festival St-Ambroise Fringe de Montréal in Montreal, Canada, in June 2015. The piece then toured to Portfringe in Portland, Maine, where it had its US premiere. The show continued to tour to Festival d'Avignon in Avignon, France, in July 2015, and the Chicago Fringe Festival in Chicago, IL, in September 2015.

## CHARACTERS AND NOTES

**LEE MAN**, a man old enough to be a father. He is simple, kind, likable, and manly (MAN LEE). Although traditional in his view of roles, he is open to growth. His mask is a blue clown nose.

**HUE MAN**, a child-sized, colorless, nose-less puppet. Another puppet that "becomes" a boy. It has human anatomy. His eyes and crotch can light up. He is a blank slate on which a MASK may be worn.

## Time

The Present

## Place

Here

## NOTES FROM THE ORIGINAL PRODUCTION

This piece was initially developed for the Center for Puppetry Arts in Atlanta, as part of their Xperimental Puppet Theater series. The play was devised to explore masculinities through the use of puppets as masks. No words are spoken in the piece with the hopes that I would work harder to communicate across cultures. The play was further developed and performed in various Fringe Festivals worldwide including Avignon, Montreal, Chicago, Portland, and Boulder.

Because of its Fringe roots, *Hue Man*'s design and development was heavily influenced by the desire to travel lightly, and set up and strike quickly. I offer the following design notes as a reference point, one possible solution to telling the story.

Within the script's depiction of action, I try to maintain a balance between describing the spirit and intent of the elements, and prescribing enough detail to keep the story clear and focused. Please use these details as references for what worked best for me, for the cultures I visited, for the time period and context in which I performed. As an artist, you may have different interpretations and designs for how you want to say these things, for your particular audiences. One element of this story was very intentional and I ask that any interpretations respect this choice: in the exploration of identities and masculinities there are no references, images, or actions specifically against women or women's behavior toward men. I believe strongly that this piece explores human concerns and that it is best to raise awareness and questions of one gender's issues without blaming or isolating another. NOTE: One moment that I recognize "walks the line" is when, during the play-within-the-play, a pregnant Barbie slaps the REAL MAN PUPPET. It is included to highlight that human violence is unacceptable and that REAL MAN is often associated with violent behavior. It is not intended to comment specifically on women's violence toward men, and should be carefully depicted as such.

**The Stage:** This play uses several theatrical spaces to tell its story: the Big Box of Blue, the Small Colorless Box, a Play Area, a World Window. The Big Box of Blue contained the Blue Baggage, which was actually a trunk. The trunk, in addition to containing props used throughout the show, also provided a sort of stage for the puppetry. The World Window is intended to quickly display images, videos, and/or shadow puppetry scenes. It is useful if this is a rear projection screen, but there are other theatrical ways to accomplish these storytelling devices and the designers should not feel limited. The Big Box of Blue is a metaphorical space in which MASK-ulinities are kept. It is large enough to move around in, yet still feels contained and lacking complete freedom. The Small Colorless Box becomes the birthplace of possibility.

**The MASK-ulinities:** Five masks were used in the production: two blue clown noses for LEE and HUE, and three MASKs that represent strong masculine stereotypes. While not inclusive of all possible masculinities, these stereotypes are meant to represent dominant masculine types that the American culture performs. There are many more masculinities and combinations that exist, and that is hopefully what the story leads one to better realize. The MASKs are selected and designed with very broad strokes in order to make a point. The MASKS should be constructed to fit both LEE and HUE, and have clear physical traits linking them to their stereotype.

**The puppets:** The main puppet, HUE MAN, can be of any type. The original production used a wooden Bunraku style puppet, and was manipulated only by the actor playing LEE. It is helpful in establishing the father-son nature of the relationship if HUE's size approximates that of a small child. Blue lights lit his eyes from within, and also came on in the puppet's crotch to signify a coming of age. There are surely other transposed theatrical ways to symbolize both the male spirit within (the eyes) and the maturing physical manifestation of manhood [*glowing crotch*] that are not distracting in their human accuracy. When HUE first appears on stage, only his head separate from the body, with one playable arm, was used. It also had a dangling blue light to indicate that it is a boy. A deflated blue balloon covered the light and was intimately involved in the circumcision. A red scarf was used for the blood effect. After the circumcision, LEE attached the head to the body on stage, as a symbol of growth and being completed, and LEE's intimate involvement in both.

Shadow puppets were used for the *Prologue* and *Epilogue*. Small hand puppets with glowing blue eyes, with faces identical to the MASKs used to represent the different masculinities, were used by LEE to perform his plays-within-the-play.

# PROLOGUE: Form and Color

[*Colorless. The stage has three main areas: The Colorless Object, The Big Box of Blue, and a projection screen called the World Window. Colorless images and video on the World Window begin to chronicle traditional masculinities and masculine roles, a narrow cultural set of reference points over time of what being a man "is" and "isn't." This is what has been. They are alike. The World Window shifts to a black silhouette of a tree against a white background. The music becomes driving, contemporary, and remains wordless. Against the colorless backdrop, a vibrant blue flower grows. Then, a different type of blue flower grows. Another. Additional and diverse blue flowers appear. They are alike. A caterpillar enters the scene, selecting and eating among only the blue flowers.*

*Full of what has been offered by nature, the caterpillar works to climb the tree and rest. He forms a cocoon. After a struggle, he emerges from the cocoon transformed into a butterfly full of blue hues. It has radiant beauty.*]

# SCENE ONE

## A "He" Volution

[*Lights up on a Big Box of Blue. On display within the Big Box of Blue are the MASKulinities, some faded MASK-uline things, and large worn-out blue MASK-uline baggage or a trunk. LEE MAN, doing what men do, is inside the Blue Box. He is dressed befitting his life's work. He wears blue. He wears blue shoes. He has a blue clown's nose. While his life's soundtrack and images play out, he pantomimes his MASK-uline life: March. Dig. Protect. Labor. Risk. Sport. Fight. Work. Repeat. He is every man progressing through all of his days. Repeat. A break whistle blows. LEE stops his pantomime, relieved. Still within the Box, he removes a small colorless lunch bag from his Blue Baggage or Trunk. He steps out of the Box. Stretches. Breathes.*]

# SCENE TWO

## Snips and Snails

[LEE *takes his break. He is pleased and pleasant. He acknowledges the audience and plays briefly with them. He is simple, charming, and likable. He does what men do on break. And he is alone. He feels lonely.* LEE *picks up and reads a comic book of Pinocchio. Flipping through the story, he gets an idea: he will not be alone anymore. Using his lunch bag, he fashions a companion. He gives it eyes to see, ears to hear, and a mouth to speak. It does not have a nose. He attempts to share his break with his companion. This proves disappointing and hollow. He is alone. The break whistle blows.* LEE *quickly crumples up his companion and, after looking around, stuffs it behind the Colorless Object. Stepping back into his Box, he repeats his MASK-uline life. After a repetition or two, there are unexpected sounds and lights. A flash. Theatrical, Blue Fairy–like Magic occurs and focuses* LEE'S *attention to the Colorless Box, which has suddenly transformed and now contains many colors, many possibilities. He steps out of his Big Blue Box and approaches the Colorless Box to find something unexpected: where his crumpled companion once fell, a small colorless, nose-less puppet has appeared. While examining the puppet, it is as if his touch or breath completes the spell. With more Theatrical Magic highlighting the moment, the puppet suddenly animates. Its eyes light up a bright blue color and the puppet is filled with life and joy. It reaches out into the world. It examines the audience. It examines* LEE. *Closely. It begins comparing itself to* LEE: *They both have eyes. They both have ears, a mouth. The puppet does not have a nose. They are not alike.* LEE *notices for the first time that the puppet is, without a doubt, a boy, and therefore like* LEE. *Initially quite pleased,* LEE *notices a problem: They are not alike. Apologizing to the audience, he immediately takes out a large pair of scissors to remedy the situation. He circumcises the unsuspecting puppet boy. There is blood. A lot. The puppet reacts.* HUE MAN, *the puppet, is now welcomed to the world, and comforted by* LEE.]

# SCENE THREE

## Boys Will Be Boys

[*Time passes and as the puppet transforms in some literal or metaphorical way, aided by* LEE, HUE *grows into a boy. A childhood rhyme, such as "What are little boys made of?" plays in the transition.*]

[LEE *teaches* HUE *to walk. They play with* HUE. *They have simple fun and are happy together. Full of life. Energy.* HUE *tries to enter the Big Box of Blue.* LEE *immediately sweeps him away, encouraging patience.* HUE *focuses on* LEE's *blue nose. He touches it. He feels his own nose-less face. It is different. They are not alike.* LEE, *thinking of something, excitedly sits* HUE *down before he himself steps inside the Box. He retrieves from his Blue Baggage a pair of blue shoes identical to the pair* LEE *currently wears on his feet, only much smaller.* LEE *returns to* HUE *and places the small blue shoes on his feet.* HUE *is thrilled. He leaps up and proudly displays how they are alike.* LEE *directs* HUE *to the Play Area, where Playtime Baggage has been left: a Blue Bag of Toys and a Pink Bag of Toys. They are both overflowing with very distinctly gender-categorized childhood playthings. Only Toys for Boys appear in the Blue Bag. Only Toys for Girls appear in the Pink Bag. They are not alike.* LEE *and* HUE *sit between the two bags.* HUE *examines items in both bags.* LEE *removes a ball from the Blue Bag and, with great excitement, introduces it to* HUE. *They play together for a moment before* HUE *is distracted by the contents of the Pink Bag.* HUE *puts down the ball and reaches for a baby doll in the Pink Bag. He plays for only a moment before* LEE, *shocked and embarrassed, quickly grabs the doll out of his hands and replaces it with a firetruck (or something similar) from the Blue Bag.* HUE *plays for a moment and then notices another fun toy in the Pink Bag: a Barbie Doll.* HUE *is only allowed to play for a very short time before* LEE *takes the Barbie out of his hands, replacing it with a Superman action figure from the Blue Bag.* HUE *engages with* LEE *for a moment in playing with the action figure, before dropping it for another item in the Pink Bag.* LEE *reluctantly tolerates this, for a bit longer this time, letting him play.* LEE *remembers the Toy Gun in the Blue Bag and quickly begins playing enthusiastically with it, trying to lure* HUE. HUE *drops the Pink Toy and immediately engages with his father in gun play. While playing together,* HUE *begins to run but trips and falls. He is lightly hurt, and as he begins to cry,* LEE *encourages him to brush it off.* HUE *continues to sob. Unsure of what to do next,* LEE *offers the boy to someone in the audience, or does some other action to indicate that he is uncomfortable dealing with these feelings.* HUE *calms down. A school bell rings. It is time for* LEE *to take* HUE *to school and then go back to doing what men do.*]

# SCENE 4

## School Blues

[*The following can be performed using some other puppet territory such as shadow puppets, toy theater, finger puppets, stop motion, or any other animation or puppets on film. The teacher, who is not* LEE, *is never seen. No words are spoken.*]

[HUE *is on a playground. He is doing what boys do. He climbs, swings, and plays freely. He is a very active boy and in his element. Joy. A school bell rings and he reluctantly leaves the playground. As he enters the classroom, he is immediately instructed to sit down. The lesson begins and* HUE *is fidgety.* HUE *is told to sit still. He tries. The lesson continues and* HUE's *attention wanders. He is told to pay attention. He tries. Really hard. Time passes. The lessons continue.* HUE *is fidgety once again, and "drops" his pencil. As he climbs out of his seat to retrieve it, he is told to sit down and be still. He is taught important life lessons in self-control and expectations. Time passes. The lessons continue.* HUE *watches the board. He watches the clock. He falls asleep. He is awakened and told to stay awake. He wants to do what he is told to do. The school bell rings. It is recess time.* HUE *is full of joy and runs outside. He does what boys do.*]

## SCENE 5

### The MASK-ulinities

[LEE *and* HUE *enter playing with the gun. Time has passed. They play slightly differently. More violently.* HUE *begins to flirt with a woman or two in the audience.* LEE *pulls him away. As* HUE *returns to play, he is suddenly awkward, uncomfortable, and tries to hide a new sensation "down below." More Blue Fairy–like Theatrical Magic occurs. The Blue Light comes on in the puppet's groin and remains lit throughout the show, to signify his coming of age.* LEE *smiles knowingly. He is proud. He offers* HUE *assurances and congratulations.* HUE *is a* MAN. *A projection of his United States Selective Service Card appears on the World Window. He is welcomed to manhood!* LEE *acknowledges that the time has come for* HUE *to enter the Big Box of Blue. It is time to select his* MASK-*ulinity.* HUE *is delighted, in a reserved way, to be let into the Box. He approaches the confined space with awe and wonder, eager to please.* LEE *chooses a* MASK-*ulinity for* HUE. *It is that of the* REAL MAN. *Proudly he presents the* MASK *to* HUE, *who appears unsure. Putting the* MASK *on himself,* LEE *demonstrates to* HUE *how this* MASK-*ulinity behaves and what it does.* HUE *is underwhelmed. Undeterred,* LEE *believes a fuller demonstration of all that a* REAL MAN *does will assure* HUE *that this is the best* MASK *to wear.*]

[*The following plays-within-the-play are performed with puppets that are a different type than* HUE. *These three puppet sequences are brief and jump quickly from Beat to Beat. They are shallow representations and highlights of their stereotypes. They are most easily performed with smaller puppets and props.*]

[LEE *takes out a small* REAL MAN PUPPET, *designed with the same face as the* REAL MAN MASK. *With a small play-within-a-play, he demonstrates with the* PUPPET *what a* REAL MAN *does. The World Window assists throughout the following performance with appropriate images for this* MASK-*ulinity: sports, balls, weights, weapons, trucks, tools, athletic men, military men, superheroes, video game legends, businessmen, film heroes, muscles, etc. The play-within-a-play reveals that* REAL MAN *is strong, and plays ball sports successfully. He wears a sports uniform. He is praised for his physical performance and strength. There is applause.* REAL MAN *is confident, daring, and drives fast vehicles.* REAL MAN *is rewarded for his assertiveness with popularity and the attention of women.* REAL MAN *"gets" a woman [perhaps using the Barbie Doll prop from earlier as the woman], and "gets" her pregnant.* REAL MAN *remains aloof when confronted with the news and gets slapped. It is funny when women try to hurt* REAL MAN! *He cannot be hurt because* REAL MAN *is always strong.* REAL MAN *appears to be on the edge of retaliating the slap with a slap. This is not funny because* REAL MAN *is strong and can hurt women. He stops himself. It is not okay for* REAL MAN *to be angry and violent. Until . . .* REAL MAN *joins the army and goes to war, trained in and praised for violence.* REAL MAN *risks his life and limbs for his country and family.* REAL MAN *fights with guns and loses a limb in battle. This is not a game.* REAL MAN *returns home, not to directly raise his family, but "chooses" to do dangerous and difficult physical labor, such as construction work, for himself and his family.* REAL MAN *hurts himself repeatedly, eventually losing another limb.* REAL MAN *sits on the couch, drinks beer, and watches TV. The play-within-a-play ends.]*

[LEE *puts the* REAL MAN PUPPET *away, and turns to* HUE *expectantly, as if to say, "Isn't this great?!" Once again he offers the* REAL MAN MASK *to* HUE, *who, with hesitation, accepts it.* HUE *puts on the mask, eager to please. Within the* MASK, *within the Big Box of Blue,* HUE *performs this* MASK-*ulinity, and does what* REAL MAN *does, executing nearly exactly the puppet demonstration he'd been given. The World Window supports him by repeating the images. Before getting very far in the performance,* HUE *stops. He rips off the* REAL MAN *mask and jumps into* LEE's *arms. Uncomfortable. This is not the* MASK-*ulinity for him.* LEE *is disappointed.]*

[*Comforted but ashamed,* HUE *begins to leave the Box, perhaps wandering toward the Pink Bag.* LEE *stops him and presents another* MASK-*ulinity. It is not his first choice, of course. It is not a popular choice at all.* LEE *is reluctant to present it, but perhaps upon seeing this particular* MASK-*ulinity,* HUE *will more readily reconsider choosing* REAL MAN. *It is the mask of* SAFE MAN. LEE *demonstrates some of the behavior and things that the* SAFE MAN MASK *can do, but soon resorts to another puppet demonstration, with* HUE *watching closely. The World Window assists the play-within-a-play with images relating to the performance of* SAFE MAN MASK-*ulinity: men with style, well-groomed, metrosexuals, men who shave their chests and legs, men with earrings, with makeup, hairdressers, dancers, fashion designers, etc.* SAFE MAN PUPPET *performs on stage in a musical. He wears a sailor costume. He dances. He is rewarded for his performance. There is applause.* SAFE MAN *becomes the painter, the musician, the artist. He is a nice guy. He has an earring. He has individuality. He walks lightly, without any intimidating strength or threat of violence. He is a safe friend.* SAFE MAN *is drawn to ballet and works hard to learn how to dance. He dances to express himself.* SAFE MAN *leads with his heart. He does not hesitate to express his kinder feelings.* SAFE MAN PUPPET *puts on a tutu and dances. There is no applause. There is laughter. Much laughter.* SAFE MAN PUPPET *retreats, hurt.* LEE *turns to* HUE *with enthusiasm.* HUE *is not sure how to react, but accepts the* MASK. *Immediately, with the World Window's assistance,* HUE *performs the* MASK-*ulinity of* SAFE MAN. *After a few moments of the experience,* HUE *stops and removes the* SAFE MAN MASK. *He looks at* LEE, *then back at the* MASK *and shakes his head.* LEE *tries to hide his relief.* HUE *is sad and unsure, but denies* LEE's *offer to try the* REAL MAN *mask again.]*

[LEE *continues with what he believes to be the only remaining* MASK-*ulinity on stage:* GENTLE MAN. *After a short attempt to entice* HUE *with the* GENTLE MAN*'s* MASK-*uline traits by wearing it and performing his role,* LEE *quickly moves to a* GENTLE MAN PUPPET *performance. The World Window assists with images to support this* MASK-*ulinity: scholars, books, brain-iacs, computers, geeks, engineers, programmers, old men, overweight men, underweight men, etc. The* GENTLE MAN PUPPET *performance begins at his graduation ceremony. He wears a black graduation cap and gown. He receives a colorless degree. He is praised for his hard work and study. There is applause. He looks out into a sea of graduates. They are alike. He considers the degree, the crowd, and the wide open future. There is uncertainty. His cap, gown, and degree are removed and he is instantly led to a cubicle among many cubicles. He is given the same computer as everyone else. He is handed some books that everyone is to learn. Resigned,* GENTLE MAN *sits and does his work. He is alone. He studies his books. After checking if anyone is looking, he reveals a Superman comic book hidden inside one of his books. He reads the comic book alone in his cubicle, looking over his shoulder from time to time. Soon he puts down his comic book and reaches into his secret place to pull out his pristine and boxed action figure collection, containing both classic and contemporary figures. The Superman action figure seen earlier is among the collection.* GENTLE MAN PUPPET *shows gentle affection for his private collection. The scene ends without much getting anywhere. There is nothing offensive here. There is nothing bold or aggressive. He is blue, but in the most beige way possible.* LEE *looks to* HUE *who is unsure of how to react.* LEE *places the* GENTLE MAN MASK *on* HUE*'s face, who transforms instantly. His performance of the* GENTLE MAN MASK-*ulinity continues a short time before he stops and removes the mask.*]

## SCENE SIX

A "He" Volution II

[LEE *approaches* HUE *and demands he choose the* MASK-*ulinity he wants to perform for life. The only options are those laid out in front of him. What else could he want to be?* HUE *looks up to* LEE. *After a small hesitation,* HUE *reaches out and gently touches* LEE*'s blue nose, then his own.* HUE *wants to be alike.* LEE *is caught off-guard and receives this with mixed emotion. He smiles proudly. He reaches into his Baggage, and takes out another blue nose. He places it on* HUE. *It looks good. It feels right. They are both pleased.* LEE *then teaches* HUE, *Beat by Beat, how to perform the* MASK-*ulinity he wears. The images, sound, and pantomime from the opening sequence is repeated, slowly at first.* HUE *learns quickly because he has watched* LEE *all of his life. After a few repetitions of the pantomime by* LEE *and* HUE, LEE *watches as* HUE *continues without his help. He gets it. He steps out of the Box for a moment to retrieve the baby doll from the Pink Bag and places it inside the Big Box of Blue, near to* HUE. *Blackout.*]

## EPILOGUE: Form and Color

[*Colorful. The World Window again shows a black silhouette of a tree against a white background. The music returns to the same driving, contemporary, wordless piece.*

*Against the colorless backdrop, a silhouette of a hand appears and sows seeds of blue and several other hues. Once again, a vibrant blue flower grows. Then, a flower of another hue grows. Then a different shade of blue, or perhaps purple, appears. More blue flowers appear and a few more flowers of different hues appear. Blue is in the majority. They are alike, and different. A caterpillar appears, selecting and eating among mostly blue flowers. It occasionally eats a flower of a different color. Full of what has been offered by nature, the caterpillar works to climb the tree and rest. He forms a cocoon. After a struggle, he emerges from the cocoon transformed into a beautiful blue butterfly, with several other hues completing him. It has radiant beauty. On the World Window, the following appears: "A MAN'S CHARACTER ALWAYS TAKES ITS HUE, MORE OR LESS, FROM THE FORM AND COLOR OF THINGS ABOUT HIM."—FREDERICK DOUGLASS]*

END OF PLAY

# Acknowledgements

The authors in this book make it what it is, and for that, they deserve all the credit. I would like to thank the artistic and administrative staff of the wonderful festivals represented in this book: Hollins-Mill Mountain Theatre Winter Festival of New Works (Roanoke, VA), the New York International Fringe Festival (NYC, NY), Women's Voices Theater Festival (DC), Hollywood Fringe Festival (Hollywood, CA), F*cking Good Plays Festival at Rattlestick Playwrights Theater (NYC, NY), Appalachian Festival of Plays and Playwrights at Barter Theater (Abingdon, VA), 2Cents Acting Out Ink Festival at the Hudson Theatres (Hollywood, CA), Portfringe (Portland, ME), St-Ambroise Fringe de Montréal (Montreal, Canada), and Chicago Fringe Festival (Chicago, IL).

Thanks, also, to the great folks at Applause Theatre & Cinema books, especially Marybeth Keating and Wes Seely. Thank you to June Clark, my agent, for supporting this project. And thank you, always, to Danielle for everything you do—seen and unseen. And finally, to Danny and Sadie, for their love and humor.